Results and Interpretations of the

2003 Mathematics Assessment

of the

National Assessment of Educational Progress

Edited by

Peter Kloosterman
Indiana University
Bloomington, Indiana

Frank K. Lester Jr.
Indiana University
Bloomington, Indiana

NATIONAL COUNCIL OF
TEACHERS OF MATHEMATICS

Library of Congress Cataloging-in-Publication Data

Results and interpretations of the 2003 mathematics assessment of the national assessment of educational progress / edited by Peter Kloosterman, Frank K. Lester.
    p. cm.
  ISBN-13: 978-0-87353-589-2
  ISBN-10: 0-87353-589-8
  1. Mathematics—Study and teaching (Middle school) —United States—Evaluation. 2. National Assessment of Educational Progress (Project) —Evaluation. 3. Mathematics—Study and teaching (Middle school) —United States—Statistics. I. Kloosterman, Peter. II. Lester, Frank K.
QA13.R4686 2007
510.71'273—dc22

2006024852

The National Council of Teachers of Mathematics is a public voice of mathematics education, providing vision, leadership, and professional development to support teachers in ensuring mathematics learning of the highest quality for all students.

This material is based on work supported by the National Science Foundation through grant number ESI 0138733 to the National Council of Teachers of Mathematics. Any opinions, findings, and conclusions or recommendations expressed in this material are those of the authors and do not necessarily reflect the views of the National Science Foundation.

Printed in the United States of America

Contents

Preface

With the enactment of the No Child Left Behind (NCLB) Act of 2001, the National Assessment of Educational Progress (NAEP) became one of the federal government's tools for measuring the progress of students toward ambitious educational goals. How times change! Before NAEP began in the 1960s, little information was available about what students were learning across the United States. The original goal for NAEP was to serve as a tool for teachers, school administrators, and curriculum developers to improve both curriculum and student learning (Kenney, 2004). NAEP was a low-stakes assessment in that students and schools suffered no consequences for poor performance. With NCLB, and its sanctions for schools that fail to make adequate yearly progress, NAEP results now generate headlines and are at the forefront of discussion of what is working in schools and what needs to be changed. Although NCLB focuses on state-defined rather than NAEP-defined levels of proficiency for students, the federal government is now using NAEP as the benchmark for assessing the quality of state achievement levels. The purpose of this volume goes back to the original goal of NAEP, namely, to identify those areas of mathematics in which students are doing well and those in which students could do better.

As the scrutiny of NAEP results has increased, the National Center for Education Statistics (NCES) has provided more detailed reporting of the results and has increased the level of security of the assessment items. Both the level of detail and the concern for item security have played prominent roles in the development of this volume. In contrast with several years ago, overall results are readily available on the NCES/NAEP Web site (nces.ed.gov/nationsreportcard/), as are reports of results in relation to background variables and the results for individual states. As with previous reports of NAEP results published by NCTM, in this monograph we report overall results, placing particular emphasis on what those results mean for teachers, school administrators, and policy makers. Specifically, because the authors have had access to the raw data, they are able to report results much differently than is possible using the Data Explorer available on the Web site.

With respect to item security, we note that our previous volume on mathematics NAEP results (Kloosterman & Lester, 2004) focused on trends in NAEP from

1990 to 2000, in part because none of the items for the 2000 assessment had been released by NCES for analysis. Moreover, at the time that volume was written, researchers were not allowed to view the secure NAEP items. Thus, although we knew how many students responded correctly to each item, we did not know exactly what the items were. As part of the release of the 2003 data, a number of items were made available to the public, and thus much of the analysis in this volume focuses on student performance on those items. Those items and the overall results were released late in 2003. The secure data set, which was necessary for analysis of the rest of the items, was not released for another year, thereby delaying production of this volume.

Further delays came when we learned that NCES would allow researchers to apply for permission to view the secure items. Although strict confidentiality of the items was still necessary, we felt that by viewing the items, we could be more confident in our interpretations of what performance on those items meant, even if we could not share the details of how we arrived at some of those interpretations. We did eventually gain access to the items, but the process that had to be followed to be allowed to view them was much more time-consuming than we had been told, thereby causing further delays in producing this volume. In short, we regret that this reporting of the 2003 results is appearing after the overall results of the 2005 assessment have been made public, but trust that the analyses here will be of value to those interested in what Grade 4 and 8 students know about mathematics. We should point out that no Grade 12 NAEP assessment was administered in 2003.

The 12 chapters of this volume are interconnected, but each stands alone, and thus readers with interest in the topics of specific chapters should be able to read those chapters without having first read earlier chapters. In brief, chapter 1 (Kenney & Kloosterman) provides background about NAEP and will be particularly useful to readers who are not familiar with the NAEP assessment program. The chapter points out changes in NAEP for the 2003 assessment as well as changes in the way the data are reported. Chapter 2 (Kloosterman & Walcott) looks at the overall 2003 results as well as results of the 2004 Long-Term Trend NAEP and the 2003 international assessments. It also summarizes NAEP results from other content areas—geography, history, and reading.

Chapters 3 through 7 deal with mathematics achievement in different content areas. Chapter 3 (Warfield & Meier) looks at students' knowledge of whole numbers. Findings include the facts that item context and availability of calculators affect performance. Rational number is discussed in chapter 4 (Kastberg & Norton) with a focus on the extent to which students are able to answer questions involving decimals and fractions and the extent to which student performance improved from Grade 4 to Grade 8. In chapter 5, Blume, Galindo, and Walcott analyze items from the Geometry and Measurement strands of NAEP. Their analysis is tied to the expectations for geometry and measurement outlined in the NCTM (2000) *Principles and Standards for School Mathematics.* Chapter

6 (Tarr & Shaughnessy) looks at performance in Data Analysis, Probability, and Statistics, placing emphasis on what students know about probability—the area in this strand that has the longest history in the NAEP program. In chapter 7, Chazan, Leavy, Birky, Clark, Lueke, McCoy, and Nyamekye report student achievement in algebra and functions. Their analyses include what we can tell about student knowledge from sets of related items and identify some of the limitations on making generalizations from NAEP data about students' knowledge of algebra.

Chapter 8 (Smith, Arbaugh, & Fi) focuses on the data from the teacher questionnaire and is thus a summary of what we know about who is teaching mathematics in United States schools and the characteristics of those school environments. Data about student perceptions of the classroom are also included. Chapters 9 (Lubienski & Crockett) and 10 (McGraw & Lubienski) deal with results from NAEP broken down by race/ethnicity and by gender. Items on which substantial discrepancies occurred in performance by race/ethnicity or gender are described in each chapter, along with such issues as SES that are connected with achievement. In chapter 11, D'Ambrosio, Kastberg, and Lambdin analyze a number of released items with the intent of understanding what performance on those items actually measures. Chapter 12 by Lester, Dossey, and Lindquist deals with changes in NAEP over the years and what those changes mean for NAEP as a tool for understanding student learning. The chapter also discusses new directions for NAEP.

Several changes have been made in the format of this monograph as compared with our previous volume on the 1990 through 2000 assessments (Kloosterman & Lester, 2004). With the release of items, the authors in this volume have returned to the practice common in earlier NAEP monographs (e.g., Kenney & Silver, 1997; Silver & Kenney, 2000) of analyzing student performance on those items. Just as the manuscripts for this volume were being prepared to be sent to NCTM headquarters for final copyediting (October 2005), results of the 2005 NAEP assessment were released, as were a number of additional items. Incorporating those results and items into the text of this volume was not possible. However, because we have added the item numbers of the released items to the tables in each chapter, readers are able to go to the NCES online Questions Tool (nces.ed.gov/nationsreportcard/itmrls/) to see those items and thus better interpret comments made in the chapters about those items. With respect to the overall 2005 results that have been released, we note that overall trends reported in this volume continued. Detailed analysis of the 2005 results will have to wait until the secure data set is made available to researchers.

Another change in this volume is that we are no longer including an appendix of available NAEP print materials. Large amounts of information are available electronically at the NAEP Web site (nces.ed.gov/nationsreportcard/), and numerous NAEP print publications are available online from NCES (nces. ed.gov/pubsearch/getpubcats.asp?sid=031). The appendix of our previous volume is still a good resource for older works, but given that those Web sites are updated continuously, we refer readers to the Web sites for information published after 2003.

Finally, NCES also released a new online Data Explorer in October 2005 (nces.ed.gov/nationsreportcard/nde/). The format of that tool is different than we had reported in our previous volume (Kloosterman, Kehle, & Koc, 2004), but the same types of analyses can be carried out using the tool. The comments about the online Data Explorer in this volume were written with the older tool in mind, but readers should have little trouble with the format of the new tool.

As we bring the project that produced this volume to a close, we want to acknowledge the help of a large number of individuals. Members of the project advisory board (James Braswell, John Dossey, Douglas Grouws, Patricia Kenney, Glenda Lappan, and Mary Lindquist) were especially helpful to us in thinking about how to move from the longitudinal focus of our previous volume to the organization presented in this monograph. When discussing secure NAEP items, we have continued to rely on descriptions provided by authors of the content chapters of the NCTM monograph on the 1996 NAEP results (Silver & Kenney, 2000). In particular, we are extremely grateful to Glen Blume, David Heckman, Vicky Kouba, Gary Martin, Michael Shaughnessy, Marilyn Strutchens, Diana Wearne, and Judith Zawojewski. Because their descriptions of secure items were already public, we are able to continue to use them without further compromising the confidential nature of those items.

Al Rogers, Ed Kulik, and Gloria Dion at the Educational Testing Service (ETS) guided us in using the secure NAEP databases. We regularly contacted them with questions, and they always responded quickly. Although we needed his help less on this monograph than on the previous one, Jon Cohen of the American Institutes for Research readily answered our questions about the AM software used to analyze NAEP data. Laura Bufford and Dana Kelly were helpful during our visit to Education Statistics Services Institute to view the secure items, and Kim Gattis advised us in what we could say about the secure items. We also wish to thank the NCTM and Indiana University staff who contributed their time, expertise, and support. Jim Rubillo acted as project director for the NCTM portion of the project, and both he and Pam Mathews were always supportive of our efforts. Ann Butterfield, NCTM copyeditor, did an excellent job of fine-tuning the writing throughout the volume. Similarly, NCTM designer Glenn Fink did an excellent job of formatting and layout.

At Indiana University, Crystal Walcott was invaluable. She ran the day-to-day operations of the project—responding to queries from the authors, making sure our security paperwork was up to date, and pointing out issues that we, as editors, needed to look into. Most important, she figured out how to run analyses from the secure data set. Because the data sets for 1996, 2000, and 2003 are organized somewhat differently, Crystal was in frequent contact with Al Rogers, Ed Kulik, Gloria Dion, and others to verify the accuracy of the statistical results we were getting. Ibrahim Budak, Jacob Feldman, and Andrew Kloosterman all spent many hours running analyses of the data under Crystal's direction. Joanne Peng served as our in-house statistician whenever we needed help interpreting the analyses we ran using the secure data set. Zac Rutledge worked on tables and formatting in many of the chapters, and Elaine Otto provided thoughtful copy-editing of the final chapters before they went to NCTM.

Finally, we express our thanks to the National Science Foundation for funding this project through grant number ESI 0138733 to the NCTM. The ideas and interpretations contained in this report are those of the authors and do not necessarily represent the position of the NSF or NCTM.

REFERENCES

Kenney, P. A. (2004). A brief history of the NCTM NAEP interpretive reports projects. In P. Kloosterman & F. K. Lester Jr. (Eds.), *Results and interpretations of the 1990–2000 mathematics assessments of the National Assessment of Educational Progress* (pp. 33–55). Reston, VA: National Council of Teachers of Mathematics.

Kenney, P. A., & Silver, E. A. (Eds.). (1997). *Results from the sixth mathematics assessment of the National Assessment of Educational Progress*. Reston, VA: National Council of Teachers of Mathematics.

Kloosterman, P., Kehle, P., & Koc, Y. (2004). Using the NAEP online tools. In P. Kloosterman & F. K. Lester Jr. (Eds.), *Results and interpretations of the 1990–2000 mathematics assessments of the National Assessment of Educational Progress* (pp. 57–68). Reston, VA: National Council of Teachers of Mathematics.

Kloosterman, P., & Lester, F. K., Jr. (Eds.). (2004). *Results and interpretations of the 1990–2000 mathematics assessments of the National Assessment of Educational Progress.* Reston, VA: National Council of Teachers of Mathematics.

National Council of Teachers of Mathematics. (2000). *Principles and standards for school mathematics.* Reston, VA: Author.

Silver, E. A., & Kenney, P. A. (2000). *Results from the seventh mathematics assessment of the National Assessment of Educational Progress.* Reston, VA: National Council of Teachers of Mathematics.

1

The 2003 NAEP Mathematics Assessment: An Ending and a Beginning

Patricia Ann Kenney and Peter Kloosterman

O FTEN referred to as "The Nation's Report Card," the National Assessment of Educational Progress (NAEP) was designed in the 1960s as a tool for monitoring precollege students' performance in a variety of subject areas. The first mathematics assessment was completed in 1973, with additional mathematics assessments following in 1978, 1982, 1986, 1990, 1992, 1996, 2000, 2003, and 2005. The focus of this monograph is the 2003 mathematics assessment, which represents both a beginning and an ending in the history of NAEP. With respect to the *ending,* the 2003 NAEP mathematics assessment is the final one that used the framework developed first in 1990 and then modified for the 1996 and subsequent assessments. Other features marked a new *beginning* for NAEP and reflected changes necessitated by the No Child Left Behind (NCLB) legislation and plans for implementing the new mathematics framework for 2005. In this chapter we present a brief overview of the 2003 NAEP mathematics assessment by focusing on what stayed the same and by showcasing the new features. For a more complete overview of NAEP, we refer the reader to the chapter by Kloosterman in the monograph that immediately preceded this one (Kloosterman & Lester, 2004).

RECENT DEVELOPMENTS IN NAEP

Over time, NAEP had evolved from a single assessment into three separate assessment programs: Main NAEP, State NAEP, and Long-Term Trend NAEP. One of the new aspects of the 2003 NAEP assessment involved the integration of Main NAEP and State NAEP into one testing program. Main NAEP was always the primary program: students were sampled from across the country, and results

Highlights

- The 2003 NAEP mathematics assessment was the final assessment that used the framework that had been developed in 1990 and modified for the previous three assessments. In line with No Child Left Behind requirements, the 2003 assessment was administered only at Grades 4 and 8.

- The 2003 NAEP included new features, such as blocks of items administered in 25-minute segments (instead of 15 minutes) and shorter versions of the student and teacher questionnaires.

- The 2003 NAEP used the same item types (multiple choice, short constructed response, extended constructed response) and the same achievement levels (basic, proficient, advanced) as NAEP assessments from 1990 through 2000.

- As mandated by the No Child Left Behind legislation, all 50 states and three jurisdictions participated in NAEP. The national sample was obtained by aggregating the samples from every state, thus making the national sample much larger than in the past. The larger sample size had an effect on statistical significance when NAEP results were compared.

- On the basis of results from the 2000 assessment that showed that including students with disabilities or other challenges had minimal effect on the overall results, all samples in 2003 included students for whom accommodations (e.g., longer testing time, bilingual test booklets) were permitted.

- The NAEP Data Explorer and NAEP Questions Tool were updated and expanded. Those tools can be found at nces.ed.gov/nationsreportcard.

were representative of the entire U.S. student population. Begun on a trial basis in Grade 8 in 1990 and expanded to include Grade 4 in 1992, State NAEP reported achievement for those two grades on a state-by-state basis using a sample of students in each state that was different from the sample tested in Main NAEP. Before the 2003 assessment, participation in State NAEP was voluntary, and some states chose to participate only at one of the two grade levels or not at all. However, because the NCLB legislation mandated that every state participate in the 2003 assessment, the samples of students for Main NAEP and State NAEP could be merged. Specifically, with all 50 states, the District of Columbia, and the Department of Defense schools participating, results reported for the nation were obtained by aggregating the samples from every state (U.S. Department of Education, 2004). Thus the distinction between Main NAEP and State NAEP samples that was made in previous monographs (e.g., Silver & Kenney, 2000; Kloosterman & Lester, 2004) is no longer applicable. In this monograph, we focus on results from the nation as a whole. For those interested in results of specific states, summaries can be found on the NAEP Web site (nces.ed.gov/nationsreportcard/). No Grade 12 assessment was administered in 2003, primarily because of the focus on Grades 4 and 8 as mandated by the NCLB legislation; the Grade 12 assessment resumed in 2005.

The third NAEP program, called Long-Term Trend, or LTT, has used the same questions and format for more than 20 years. Because the LTT program has not changed over time, it is a good indicator of how well students today do in comparison with their peers 20 to 30 years ago *on the types of items that were typical in mathematics classes in the 1970s*. In contrast with the sample for Main NAEP, LTT has a small sample, results are reported only for the nation as a whole, and the sample for LTT is chosen by age level (9-year-olds, 13-year-olds, and 17-year-olds) instead of grade level. Moreover, because of the content of the items, LTT is not as appropriate as Main NAEP for assessing topics new to the elementary and middle school mathematics curriculum, such as algebraic thinking and reasoning and interpreting from data in charts and graphs. A summary of the results from LTT NAEP is included in chapter 2. For the first time since its creation, samples of LTT NAEP items were made available to the public; those items can be found by using the online NAEP Questions Tool described later in this chapter.

Another factor with respect to NAEP testing and reporting of data involves assessment of students with disabilities or limited proficiency in English. Before 1996, such students were tested the same way as other students (i.e., no accommodations were made) or were not tested at all. In keeping with national legislation that requires inclusion of all students in large-scale academic assessments, in the 1996 and 2000 mathematics assessments students in some schools were given the same types of accommodations they would receive in the regular classroom. For example, students with a learning disability in reading may have had directions read to them, students with problems concentrating may have been tested in small groups or individually, and students with limited proficiency in English may have been tested using bilingual test booklets. The reason for allowing some schools to provide accommodations and not others was to see how much of a difference the accommodations made in overall performance. The result from the 1996 and 2000 assessments clearly showed that including students with disabilities had minimal effect on the overall results. In 2000, for example, composite-scale scores of the accommodations-not-permitted sample were 2 scale-score points higher than the accommodations-permitted sample in 4th grade and 8th grade, and in 1996, the 4th-grade scores for the accommodations-permitted and not-permitted groups were the same (see chapter 2). For the 2003 assessment, all samples included students for whom accommodations were permitted. For that reason, all scores reported in this volume are for samples in which accommodations were permitted unless otherwise noted.[1]

---

[1] In the Kloosterman and Lester (2004) monograph on the 1990–2000 NAEP assessments, results were reported for accommodations-not-permitted samples, and thus scale scores and percentage correct on individual items reported in this monograph may vary slightly from those reported in that volume.

As in previous years, the 2003 NAEP included students from both public and private schools. The results reported in this volume include students from both types of schools. However, because the number of private school students sampled in some states was very small, *NAEP results for individual states are based on public school students only.* Thus, when comparing the results for students in one state with the results for the nation as a whole, a more accurate comparison is made by using national results for students from public schools only. However, national results based on public and private school students as a group tend to be only 1 or 2 scale points different from national results for public school students only.

NAEP CONTENT STRANDS

The mathematics content tested on the NAEP assessments and the types of items used are defined by the framework developed under the auspices of the National Assessment Governing Board (NAGB) (see Kenney, 2000; NAGB, n.d.). The assessment includes items from five content areas, including a few items that have been classified in more than one area. The five areas are (a) Number Sense, Properties, and Operations, (b) Measurement, (c) Geometry and Spatial Sense, (d) Data Analysis, Statistics, and Probability, and (e) Algebra and Functions. These five areas are similar to those in the National Council of Teachers of Mathematics (NCTM) *Standards* documents (1989, 2000). However, the NAEP framework was constructed after much public input and is the result of consensus of the development committee rather than an intentional effort to align with the *Standards*. Although NCTM is one of the sponsors of this monograph, the NAEP assessment program is sponsored by the United States government and is not accountable to any individual interest group.

Because this monograph reports on the Grade 4 and Grade 8 results, we describe only the framework for the content strands at those two grade levels. Figure 1.1 summarizes aspects of each of the five content strands. We direct the reader to the framework document (NAGB, n.d.) and to chapter 1 (Kloosterman, 2004) in the previous monograph for a more complete description. Additional information about the content strands and samples items can be found in this monograph, as follows:

- Number Sense, Properties, and Operations: whole number results in chapter 3 and rational number results in chapter 4

- Measurement; and Geometry and Spatial Sense: results combined in chapter 5

- Data Analysis, Statistics, and Probability: results reported in chapter 6

- Algebra and Functions: results reported in chapter 7

Number Sense, Properties, and Operations	• Strand classifies about 40% of Grade 4 and 25% of Grade 8 items • Includes understanding of whole numbers, fractions, decimals, integers, and real numbers and their properties • Focuses on numerical relationships (e.g., ratio, proportion, percentage) • Assesses use of estimation and computational algorithms in mathematical and applied contexts
Measurement	• Strand classifies about 20% of Grade 4 and 15% of Grade 8 items • Focuses on understanding of measurement processes to compare mathematical and real-world objects • Includes units of measurement, use of measurement tools, and such applications as money, temperature, length, width, perimeter, area, capacity, mass, angular measure, volume, and surface area
Geometry and Spatial Sense	• Strand classifies about 15% of Grade 4 and 20% of Grade 8 items • Includes identification of geometric shapes and transformations • Assesses informal construction and geometric reasoning • Includes overlap with measurement concepts
Data Analysis, Statistics, and Probability	• Strand classifies about 10% of Grade 4 and 15% of Grade 8 items • Includes skills in data collection, organization, representation, and interpretation • Assesses probability concepts in mathematical and real-world contexts • Focuses on graphical representation of data and explanation of statistical claims
Algebra and Functions	• Strand classifies about 15% of Grade 4 and 25% of Grade 8 items • Grade 4 items: focus on recognition and generalization of patterns • Grade 8 items: focus on more sophisticated patterns as well as on solving basic equations and inequalities using algebraic and graphical methods

Figure 1.1. Summary of content strands in the NAEP mathematics framework for 2003.

MATHEMATICAL POWER AND ABILITY LEVELS

In addition to defining the five NAEP content strands, the mathematics framework calls for the assessment of "mathematical power" at three "ability levels" (NAGB, n.d.). According to NAGB, "mathematical power is characterized as a student's overall ability to gather and use mathematical knowledge through exploring, conjecturing, and reasoning logically; through solving nonroutine problems; through communicating about and through mathematics; through connecting mathematical ideas in one context with mathematical ideas in another context or with ideas from another discipline in the same or related contexts" (p. 35). To assess mathematical power, NAEP looks at ability to *reason* in mathematical situations and to *communicate* in writing the logic used in solving problems. Some items also require students to *connect* mathematical ideas across contexts. The three interconnected ability levels specified by NAGB are "conceptual understanding," "procedural knowledge," and "problem solving."

Figure 1.2 includes a brief summary of the salient aspects of each ability level. For a more complete description, the reader can again consult the NAEP framework document (NAGB, n.d.) and the first chapter (Kloosterman, 2004) in the previous monograph.

Conceptual understanding	• Knowledge about a mathematical topic or procedure • Demonstrated by identification or generation of examples; knowledge and application of facts, definitions, and principles; and recognition of relationships • Involves communication of understanding of mathematics
Procedural knowledge	• Knowledge about how mathematics is done • Involves selection and application of mathematical procedures, explanations of those procedures, and adaptation of procedures to particular situations • Includes creation of graphs and visual representations, use of computational algorithms, and performance of noncomputational procedures, such as estimating
Problem solving	• Application of conceptual understanding and procedural knowledge to new and complex situations • Includes understanding of problems, formulation of solutions, and reflection on the efficacy and reasonableness of answers • Involves connections between procedures and concepts through communication of mathematical thinking

Figure 1.2. Summary of ability levels in the NAEP mathematics framework for 2003.

NAEP ITEM FORMATS

As has been true for the past four mathematics assessments, the 2003 NAEP used three item formats. The first is a standard multiple-choice format, with each 4th-grade item having four choices and 8th-grade items having either four or five choices; NAEP does not use the choices "all of the above" or "none of the above." The second format, which has two variants, is called short constructed response. In the first variant, students simply write their answers in the space provided and are given full credit for a correct response and no credit for an incorrect response. In the second variant, students answer multiple questions or must provide a brief rationale for the response they give. Students may earn partial credit on those items. The third type of item format is the extended constructed response. On those items, focused holistic rubrics allowing partial credit are used. Extended constructed-response items are always placed at or near the end of the set of items to ensure that students do not spend so much time computing or justifying answers that they do not get to the rest of the items in the set. Overall, time is an issue, although not a major one, because at each grade level most students answer most if not all the questions. In the 2003 NAEP, 114 out of 181 4th-grade items were multiple choice, 59 were short constructed response, and 8 were extended constructed response. At the 8th-grade level, 129 out of the 197 items were multiple choice, 58 were short constructed response, and 10 were extended constructed response. In all previous NAEP mathematics assessments, some items were used at more than one grade level to permit analysts to determine how much better students become as they progress through school. In 2003, 50 items appeared at both Grades 4 and 8.

Figures 1.3 through 1.6 present samples of each of the item formats and scoring; all were released from the 2003 assessment. The multiple-choice item in Figure 1.3 was classified as a problem-solving item within the Measurement content strand for Grade 4. Time is considered to be part of the Measurement strand in the NAEP framework. Forty percent of the 4th graders in the national sample answered the item correctly.

Ted went to the beach at 10:30 a.m. and came home at 2:00 p.m. How many hours was he gone?

A) 8 1/2
B) 4 1/2
C) 3 1/2
D) 2 1/2

Answer: C

Figure 1.3. Multiple-choice item (2003-4M7 #17) given to 4th-grade students.

The short constructed-response item scored as correct or incorrect shown in Figure 1.4 was classified as a Data Analysis, Statistics, and Probability item testing procedural knowledge. The item was used at 8th grade, and only 19% of the students correctly answered it.

Score	Number of Students
90	1
80	3
70	4
60	0
50	3

The table above shows the scores of a group of 11 students on a history test. What is the average (mean) score of the group to the nearest whole number?

Answer:_____

Answer: 69

Figure 1.4. Correct-incorrect short constructed-response item (2003-8M7 #13) given to 8th-grade students.

Figure 1.5 is an example of a partial credit short constructed-response item given only to 8th-grade students. It tested conceptual understanding of an Algebra and Functions concept. Nineteen percent of students received full credit on the item, and another 31% received partial credit.

Figure 1.6 is an example of an extended constructed-response task that was administered to 4th-grade students and categorized as problem solving in the Number Sense, Properties, and Operations content strand. As is explained in the solutions portion of Figure 1.6, five score levels were used to rate a student's response to the item. In addition to the 7% who did not attempt the item, 6% of the responses were incorrect, 36% were scored at the minimal level, 21% at the partial level, 11% at the satisfactory level, and 19% at the extended level (which means that all five parts were answered correctly).

QUESTIONNAIRES

After completing the actual items, all students completed a background questionnaire. The first part of the questionnaire focused on demographics and included questions about race and ethnicity, mother's and father's level of education, reading materials at home, homework, attendance, and use of computers at home. The second part focused on mathematics background and courses taken or planned (Grade 8 only), instructional experiences, use of calculators and other resources in class, and beliefs about the usefulness of mathematics and about one-

Two large storage tanks, T and W, contain water. T starts losing water at the same time additional water starts flowing into W. The graph below shows the amount of water in each tank over a period of hours.

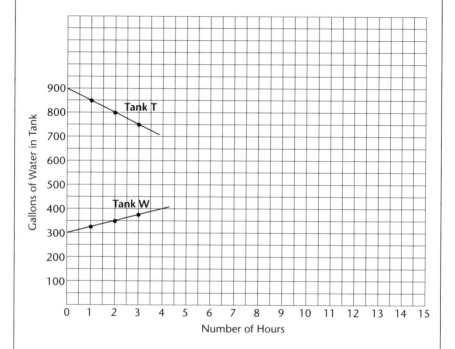

Assume that the rates of water loss and water gain continue as shown. At what number of hours will the amount of water in T be equal to the amount of water in W?

Show or explain how you found your answer.

Answer: 8 hours

Graphical Solution: Extend both lines to the right until they intersect. Then read the horizontal coordinate of the point of intersection.

(continued)

Figure 1.5. Partial credit short constructed-response item (2003-8M10 #13) and scoring guide used with 8th-grade students.

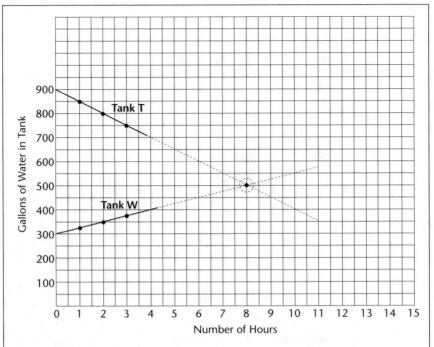

Note: If lines are extended correctly until they intersect, this will serve as sufficient justification. No words are required in this situation.

Algebraic Solution:

Equation of lines: T: $y = -50x + 900$
                      W: $y = 25x + 900$

Point of intersection (8 hrs., 500 gal.)

This question could be solved using either a numerical, graphical, or algebraic approach. Whatever solution path was selected required the student to recognize that the water in tank T is decreasing at a rate of 50 gallons per hour and the water in tank W is increasing at a rate of 25 gallons per hour. These rates could be used to determine when there are equal amounts of water in the two tanks by using any one of several methods, for example, by numerically comparing values for the amount of water in the tanks at different times, by extending the given graphs until they intersect, or by setting up and solving an equation.

A partially correct response could involve either the number of hours being incorrect but falling between 6 1/2 and 8 1/2 and a correct procedure or a correct number of hours with an insufficient or missing justification.

Figure 1.5 (continued). Partial credit short constructed-response item (2003-8M10 #13) and scoring guide used with 8th-grade students.

The shaded part of each strip below shows a fraction.

A.

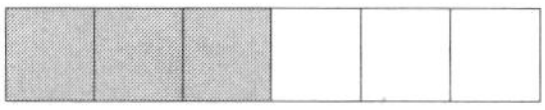

This strip shows 3/6.

B.

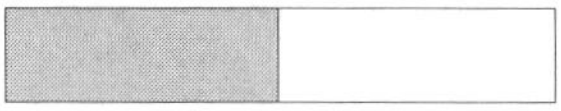

What fraction does this strip show? _____

C.

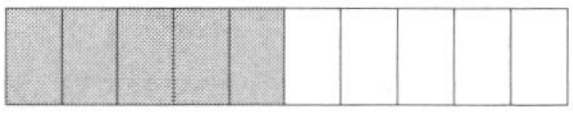

What fraction does this strip show? _____

What do the fractions shown in A, B, and C have in common?

_____

Shade in the fraction strips below to show two different fractions that are equivalent to the ones shown in A, B, and C.

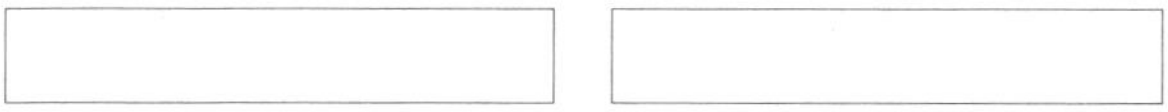

Solution:

Five responses are required for this problem:

Response 1:
        Part 1(B): 1/2.
Acceptable forms of 1/2: 1 out of 2, one half; 1:2, 1÷ 2, 50%, 1\2. If student draws a model for B or C and names it correctly, it will be accepted.

Response 2:
        Part 1C: 5/10 or 1/2.

Response 3:
        Part 2: There are many possible answers:
        They are equivalent fractions.
        They all equal 1/2.
        They are all equal.
        They are all the same size.
        They all end at the same place.
        They are all 3 centimeters long.
        The bottom number is twice the top number.

Responses 4 and 5:
        Part 3: Any fraction equivalent to 1/2, other than those shown in Part 1
        (two different responses required).

Scoring Guide:
        Extended: All five responses correct.
        Satisfactory: Any four responses correct.
        Partial: Any three responses correct.
        Minimal: Any one or two responses correct.

Figure 1.6. Extended constructed-response item (2003-4M10 #18) and scoring guide used with 4th-grade students.

self as a mathematics learner. Student responses to some questionnaire items are included in subsequent chapters in this volume. The items are all available using the online NAEP Data Explorer (nces.ed.gov/nationsreportcard/nde/), although they are not presented in the order in which they were presented to students. The most recent background questionnaires for each NAEP assessment, in the exact form they were given to students, are also available on the NAEP Web site (nces.ed.gov/nationsreportcard/bgquest.asp). At the time this chapter was being prepared, NCES made available the 2005 background questionnaires, which were somewhat abbreviated but similar in format to the 2003 questionnaires.

Teachers of 4th- and 8th-grade students were also asked to complete a 20-minute questionnaire. Many of the results from the teacher questionnaires are reported in chapter 8, although additional results are included as appropriate in other chapters. When examining the results from the teacher questionnaires reported in this volume, readers should note that most results are labeled as the "percentage of students who have teachers" who fall into a particular category. Such wording is necessary because NAEP is based on a representative sample of students rather than teachers. If results were reported in terms of the actual percentage of teachers responding in a certain way, they would not necessarily be an accurate representation of the total population of teachers.

The teacher questionnaires were different for 4th- and 8th-grade teachers. The 4th-grade teacher questionnaire consisted of four sections. The first section contained items about a teacher's background, education, general questions on demographics, and more specific questions about the teachers' training in language arts and mathematics.[2] The second section asked teachers about their classroom organization, including number of students, the teacher's role in language arts and mathematics instruction, the way those subjects are taught (e.g., as discrete subjects, integrated with other subjects), and the number of hours a week each subject is taught. The final two sections were devoted to questions about reading and mathematics instruction, respectively. For the mathematics section, teachers were asked about the ways they assessed student progress, the use of computers, ability grouping, amount of homework assigned, amount of emphasis on topics in mathematics (e.g., geometry, data analysis), and the use of calculators. The 8th-grade questionnaire was shorter than the 4th-grade questionnaire because the focus was restricted to mathematics and because the only question asked about classroom instruction was about the amount of time spent each week on mathematics. Like the student questions, the teacher questions can be found in the NAEP Data Explorer.

A final 20-minute questionnaire was completed by an administrator for each school in the NAEP sample. That questionnaire, often referred to as the "school"

---

[2] Questions about both language arts and mathematics appear on the 4th-grade teacher questionnaire because an individual teacher would be likely to teach both subjects, so some of the students in his or her class would take the NAEP reading assessment while others would take the NAEP mathematics assessment.

questionnaire, focused on size and type of school (private religious, private independent, public magnet, etc.), school organization, parental involvement, expectations of students, absenteeism, retention rates, stability of the student and teacher populations, and percentage of students in special programs, including those for the gifted, limited English proficient, and disabled. Statistics about percentage of students receiving free lunch, which are often used as an indicator of socioeconomic level of a school, also come from administrators' responses to the questionnaire. Items from the school questionnaire can be found on the NAEP Web site.

SAMPLES OF STUDENTS AND ADMINISTRATION PROCEDURES

All 50 states and three jurisdictions participated in the NAEP mathematics assessment in 2003. Approximately 190,000 4th-grade students from 7,500 schools and 153,000 8th-grade students from 6,100 schools were assessed. As reported in the NAEP highlights document (U.S. Department of Education, 2004, p. 20), the national samples were larger than in the past because they were based on the combined public school samples from the states plus additional samples of students attending private schools; no separate national sample was selected. A shift occurred in the racial/ethnic[3] composition of the NAEP samples, as follows:

- An increase in the percentage of Hispanic students, from 6% in 1990 to 18% in 2003 at Grade 4, and from 7% to 15% at Grade 8
- A decrease in the percentage of white students from 75% in 1990 to 60% in 2003 at Grade 4, and from 73% to 63% at Grade 8
- No significant change in the percentage of black students, who make up about 17% of the sample at Grade 4 and 16% at Grade 8

Regarding administration of the NAEP items to students, in the NAEP design no student takes all items at a particular grade level. Instead, the items are divided into blocks, that is, sets of items that always remain together. In 2003, each grade-level test had two blocks of items, which were assembled into booklets along with the student questionnaire. Students had 25 minutes to complete each of the two blocks of items, representing a departure from the practice used in previous NAEPs, which encompassed three shorter blocks of items and gave students 15 minutes to complete each block (see Kloosterman, 2004). The timing change was made so that the time limits for the mathematics assessment matched those for the reading assessment (which for a number of years had been 25 minutes per block), thus allowing some students in a class to be completing items from the mathematics assessment while others were completing items from the reading

---

[3] NAEP reports race/ethnicity by six categories: white, black, Hispanic, Asian/Pacific Islander, American Indian, and unclassified. In this volume, we report data for all categories except unclassified. Because of the small sample sizes for Asian/Pacific Islander and American Indian students, the bulk of reporting done by NAEP by race/ethnicity includes only white, black, and Hispanic students.

assessment. NAEP limits the time any one student spends on any assessment to an hour, so no student completes more than one content area. Administering the reading and mathematics assessments at the same time is also reflected in the 4th-grade teacher questionnaire, which contains questions about the teacher's background and instructional practices in both subjects.

Three blocks of 2003 items from each grade-level test were made available on the NAEP Web site and thus were available as sample items for the chapters in this monograph. We received permission from the National Center for Education Statistics (NCES) to view the nonreleased items, and that access facilitated descriptions of items and scoring guides (for constructed-response questions) that appear within the chapters. To maintain confidentiality of the nonreleased items, descriptions of those items throughout this volume are necessarily vague. Also note that the released items are not representative of NAEP as a whole, as indicated by the NAEP Questions Tool Web site (nces.ed.gov/nationsreportcard/itmrls). Although we were not able to thoroughly analyze the nonreleased items, as a group they appear to require more analysis and more conceptual understanding and to cover a broader range of mathematics concepts than the released items as a group. The four released items presented earlier in this chapter are typical of the range of items that students see on NAEP.

REPORTING RESULTS:
SCALE SCORES AND ACHIEVEMENT LEVELS

In the early years of NAEP, performance was reported by item or cluster of items, but no overall composite achievement score was determined. Beginning with the fourth mathematics assessment in 1986, NAEP began reporting a composite scale score for student achievement (NAEP results from 1973, 1978, and 1982 were also scaled in 1986 to facilitate reporting of performance over time). The NAEP scaling system is independent of grade level, and scores range from 0 to 500. The system, based on item-response theory (Braswell et al., 2001), allows scores on multiple-choice and constructed-response items of varying difficulty to be combined into a single, meaningful score.

Another important factor with respect to the NAEP assessment design is that it is very different from those used in most state and local systems. NAEP is designed to get a sense of the performance of the nation as a whole rather than the performance of individual students. Thus it yields no reliable individual student scores; one can use NAEP data to get a sense of average student performance in a state or region but not to quantify or compare individual student performance.

In addition to reporting results by scale score, NAEP also uses what are called "achievement levels"—basic, proficient, and advanced—which are set by NAGB. The No Child Left Behind legislation stipulates that all students must be at the proficient level on their state assessment by 2014, and thus the NAEP achievement levels have become important from a policy prospective. Figure 1.7

provides a brief description of the NAEP achievement levels for Grade 4 and Grade 8 along with the scale score that identifies the cutoff score for each level. Additional information about the achievement levels can be found in Braswell et al. (2001) and Loomis and Bourque (2001).

NAEP MATHEMATICS ACHIEVEMENT LEVELS: GRADE 4

BASIC (214)

Fourth-grade students performing at the basic level should show some evidence of understanding the mathematical concepts and procedures in the five NAEP content strands.

PROFICIENT (249)

Fourth-grade students performing at the proficient level should consistently apply integrated procedural knowledge and conceptual understanding to problem solving in the five NAEP content strands.

ADVANCED (282)

Fourth-grade students performing at the advanced level should apply integrated procedural knowledge and conceptual understanding to complex and nonroutine real-world problem solving in the five NAEP content strands.

NAEP MATHEMATICS ACHIEVEMENT LEVELS: GRADE 8

BASIC (262)

Eighth-grade students performing at the basic level should exhibit evidence of conceptual and procedural understanding in the five NAEP content strands. This level of performance signifies an understanding of arithmetic operations—including estimation—on whole numbers, decimals, fractions, and percent.

PROFICIENT (299)

Eighth-grade students performing at the proficient level should apply mathematical concepts and procedures consistently to complex problems in the five NAEP content strands.

ADVANCED (333)

Eighth-grade students performing at the advanced level should be able to reach beyond the recognition, identification, and application of mathematical rules in order to generalize and synthesize concepts and principles in the five NAEP content strands.

For more complete descriptions, see Braswell et al. (2001, pp. 10–11).

Figure 1.7. NAEP mathematics achievement levels and cutoff scores for Grades 4 and 8.

As noted in previous NAEP monographs published by NCTM (Kenney, 2000; Kloosterman, 2004) and elsewhere (Linn, Baker, & Betebenner, 2002; Pellegrino, Jones, & Mitchell, 1999), the need for clearly defined achievement levels is reasonably well accepted, but considerable controversy has arisen about where on the NAEP scaling system the basic, proficient, and advanced levels should be set. Part of the controversy comes from the fact that NAEP items were not written to be representative of specific achievement levels, and thus the determination of the cutoff score for each achievement level is somewhat arbitrary.

To provide another perspective on what students at different levels are able to do, we include "item maps" (Figures 1.8 and 1.9) showing item difficulty for Grades 4 and 8. The items maps include the achievement-level cutoff scores for the basic, proficient, and advanced levels. Statistics on the percentage of students currently meeting each achievement level are presented in chapter 2.

Figure 1.8 is the item map for the 4th-grade NAEP items on the 0 to 500 scale. According to the map, a 4th-grade student who was at the 250 level overall would likely be able to solve a simple probability problem (calculator available) (244) and very likely to be able to add two 3-digit numbers (172). The same student would have more difficulty locating two points on a grid given the coordinates (265) and would probably not be able to solve a story problem involving fractions (314). In 2003, the composite (overall) scale score for Grade 4 was 235.

Figure 1.9 is the item map for the 8th-grade items. Looking at a hypothetical student at the 300 level, we can see that he or she would probably be able to correctly solve and explain a word problem involving remainders (296) and very likely to be able to solve a problem using data given in a pie chart (256). By comparison, the same student would probably have considerable difficulty recognizing the meaning of "isosceles" in an unusual context (351) and would have a very small chance of determining the surface area of a given rectangular solid even with a calculator available (388). In 2003 the average composite scale score for Grade 8 was 278.

NAEP ONLINE DATA EXPLORER AND QUESTIONS TOOL

Since the release of the 2000 data, much more about the NAEP assessment and results has become available to the public on the NAEP Web site. The Data Explorer and Questions Tool noted previously in this chapter and reported by Kloosterman, Kehle, and Koc (2004) have been updated and expanded. Results are now available by state and for the nation as a whole, and the user has multiple options for viewing the data in relation to demographic and other background variables. In addition, results from the trial urban assessment are available, as are the results of the 2003 data, which show charter school students performing somewhat below their public school peers (nces.ed.gov/nationsreportcard/studies/charter/results.asp). As noted previously in this chapter, the national sample includes students from private schools, whereas state samples do not and thus all state results are reported for public school students only.

The user has two main options to view state data. One can go to nces.ed.gov/ nationsreportcard, click on "state profiles" in the upper-right-hand corner, and select a state from the U.S. map. To get more detail than the profiles provide, click on "analyze data" (just to the left of state profiles), click on "go to quick start,"

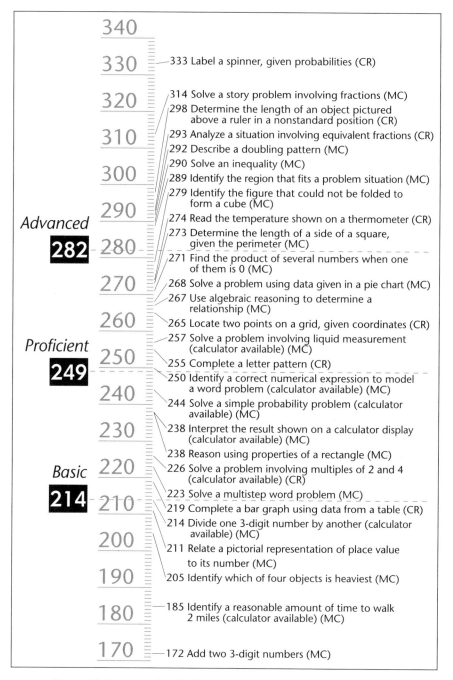

340

330 ──333 Label a spinner, given probabilities (CR)

320 ╱314 Solve a story problem involving fractions (MC)
    298 Determine the length of an object pictured
        above a ruler in a nonstandard position (CR)

310 ╱293 Analyze a situation involving equivalent fractions (CR)
    292 Describe a doubling pattern (MC)
    290 Solve an inequality (MC)

300 289 Identify the region that fits a problem situation (MC)
    279 Identify the figure that could not be folded to
        form a cube (MC)

290 274 Read the temperature shown on a thermometer (CR)

Advanced   273 Determine the length of a side of a square,
                    given the perimeter (MC)

282 280 271 Find the product of several numbers when one
            of them is 0 (MC)

270 268 Solve a problem using data given in a pie chart (MC)
    267 Use algebraic reasoning to determine a
        relationship (MC)

260 265 Locate two points on a grid, given coordinates (CR)
    257 Solve a problem involving liquid measurement
        (calculator available) (MC)

Proficient 250 255 Complete a letter pattern (CR)

249 250 Identify a correct numerical expression to model
            a word problem (calculator available) (MC)

240 244 Solve a simple probability problem (calculator
        available) (MC)

230 238 Interpret the result shown on a calculator display
        (calculator available) (MC)
    238 Reason using properties of a rectangle (MC)

Basic 220 226 Solve a problem involving multiples of 2 and 4
                (calculator available) (CR)

214 210 223 Solve a multistep word problem (MC)
        219 Complete a bar graph using data from a table (CR)
        214 Divide one 3-digit number by another (calculator
            available) (MC)

200 211 Relate a pictorial representation of place value
        to its number (MC)

190 205 Identify which of four objects is heaviest (MC)

180 ──185 Identify a reasonable amount of time to walk
            2 miles (calculator available) (MC)

170 ──172 Add two 3-digit numbers (MC)

Figure 1.8. Item map for Grade 4, 2003 NAEP mathematics assessment.

Source. U.S. Department of Education, 2004; retrieved from nces.ed.gov/
nationsreportcard/itemmaps/index.asp?grade=4&subj=Mathematics.

Note. MC = multiple choice; CR = constructed response.

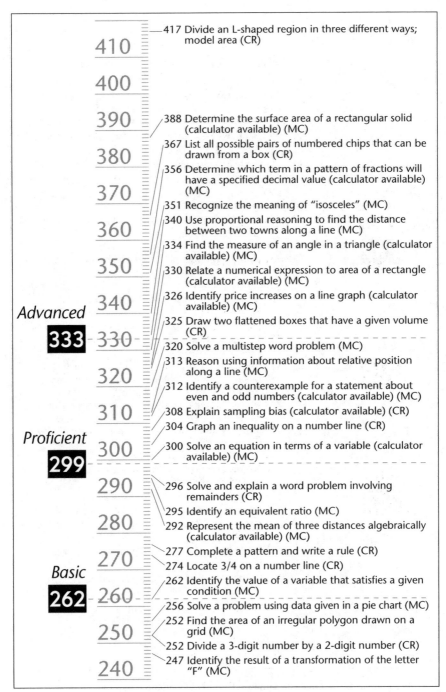

410

400

390 ——— 388 Determine the surface area of a rectangular solid (calculator available) (MC)

380 ——— 367 List all possible pairs of numbered chips that can be drawn from a box (CR)

——— 356 Determine which term in a pattern of fractions will have a specified decimal value (calculator available) (MC)

370 ——— 351 Recognize the meaning of "isosceles" (MC)

——— 340 Use proportional reasoning to find the distance between two towns along a line (MC)

360 ——— 334 Find the measure of an angle in a triangle (calculator available) (MC)

350 ——— 330 Relate a numerical expression to area of a rectangle (calculator available) (MC)

——— 326 Identify price increases on a line graph (calculator available) (MC)

340 ——— 325 Draw two flattened boxes that have a given volume (CR)

Advanced

333 330 ——— 320 Solve a multistep word problem (MC)

——— 313 Reason using information about relative position along a line (MC)

320 ——— 312 Identify a counterexample for a statement about even and odd numbers (calculator available) (MC)

310 ——— 308 Explain sampling bias (calculator available) (CR)

——— 304 Graph an inequality on a number line (CR)

Proficient

299 300 ——— 300 Solve an equation in terms of a variable (calculator available) (MC)

290 ——— 296 Solve and explain a word problem involving remainders (CR)

——— 295 Identify an equivalent ratio (MC)

280 ——— 292 Represent the mean of three distances algebraically (calculator available) (MC)

270 ——— 277 Complete a pattern and write a rule (CR)

——— 274 Locate 3/4 on a number line (CR)

Basic

——— 262 Identify the value of a variable that satisfies a given condition (MC)

262 260 ——— 256 Solve a problem using data given in a pie chart (MC)

——— 252 Find the area of an irregular polygon drawn on a grid (MC)

250 ——— 252 Divide a 3-digit number by a 2-digit number (CR)

240 ——— 247 Identify the result of a transformation of the letter "F" (MC)

Figure 1.9. Item map for Grade 8, 2003 NAEP mathematics assessment.

Source. U.S. Department of Education, 2004; retrieved from nces.ed.gov/ nationsreportcard/itemmaps/index.asp?grade=8&subj=Mathematics.

Note. MC = multiple choice; CR = constructed response.

and then on "I agree to the terms above" for the NCES data usage agreement. At this point, choose a grade level (step 1) and subject area (step 2), and then click on the plus sign next to "state/jurisdiction" (step 3) to get a list of states. To study gender differences in the Indiana data, for example, selecting Grade 8, mathematics, Indiana, gender (under step 4, "variables"), all years available (step 5) and then results brings one to a table listing average scale scores of females and males for each year that NAEP was administered in Indiana. Switching to advanced mode brings far more options for looking at results in relation to demographic and other background variables. For example, the "format table" option leads to a drop down menu allowing analyses by content strand (e.g., Algebra and Functions; or Data Analysis, Statistics, and Probability).

Also available online are all the NAEP items that have been released to the public since 1990 and links to other NAEP publications. To see items from the main NAEP page, click on sample questions and then on search options. We find the option for searching by block is the easiest for finding items mentioned in this monograph; after selecting mathematics and a grade level, the user is given block numbers that correspond to the first digits of the numbers provided with each released item. The basic search option is useful because it permits the user to search by content area and grade level, and the advanced search is useful for finding extended constructed-response items or for identifying particularly easy or difficult items. Along with actual items, the Questions Tool provides sample student responses and data on each item by demographic subgroup. Because student performance rates on the items are included, teachers who want to know how their students compare with a national sample can select items, administer them, and then compare the results with those of the nation as a whole. Finally, additional NAEP publications can be downloaded by going to the publications area on the main NAEP page and then clicking on mathematics. Like the student characteristic options on the Data Explorer, the publications are most likely to be of value primarily to researchers.

SAMPLE SIZE AND DIFFERENCES
IN SUBGROUP PERFORMANCE

In response to NCLB and the need to have accurate data for each state and for demographic subgroups in each state, the sample size for NAEP increased dramatically in 2003. At Grade 4, the sample of students completing mathematics questions grew from 3,423 students in 1990 to 13,542 in 1996, to 27,366 in 2000 (Braswell et al., 2001), and to approximately 190,000 in 2003 (U.S. Department of Education, 2004). At Grade 8, the sample grew from 3,431 in 1990 to 14,260 in 1996, to 31,624 in 2000, and to approximately 153,000 in 2003. An important point to keep in mind is that because any one student takes only a subset of the NAEP items, the number of students completing any given item is substantially smaller. Specifically, the number of students completing each item grew from approximately 1,500 in the 1990s to about 38,000 in Grade 4 and about 31,000 in Grade 8 in 2003.[4]

Related to sample size is the issue of comparing the performance of demographic subgroups. Traditionally, researchers have looked at statistical significance as one measure of the extent to which differences across subgroups are meaningful. Most of the NAEP analyses reported in Kloosterman and Lester (2004), for example, used the .05 level of statistical significance, that is, when the difference between two groups was large enough that the chance was less than 5% that the difference was due to sampling errors rather than true difference between the groups, one group was said to have done better than another. Accurate measurement of statistical significance is dependent in part on random selection of students tested, and NAEP sampling is done very carefully in that regard (see nces.ed.gov/nationsreportcard/about/nathow.asp).

Another contributing factor is the size of the sample. With the large sample size for the 2003 NAEP, almost all differences between larger subgroups are significant and thus representative of true differences between the groups. In 2000, for example, the overall scale score for female 4th-grade students was 224 and the corresponding score for male students was 227. That difference was not statistically significant, and the conclusion that males and females performed equally was appropriate. In 2003, female scores rose to 233 and male scores rose to 236, yet because of the larger sample size, the 3-point difference was statistically significant. In other words, the difference between males and females was 3 points in 2000 and again in 2003, but because more students were assessed in 2003, we can be more confident that the difference was more than just random chance. A more dramatic example comes from the 2003 Grade 8 data, in which the overall scale score for females was 277 and the score for males was 278. The 1-point difference is statistically significant. Thus, although the difference between 8th-grade females and males in 2003 was very small, it was a true difference that would likely show up again if a new sample was selected. Sample sizes for subgroups based on race/ethnicity—particularly the Asian/Pacific Islander and Native American samples—are still small enough that many differences are not statistically significant. For example, the overall scale score for Native American students in Grade 8 was 4 points higher than the score for corresponding Hispanic students, but that difference is not statistically significant. In brief, the large sample size for 2003 makes the question of statistical significance less important than the question of whether a gap between groups of 2 or 3 points is enough to be concerned about. Such gaps may be cause for concern, but for reasons beyond statistical significance. More discussion of subgroup differences can be found in chapters 9 and 10.

---

[4] These numbers were obtained by examining a selected set of items from the NAEP Data Explorer. The Data Explorer has been changed, however, and no longer provides sample sizes for items.

CONCLUSION

As we noted in the title of this chapter, the 2003 NAEP mathematics assessment marked both an ending and a beginning. A number of features that had existed for over a decade were discontinued and replaced by a new set of features in the 2005 NAEP. In particular, and perhaps most important, the 2003 NAEP was the last time that the framework that had been used since 1990 was used to develop and organize the item blocks. The new features included (a) longer item blocks administered in a 25-minute time frame, (b) dramatically larger sample sizes and a different distribution of students by race/ethnicity for Hispanic and white students, (c) the requirement that all states participate in NAEP, (d) a reporting system that included students with accommodations, and (e) a reduced set of questions for the student and teacher questionnaires. Many of the new features were adopted for use in the 2005 NAEP mathematics assessment, which was based on a new framework (nces.ed.gov/nationsreportcard/frameworks.asp).

Although the changes in NAEP content and format have been significant over the years, an additional striking change in the past several years has been the attention paid to NAEP. In the early years of NAEP, researchers and curriculum developers and some classroom teachers were interested in NAEP results, but the general public and policy makers paid little attention. The introduction of scale scores in the mid-1980s permitted comparison of performance over time, resulting in a modest increase in interest in NAEP. State results began to appear in the 1990s, again leading to increased attention to NAEP findings. The passage of the No Child Left Behind legislation in 2001, however, moved NAEP into national prominence. Despite the fact that the legislation says that states are to use their own curriculum frameworks rather than those of NAEP, the legislation also mentions NAEP as the primary benchmark for determining the quality of state frameworks and state measures of student achievement. In addition to classroom teachers and school administrators, policy makers are now paying very close attention to NAEP results to determine whether students are improving. Closing the achievement gap between white and black and between white and Hispanic students is essential if the requirements of NCLB are to be met, and, again, NAEP data are being used as a primary indicator of success. For at least the next 10 years, NAEP will be administered in Grades 4 and 8 in mathematics and reading every other year to monitor progress of all states and groups of students. NAEP results will have a bearing on schools and public policy throughout that period.

One thing that remains the same across the NAEP mathematics assessments—beginning with the first assessment in 1973—is NCTM's commitment to examining NAEP results and learning from them about the progress that U.S. students are making in mathematics. We hope that continuing the tradition of the NCTM NAEP interpretive reports will have an impact on the mathematics education community. In particular, for classroom teachers, school administrators, teacher educators, and policy makers, the in-depth interpretive look at the results from the 2003 NAEP mathematics assessment contained in this volume provides valuable information about student strengths in mathematics and areas that need additional attention.

REFERENCES

Braswell, J. S., Lutkus, A. D., Grigg, W. S., Santapau, S. L., Tay-Lim, B. S.-H., & Johnson, M. S. (2001). *The nation's report card: Mathematics 2000.* Washington, DC: National Center for Education Statistics. Retrieved November 6, 2005, from nces.ed.gov/pubsearch/pubsinfo.asp?pubid=2001517

Kenney, P. A. (2000). The seventh NAEP mathematics assessment: An overview. In E. A. Silver & P. A. Kenney (Eds.), *Results from the seventh mathematics assessment of the National Assessment of Educational Progress* (pp. 1–21). Reston, VA: National Council of Teachers of Mathematics.

Kloosterman, P. (2004). Interpreting the 2000 NAEP mathematics data: Issues and mono-graph overview. In P. Kloosterman & F. K. Lester Jr. (Eds.), *Results and interpretations of the 1990–2000 mathematics assessments of the National Assessment of Educational Progress* (pp. 3–32). Reston, VA: National Council of Teachers of Mathematics.

Kloosterman, P., Kehle, P., & Koc, Y. (2004). Using the NAEP online tools. In P. Kloosterman & F. K. Lester Jr. (Eds.), *Results and interpretations of the 1990–2000 mathematics assessments of the National Assessment of Educational Progress* (pp. 57–68). Reston, VA: National Council of Teachers of Mathematics.

Kloosterman, P., & Lester, F. K., Jr. (Eds.). (2004). *Results and interpretations of the 1990–2000 mathematics assessments of the National Assessment of Educational Progress.* Reston, VA: National Council of Teachers of Mathematics.

Linn, R. L., Baker, E. L., & Betebenner, D. W. (2002). Accountability systems: Implications of requirements of the No Child Left Behind Act of 2001. *Educational Researcher, 31*(6), 3–16.

Loomis, S. C., & Bourque, M. L. (Eds.). (2001). *National Assessment of Educational Progress achievement levels: 1992–1998 mathematics.* Washington, DC: National Assessment Governing Board. Retrieved August 27, 2005, from www.nagb.org/pubs/mathbook.pdf

National Assessment Governing Board (NAGB). (n.d.). *Mathematics framework for the 2003 National Assessment of Educational Progress.* Washington, DC: Author. Retrieved August 27, 2005, from www.nagb.org/pubs/math_fw_03.pdf

National Council of Teachers of Mathematics. (1989). *Curriculum and evaluation stan-dards for school mathematics.* Reston, VA: Author.

National Council of Teachers of Mathematics. (2000). *Principles and standards for school mathematics.* Reston, VA: Author.

Pellegrino, J. W., Jones, L. R., & Mitchell, K. J. (Eds.). (1999). *Grading the nation's report card: Evaluating NAEP and transforming the assessment of educational progress.* Washington, DC: National Academy Press.

Silver, E. A., & Kenney, P. A. (Eds.). (2000). *Results from the seventh mathematics assessment of the National Assessment of Educational Progress.* Reston, VA: National Council of Teachers of Mathematics.

U.S. Department of Education. (2004). *The nation's report card: Mathematics highlights 2003.* Washington, DC: National Center for Education Statistics. Retrieved August 27, 2005, from nces.ed.gov/pubsearch/pubsinfo.asp?pubid=2004451

2

The 2003 NAEP Mathematics Assessment: Overall Results

Peter Kloosterman and Crystal Walcott

T HE LATEST results from National Assessment contain good news for anyone interested in mathematics teaching in the United States. At Grades 4 and 8, the only grades assessed in 2003, scores increased significantly from the 2000 assessment. Results from the 2004 Long-Term Trend NAEP assessment were also quite promising, as scores rose to substantially higher levels than ever before. In this chapter, we report the overall findings of the 2003 Main NAEP and briefly discuss findings by content area and demographic subgroup. We then discuss the results of the 2004 Long-Term Trend assessment and results of international assessments administered in 2003. We end with an analysis of achievement trends over time for the various content areas that NAEP assesses.

OVERALL GAINS IN GRADES 4 AND 8

In 2003, the average 4th-grade scale score on Main NAEP was 235, up from 226 in 2000 and 224 in 1996 (Figure 2.1). The average 8th-grade score was 278, up from 273 in 2000 and 270 in 1996 (Figure 2.1). To project backward from 1996, we need to look at scores from samples in which no accommodations for students with disabilities were permitted (see chapter 1 for a discussion of accommodations). Figure 2.1 shows that the scores from the samples of students for whom accommodations were not permitted differs by no more than 2 points from the scores of samples in which accommodations were permitted. Thus switching between the two types of scores has little effect on interpretations. With that caveat in mind, the gain since 1996 is half the 22-point gain since 1990

Highlights

- Overall scale scores in Grades 4 and 8 improved significantly from 2000 to the highest levels ever recorded.

- At Grade 4, the greatest gains since 1990 were in the area of Algebra and Functions and the next greatest gains were in Number Sense, Properties, and Operations. In contrast, 8th-grade students' gains in Number Sense, Properties, and Operations were lower than in any other content strand.

- At Grade 4, the gap between the lowest and highest achievers was relatively stable in the 1990s but narrowed significantly between 2000 and 2003. At Grade 8, the gap between lowest and highest achievers has remained relatively stable since 1990.

- Between 1996 and 2003, the gap in scale scores between black and white students lessened at both Grades 4 and 8. The gap in scale scores between Hispanic and white students was relatively stable although considerably smaller than the gap between black and white students. Similar results were found in the 2004 Long-Term Trend NAEP.

- Long-Term Trend NAEP assesses the mathematics of the 1970s and 1980s. As with Grades 4 and 8 in Main NAEP, the scores of 9- and 13-year-old students on Long-Term Trend NAEP are increasing. The scores of 17-year-olds are relatively stable.

- At Grades 4 and 8, U.S. students scored higher than the international average on the 2003 Trends in Mathematics and Science Study (TIMSS). Fifteen-year-old U.S. students scored lower than the international average on the 2003 Program for International Student Assessment (PISA).

- Gains on NAEP scores in mathematics over the past 10 years have been greater than gains in any other subject area assessed by NAEP. A number of factors, including the NCTM Standards documents (1989, 1991, 1995, 2000) and the efforts of NCTM members, are likely to have contributed to that improvement.

for Grade 4 and a little less than half the 15-point gain since 1990 for Grade 8. Given the 500-point scale used by NAEP, these gains may not seem significant, but in fact they are quite substantial.

One way to interpret gains over time is to look at gains in relation to average scores at different grade levels. The NAEP scaling system was not designed for analyzing performance across grade levels, but a number of the same items have been used at more than one grade level and the same scoring and scaling system was used regardless of whether the students were in 4th, 8th, or 12th grade. Figure 2.1 shows that the difference between the average scores for 4th and 8th grade ranged from a high of 50 points in 1990 to a low of 43 points in 2003. Figure 2.1

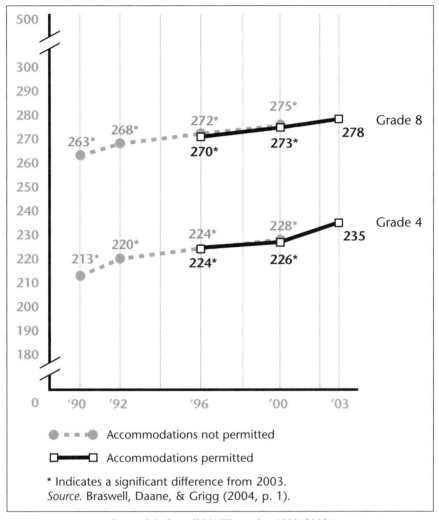

Figure 2.1. Overall NAEP results, 1990–2003.

also shows that 4th graders gained 11 points between 1996 and 2003. That 11-point gain is roughly one-fourth of the difference between the 4th- and 8th-grade scores for the various administrations of NAEP. To put that finding another way, an average student would gain about 11 points a year from 4th to 8th grade, so the 11-point gain in 4th grade from 1996 to 2003 can be thought of as roughly one grade level, and the 22-point gain since 1990, as roughly two grade levels. That observation suggests that in 2003, Grade 4 students performed about one grade level higher than students in 1996 and about two grade levels higher than students in 1990.

Similar reasoning can be applied to the 8th-grade results. About 8 points of gain per year were necessary to get from the 8th- to 12th-grade average in 2000, the last time both those levels were assessed (see Kehle, Wearne, Martin, Strutchens, & Warfield, 2004, for the 12th-grade data). Thus the 8-point gain in 8th-grade scores from 1996 (accommodations permitted scale score of 270) to 2003 (scale score of 278) is also about one grade level. The 15-point gain in 8th-grade scores since 1990, like the gain in 4th-grade scores, is roughly equivalent to two grade levels. Again, the NAEP scaling system was not intended to provide grade-level equivalents, and thus the improvement of two grade levels since 1990 is an approximation, but we view that approximation as evidence that dramatic improvement was made in 4th- and 8th-grade NAEP mathematics scores during the 1990s.

GAIN BY MATHEMATICS CONTENT AREA

As is explained in chapter 1, NAEP assesses five content areas in mathematics: (a) Number Sense, Properties, and Operations; (b) Measurement; (c) Geometry and Spatial Sense; (d) Data Analysis, Statistics, and Probability; and (e) Algebra and Functions. Details on performance in each individual content area can be found in chapters 3–7. At the 4th-grade level, the largest gain in any content area since 1990 was 27 points in Algebra and Functions. That gain may be attributable to the fact that algebraic reasoning has been emphasized in elementary school for the past 15 years. The second largest gain in 4th grade was in Number Sense, Properties, and Operations (23 points). That gain is likely attributable to the current substantial emphasis on basic skills at the elementary school level. At the 8th-grade level, students gained 10 points since 1990 on Number Sense, Properties, and Operations and 15–19 points in each of the other areas. The significant improvement in such areas as data analysis and algebraic thinking is encouraging in view of increased curricular emphasis on those topics.

ACHIEVEMENT BY SUBGROUPS

Lowest and Highest Achievers

How are the strongest and the weakest students doing? Is the gap between them increasing, decreasing, or remaining stable? Figure 2.2 shows scores between 1990 and 2003 for 4th- and 8th-grade students at the 10th, 25th, 50th, 75th, and 90th percentiles of NAEP. In 4th grade, the gap between the lowest and highest achievers is narrowing modestly, with the difference of 82 points between the 10th and 90th percentiles in 1990 falling to 73 points in 2003. Closer analysis of Figure 2.2 shows that almost all the reduction in the 4th-grade gap came between 2000 and 2003. Although the gap between the lowest and highest achievers is

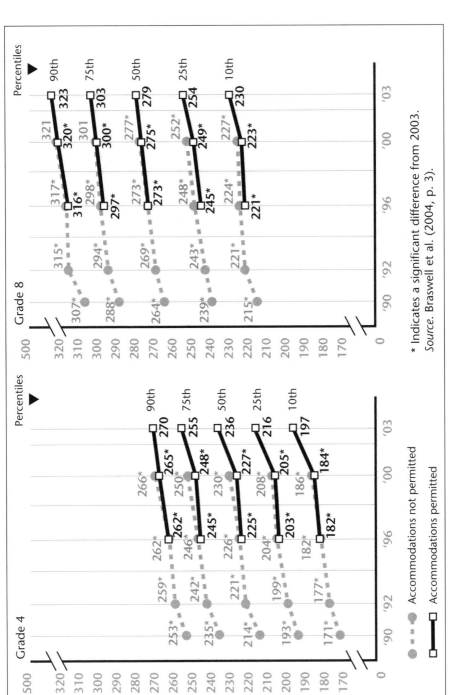

Figure 2.2. Overall NAEP results by percentile, 1990–2003.

* Indicates a significant difference from 2003.
Source. Braswell et al. (2004, p. 3).

still high, the substantial reduction in that gap between 2000 and 2003 shows that efforts to raise the skills of the lowest achievers in the primary grades have been successful—fewer young children are failing to master basic mathematics. Although NAEP does not supply data on why such improvement may be occurring, it makes intuitive sense that programs to reduce class size in primary grades and increased emphasis on early remediation are having a positive effect.

The gap between lowest and highest achievers has been more stable at Grade 8, rising from 92 points in 1990 to 97 points in 2000 (with accommodations permitted) and falling back to 93 points in 2003 (Figure 2.2). For both grades, the substantial increase in the scale score for students at the 10th percentile is encouraging. The Grade 8 gap is still more than the Grade 4 gap, but that discrepancy is not surprising given that gaps between the lowest and highest achievers on almost any type of assessment increase with the number of years students are in school.

Gender, Ethnicity, and Socioeconomic Status

Gaps between demographic groups are analyzed in detail in chapters 9 and 10. In brief, 4th-grade males outperformed 4th-grade females by 1 point in 1996 and 3 points in 2000 and 2003. That difference was statistically significant at the $p < .05$ level only in 2003, but the change in significance could be due to the larger sample size in 2003 as opposed to any real change in the gender gap. Differences in average score by racial or ethnic subgroup are large, although the gap between black and white students appears to be closing slowly. Specifically, the gap between black and white 4th graders dropped from 34 points to 27 points between 1996 and 2003 (Table 2.1), and the corresponding gap for 8th graders dropped from 41 to 36 points (Table 2.2). The gap between Hispanic and white students was 21 points in Grade 4 and 29 points in Grade 8 in 2003. Those gaps are smaller than the corresponding black-white gaps but not significantly different from the Hispanic-white gaps in 1996 (Tables 2.1 and 2.2). A substantial positive correlation occurs between achievement based on race/ethnicity and that based on socioeconomic status (see chapter 9), although the achievement gap based on students' receiving versus not receiving free or reduced price lunch has been relatively stable (Grade 4 gaps of 25 points in 1996, 27 points in 2000, and 23 points in 2003; Grade 8 gaps of 27 points in 1996, 30 points in 2000, and 28 points in 2003).

ACHIEVEMENT LEVELS

As in all recent NAEP assessments (see chapter 1), results in 2003 were reported in terms of the percentage of students reaching predetermined achievement levels. NAEP uses the levels of below basic, basic, proficient, and advanced. Interest in achievement at each level has become more important given the No Child Left Behind (NCLB) requirement that all children must meet a state-

Table 2.1
Grade 4 Scale Scores by Demographic Subgroup

	1996	2000	2003
All students	224*	226*	235
Male	224*	227*	236
Female	223*	224*	233
White	232*	234*	243
Black	198*	203*	216
Hispanic	207*	208*	222
Asian/Pacific Islander	229*	Insufficient data	246
American Indian/Alaska Native	217	208*	223
Eligible for free/reduced price lunch	207*	208*	222
Not eligible for free/reduced price lunch	232*	235*	244

* Indicates that the scale score is significantly different from the 2003 scale score for this group.

Table 2.2
Grade 8 Scale Scores by Demographic Subgroup

	1996	2000	2003
All Students	270*	273*	278
Male	271*	274*	278
Female	269*	272*	277
White	281*	284*	288
Black	240*	244*	252
Hispanic	251*	253*	259
Asian/Pacific Islander	Insufficient data	288	291
American Indian/Alaska Native	Insufficient data	259	263
Eligible for free or reduced price lunch	250*	253*	259
Not eligible for free or reduced price lunch	277*	283*	287

* Indicates that the scale score is significantly different from the 2003 scale score for this group.

defined level of proficiency by 2014. Table 2.3 shows the percentage of students scoring at the four NAEP achievement levels. Note that the percentages of students at or above the proficient levels in these tables include those students who are at the proficient level and at the advanced level. The percentages of students at or above the basic level includes those at the basic, proficient, and advanced levels. From the perspective of NCLB, it is encouraging that the percentages of students reaching basic, proficient, and advanced are increasing each year while the percentage of those below the basic level is decreasing. However, although the percentage of 4th-grade students reaching the proficient level has risen from 21% in 1996 to 32% in 2003, the current rate of gain is less than 2% per year and thus much too low to meet the NCLB goal of all students' attaining the proficient level by 2014. At Grade 8, the rate of gain is only about 1% per year. Thus, with just 29% of 8th graders currently performing at the proficient level, meeting the goal of all students' achieving at the proficient level by 2014 seems highly unlikely. Because NCLB requires students to meet state-defined rather than NAEP levels of proficiency, analysts might argue that meeting state-defined levels may yet be possible. However, NCLB also says that NAEP will be used as an indicator of state standards. So, regardless of how one defines proficiency, the noble goals of NCLB seem to be unattainable even if the substantial rates of improvement in mathematics achievement continue.

Table 2.3
Percentage of Students at Various Achievement Levels

	Grade 4			Grade 8		
	1996	2000	2003	1996	2000	2003
At advanced	2*	3*	4	4*	5	5
At or above proficient	21*	24*	32	23*	26*	29
At or above basic	63*	65*	77	61*	63*	68
Below basic	37*	35*	23	39*	37*	32

Note. Percentages for basic and proficient include those at or above these levels, and thus the only levels that sum to 100 are the below-basic level and the at-or-above-basic level. Minimum scale scores for the basic, proficient, and advanced levels at Grade 4 are 214, 249, and 282, respectively, and corresponding scores at Grade 8 are 262, 299, and 333.

* Indicates the percentage is significantly different from the 2003 percentage for this group.

LONG-TERM TREND RESULTS

The main focus of this volume is Main NAEP, which is updated to include new items with each administration. A second NAEP assessment, known as the Long-Term Trend (LTT) assessment, uses items from the 1970s and early 1980s and has not changed at all in 20 years. Because the items have not changed, LTT NAEP is representative of the mathematics that was taught and assessed in the 1970s more so than Main NAEP, which today includes more algebraic thinking, more statistical thinking, and a number of more complex items than was true of Main NAEP 20 or more years ago. Although LTT NAEP has both multiple-choice and short constructed-response items, extended constructed-response items (see chapter 1) appear only in Main NAEP. NAEP administers the LTT to a relatively small national sample, and thus insufficient data are generated to provide state-level results. In addition, LTT NAEP uses the sampling procedures and age levels that were used in the NAEPs of the 1970s. That is, LTT NAEP is given to 9-, 13-, and 17-year-old students rather than to students at Grades 4, 8, and 12. Although the content of LTT NAEP is dated, because it has not changed, it can be used to determine how students today perform on the more computationally oriented mathematics of the 1970s and how that performance has changed over time.

LTT NAEP was administered in mathematics in 1973, 1978, 1982, 1986, 1990, 1992, 1994, 1996, 1999, and 2004. Figure 2.3 shows the overall mathematics scores for each of those years. Age 9 scores climbed substantially between 1986 and 1990 and again between 1999 and 2004. Age 13 scores climbed 5 points between 1978 and 1982 and 5 more between 1999 and 2004, with a 6-point gain from 1990 to 1999. The scores of 17-year-old students have been relatively stable throughout the history of NAEP.

The lack of gain by 17-year-old students on LTT NAEP since 1990 is mirrored by a similar lack of gain by Grade 12 students on Main NAEP and may partly be the result of students' failing to take the NAEP exam seriously (see Kehle et al., 2004). However, the lack of gain by high school students is almost certainly due to more than just the extent to which students take the assessment seriously and thus must be viewed with concern. The very modest gains by 9- and 13-year-old students on LTT NAEP in the 1990s were somewhat surprising given the substantial gains by 4th- and 8th-grade students on Main NAEP during the same period (Figure 2.1). However, the largest proportion of the gain over that decade in Grade 4 was in the areas of patterns and algebraic thinking and graphing (Kloosterman et al., 2004), and a substantial proportion of the gain in Grade 8 was in the areas of data analysis and algebra and functions (Sowder, Wearne, Martin, & Strutchens, 2004). Those areas have had increased emphasis in the curriculum of the 1990s and are not well represented in the LTT assessment. Thus the modest gains of 9- and 13-year-olds on LTT over that period are likely to be a function of the nature of the LTT assessment rather than lack of overall improvement of elementary and middle school students. The increases for 9- and 13-year-old students on LTT from 1999 to 2004 are similar in magnitude to those on Main NAEP from 2000 to 2003. An increased emphasis on "basic skills" in mathematics in recent years could account for the recent improvement on LTT. Regardless, performance has clearly increased on basic skills as well as on more complex skills including algebraic thinking and data analysis.

A detailed analysis of the 2004 LTT results is beyond the scope of this volume, but interested readers can find a summary at the NCES Web site (nces.ed.gov/nationsreportcard/). One trend in the 2004 LTT data is worthy of note. As also occurred with Main NAEP, some of the score gaps based on race/ethnicity have decreased since the previous assessment. As can be seen in Figure 2.4, black and white 9-year-old students improved from 1999 to 2004, but the rate of improvement was higher for black students and thus the gap narrowed to 23 points—the smallest ever recorded, although only 2 points smaller than the gaps in 1986,

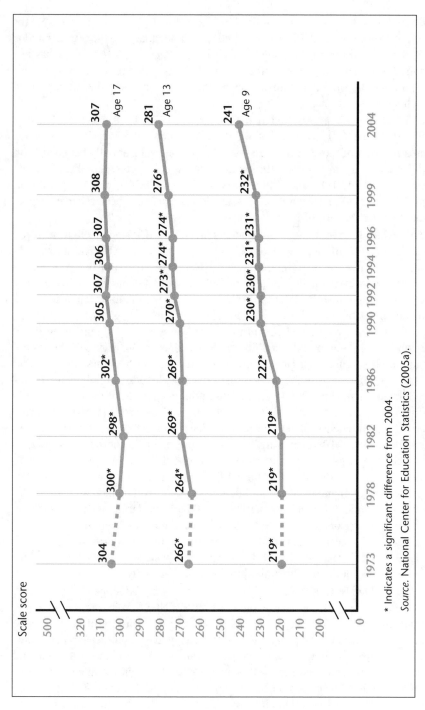

Scale score

* Indicates a significant difference from 2004.

Source. National Center for Education Statistics (2005a).

Figure 2.3. Results of the 1973–2004 Long-Term Trend assessment in mathematics.

1994, and 1996. For 13-year-olds, the 27-point score gap was substantially smaller than the gap in 1999 but still higher than the 24-point gap in 1986 (Figure 2.5). Although not shown in the figures, the 28-point gap for 17-year-olds has been relatively stable—down 3 points in 2004 but still within the range of 21–31 points that has been evident since 1986.

Like Main NAEP, gaps between white and Hispanic students on LTT NAEP have always been less than gaps between white and black students. The white-Hispanic gap in 2004 for 9-year-olds was the smallest ever recorded (Figure 2.6). Between 1999 and 2004, the gap shrank one point for 13-year-olds but is within the range of 19–25 points that has been evident since 1982 (Figure 2.7). The white-Hispanic score gap of 24 points for 17-year-olds was up 2 points since 1999 but still within the range of 20–27 points that has existed since 1982.

INTERNATIONAL ACHIEVEMENT RESULTS

Although not a focus of this volume, the achievement of U.S. students in mathematics can be considered in relation to the achievement of students from other countries. In addition to NAEP, representative samples of students in the United States participated in two international assessments in 2003. We briefly review the results from those assessments.

Trends in Mathematics and Science Study

Like NAEP, the Trends in Mathematics and Science Study (TIMSS) assessment has been given in various forms since the 1960s (see Gonzalez et al., 2004; Robitaille & Travers, 1992). Although not administered as frequently as NAEP, TIMSS is somewhat similar in format and content. In 2003, it was given at Grades 4 and 8 and included a combination of multiple-choice and short constructed-response items based on a framework that is similar but not identical to the framework used by NAEP (Sztajn et al., 2004). At Grade 4, U.S. students performed significantly above the international average, as they did in 1995, the last time that TIMSS was administered at that level. Eleven countries performed significantly better than the United States, and 13 performed significantly worse in 2003 (Gonzalez et al., 2004). In contrast with the gains seen by U.S. 4th-grade students on Main NAEP, 4th graders' scores on TIMSS did not change between 1995 and 2003.

TIMSS was administered at the 8th-grade level in 1995, 1999, and 2003. U.S. students scored significantly above the international average in all three years, and the 2003 scores were significantly higher than those in 1995. More countries participated in TIMSS at Grade 8 than at Grade 4, and 9 of those countries scored better than the United States at that level, 10 scored statistically equivalent to the United States, and 25 scored significantly below the United States (Gonzalez et al., 2004). The most recent TIMSS administration for high school students took

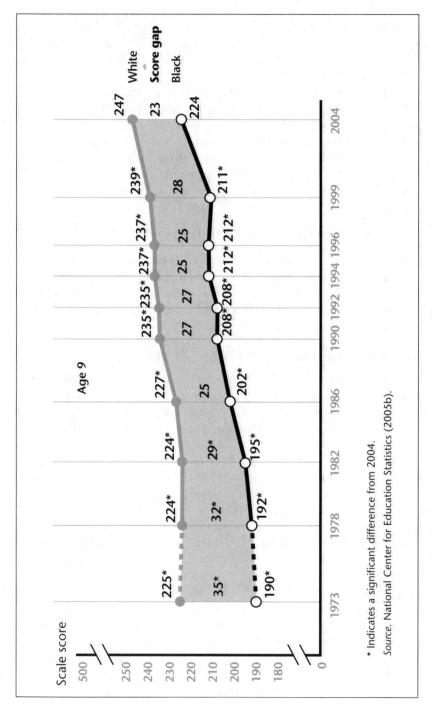

Figure 2.4. LTT achievement gap between age 9 white and black students, 1973–2004.

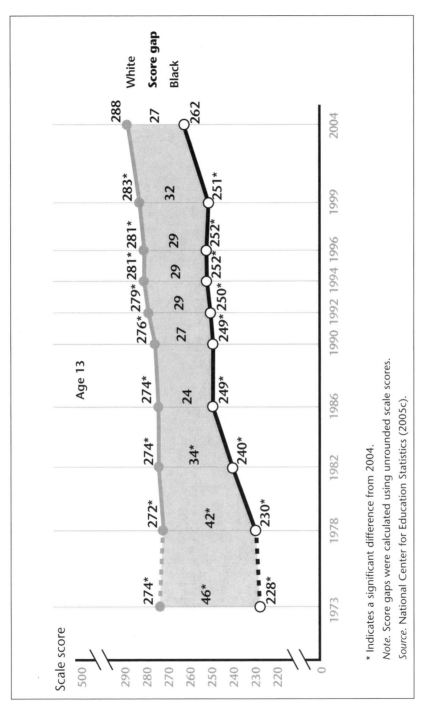

Scale score

Age 13

White
Score gap
Black

274* 272* 274* 274* 276* 279*281* 281* 283* 288

46* 42* 34* 24 27 29 29 29 32 27

228* 230* 240* 249* 249*250* 252*252* 251* 262

1973 1978 1982 1986 1990 1992 1994 1996 1999 2004

500
290
280
270
260
250
240
230
220
0

* Indicates a significant difference from 2004.

Note. Score gaps were calculated using unrounded scale scores.

Source. National Center for Education Statistics (2005c).

Figure 2.5. LTT achievement gap between age 13 white and black students, 1973–2004.

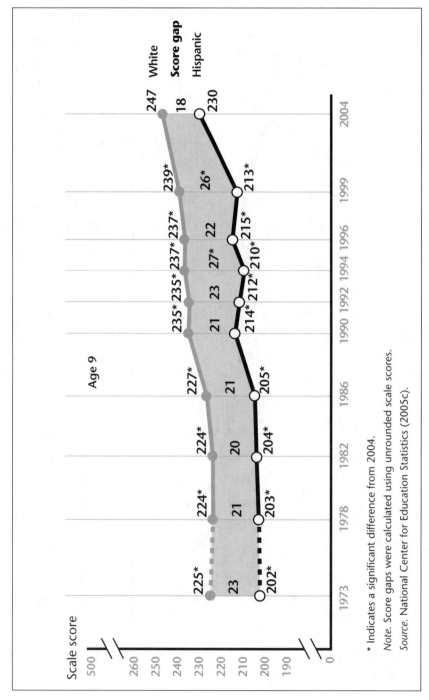

Scale score

Age 9

White

Score gap

Hispanic

247

18

230

239* 26* 213*

237* 237* 22
235* 235* 27* 215*
235* 23 212* 210*
227* 21 214* 210*
224* 205*
224* 20
224* 21 204*
225* 203*
23 202*

1973 1978 1982 1986 1990 1992 1994 1996 1999 2004

500
260
250
240
230
220
210
200
190
0

* Indicates a significant difference from 2004.

Note. Score gaps were calculated using unrounded scale scores.

Source. National Center for Education Statistics (2005c).

Figure 2.6. LTT achievement gap between age 9 white and Hispanic students, 1973–2004.

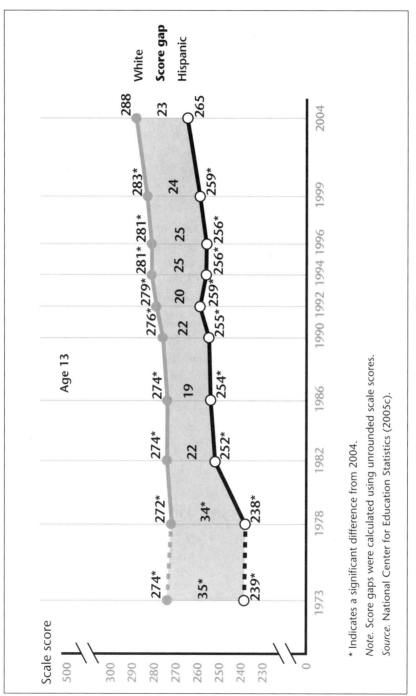

Figure 2.7. LTT achievement gap between age 13 white and Hispanic students, 1973–2004.

Scale score

Age 13

White
Score gap
Hispanic

2004   288   23   265

1999   283*   24   259*

1994 1996   281* 281*   25 25   256* 256*

1990 1992   276* 279*   22 20   255* 259*

1986   274*   19   254*

1982   274*   22   252*

1978   272*   34*   238*

1973   274*   35*   239*

* Indicates a significant difference from 2004.

Note. Score gaps were calculated using unrounded scale scores.

Source. National Center for Education Statistics (2005c).

place in 1995. On that assessment, as on previous TIMSS assessments, U.S. 12th-grade students scored significantly below the international average (Mullis, Martin, Beaton, Gonzalez, Kelly, & Smith, 1998).

Program for International Student Assessment

The second international study in which U.S. students participated in 2003 was the Program for International Student Assessment (PISA). In contrast with NAEP and TIMSS, which were developed to assess student performance on skills they were learning in school, PISA was designed to assess literacy skills in real-world contexts. Thus, whereas NAEP and TIMSS contain items that are typical of what students see in school, all PISA items are set in a real-world context and require students to extract information from the context to answer questions (Sztajn et al., 2004). PISA is given only to 15-year-old students and has foci in reading, mathematics, and science. Started in 2000 with plans to do assessments every three years, PISA is designed with a heavy emphasis on one of the three areas each time it is given. Mathematics was the assessment focus in 2003, and U.S. students scored significantly below the international average. Specifically, of 38 comparison countries, 23 scored higher than the United States on the mathematics literacy portion of PISA and 25 scored higher than the United States on the mathematics problem-solving portion of the assessment (*Learning for Tomorrow's World,* 2004). Those results are consistent with previous international studies that have shown that U.S. high school students lag behind international peers in mathematics (Gonzalez et al., 2004). The fact that U.S. 8th-grade students scored above the international average on TIMSS in 2003 whereas students only a couple of years older scored below the international average on PISA may also be related to the context and problem-solving aspects of PISA. Specifically, students in other countries may be exposed to more problems that go beyond practice of previously learned skills or are set in a real-world context (Hiebert et al., 2003) and thus are better prepared to succeed on those types of problems.

ACHIEVEMENT OUTSIDE OF MATHEMATICS

As explained in Kloosterman (2004), NAEP has been administered at intervals of 2 to 7 years over the past 30 years in the areas of reading, writing, science, history, geography, and civics. Even though item formats differ from one content area to another, the same type of scaling system and the same scale anchors were used in NAEP assessments of geography, history, mathematics, and reading achievement. Table 2.4 shows average scale scores for Main NAEP for geography, history, mathematics, and reading between 1994 and 2003. Scale score gains in mathematics are larger than in the other three areas. Note that because the type of scaling system is the same, a comparison of growth over time is possible in those four subject areas. However, scale scores cannot appropriately be used to compare achievement levels across subject areas. For example, even though the average mathematics scale score for 4th graders in 2003 was 235 on a scale ranging from 0 to 500 and the average reading scale score was 218, we cannot say that 4th-grade students are doing better in mathematics than reading. Science was assessed in 1996 and again in 2000, but different scale anchors were used for reporting the science Main NAEP, and thus all that we can conclude is that from 1996 to 2000, average science scores of 4th- and 8th-grade students were stable. Similarly, writing was assessed in 1998 and 2000 using a separate scaling system. In contrast with science, a statistically significant increase was seen in writing scores in Grades 4 and 8 over that period.

Table 2.4
Average Scale Scores for Various Main NAEPs, 1994–2003

Subject	Grade	1994	1996	1998	2000	2001	2002	2003
Geography	4	206*				208		
	8	260				260		
History	4	205*				209		
	8	259				260		
Mathematics	4		224*		226*			235
	8		270*		273*			278
Reading	4	214*		215*	213*		219	218
	8	260*		263			264*	263

Note. Scores from 1994 are for samples for which accommodations were not permitted. The 1994 data were included to make growth patterns in geography, history, and reading more apparent. None of the areas listed were assessed in 1995, 1997, or 1999.

* Indicates significant difference from the most recent assessment.

CONCLUSION

For those involved in mathematics education, the 2003 NAEP results are clearly cause for optimism. Scores at Grades 4 and 8 are up significantly since 2000, and gains are seen in all five mathematics content areas assessed by NAEP. The achievement gap between white and black students appears to be narrowing, fueled in part by the substantial improvement by students at the lowest end of the achievement distribution. Scores for 9- and 13-year-old students on the 2004 Long-Term Trend assessment were also up significantly, indicating that traditional mathematics skills are improving along with the more complex skills measured by Main NAEP at the elementary and middle school levels. On TIMSS, U.S. 4th- and 8th-grade students scored above the international average, although 15-year-old students scored below the international average on PISA. The PISA results imply that U.S. high school students need more experience solving problems beyond those seen in traditional textbooks.

What has happened in classrooms to help children improve in mathematics? Later chapters in this volume pinpoint some of the types of mathematics tasks on which gains have been the greatest and explore specific curricular and pedagogical reasons for those gains. In this chapter, we have focused on overall gains and thus speculate only on general curricular and policy influences on mathematics achievement.

At the elementary school level, where teachers have control over the amount of time spent on mathematics, a reasonable hypothesis is that students are spending more time on mathematics. Support for that hypothesis comes from the NAEP teacher questionnaires, which indicate that the percentage of Grade 4 students who spend 4 or more hours a week getting instruction in mathematics increased from 66% in 1996 to 72% in 2000. The teacher question about time spent was reworded in 2003, making comparison with 2000 impossible, but 52% of the 4th-grade students had teachers who reported spending 7 hours or less on mathematics and 37% had teachers who reported spending 7 to 9.9 hours a week on mathematics instruction with one class. No comparable data are available on time spent in Grade 8, but the lack of improvement by 17-year-old students on LTT NAEP may be due in part to the fact that length of classes in high school has been relatively stable.

Related to the amount of time spent on mathematics is what is actually happening in class. Since the publication of *Curriculum and Evaluation Standards for School Mathematics* (National Council of Teachers of Mathematics [NCTM], 1989), more emphasis has been placed on such topics as algebraic thinking and data analysis and on different ways of approaching some of the more traditional topics in mathematics. The NCTM document has likely played a significant role in the rise in NAEP scores. At the time the 2003 Main NAEP results and the 2004 LTT NAEP results were released, a number of comments by politicians and White House officials indicated that the gain in scores was attributable to the No Child Left Behind legislation of 2001. However, given the short time that legislation had been in effect before the NAEP assessments were administered, it was unlikely to have made a difference in the NAEP results.

Other factors are also at play. Some states have pressed for smaller class sizes in the primary grades. We have no way of knowing how much smaller classes have helped NAEP scores, but they could be a factor. Considerable debate is taking place about accountability and how much children should be assessed. Simply assessing children does not improve performance, but accountability in general may be a factor affecting achievement. NAEP, unfortunately, fosters no insight into that issue. In some areas of the country, a push has been exerted to hold children back from kindergarten until they are ready. Indiana, for example, requires children to be 5 years old by July 1 to start school. Fourth-grade students in Indiana score above the national average in mathematics, but we have no way of knowing whether they score higher because of curricular and pedagogical influences in Indiana schools or because they are 2 or 3 months older than their peers in other states. Another factor may be teacher professional development. Although modest, increased funding has been allotted for in-service development of mathematics teachers over the past decade, and that in-service work has likely resulted in better teaching. In brief, improvements in performance can be linked with numerous factors, many of which interact. Thus a determination of which factors have been the most influential is virtually impossible.

Although room for improvement remains in mathematics teaching and learning, the news from the 2003 NAEP is very good. The position of NCTM has been that every child can and should learn mathematics, and the NAEP data show that all groups are making significant progress. Moreover, the NAEP data show that we can teach basic skills and problem solving at the same time. No evidence would indicate that we need to wait until students master the basics before giving them more complex mathematical problems to solve. Overall, NAEP results show dramatic improvements in mathematics learning, and we should take a few minutes to acknowledge our success.

REFERENCES

Braswell, J. S., Daane, M. C., & Grigg, W. S. (2004). *The nation's report card: Mathematics highlights 2003.* Washington, DC: National Center for Education Statistics. Retrieved November 6, 2005, from http://nces.ed.gov/nationsreportcard/pdf/main2003/2004451.pdf

Gonzalez, P., Guzman, J. C., Partelow, L., Pahlke, E., Jocelyn, L., Kastberg, D., & Williams, T. (2004). *Highlights from the Trends in International Mathematics and Science Study (TIMSS) 2003.* Washington, DC: National Center for Education Statistics.

Hiebert, J., Gallimore, R., Garnier, H., Givvin, K. B., Hollingsworth, H., Jacobs, J., Chui, A. M., Wearne, D., Smith, M., Kersting, N., Manaster, A., Tseng, E., Etterbeek, W., Manaster, C., Gonzalez, P., & Stigler, J. (2003). *Teaching mathematics in seven countries: Results from the TIMSS 1999 video study.* Washington, DC: National Center for Education Statistics.

Kehle, P. Wearne, D., Martin, W. G., Strutchens, M., & Warfield, J. (2004). What do 12th-grade students know about mathematics? In P. Kloosterman & F. K. Lester Jr. (Eds.), *Results and interpretations of the 1990–2000 mathematics assessments of the National Assessment of Educational Progress* (pp. 145–174). Reston, VA: National Council of Teachers of Mathematics.

Kloosterman, P. (2004). Interpreting the 2000 NAEP mathematics data: Issues and monograph overview. In P. Kloosterman & F. K. Lester Jr. (Eds.), *Results and interpretations of the 1990–2000 mathematics assessments of the National Assessment of Educational Progress* (pp. 3–32). Reston, VA: National Council of Teachers of Mathematics.

Kloosterman, P., Warfield, J., Wearne, D., Koc, Y., Martin, W. G., & Strutchens, M. (2004). Fourth-grade students' knowledge of mathematics and perceptions of learning mathematics. In P. Kloosterman & F. K. Lester Jr. (Eds.), *Results and interpretations of the 1990–2000 mathematics assessments of the National Assessment of Educational Progress* (pp. 71–103). Reston, VA: National Council of Teachers of Mathematics.

Learning for tomorrow's world: First results from PISA 2003 (2004). Paris: Organisation for Economic Co-operation and Development. Retrieved Oct. 19, 2005, from www.pisa.oecd.org

Mullis, I. V. S., Martin, M. O., Beaton, A. E., Gonzalez, E. J., Kelly, D. L., & Smith, T. A. (1998). *Mathematics and science achievement in the final year of secondary school: IEA's Third International Mathematics and Science Study (TIMSS)*. Chestnut Hill, MA: TIMSS International Study Center.

National Center for Education Statistics (2005a). *National trends in mathematics by average scale scores*. Retrieved November 6, 2005, from http://nces.ed.gov/nationsreport-card/ltt/results2004/nat-math-scalescore.asp

National Center for Education Statistics (2005b). *Trends in average mathematics scale scores by race/ethnicity: White-black gap*. Retrieved November 6, 2005, from http://nces.ed.gov/nationsreportcard/ltt/results2004/sub-math-race.asp

National Center for Education Statistics (2005c). *Trends in average mathematics scale scores by race/ethnicity: White-Hispanic gap*. Retrieved November 6, 2005, from http://nces.ed.gov/nationsreportcard/ltt/results2004/sub_math_race2.asp

National Council of Teachers of Mathematics (1989). *Curriculum and evaluation standards for school mathematics*. Reston, VA: Author.

National Council of Teachers of Mathematics (1991). *Professional standards for teaching mathematics*. Reston, VA: Author.

National Council of Teachers of Mathematics (1995). *Assessment standards for school mathematics*. Reston, VA: Author,

National Council of Teachers of Mathematics (2000). *Principles and standards for school mathematics*. Reston, VA: Author.

Robitaille, D. F., & Travers, K. J. (1992). International studies of achievement in mathematics. In D. A. Grouws (Ed.), *Handbook of research on mathematics teaching and learning* (pp. 687–709). New York: Macmillan.

Sowder, J. T., Wearne, D., Martin, W. G., & Strutchens, M. (2004). What do 8th-grade students know about mathematics? Changes over a decade. In P. Kloosterman & F. K. Lester Jr. (Eds.), *Results and interpretations of the 1990–2000 mathematics assessments of the National Assessment of Educational Progress* (pp. 105–143). Reston, VA: National Council of Teachers of Mathematics.

Sztajn, P., Anthony, H. G., Chae, J., Erbas, A. K., Hembree, D., Keum, J., Klerlein, J. T., & Tunc-Pekkan, Z. (2004). NAEP, TIMSS, and PISA: What can we learn? In P. Kloosterman & F. K. Lester Jr. (Eds.), *Results and interpretations of the 1990–2000 mathematics assessments of the National Assessment of Educational Progress* (pp. 383–418). Reston, VA: National Council of Teachers of Mathematics.

3

Student Performance in Whole-Number Properties and Operations

Janet Warfield and Sherry L. Meier

BEFORE 1996, the mathematics framework for the National Assessment of Educational Progress called for 50% of the items to deal with Number Sense, Properties, and Operations. Since 1990, the emphasis of the mathematics framework has shifted to a more balanced distribution of items across the five content strands. At the 4th-grade level in 1990 and 1992, the framework stipulated that 45% of the items should be classified as Number Sense, Properties, and Operations. In 1996, 2000, and 2003, the framework called for number sense items to be 40% of the total number of items. At the 8th-grade level, the percentage of items recommended for number sense dropped from 30% in 1990 and 1992 to 25% in 1996, 2000, and 2003 (National Assessment Governing Board [NAGB], 2002).

In 2003, 75 of the 182 4th-grade items were classified as Number Sense, Properties, and Operations. Of those, approximately 55%, or about 23% of the items used at the 4th-grade level, dealt with whole numbers. Of the 200 8th-grade items, 51 were classified as Number Sense, Properties, and Operations. Approximately 34% of those, or 8.5% of the items used at the 8th-grade level, involved whole numbers. Other items in the category dealt with fractions, decimals, and percentage and are discussed chapter 4.

Although the percentage of total items classified as Number Sense, Properties, and Operations that involve whole numbers has diminished over time, many items in other NAEP content strands require students to use computation involving whole numbers or concepts related to whole numbers. Such items were included among those analyzed for this chapter.

The remainder of this chapter is divided into two sections. First, we discuss student performance on the items classified as Number Sense, Properties,

Highlights

- About 65% of 4th graders are able to identify odd and even numbers. Only about 46% of 8th graders are able to reason about properties of, and operations with, odd and even numbers.
- About 75% of 4th graders have basic understanding of place value.
- Fourth-grade students do better on addition than subtraction.
- Fourth- and 8th-grade students do better on numeric addition, subtraction, multiplication, and division problems than on word problems and better on routine one-step word problems than on nonroutine or multistep problems.
- Fourth- and 8th-grade students perform better on addition and subtraction problems than on multiplication and division problems.
- Fourth-grade students do not do as well on extended constructed-response items as they do on other item types.
- Students do better on whole-number items in noncalculator blocks than on whole-number items in calculator blocks. Apparently other variables had an influence on performance on those items.

and Operations that involved whole numbers. Second, we discuss factors that may have influenced students' performance; for this purpose we include items that dealt with whole numbers but that were not classified as Number Sense, Properties, and Operations.

DEALING WITH WHOLE NUMBERS

In this section, we address only items that were classified by NAEP as Number Sense, Properties, and Operations and that dealt only with whole numbers. Although we examined all the items in that category, we do not discuss all of them. We have divided the items into six clusters: (1) factors and multiples, (2) place value, (3) whole-number addition and subtraction (including purely numeric problems and one-step word problems), (4) problem solving using whole-number addition and subtraction, (5) whole-number multiplication and division (including numeric items and number sentences), and (6) whole-number multiplication and division word problems.

Factors and Multiples

A group of items dealt with factors and multiples (see Table 3.1), including six that dealt with even and odd numbers. Of those six items, three were given only to 4th-grade students and three were given only to 8th-grade students.

The 4th-grade items were quite different from those given to 8th-grade students. The 4th graders were asked to classify two two-digit numbers and one three-digit

Table 3.1
Performance on Items Involving Factors and Multiples

		Percentage Correct	
Item Description		Grade 4	Grade 8
Even- and Odd-Number Items			
1.	Classify numbers as even or odd.	65	
2.	State the greatest even number less than a given number less than 50. (2005-4M12 #9)[a]	71	
3.	Recognize odd-number property in a word problem.	55	
4.	Identify properties of the sum of prime numbers, relative to even and odd.		55
5.	Consider the statement "If n is an even number, then n is two times an odd number." For which of the following values of n is the statement FALSE? (Choices are 2, 6, 8, 10, 14.) (2003-8M7 #11)		48
6.	Choose an operation that always results in odd integers.		34
Other Factors and Multiples Items			
7.	Two whole numbers, each greater than 2, are multiplied together. The product is 126. What could the two numbers be? (2003-4M7 #18)	15	
8.	Six students bought exactly enough pens to share equally among themselves. Which could be the number of pens they bought? (Choices are 46, 48, 50, or 52). (2003-4M6 #11, 2003-8M6 #11)	51	83

Note. Items 4, 5, 6, and 8 were multiple-choice items. Items 1, 2, 3, and 7 were short constructed-response items. Calculators were allowed on Items 4, 5, and 7.

[a]2005 items were released while this volume was in production. Block and item numbers were added so that interested readers can find the relevant 2005 items using the online Questions Tool.

number as either even or odd (Item 1), to give the greatest even number less than a given number (Item 2), and to solve a word problem about students walking in pairs. About two-thirds of the 4th graders were able to answer Items 1 and 2 correctly. However, only 55% were able to use their understanding of even and odd numbers to correctly solve a word problem.

The 8th-grade items required students to reason about properties and operations with even and odd numbers. Item 4 was a multiple-choice item that required students to reason about prime numbers. Only 55% of 8th graders answered this item correctly. Item 5 in the table was a released item, and, observing the convention that is used throughout this volume, it is followed in the table by the block and item number so that interested readers can find the item and additional information about that item using the NAEP online Questions Tool (nces.ed.gov/nationsreportcard, see chapter 1). On Item 5, 48% selected the correct answer of 8. No apparent pattern was seen in the incorrect responses (17% chose 2, 13% chose 6, 8% chose 10, 14% chose 14), clouding any hypothesis about why students missed this item other than to suggest that they might not have understood the statement in the problem. Item 6, for which students were to select an operation that would always result in an odd integer, was even more difficult for the students; only 33% answered it correctly.

The last two items in Table 3.1 dealt with factors other than 2. Both of those were released items. Item 7, which was given to only 4th graders, was a short constructed-response item on which students were allowed to use calculators. Only 15% of the students gave a correct answer, and another 8% gave the answer of 2 and 63, which was considered to be partially correct. The difficulty posed by the problem in Item 7 is puzzling, inasmuch as students had calculators available and four appropriate solutions were possible. One possible explanation is that the students may not have understood the mathematical language used in the problem, that is, they may not have known what is meant by *whole numbers* or by *product*. Another possibility is that students may not have seen items phrased similarly to this item in 4th-grade textbooks.

Item 8 is the only item in this category that was given to both 4th- and 8th-grade students. Fifty-one percent of 4th graders and 83% of 8th graders chose the correct answer. The most commonly chosen incorrect answer to this multiple-choice question was 46; it was selected by 29% of the 4th graders and 10% of the 8th graders. Since this choice was the only response other than the correct one that falls between 40 and 50, students may have known an approximate answer for 6×8 but had not memorized the fact and were not able or did not attempt to derive it.

Place Value

Table 3.2 shows students' performance on items dealing with place value. Of the six items shown in the table, four were given to 4th graders only, one was given to 8th graders only, and one was given to both 4th and 8th graders. As can be seen in Table 3.2, approximately three-fourths of 4th-grade students responded correctly to the first four items listed, all of which were multiple-choice items.

Items 3 and 5 in Table 3.2 were similar, and the high percentages of students choosing the correct answers indicate that students are good at translating large numbers in words into numerals. Students' performance on Item 6 in the table is somewhat puzzling. Although not released, Kouba and Wearne (2000) described this item by saying that it involved asking students to write a number given three digits (for example, 7, 2, and 5) and place values of two of those digits

Table 3.2
Performance on Place Value Items

	Item Description	Percentage Correct	
		Grade 4	Grade 8
1.	Choose the number represented in a picture of base ten blocks. (2003-4M10 #6)	83	
2.	Given a set of four-digit numbers, choose which is greatest.	72	
3.	Ron was listening to the radio and heard, "One hundred twenty-four thousand sixty-five books have been donated to the library." What is this number? (Choices are 12,465; 124,065; 124,650; 100,024,065). (2003-4M10 #3).	77	
4.	Choose a number that is 10 more than a given four-digit number.	76	
5.	Identify large number.		80
6.	Write a three-digit number given digits and condi-tions related to their place value.	65	63

Note. Item 6 was a short constructed-response item. The others were multiple-choice items.

(for example, there are 7 tens and 5 hundreds). This item has appeared on every NAEP assessment since 1990. The scores on this item since 1990 are shown in Table 3.3.

Kouba and Wearne wrote about performance on Item 6 in the 1996 NAEP. "Only 58 percent of the 4th-grade students correctly produced a number that met the given conditions. It is somewhat surprising that 8th-grade students did only slightly better on this task" (2000, p. 148). The results for Item 6 are even more

Table 3.3
Performance on Item 6 in Table 3.2

	Percentage Correct				
Grade	1990	1992	1996	2000	2003
4th	50	54	58	67	65
8th	55	60	60	62	63

Note. The percentage correct for 1990 and 1992 is for samples in which accommodations were not permitted. The percentage correct in 1996 was 58 for Grade 4 for the sample with accommodations not permitted.

surprising when viewed across time. Although the percentage of students correctly answering the question remains low, the percentage of 4th graders giving a correct response has gradually increased since 1990 while the percentage of 8th graders giving a correct response has remained steady or increased only slightly. The result is that in 2003 a higher percentage of 4th graders than 8th graders answered the item correctly. As Kouba and Wearne also pointed out, we do not have access to student responses on this short constructed-response item. Therefore, we cannot identify why it is difficult for students (2000). We can hypothesize, however, that place value is being emphasized more in the lower grades than in the past. This emphasis could account for the increased performance of 4th graders. We can also hypothesize that the 8th graders thought they knew place value so well that they did not read the problem carefully and thus did not notice that the hundreds and tens place values were reversed in the words in the problem.

Addition and Subtraction Operations With Whole Numbers

Most of the whole-number items on the 2003 NAEP required students to add, subtract, multiply, or divide whole numbers. We discuss addition and subtraction items first. We have divided these items into two clusters: (1) numeric items and word problems that could be solved by adding or subtracting the numbers given in the problem, and (2) items that required more abstract problem solving. Table 3.4 shows the first cluster of items.

Three numeric addition and subtraction items were given, the first only to 4th-grade students and the second and third to both 4th- and 8th-grade students. The second problem was a multiple-choice item, and the other two were short constructed-response items. Students did well on these problems, with approximately 80% of 4th graders and 90% of 8th graders giving correct responses. The only released item in this category was Item 2 in Table 3.4. The correct answer for this item was chosen by 89% of 4th graders and 91% of 8th graders.

Higher percentages of 4th-grade students gave correct responses to Item 2 than to either Item 1 or Item 3. For 4th graders, approximately 10% fewer students were able to answer those items correctly. Two explanations for this deficiency are possible. First, Items 1 and 3 were short constructed-response items and thus may have been more difficult than Item 2, which was a multiple-choice item (this aspect is discussed in more detail later in the chapter). A second, and probably more likely, explanation is that Item 2 required addition with regrouping, whereas Items 1 and 3 required subtraction with regrouping. We do not have data that allow us to determine the sorts of errors students made on Items 1 and 3. However, when Kouba and Wearne (2000) examined responses to Item 3 on the 1996 NAEP, they found three common errors: (1) students subtracted the smaller digit from the larger, regardless of whether the digits were in the minuend or subtrahend; (2) students made errors in regrouping; and (3) students added instead of subtracted. Although we cannot say whether students made similar mistakes in 2003, they were likely to have done so.

Table 3.4

Performance on Whole-Number Addition and Subtraction Items: Numeric and Word Problems

	Percentage Correct	
Item Description	Grade 4	Grade 8
Numeric Problems		
1. Subtract a one-digit from a two-digit number with regrouping.	80	
2. Add: 238 + 462 (Choices are 600, 690, 700, 790). (2003-4M6 #1, 2003-8M6 #1)	89	91
3. Subtract a two-digit from a three-digit number with regrouping. (2005-4M4 #1)	77	89
Word Problems		
4. The band members have a goal to sell 625 candy bars. If they have sold 264 so far, how many more candy bars do they have to sell to reach their goal? (2003-4M10 #9)	63	
5. Subtract a six-digit number from a seven-digit number with regrouping.	34	
6. Solve a word problem involving coins.	60	
7. Interpret a Venn diagram, and solve a word problem. (2005-4M12 #4)	78	
8. Subtract five-digit numbers with regrouping (answer expressed as an estimate).	49	83

Note. Items 2, 6, 7, and 8 were multiple-choice items. The others were short constructed-response items. Calculators were allowed on Item 5.

As in previous NAEP administrations, students did not perform as well on word problems as on numeric items (Kloosterman, Warfield, Wearne, Koc, Martin, & Strutchens, 2004). The difficulty of word problems would seem to lie in the fact that students need to determine which operation to use. However, the particular items in Table 3.4 may have been difficult for reasons other than simply that they were word problems.

Item 4 in Table 3.4 may have been difficult not only because it was a word problem but because of the hypothetical nature of the story in the problem. Instead of saying the students have 625 candy bars to sell, the problem says their goal is to sell 625 candy bars, and instead of saying they have sold 264, the problem says, "If they have sold 264." That is, the problem might have been easier if it had read, "The band members had 625 candy bars. They sold 264 of those. How many candy bars do they still have?" Research has shown that students typically find problems describing a clear action easier to solve than those in which the action is not clear (Carpenter, Fennema, Franke, Levi, & Empson, 1999).

Item 5 in Table 3.4, which required students to subtract a six-digit number from a seven-digit number, was the most difficult addition or subtraction word problem for 4th graders, even though they were allowed to use calculators. The difficulty was likely due to the fact that the seven-digit number in the problem was written in words rather than numerals. If students were unable to translate from words to numerals, they were thus unable to enter the correct numeral into the calculator. Item 6, a word problem involving money, required students to translate from names of coins to amounts of money. This requirement may have contributed to the difficulty of the problem. Finally, Item 7 required students to work with large numbers to estimate an answer. If students knew to round the given numbers and subtract to get an estimate, the problem was not difficult. Students may have run into difficulty because they attempted to do the standard subtraction algorithm, which required regrouping three times. Although the evidence clearly shows that students do not perform as well on word problems as on numeric problems, we can reasonably conclude that factors embedded in the specific word problems might lead to the difficulty. Unfortunately, we do not have more information about student responses to those items; such information could help us understand the difficulties students have with the items.

Some items required students to use more than one operation, complete more than one step, or use more complex reasoning than the items shown in Table 3.4. Those items are listed in Table 3.5. Five such items were given to 4th graders, and one was given to 8th graders.

The percentages of 4th-grade students correctly answering the numeric items were low. Only 47% gave a correct response for Item 1, and 32% gave a correct response for Item 2, both of which were short constructed-response items. In Item 1, students were given a set of five digits and asked to use them to write a subtraction problem with a given answer. Item 3 consisted of a number sentence in which four one-digit numbers were added or subtracted to arrive at a specific two-digit result. Two of the one-digit numbers were missing, and students were to give two different sets of numbers that could be used in the blanks. Both of those items required students to reason about the numbers used rather than to apply an algorithm as required for the numeric items in Table 3.4.

The results for the word problems in Table 3.5 were inconsistent. Seventy-eight percent of 4th graders answered Item 3 correctly, but only 42% answered Item 4 correctly and 27% answered Item 5 correctly. Item 3 is a missing-addend problem. Students are given two addends (6 and 12) and the sum and are asked to find a third addend. The relatively small size of the numbers may have contributed to students' finding the problem easier than Items 4 and 6, which were also missing-addend problems. It also might have been easier because it was the only multiple-choice

Table 3.5
Performance on Whole-Number Addition and Subtraction Items: Problem Solving

| | Percentage Correct | |
Item Description	Grade 4	Grade 8
Numeric Problems		
1. Construct a subtraction problem given digits and a target difference. (2005-4M4 #11)	47	
2. Find pairs of missing one-digit terms in an addition-and-subtraction equation. (2005-4M4 #12)	32	
Word Problems		
3. On Thursday Becky made some popcorn balls. On Friday she made 6 popcorn balls. On Saturday she made 12 popcorn balls. Becky took all 23 popcorn balls that she made to a party. How many popcorn balls did she make on Thursday? (Choices are 5, 11, 17, and 41). (2003-4M10 #7)	78	
4. Solve a multistep word problem involving three-digit numbers. (2005-4M4 #8)	42	
5. Solve a nonroutine, multistep problem, and explain.	27	
6. Solve a multistep word problem involving two- and three-digit numbers.		43

Note. Item 3 was a multiple-choice item. The others were short constructed-response items. Calculators were allowed on Items 5 and 6.

item in the group, and on missing-addend problems in particular, students who are having difficulty approaching the problems directly can look at the answer choices and figure out which one works.

Clearly, 4th graders performed better on one-step numeric problems using addition and subtraction than on simple word problems, and better on simple word problems than on nonroutine problems. They did not exhibit much difference in their performance on nonroutine numeric problems and nonroutine word problems. Similar results are true for 8th-grade students, although we do not have evidence for their performance on nonroutine numeric problems. The 2003 results are comparable to those on previous NAEP examinations (Kloosterman et al., 2004; Kouba & Wearne, 2000).

Multiplication and Division Operations With Whole Numbers

We separated items related to multiplication and division of whole numbers into two clusters: (1) numeric situations and number sentences and (2) word problems. Table 3.6 shows the percentage of students giving correct responses for the first cluster.

The first item in Table 3.6 required students to multiply two two-digit numbers and then divide by a third two-digit number. Calculators were allowed on Item 1, so the fact that it was answered correctly by a higher percentage of 4th-grade students than any other item in Table 3.6 is not surprising. What is somewhat sur-

Table 3.6

Whole-Number Multiplication and Division Items: Numeric Situations and Number Sentences

	Percentage Correct	
Item Description	Grade 4	Grade 8
Numeric Situations		
1. Multiply and divide two-digit numbers.	84	
2. $4 \times 0 \times 5 \times 9 =$ (Choices are 0, 36, 45, and 180). (2003-4M10 #11)	53	
3. Divide 504 by 21. (2003-8M10 #1)		73
Number Sentences		
4. Sam placed cookies on a cookie sheet to form 2 rows with 6 cookies in each row. Which of the following number sentences best describes this situation? (2003-4M7 #4)	83	
5. Kim wants to give 7 stickers to each of her 5 friends. To find out how many stickers she needs, she writes the number sentence $7 + 7 + 7 + 7 + 7 = $ _____. Write a number sentence with multiplication that she could use to find the number of stickers she needs. (2003-4M10 #5)	71	
6. Pat has 3 fish bowls. There are 4 plants and 5 fish in each bowl. Which gives the total number of fish? (2003-4M7 #11).	57	
7. Carla has 12 boxes, each weighing the same amount. What would be a quick way for her to find the total weight of the 12 boxes? (Choices are: add 12 to the weight of one of the boxes; subtract 12 from the weight of one of the boxes; divide the weight of one of the boxes by 12; multiply the weight of one of the boxes by 12). (2003-4M6 #9, 2003-8M6 #9)	57	81
8. Choose extraneous information in a multistep word problem with one-digit numbers. (2005-8M3 #8)	35	64

Note. Items 2 and 5 were short constructed-response items. The others were multiple-choice items. Calculators were allowed on Items 1, 4, and 6.

prising is that only 84% of students chose the correct answer. Fifty-three percent of 4th graders chose 0, the correct answer for Item 2. Two percent chose 36, 32% chose 45, and 11% chose 180. The 32% who chose 45 probably multiplied 4 × 0 and 5 × 9 and chose to ignore the result of the first multiplication in determining the answer. Another 11% ignored the 0 entirely and multiplied the numbers 4, 5, and 9 to get an answer of 180. Clearly, nearly half of the 4th graders tested did not understand the role of zero in a multiplicative situation.

The second group of items in Table 3.6 required the students to write or choose correct number sentences for multiplication or division word problems. Eighty-three percent of 4th graders correctly answered Item 4, and 71% of 4th graders correctly answered Item 5. Worth noting here is the fact that 18% of students were considered to have given partially correct responses to Item 5. The responses considered partially correct were 35, $7 + 7 + 7 + 7 + 7 = 35$, $7 \times 7 = 35$, and $7 \times 5 = 30$. We mention this aspect of the scoring because we fail to understand why any of those responses were considered partially correct.

Fourth graders did not perform as well on Items 6 and 8, which required them to attend to extraneous information. They also did not perform well on Item 7, possibly because they were not given the weight of one box. Eighth graders performed better on Items 7 and 8 than did 4th graders. However, only 64% of 8th graders responded correctly to Item 8, on which they needed to attend to extraneous information, and only 81% selected the correct response to Item 7.

Table 3.7 shows student performance on multiplication and division word problems. The items are divided into two categories. The first three were one-step word problems and were given only to 4th graders. The others involved more than one step; of those, four were given only to 4th graders, two were given only to 8th graders, and one was given to both 4th and 8th graders.

As might be expected, 4th graders performed better on one-step word problems than on multistep or nonroutine problems. Surprisingly, students did better on Item 3, which was a division problem, than on Items 1 and 2, which were multiplication problems. All three of the items were multiple choice, and calculators were allowed on all three. Item 1 may have been difficult because of the measurement context. The most frequently chosen incorrect answer, 4, was chosen by 21% of the students, indicating that they were not sure whether to multiply or divide. Item 3, by contrast, was an equal-sharing problem in which a given number of students were to be put into equal groups. This context may have been more familiar to 4th graders.

Fourth graders found the multistep and nonroutine word problems shown in Table 3.7 quite difficult. Slightly more than one-third of the 4th graders answered Items 4, 5, and 6 correctly. Only 34% of 4th graders selected the correct answer (20) for Item 6. Fifty-three percent selected 30; those students apparently answered the question "How many boys are in the class?" rather than the question in the problem. Item 7 was answered correctly by only 7% of 4th graders. Item 7 was similar to Item 6; however, two numeric answers and an explanation were required.

Table 3.7

Performance on Whole-Number Multiplication and Division Word Problems

		Percentage Correct	
	Item Description	Grade 4	Grade 8
One-Step Word Problems			
1.	At a picnic, cider is served in cups. If 1 pint will fill 2 cups, how many cups can be filled from 8 pints of cider? (2003-4M7 #8)	61	
2.	Choose the correct answer for a word problem involving multiplication of a two-digit number by a one-digit number.	52	
3.	Choose the correct answer to a division word problem involving a three-digit number divided by a one-digit number.	71	
Multistep and Nonroutine Word Problems			
4.	Solve a multioperational problem involving division with remainders and two-digit numbers.	34	
5.	Kirstin wants to buy a flute that costs $240. She has saved $20 each week for 3 weeks. How many more weeks does Kirstin need to save money if she continues to save $20 each week? (2003-4M7 #14)	39	
6.	In Jean's class there are twice as many boys as girls. If there are 10 girls in the class, how many boys and girls are there in the class? (Choices were 15, 20, 25, and 30). (2003-4M7 #16)	34	
7.	Choose the correct answer to a multioperational problem involving one-digit to three-digit numbers.	7	
8.	A high school orders 11 buses to transport 418 students. If each bus can seat 35 students, will the number of buses ordered be enough to provide a seat for each student? Explain. (2003-8M10 #5)		77
9.	Fifteen boxes each containing 8 radios can be repacked in 10 larger boxes each containing how many radios? (Choices were 8, 10, 12, 80, 120). (2003-8M7 #9)		47
10.	Carla has 3 empty egg cartons and 34 eggs. If each carton holds 12 eggs, how many more eggs are needed to fill all 3 cartons? (2003-4M6 #12)	46	80

Note. Items 4 and 8 were short constructed-response items. Item 7 was an extended constructed-response item. The others were multiple-choice items. Calculators were allowed on Items 1, 2, 3, 5, 6, 7, and 9.

Eighth graders were not given any one-step multiplication or division problems. They performed better than 4th graders on the multistep word problems. About 80% correctly answered two of the three items they were given. Surprisingly, they did not do nearly as well on Item 9.

STUDENTS' PERFORMANCE ON ALL ITEMS DEALING WITH WHOLE NUMBERS

In this section we discuss all items that required the students to understand whole-number concepts or to carry out whole-number computation. Our discussion includes items that were classified by NAEP as being in a category other than Number Sense, Properties, and Operations.

Overall Cross-Grade Comparison on Items Involving Whole-Number Operations

Some items involving whole-number operations or place value were given to both 4th and 8th graders. On those items, 8th graders typically performed better than 4th graders. Although this finding might be expected, the amount of increase and variation in the amount of increase across problems were interesting. The average percent of increase from 4th to 8th grade across twenty items was 41%. However, the range of the percent of increase was large, with a low of –3.5% and a high of 164%. The item on which 3.5% fewer 8th-grade students got the correct answer than 4th-grade students was a relatively simple place-value question (Item 5 in Table 3.2—see our previous discussion of this item). On the other extreme, the item that showed an increase of 164% was a multiple-choice item that required students to identify the set of whole numbers that made an inequality true. Less than 24% of 4th graders completed the task successfully, whereas more than 63% of 8th graders did so. The discrepancy in the results on the inequality problem is perhaps expected, since 8th-grade students are likely to be more familiar with inequalities than 4th-grade students. However, we continued to wonder whether other factors may also have influenced student performance on such tasks across grade levels.

Other Factors Influencing Students' Performance on Items Involving Whole Numbers

As we examined the variety of questions on the NAEP assessment that required the use of whole-number computation, we found several variables that we believe could have influenced student performance. Although in the past, item difficulty has been discussed in relation to number size, operations required, and whether the item required a single or multiple steps, other characteristics of the questions have not been as fully investigated or reported. Other characteristics that could have affected student performance fascinated us, and we decided to look at some of those characteristics more closely. We identified three main characteristics as variables that might have an impact on performance: (1) the type of item response required of the student, (2) whether a calculator was allowed, and (3) the context of the problem. As a result, we decided to investigate whether any patterns existed in student performance according to those three variables across 4th and 8th grades. To examine those variables, we needed accurate and specific descriptors for each item, including information on whether a calculator was allowed on each. We had adequate detail on most but not all of the nonreleased items, so the following analysis is based only on those items on which exact analysis was possible. Although this constraint slightly reduced our item pool for analysis, the results are still noteworthy.

Item Response Type

NAEP includes items that require three types of responses. The first of these is the typical multiple-choice (MC) item, for which a student must pick the correct answer from among four or five choices. Such items are designed to contain distracters that represent incorrect answers students will get if they make a common error (see chapter 1). The second type of items is short constructed-response (SCR) items. Such items require a student to calculate an answer and provide that answer in a specified location in the answer booklet (see Figure 3.1).

The third type of items, extended constructed-response items (ECR), were first included on the 1992 assessment and were designed to require students not just to communicate their ideas by writing in their answers but also to demonstrate their reasoning by showing their work or writing explanations (NAGB, 2002). Figure 3.2 presents an example of an ECR item.

The NAGB believed that the ECR and SCR items would provide a more complete picture of student performance. Our analysis was designed with that idea in mind. By examining performance according to the format of the problem as well as its context, we hoped to obtain a more complete picture of student achievement as well as to examine test variables that might influence student performance.

Table 3.8 provides the mean percentage of whole-number-related items correct by grade level on the basis of the type of response required. As we examined the whole-number items on the 2003 assessment, we found that the number of SCR and MC items were fairly well balanced at the 4th-grade level, but at the 8th-grade level the number of MC items was still more than double that of the SCR items. Although the number of ECR items did increase to four at the 4th grade, no ECR items related to whole-number computation or place value were administered at the 8th-grade level. Because of this discrepancy, we are unable to get a clear picture of any overall growth in reasoning with whole numbers between 4th and 8th grade. Unfortunately, growth is desperately needed in this area.

The 4th graders scored very poorly on the ECR items, a result that one might expect on the basis of earlier studies, which show that students have more difficulty solving complex mathematical problems. However, recent trends toward

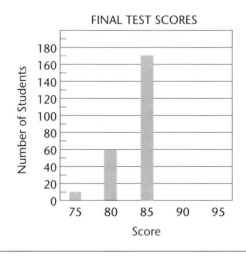

FINAL TEST SCORES	
Score	Number of Students
95	50
90	120
85	170
80	60
75	10

Use the information in the table shown to complete the bar graph below.

Figure 3.1. Example of a short constructed-response item (2003-8M6 #6).

Table 3.8
Student Performance on Whole-Number Items by Type of Response

Grade	Extended Response		Multiple Choice		Short Constructed Response	
	N	% correct	N	% correct	N	% correct
4	4	4%	51	57%	29	53%
8	0	n.a.	40	57%	18	58%

Note. N is the number of items requiring the indicated type of response. % correct is the mean percentage of students getting those items correct.

The table below shows how the chirping of a cricket is related to the temperature outside. For example, a cricket chirps 144 times each minute when the temperature is 76°

Number of Chirps per Minute	Temperature
144	76°
152	78°
160	80°
168	82°
176	84°

What would be the number of chirps per minute when the temperature outside is 90° if this pattern stays the same?

Answer: _____

Explain how you figured out your answer.

Figure 3.2. Example of an extended constructed-response item (2003-4M7 #20).

including more of this type of question on state assessments led us to hope that performance in this area would have improved. Unfortunately, the mean percentage of students getting whole-number ECR items correct in 2003 was less than 4.5%, which is a very disheartening outcome. If the ECR items truly measure students' reasoning with whole numbers and place value, then students are woefully inept at reasoning. Because of the lack of extended constructed-response items related to whole-number computation or place value at 8th grade, we do not know whether student responses on items in that format would improve over time. However, we do know that at 8th grade, other MC and SCR items were written to measure reasoning with whole numbers and place value (see our previous discussion of factors and multiples), and the mean percentage of students who answered those items correctly was almost 46%. The lack of similar MC or SCR items at 4th grade causes difficulty in determining whether the students' performance at 4th grade was primarily influenced by the extended response format or whether the students truly were not able to reason with whole numbers. Likewise, the lack of ECR items at 8th grade makes impossible any investigation into whether the format of the questions would have had the same negative impact on the students' ability to answer the question correctly as it had for 4th graders.

We looked at patterns in the results on the different types of questions and found that 4th graders did not perform as well on the short constructed-response items as they did on the multiple-choice items. Although one might expect that random guessing would produce a higher percentage of correct responses on multiple-choice items, this outcome was not true across grades, so other factors may also be present. Perhaps the distracters on the multiple-choice items did not have much influence on the 4th graders, and they may be slightly more adept at recognizing a correct answer than they are at producing the answer themselves. By 8th grade, the students seem to have overcome this problem. Eighth graders performed nearly identically on those two types of items. Although we would like to think the 8th graders would also have overcome some of the difficulty that 4th graders had with the ECR items, we have no means of measuring that growth with whole numbers. Clearly, the influence of different types of items on student achievement is in need of further research, and the NAGB needs to consider balancing the 8th-grade whole-number items as they have the 4th-grade items.

Items for Which a Calculator Was Allowed

Since 1996 NAEP assessments have included blocks of items for which calculators are allowed and provided for student use. "In the 1996, 2000, and 2003 assessments, calculators were provided on about one-third of the assessment. Students do not have access to a calculator on about two-thirds of the exam" (NAGB, 2002, p. 17). The intent was to measure the students' ability to use calculators in mathematical situations. To obtain a clear picture on the impact of calculator presence, some items in the calculator block required students to demonstrate skills in which a calculator is not needed or necessarily helpful. We found interesting results when we examined the items in the blocks for which calculators were allowed and compared them with the student results on similar items across blocks for which calculators were and were not allowed.

One would assume that allowing a calculator on items that involved whole-number computation and number sense would increase the ability of students to get correct numerical answers. This outcome was not necessarily true. In fact, for 4th graders, the mean percentage of students getting items correct in the non-calculator blocks was 55%, whereas the mean percentage getting items correct in the calculator block was only 46%. Similarly, the mean percentage of 8th-grade students getting items correct in the noncalculator blocks was 60%, whereas the mean percentage correct in the calculator block was only 49%. These percentages appear to be counter to what one might expect, so further examination of the specific items was needed.

The 2003 assessment had several items across grade levels that required pure numeric computation and allowed the use of the calculator. As would be expected, on those items, the students scored higher with the use of the calculator. For example, 8th graders were given parallel multiple-choice items on a calculator-allowed block and a noncalculator block that asked students to compute using order of operations. On the calculator-based item, 93% of the students were successful. On a similar item for which a calculator was not allowed, less than 52%

of the students were successful. That result is more what one might expect to find when calculators are allowed for items involving whole numbers and number sense. So those items do not explain the direction of the overall differences present in the calculator-noncalculator comparisons.

The test also included items for which the calculator would not have helped or would have hindered the students' success at answering the questions. Examples of this type of item would be word problems in which the student is asked to identify the appropriate operation or number sentence to answer a question but not to perform the computation. Two such items are presented at the 4th-grade level—one in a calculator-based block and another in a noncalculator block. The students were able to answer both items correctly 56.5% of the time. The calculator had absolutely no impact on their ability to answer the question correctly. Again, this result does not help explain the differences. Therefore, we needed to examine items on which students scored poorly with the use of the calculator and were more successful without the use of the calculator.

As we searched for items of this type, we looked for items that were within the same content strand. We found that in situations in which the students scored worse on the calculator-based items, the results were probably more indicative of the higher level of difficulty of the item than of whether a calculator was available to the students. Compare two 8th-grade items from the Data Analysis, Statistics, and Probability strand that involve whole-number understanding or computation.

The item shown in Figure 3.3 allowed a calculator, but only 19.5% of the students got the item correct. In contrast, the item shown in Figure 3.1 did not allow a calculator, and 89.1% of the students got it correct. Further examination of the two items clearly shows that one is much simpler than the other. One requires students to use data from a table to calculate a weighted average. The other requires students simply to finish an incomplete bar graph from a given data set. Although both tasks started with a similar data set and contextual setting, the concept involved in one is much more difficult than the other. Thus the fact that students scored poorly on the more difficult item, regardless of whether they had access to a calculator, is not surprising. No similar items of similar difficulty were found in the noncalculator blocks. Such items have a distinct impact on the mean percentage of students getting the items correct in the calculator versus noncalculator blocks of the test, rendering difficult any attempt to measure the impact of allowing a calculator on the test.

Overall, we identified several issues as problematic for determining the impact of the availability of calculators on student performance. First, the number of items that involved whole-number operations in calculator blocks is relatively small. The small item pool makes detailed statistical analysis for significance difficult. Second, the lack of items of comparable difficulty in each block is problematic. Finally, we found several items that had not been in calculator blocks in the past but that were in calculator blocks in 2003. We also identified a few items

Score	Number of Students
90	1
80	3
70	4
60	0
50	3

The table above shows the scores of a group of 11 students on a history test. What is the average (mean) score of the group to the nearest whole number?

Answer: _____

Figure 3.3. An item (2003-8M7 #13) for which a calculator was allowed but on which 8th-grade students scored poorly.

that were in calculator blocks in the past but that were not in calculator blocks in 2003. Such discrepancies muddy any attempts at examining those items for performance trends over time.

On the basis of these issues and findings, we believe the rationale for allowing calculators for some sections and not for others and the content of the items in those sections need further study. If we truly want to measure the impact of calculator use on an item, a pool of items will need to be administrated both with and without calculator use during the same testing period, to allow examination of the effects of calculator use on specific items. Otherwise we are trying to judge the impact of the use of the calculator across a variety of items of varying difficulty, or we are muddying the data regarding the tracking of specific items across time by permitting or not permitting calculator use from administration to administration.

Item Context

A growing body of research tells us that the context of a mathematics problem can affect the ability of students to solve the problem (e.g., chapter 11; Hembree, 1992). Yet much remains that we do not know about the impact of specific contexts, and past analyses of the NAEP whole-number items have not addressed this issue. As we examined item context, four types of contextual situations appeared; some items had no context, some had a real-world context, some had a mathematical context, and some had both a mathematical and real-world context. The four item types are more fully defined below.

No Context

The most obvious items that fit this category were "naked number" items, for which absolutely no context was included, just numbers and symbols. Clearly, the only situation or context present in these problems is the meaning of the numbers and the operation. No other information or knowledge could influence the students' ability to answer the question. Some questions were posed in word format in which the words related only to the numbers, operations, or procedures and had no real context (e.g., Item 7 in Table 3.1). This example again shows that the question relies strictly on the students' knowledge of number and operations, and the associated terminology, to solve the problem.

Mathematical Context

Word problems and other questions that were not situated in any real-life setting but that did require knowledge of other mathematical concepts to select appropriate computational operations were classified as having a mathematical context. In those problems, the use of whole-number operations or place-value concepts was required to solve the problem, yet the question was often situated within another mathematical strand. For example, in the problem shown in Figure 3.4, the student clearly needs to know what a square is, that it has four sides of the same length, and that the perimeter is the distance around the object. These geometry and measurement ideas are necessary but not sufficient to obtain the correct answer. The student still needs to be able to successfully divide 36 by 4 to get the correct solution. Hence the whole-number computational aspects of the problem are set in a mathematical context.

The perimeter of a square is 36 inches. What is the length of one side of the square?

    A)   4 inches
    B)   6 inches
    C)   9 inches
    D)   18 inches

Figure 3.4. An example of a problem with a mathematical context (2003-8M6 #10).

Real-World Context

Items in which the question is framed in a real-world situation that gives direct meaning to the whole-number operation or place-value idea central to solving the problem are categorized as having a "real-world context." In Item 8 of Table 3.1, for example, the students must visualize what is needed to share equally among six students, and they can connect the question with a real-world experience. Items in which the computation or numerical meaning of the problem is grounded in a situation that students can relate to their real-life activities were classified as having a real-world context.

Indirect Real-World and Mathematical (IRM) Context

The final category is a composite of the previous two. The questions had some connections with the real-world, so the students could relate the information to their own experiences, but the context was more closely related to another area of mathematics in which the computational aspects of the problem were situated. These questions were typically framed in a real-world situation that lent meaning to the mathematical idea or concept other than whole-number operation or place value, but they also required whole-number operation or place-value knowledge and understanding to solve the problem successfully. Figure 3.3 shows an example of this type of problem. The question gives information about a group of students' scores on a test, providing a context for the data and a statistical situation that requires whole-number computation. The context allows students to understand the meaning of the data table in a more concrete manner but does not necessarily relate to the numerical operations needed to complete the problem successfully. Thus the question contains both a real-world and a mathematical context that can affect the ability of the student to complete the task.

Analysis by Context Category

We found that both the number of each type of item and the percentage of students responding correctly to that type of item showed some interesting patterns across grade levels. Table 3.9 shows the mean percentage of students giving correct responses across item context types and across grade levels. We discuss first the distribution of the items and then the performance of students by context category.

Table 3.9
Student Performance on Items by Context

Grade Level	No Context		Direct Real-World Context		Indirect Real-World and Mathematical (IRM) Context		Mathematical Context	
	N	% correct	N	% correct	N	% correct	N	% correct
4	25	60.9	33	49.2	9	58.1	17	45.2
8	15	65.8	14	64.1	8	51.3	20	48.3

Note. N is the number of items requiring the indicated type of response, and % correct is the mean percentage of students getting those items correct.

In 4th grade, most items fell into two categories: items having no context and items having a real-world context. Although the real-world problems occurred most frequently for 4th graders, the frequency of items having no context was a close second. We found that a large number of the 4th-grade items that were new in the 2003 administration had no context. Possibly the item developers were attempting to balance the 4th-grade-level number of items having no context with those having a real-world context.

In contrast, by 8th grade the largest number of items occurs in the mathematical context category. This preponderance is perhaps understandable, as 8th graders would commonly be expected to solve problems in other mathematical strands that would involve using whole-number computation. The number of real-world problems and items that had no context were nearly equal for 8th graders and made up the next most common context areas.

Across both grades the actual number of items classified as having IRM context was relatively small but consistent. IRM items made up a greater percentage of items for the 8th-grade students, possibly reflecting the increased number of numeration items having no context or real-world contexts that would require fraction or decimal computation rather than whole-number computation.

Performance trends across context categories were interesting. Although the number of items in each category was fairly small, making detailed statistical analysis of student performance impractical, some patterns are worthy of discussion. At both grades, students performed best on items having no context and worst on items having a strictly mathematical context. This result seems to indicate a lack of connections between computation skills and both real-world situations and other mathematical concepts on the part of students. This outcome is perhaps not surprising, given the lack of connections still present in many traditional elementary or middle-grade programs.

Although for 8th-grade students the presence of a real-world context appears to have considerably less impact on their ability to get a correct answer than it does for 4th graders, the inconsistencies in that growth in the other contextual categories are interesting. Whereas the 8th graders were slightly better at handling items with a mathematical context, the 4th graders seemed to be more able to handle the IRM contexts. Because of that apparent inconsistency, we examined the mathematical context and IRM items for the type of mathematical connections they involved to determine whether that aspect could account for some of the differences.

As we examined the items classified as IRM, we found that the vast majority of them were related to the Data Analysis, Statistics, and Probability strand, whereas in contrast many of the mathematical context items were related to the Measurement or Geometry and Spatial Sense strands. Past international analyses have shown that students perform slightly better on data tasks than on tasks in measurement or geometry (Kilpatrick, Swafford, & Findell, 2001). We also know that nationally a marked increase has recently occurred in the amount of data and statistics included in the elementary curriculum (Kloosterman et al., 2004). Perhaps that curricular emphasis accounts for some of the difference in the students' performance on the IRM items in comparison with the items having a purely mathematical context. Another possible explanation is that the nature of the real-world connections of the IRM questions varied between 4th and 8th grade, with some being more familiar to the students than others.

The role and impact of context are indeed complex, and more research needs to be done that relates aspects of various contextual settings to student performance. In the meantime, the balance between contextual problems of various types should be monitored and evaluated for any trends in student performance over time.

CONCLUSIONS

Although scores on NAEP 4th- and 8th-grade assessments continue to increase over time (see chapter 2; Kloosterman et al., 2004; National Center for Education Statistics, 2005; Sowder, Wearne, Martin, & Struchens, 2004), patterns of achievement have remained roughly the same. Students in 4th and 8th grades continue to do well on simple numeric whole-number problems and one-step word problems. However, they do not do as well on numeric and word problems involving more complex reasoning. Clearly, the overall results are promising, but the inability of students to deal successfully with items requiring complex reasoning is a concern.

We examined three factors (availability of calculators, type of response, and item context) that might play a role in students' achievement on NAEP. We found that the pattern of items on NAEP made this analysis difficult to carry out. For example, the items in calculator and noncalculator blocks were not comparable. Nonetheless, we found some interesting patterns. Both 4th- and 8th-grade students performed better on items for which calculators were not allowed than on items for which calculators were allowed. Fourth graders performed best on whole-number multiple-choice items, slightly less well on short constructed-response items, and very poorly on extended constructed-response items. Eighth graders performed similarly on whole-number short constructed-response items and multiple-choice items. They were not given any whole-number extended constructed-response items. Both 4th and 8th graders performed well on items having no context and worst on items having a purely mathematical context. More analysis of the foregoing three factors and other factors that might influence student performance would be helpful for both researchers and teachers.

REFERENCES

Carpenter, T. P., Fennema, E., Franke, M. L., Levi, L., & Empson, S. B. (1999). *Children's mathematics: Cognitively guided instruction.* Portsmouth, NH: Heinemann.

Hembree, R. (1992). Experiments and relational studies in problem solving: A meta-analysis. *Journal for Research in Mathematics Education, 23,* 242–273.

Kloosterman, P., Warfield, J., Wearne, D., Koc, Y., Martin, W. G., & Strutchens, M. (2004). Fourth-grade students' knowledge of mathematics and perceptions of learning mathematics. In P. Kloosterman & F. K. Lester Jr. (Eds.), *Results and interpretations of the 1990–2000 mathematics assessments of the National Assessment of Educational Progress* (pp. 71–103). Reston, VA: National Council of Teachers of Mathematics.

Kouba, V. L., & Wearne, D. (2000). Whole number properties and operations. In E. A. Silver & P. A. Kenney (Eds.), *Results from the seventh mathematics assessment of the National Assessment of Educational Progress* (pp. 141–161). Reston, VA: National Council of Teachers of Mathematics.

National Assessment Governing Board (NAGB) (2002). *Mathematics framework for the 2003 National Assessment of Educational Progress.* Washington, DC: Author. Retrieved June 18, 2005, from www.nagb.org/pubs/math_fw_03.pdf

National Center for Educational Statistics (NCES) (2005). *National Assessment of Educational Progress: The nation's report card.* Washington, DC: Author. Retrieved June 18, 2005, from http://nces.ed.gov/nationsreportcard/

Kilpatrick, J., Swafford, J., & Findell, B. (Eds.). (2001). *Adding it up: Helping children learn mathematics.* Washington, DC: National Academy Press.

Sowder, J. T., Wearne, D., Martin, W. G., & Strutchens, M. (2004). What do 8th-grade students know about mathematics? Changes over a decade. In P. Kloosterman & F. K. Lester Jr. (Eds.), *Results and interpretations of the 1990–2000 mathematics assessments of the National Assessment of Educational Progress* (pp. 105–143). Reston, VA: National Council of Teachers of Mathematics.

Building a System of Rational Numbers

Signe E. Kastberg and Anderson Norton III

STUDENTS' rational number understanding has been the focus of a significant amount of research activity over the years (Carpenter, Fennema, & Romberg, 1993; Hiebert, 1985; Hiebert & Wearne, 1985, 1988; Hiebert, Wearne, & Taber, 1991; Moss & Case, 1999; National Research Council, 2001; Pitkethly & Hunting, 1996; Resnick, Nesher, Leonard, Magone, Omanson, & Peled, 1989; 1997; Steffe, 2002; Steffe, Cobb, & von Glasersfeld, 1988). Of particular importance in existing literature is the idea that students' understandings of units play a significant role in their performance on rational number items. In this chapter, we draw insights from the research literature as we interpret students' responses to NAEP multiple-choice and constructed-response items and report on the general findings that result from the interpretations.

In an analysis of student performance on rational number items from the 1996 NAEP mathematics assessment, Wearne and Kouba (2000, pp. 188–189) drew several conclusions:

- when students at multiple grade levels are given the same task, older students are more successful than younger students;

- students at all grade levels are more successful in solving routine one-step tasks than nonroutine and multistep tasks; and

- students' notions of what constitutes the unit appears to be at the root of many of the difficulties they have with rational numbers.

These conclusions provided a baseline for our work. To gain a view of the landscape of students' success with rational number items on the 2003 NAEP mathematics assessment, we examined trends in performance on released items and those items not yet released but described in Wearne and Kouba's (2000) analysis and in Kloosterman and Lester (2004). Although these items may not

Highlights

- Overall Grade 4 student performance on decimal items has improved statistically significantly since 1996 except on multiplication items.

- Grade 8 students have shown consistent performance on decimal items since 1996. Most students can perform computations with decimals but have greater difficulty using their understanding of decimals on items in context, such as those drawn from other strands including data analysis.

- Fractions had not yet become measurable items for many of the students at either grade, although students do seem to move toward such a conception between Grades 4 and 8.

- Grade 4 students' performance on fraction items has improved significantly except on items that require students to consider whole numbers and simple fractions as measurable extents.

- Grade 8 students' successful performance on measurement items that require fraction knowledge has decreased since 1996 while their successful performance on part-whole items has increased.

exhaust the database used on the 2003 assessment, they represented sufficient variety in the difficulty of the items and the contexts in which they were presented to reveal trends in student performance on rational number tasks.

DECIMALS

An examination of student performance on decimal items suggests that conclusions drawn by Wearne and Kouba (2000) regarding student performance in 1996 also apply to students' performance on rational number items drawn from the 2003 NAEP mathematics assessment. Table 4.1 contains evidence that "given the same task, older students are more successful than younger students" (p. 188). Student performance on two released items and one unreleased item illustrates that, whereas many Grade 4 students struggle to identify a decimal and to use quantities that involve decimals to compute prices or change, most Grade 8 students are successful with these tasks. To make more sense of changes that might be occurring in student thinking between Grades 4 and 8, we take a closer look at student performance on the two released items (Items 2 and 3).

The results on released items illustrate that the vast majority of Grade 8 students were able to compute with decimal quantities involving money. Even when the item seemed to demand more than one operation (Item 2), most Grade 8 students were successful. Performance on this item was statistically significantly higher in comparison with the performance of Grade 8 students on the same item in 1996 (see Table 4.4 for more evidence of Grade 8 student computational performance with decimals).

Table 4.1
Student Performance on Items Involving Decimals

	Percentage Correct	
Item Description	Grade 4	Grade 8
1. Place a decimal number on a portion of a number line with divisions not 0.1 apart. (2005-4M4 #8, 2005-8M4 #8)[a]	55	88
2. How much change will John get back from $5.00 if he buys 2 notebooks that cost $1.80 each? (2003-4M6 #15, 2003-8M6 #7)		
A. $1.40 (correct response)	35	73
B. $2.40	19	13
C. $3.20	23	6
D. $3.60	22	7
3. The Breakfast Barn bought 135 dozen eggs at $0.89 per dozen. What was the total cost of the eggs? (2003-4M7 #12, 2003-8M7 #2)		
A. $116.75	10	2
B. $120.15 (correct response)	59	85
C. $135.89	21	5
D. $151.69	7	8

Note. Item 1 was a short constructed-response item, and the rest were multiple-choice items. Calculators were allowed on Item 3.

[a]2005 items were released while this volume was in production. Block and item numbers were added so that interested readers can find the 2005 items using the online Questions Tool.

Analyses of distracters and shifts in distracter selection when comparing the performance of Grade 4 and Grade 8 students may provide evidence that explains shifts in reasoning. On the notebook item (Item 2, Table 4.1), comparable percentages of Grade 4 students seemed to select incorrect distracters that appear to align with typical computation or reading errors. Distracter B may have been appealing to students who had difficulty regrouping ($2.40 = $5.00 − $3.60), whereas distracters C and D may have appealed to students who had difficulty reading ($3.20 = $5.00 − $1.80, $3.60 = 2($1.80) or $1.80 + $1.80). In response to the notebook item, 45% of Grade 4 students selected $3.20 or $3.60, in contrast with only 13% of Grade 8 students. The shift in distracter selection suggests that Grade 8 students were less likely to choose either distracters indicative of incorrect readings of the problem or of a contextually unrealistic answer to the problem. Most Grade 8 students seemed to know that the change from the purchase of two notebooks costing nearly $2.00 each would be less than $3.00.

Thirteen percent of Grade 8 students still selected $2.40 (distracter B), an answer that either appeared realistic because the price of a notebook was less than $2.00 or that stemmed from a regrouping error during the application of the standard algorithm (calculating $5.00 – $3.60 as $2.40).

We also assert that students could be successful on this item without any understanding of rational numbers. Performing the computations as whole numbers and then selecting the distracter with the same digits: $500 – 360 = 140$, results in a correct answer. None of the distracters were given as whole numbers, so we could not easily determine whether whole-number reasoning was used by very many students. Later in this chapter we discuss evidence drawn from Grade 8 student work on released items (see Figures 4.1 and 4.2) that illustrates how students may use that approach with success.

A similar shift in distracter selection can be seen in the comparison of Grade 4 and 8 student performance on the egg item (Item 3, Table 4.1). The distracters for this item include answers that could be generated by simply computing with the numbers given in the problem: $135.89 = 135 + $0.89 (distracter C), $151.69 = 135/$0.89 (distracter, D). These distracters were selected by more than a quarter of Grade 4 students. As with the notebook item, the percentage of Grade 8 students selecting these distracters (13%) declined. It seems that the majority of Grade 8 students understood that quantities and rates should not be added; however, approximately the same percentage of Grade 4 and Grade 8 students incorrectly selected distracter D.

Comparing student performance on three items (Table 4.1) suggests that, as expected, Grade 8 students were more successful than Grade 4 students on decimal items given at both grade levels. Grade 4 students' performance on these items suggests that many had difficulty with decimals even when problems were set in contexts that support selecting an appropriate answer. They seemed to have the most success when a calculator was provided and only one step was needed to produce an answer (as in Item 3 from Table 4.1). The majority of Grade 8 students were successful when faced with decimal computation problems. They were successful at either computing solutions or using problem contexts to eliminate unrealistic distracters.

To further investigate the performance of Grade 8 and Grade 4 students on decimal items and their thinking about decimal items, we discuss a collection of items described in previous monographs (Kloosterman & Lester, 2004; Silver & Kenney, 2000) or released in 2003. In particular, in the next two sections we explore how the students may have been interpreting the decimal representations of a rational number and how they may have made sense of decimal units $(0.1, 0.01, 0.001, ...)$.

Grade 4

Table 4.2 provides evidence of Grade 4 students' performance on NAEP decimal items since 1996. Overall Grade 4 student performance on decimal items has improved statistically significantly since 1996. Despite that improvement, a rather large percentage of students appear to have had difficulty with decimal items.

The two items for which Grade 4 student performance has statistically significantly declined since 1996 require students to multiply decimals. Students were allowed to use a four-function calculator for both items. Item 5 was multiple choice and set in context, and Item 3 was a constructed-response context-free item that required multiplication of two-digit numbers. Student performance on these items does not reveal much about student thinking; however, it does illustrate that simply providing students with a calculator does not ensure success. We hypothesize that students may not have known how to enter the decimals into the calculator or read the display. Both of those skills involve differentiating between whole-number and decimal notations, a distinction that may stem from an understanding of decimals as parts of units (for example, $0.89 as part

Table 4.2
Grade 4 Student Performance on Items Involving Decimals

	Item Description	Percentage Correct		
		1996	2000	2003
1.	Identify the decimal number for a given representation.	53*	54	57
2.	Place a decimal number on a portion of a number line with divisions not 0.1 apart. (2005-4M4 #5)	41*	51*	55
3.	Multiply decimals.	73*	72*	63
4.	184 divided by 115 = 1.6. (2003-4M7 #1)	71*	78	79
5.	Find the cost of 135 dozen eggs at $0.89 per dozen. (2003-4M7 #12)	64*	61	59
6.	Berries cost 87¢ per pint. How many dollars would 6 pints cost? (2003-4M7 #9)	63*	67*	70
7.	Given data in a table, find the total amount of rain in a week. (2003-4M7 #3)	n.a.	79	79
8.	How many one-dollar bills are needed to buy 2 notebooks at $2.79 each? (2003-4M10 #15)	26*	27*	31
9.	Identify change from $5.00 if 2 books cost $1.80 each. (2003-4M6 #15)	28*	34	35

Note. n.a. indicates the item was not administered this year. Items 2 and 3 were short constructed-response items, and the rest were multiple-choice items. Calculators were allowed on Items 3 through 7.

* Indicates the percentage correct is significantly different from the 2003 percentage correct.

of $1.00). Declining performance on these items may also be the result of in-experience with calculators. Data from student and teacher questionnaires sug-gests that in 2003, students may indeed have had less access to calculators than did their peers in 1996 and 2000. Thirty-seven percent and 44% of Grade 4 stu-dents taking the NAEP mathematics assessments in 1996 and 2000, respectively, reported never or hardly ever using a calculator for classwork. In 2003, 67% of students noted that they never or hardly ever used a calculator for classwork. Questions focused on the use of calculators on tests or quizzes yielded similar results. Limited access was also reported by the teachers of students who were assessed in 2003. Only 9% reported that they permit the use of calculators for tests, and 6% reported that they permit unrestricted use of calculators in class.

To gain further insight into Grade 4 students' possible interpretations of deci-mals and computations with them, we explore student performance on a calcula-tor item and a paper-and-pencil item (Table 4.3).

Table 4.3
Grade 4 Student Performance on Items Involving Interpretations of Money

Item	Percentage Responding
1. Mrs. Jones bought 6 pints of berries. Each pint cost 87¢. Mrs. Jones used her calculator to find the cost of the ber-ries and the display showed 522. What was the cost of the berries? (2003-4M7 #9)	
A. $522	20
B. $52.20	6
C. $5.22 (correct response)	70
D. $0.52	3
2. Estela wants to buy 2 notebooks that cost $2.79 each, including tax. If she has one-dollar bills and no coins, how many one-dollar bills does she need? (2003-4M10 #15)	
A. 3	41
B. 4	13
C. 5	14
D. 6 (correct response)	31

Students were given a calculator to compute answers for Item 1 (Table 4.3). Still, more than a quarter of the students selected mathematically and contextu-ally unrealistic answers of $522 and $52.20. These students may have focused on the illustration of a calculator in the item or simply performed the computation on the cents as if they were whole numbers with a "point." Another source of understanding in this problem is the use of context. Berries that cost over $50.00 or under $1.00 may seem unrealistic if one thinks of the price of berries (87¢) as a part of $1.00. Answers over $50.00 are reasonable if the numerals in the problem are thought of as whole numbers. Those students (26%) who chose answers over $50.00 may have been struggling to develop a relationship between dollars as a unit and cents as a part of a unit.

In a related item, students were asked to select the whole number of dollars needed to purchase two notebooks that cost $2.79 each (Item 2, Table 4.3). The most popular distracter, three dollars, was selected by 41 percent of the students. Students may have estimated the number of dollars needed to purchase only one notebook, an error that stems from difficulties reading the item. Those who selected four dollars may have considered only the whole-dollar amount in the price ($2.00 + $2.00), whereas those who selected five dollars may have reasoned that the cents needed for a single notebook was a part of a dollar, perhaps a half. Alternatively, the students may have simply added the two numbers in the problem, 2 + $2.79. That argument seems most plausible in light of the performance of some students on the calculator item that involves purchasing 135 dozen eggs.

We can be sure of very little about Grade 4 students' understandings of decimals on the basis of this small collection of multiple-choice items. No released item provides a view of how decimal numerals are being interpreted as quantities. Instead, we are able to see that the majority of students performed well on decimal items if a calculator was present and the item required only a one-step computation. We also saw indications that some students may have treated the decimals in a money context as whole numbers of dollars and whole numbers of cents. In that thinking, the decimal point signifies a separation of dollars and cents but does not signify that cents are parts of dollars. That finding indicates that although students were generally more successful than their counterparts in 1996, they still had difficulty making sense of decimals as parts of a whole.

Grade 8

Mathematics educators can safely assume that Grade 8 students have experienced instruction regarding decimal notation and computation. Assuming that a major goal of instruction is the development of understanding, Grade 8 students should understand a decimal as a part of a whole and should be able to use that thinking in a variety of situations. An examination of student performance on the decimal items described in Table 4.4 allows us to identify strengths in their performance and provides evidence for hypotheses about student reasoning.

Although Grade 8 student performance on decimal items has generally held steady since 2000, on four items (2, 7, 8, 11) the percentage of students who were successful statistically significantly decreased. Three of the items (2, 7, 11), and indeed the majority of items described in previous monographs or released in

Table 4.4
Grade 8 Student Performance on Items Involving Decimals

		Percentage Correct		
	Item Description	1996	2000	2003
1.	Place a decimal number on a portion of a number line with divisions not 0.1 apart. (2005-8M4 #5)	86	88	88
2.	Given a table in which some items are to be added and others subtracted, identify the result.	60*	65*	58
3.	Identify the number of a unit, given in cents, that could be purchased with a given number of dollars.	57*	61	62
4.	Given a table of values for a linear function described in a real-world context, complete a table for values of x and $f(x)$ and produce a symbolic function rule.	19*	25	24
5.	Read line graphs and perform calculations. (2005-8M4 #20)	n.a.	11	10
6.	Find the cost of 135 dozen eggs at $0.89 per dozen. (2003-8M7 #2)	82	84	85
7.	Find increases exceeding 10 cents from a line graph with prices given in dollars. (2003-8M7 #8)	46	50*	45
8.	The diameter of a red blood cell, in inches, is 3×10^{-4}. This expression is the same as which of the following numbers? (2003-8M7 #16)	40	46*	41
9.	While she was on vacation, Tara sent 14 friends either a letter or a postcard. She spent $3.84 on postage. If it costs $0.20 to mail a postcard and $0.33 to mail a letter, how many letters did Tara send? Show what you did to get your answer. (2003-8M7 #19)	n.a.	11	10
10.	Identify change from $5.00 if 2 books cost $1.80 each. (2003-8M6 #7)	67*	71	73
11.	Movie tickets cost $5.25 each. If 100 tickets were sold, how much money was collected? (2003-8M10 #2)	72*	74*	69

Note. n.a. indicates the item was not administered this year. Items 1, 4, and 11 were short constructed-response, Items 5 and 9 were extended constructed-response, and the rest were multiple choice. Calculators were allowed on Items 2, 3, 4, 6, 7, 8, and 9.

* Indicates the percentage correct is significantly different from the 2003 percentage correct.

2003, ask students to compute with decimals that represent money or interpret graphs that include decimals that represent money.

We hypothesized that constructed-response items had the potential to provide additional evidence regarding Grade 8 students' understanding of decimals, at least as they represent money. The two constructed-response items released in 2003 appear in Table 4.4. Item 11 (movie-tickets item) was drawn from the Number and Operations strand, and item 9 (vacation letters) was drawn from the Algebra and Functions strand. Students were provided with a scientific calculator to support their work on the vacation-letters item.

The work of Hiebert and Wearne (1985) led us to predict that students would attempt to solve the movie-ticket item using the standard algorithm and might make errors at algorithm decision points, such as where to put the decimal point. Sixty-nine percent of students responding to this item arrived at a correct answer, whereas 28% of the students' answers were incorrect. An examination of the student work samples available on the Questions Tool illustrates difficulties that students may have had with decimals.

The correct student work in Figure 4.1 demonstrates use of the standard algorithm, including the multiplication of $5.25 by 0 twice and by 1 once. The student whose work was graded as incorrect may have multiplied 525 by 100 and then simply appended a decimal point and zeros. Looking only at the student work shown here, we see the difficulty some students had in understanding the impact that a multiplicand of a power of 10 can have on a decimal unit (here, $5.25). The student whose answer was correct felt compelled to perform the multiplication algorithm, whereas the student whose answer was incorrect became confused as to the position of the decimal point. Both approaches suggest a weak or absent understanding of place value for quantities involving decimals.

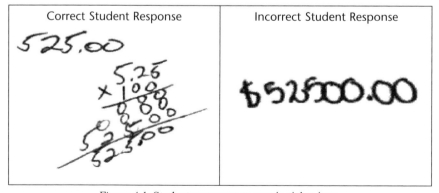

Figure 4.1. Student responses to movie-ticket item.

We approached the vacation-letter item with less certainty. Although students might easily solve the problem using trial and error, only 10% of responses were scored as correct. We predicted that many Grade 8 students would use trial and error and multiples of the stamp prices ($0.20 and $0.33) to approximate the total amount spent on postage. An example of that approach, using $1.00 as a unit of postage for five postcards, was depicted in a sample extended (i.e., very complete) response from the Questions Tool. The student used a heuristic to determine the number of letters Tara sent (see Figure 4.2). The price of postage for a collection of letters was calculated, to which multiples of $0.20 were added. If a comparison of the sum to the total cost of postage results in a significant difference (example: $2.95 + $0.33 = $3.28 < $3.84), the cost of postage for a single letter is again added to the sum. That work suggests that the student did not use a calculator, as evidenced by the consistent error in the addition algorithm when $0.30 was added (see arrows in Figure 4.2).

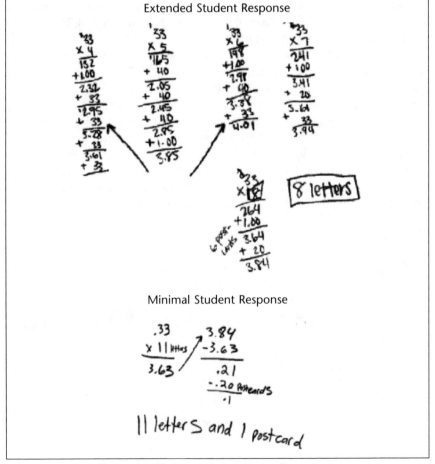

Figure 4.2. Student work for vacation-letters item.

The work in Figure 4.2 also suggests that the student may have been working with the quantities as whole numbers. Each multiple of 33 cents appears in the algorithm as a whole number without a decimal point. The student appears to have the understanding that the problem involves dollars and cents, but that understanding did not play a role in the majority of the computations. The rather loose attention to the decimal point may indicate a focus on the computation itself but may also suggest that the student merely used the notation of dollars and cents given in the problem without understanding the complex relationships between the whole (here, the dollar) and its parts. Further evidence of students' difficulty with the relationships between the dollar and parts of a dollar is provided in the student response graded as minimal (see Figure 4.2). Here, the work suggests that the student was thinking about the maximum number of letters that could be mailed for $3.84 and used the remaining money for one postcard. Although the computation of the total cost for 11 letters may have been performed with a calculator, we cannot know whether the student used a calculator. We can see the difference between 21 and 20 cents calculated by the student. The 1 cent difference was recorded by the student as ".1." That representation hints at a familiar difficulty, the representation of a hundredth of a unit: in this instance, the representation of 1 cent as a tenth of $1.00.

Students' written responses to the previous two items detail what performance data often hide. Responses to the vacation-letters item that earned some credit suggest difficulties beyond the obvious challenges of algebraic reasoning. We are able to see the dangers of overreliance on taught algorithms (Kamii & Lewis, 1993) and the learning that can result when syntactic approaches take precedence over symbolic ones (Hiebert & Wearne, 1985). Even those students who arrived at correct answers exhibited a struggle with computation that appears to stem from an inadequate attention to the development of a complex system of relationships represented by decimal numbers.

Further investigation of the application of decimal understanding is afforded by the release of an item that requires an understanding of decimals and skill at reading and interpreting graphs. Curcio (1987) identified several skills associated with graph sense, including reading and interpreting graphs. In analyses of student performance on 1996 and 2000 NAEPs, Zawojewski and Shaughnessy (2000) and D'Ambrosio, Kastberg, McDermott, and Saada (2004) identified items that involved interpreting graphs as more challenging for students. The multiple-choice item includes a graph of yearly hamburger prices in dollars. Students were asked to identify the number of yearly increases that exceed 10 cents (see Table 4.5). To read the graph, it is necessary for students to interpret 10 cents as a tenth of $1.00 ($0.10).

Almost half the students were able to read the graph and use their understanding of decimals in monetary representations to craft their responses. Interestingly, 22% of the students selected the distracter that asserted no yearly increases of 10 cents or more were pictured. One interpretation of these students' reasoning is

Table 4.5
Grade 8 Data Analysis Item That Requires an Understanding of Decimals

Item	Percentage Responding

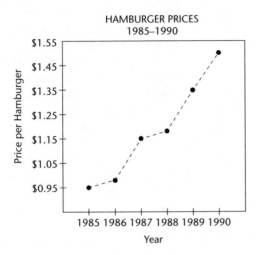

HAMBURGER PRICES
1985–1990

According to the graph above, how many times did the yearly increase of the price of a hamburger exceed 10 cents? (2003-8M7 #8)

A. None	22
B. One	7
C. Two	14
D. Three (correct response)	46
E. Four	11

Note. Calculators were allowed.

consistent with the student work from the vacation-letters problem (Figure 4.2). In the graph of the price increases, the digit in the hundredths place remains unchanged while the digit in the tenths place increases by 1 with each increment on the axis. The indication of a 10 cent increase in the price may be difficult or impossible to interpret if one thinks that ".1" represents one cent, as was suggested in our analysis of the vacation-letters problem.

The Grade 8 items released in 2003 focus almost exclusively on the use and understanding of decimal notation as it represents money. However, one item (Item 8, Table 4.4) goes beyond that application to help provide evidence of students' understanding of scientific notation as it relates to decimals. Representation of decimals in scientific notation may be relatively new and difficult for students, as performance suggests. Again, students had access to a scientific calculator as they attempted to compute the diameter of a red blood cell given in scientific notation.

Forty-one percent of the students correctly selected 0.0003 as the diameter of a red blood cell, and another 22% may have used an incorrect procedure (move the decimal point) to arrive at their answer of 0.00003. That order-of-magnitude error is hard to detect in representations that students may link only procedurally. However, even those students who had no procedure for this particular problem were likely to select 0.00003, 0.0003, or 0.003 because only these distracters indicate that a red blood cell is less than an inch in diameter. Indeed, 78% of students selected one of these answers. Still, 22% of the students selected unrealistic answers of 3,000 or 30,000 inches as the diameter of a red blood cell. Such answers may have been the result of incorrect procedures (move the decimal point four places to the right) and a focus on the mathematics without attention to problem context. Students' focus on procedure indicates once again that, whereas some students can perform simple computations with decimals, their conceptual understanding of the objects that the decimals are meant to signify may still be developing.

Decimal Summary

Student performance on items that involve computation with decimals has generally held steady since 1996 with a few exceptions. Grade 4 students have shown improved performance on computation with, and representation of, decimal quantities, with the exception of multiplying decimals. We hypothesize that difficulty in identifying or recording a product may be the result of students' inattention to the decimal point as significant in the representation. That approach to decimal may indicate that some students are still developing an understanding of a decimal fraction as a part of a whole. Other plausible explanations for students' declining performance on multiplication items when a calculator is available include limited access to that important tool and few opportunities during mathematics instruction to reason multiplicatively with decimals.

Grade 8 students have shown consistent performance on decimal items since 1996. Most students can compute with decimals but have greater difficulty using mathematics from two domains. The vacation-letters item (see Table 4.4) from the Algebra and Functions strand illustrates that difficulty. Students struggled to use their understanding of decimals and their algebraic reasoning to craft correct responses. Our analysis of student work also suggests that although Grade 8 students may understand that digits to the right of a decimal point are parts of a whole, they may have difficulty distinguishing between units less than 1 (e.g., $0.1 and $0.01) or moving between representations (10 cents as $0.1 or 3×10^{-4} as 0.0003).

We next turn to an analysis of student reasoning and performance on fraction items.

FRACTIONS

We identified eight released items that involved fraction knowledge. Of those, three were multiple-choice items and five were constructed-response items. We can begin to make sense of students' fraction knowledge by considering the distracters and percentage of correct solutions for the multiple-choice and constructed-response items.

We first investigate student performance on three items that include the fraction 3/4. Their responses to the item in Figure 4.3 illustrate that most students had, at least, a visual pattern for fractions such as 3/4. That pattern seems to have been evoked when students recognized the need for equal pieces. Even in Grade 4, 83% of the responses were correct. The only distracter that drew more than 2% of responses showed an equally partitioned whole (distracter A); 13% of Grade 4 students and 4% of Grade 8 students chose that distracter. That selection indicates that students' conceptions of fractions include the need for equal pieces in the whole (equi-partitioning), even if only a superficial relationship exists between the numbers in the fraction and the number of pieces shown in the shaded part and the whole (the item in Figure 4.3 involved three shaded and four unshaded pieces).

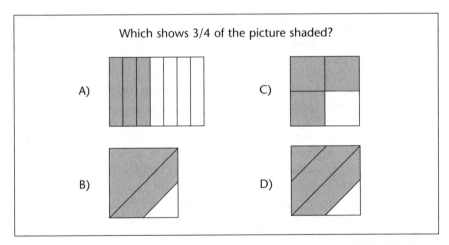

Figure 4.3. Grade 4 item assessing children's fraction knowledge. (2003-4M6 #2)

The item in Figure 4.4 required students to place a mark for 3/4 on a number line. The percentage correct for Grade 4 and Grade 8 students was remarkably similar: 57% and 64%, respectively. A typical incorrect response for Grade 4 students was marking 3/8 as 3/4, presumably because it represented three out of four marks in the first half of the unit. Among Grade 8 students, an illustrative incorrect response involved finding 1/2, setting it equal to 2/4, and counting on one more mark to the right. A student giving such a response conceives of 3/4 as one more than 2/4, but because the units indicated are eighths, uses one more *eighth,* marking 5/8 instead of 3/4. That misconception further supports the conclusion that Grade 4 and Grade 8 students' responses illustrate an equi-partitioning conception of fractions (at least for such fractions as 3/4) with little regard for what should be the whole. Beyond that, the Grade 8 students employed more of their procedural knowledge, such as equating 1/2 with 2/4, without recognizing that the small segments were eighths or relative *extents* of a given whole. Lacking a genuine understanding of 1/8 as a relative extent of a given whole, Grade 8 students' success in short constructed-response items was little better than that of Grade 4 students.

On the portion of the number line below, a dot shows where 1/2 is.
Use another dot to show where 3/4 is.

0   1

Figure 4.4. Item assessing students' abilities to place 3/4 on a number line. (2003-4M6 #16, 2003-8M6 #16)

The item in Table 4.6 required students to resolve a word problem involving the division of 3/4 into eighths. The remarkable difference in the performance of Grade 8 students compared with Grade 4 students indicates that either students were using procedures for division of fractions, such as invert and multiply ("keep-change-flip"), or Grade 8 students may have begun to understand 3/4 as three fourths, each of which is composed of two eighths. Given that the percentage of Grade 8 students choosing distracters of 3 and 4 (A and B) remained high while the largest shift was from Distracter D to C, the increased performance among Grade 8 students seems to have been due in large part to rote mastery of procedures. Otherwise, we would expect to see a bigger shift from the superficial Distracters A and B rather than from the more reasonable response of D.

Whereas the items in Table 4.6 provide opportunity for insight, we hesitate to make generalizations about all fractions on the basis of students' work with 3/4. Children may be familiar with halves, fourths, and eighths as a result of their experiences with paper folding and sharing (Sharp & Adams, 2002) but have far less experience with other fractions, many of which cannot be generated using folding.

We consider the next three items (seen in Table 4.7 and Figures 4.5 and 4.6) together because the disparities in correct responses on these similar items introduce some surprises about students' concepts of fractions. Only two distracters in the item in Table 4.7 appear reasonable. Response A, 8 1/2 hours, seems unreasonably long. Distracter B overcounts the 1-hour intervals by one (perhaps

Table 4.6
Students' Understanding of Division of Fractions (2003-4M6 #17, 2003-8M6 #17)

	Percentage Responding	
Item	Grade 4	Grade 8
Jim has 3/4 of a yard of string which he wishes to divide into pieces, each 1/8 of a yard long. How many pieces will he have?		
A. 3	19	15
B. 4	30	21
C. 6 (correct response)	27	55
D. 8	21	8

attracting students who began counting 10:30 as 1, 11:30 as 2, etc.). Distracter D undercounts the intervals by one and, furthermore, suspiciously implicates the 2:00 p.m. hour. Surprisingly, almost the same percentage of students chose Distracter D as those who chose the "unreasonable" Distracter A. Therefore, overcounting is the only significant distracter, accounting for 38% of responses. We were surprised that many more students responded appropriately to this time item than to the toothpick item depicted in Figure 4.5.

The item in Figure 4.5 asked students to find the length of a toothpick. Only 20% of Grade 4 students responded appropriately with 2 1/2 or an equivalent fraction. Although this problem was a constructed-response item and we might be inclined to attribute the relative lack of success to the item format, nearly all responses could be accounted for among three choices. The most common response (42%) among Grade 4 students was that the toothpick measured

Table 4.7
Using Simple Fractions to Solve a Problem Involving Time (2003-4M7 #17)

	Percentage Responding
Item	Grade 4
Ted went to the beach at 10:30 a.m. and came home at 2:00 p.m. How many hours was he gone?	
A. 8 ½	11
B. 4 ½	38
C. 3 ½ (correct response)	40
D. 2 ½	10

Note. Calculators were allowed.

10 1/2 inches. That choice indicates that many Grade 4 students seemed to rely on reading the ruler at the right end of the toothpick. Their use of 1/2 indicates the simple conception of fractions as being between two whole numbers (perhaps exactly between). Even whole numbers seem not to have been used as extents among Grade 4 students, who still seemed to consider numbers predominantly as counting tools. That perception would explain the relative success that Grade 4 students experienced in solving the time item (Table 4.7); they could correctly respond to the item not by measuring a continuous extent of time but rather by counting the hours.

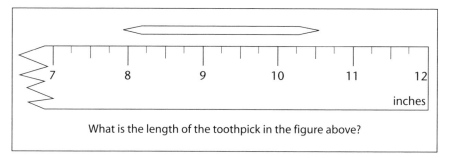

What is the length of the toothpick in the figure above?

Figure 4.5. Item assessing measurement using fractions (2003-4M6 #18, 2003-8M6 #18).

The time item (Table 4.7) would seem to be more complicated than the toothpick item because it involves the conversion of 30 minutes into half an hour and because of the difficulty of dealing with noon. However, the units in the time item are clear, related to daily experience, and call for no conception of number as extent. The hours are items to be counted, and the only common mistake students seemed to have made was to count both the 10:30 a.m. hour and the 2:00 p.m. hour, thus overcounting. So students seem to have had an affinity for count rather than extent, a conception that explains their difficulty with the toothpick item.

Fifty-eight percent of Grade 8 students measured the toothpick (Figure 4.5) correctly. That statistic indicates that students' understanding of whole numbers moves from simple readings of numerals, to counts of increments, to using whole-number measures of extent. Still, the fractional parts of the extent, as with decimals, may be nothing more than an appended afterthought, especially in the instance of the simple fraction 1/2. We will see that students traverse a similar path in their developing understanding of fractions: from reading fractions (by pattern recognition or as a mark between two whole numbers), to counting them (as so many equal pieces out of so many in the whole), to using them as measures of relative extent. We have already seen evidence of that developmental trajectory in student responses to the item in Figure 4.4. A common mistake for Grade 4 students was to count three out of the first four marks in labeling 3/4. Typical Grade 8 mistakes included marking 3/4 as the extension that was one more mark beyond 1/2. Accordingly, for Grade 8 students, 1/2 may have become an extent that could then be converted to 2/4, but 3/4 was still perceived as a counting item that is one more than 1/2.

Student responses to the constructed-response item in Figure 4.6 illustrate that for many Grade 8 students, fractions may yet be "in between" numbers. Eighty-two percent of the Grade 8 students responded correctly that the scale measures 6 1/2 ounces. Only 17% seemed confused by the inversion of the scale, respond-ing with 7 1/2. So the 24-point disparity between the percentage correct on this item and that on the toothpick item is likely attributable to Grade 8 students' lin-gering conceptions of measure as a simple reading of a position on the measuring device (e.g., 6 1/2 as the numerical reading that is between 6 and 7).

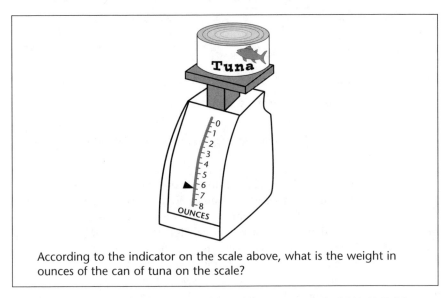

According to the indicator on the scale above, what is the weight in ounces of the can of tuna on the scale?

Figure 4.6. Item assessing reading simple fractions on a scale (2003-8M7 #4).

Evaluation of Constructed-Response Items Using a Partial Credit Scale

Student responses to the Grade 4 item Figure 4.7 were scored as "correct," "partial," or "incorrect." We predicted that students would respond to this item by coordinating the relations among the three numbers 20, 1/4, and 15. The sample response included in Figure 4.7 illustrates one such approach.

The sample student response demonstrates the coordination of a concept of 1/4 as 5 out of 20 and a concept of 15 out of 20 as 3/4. The student conceived of fractions as relative extents of the whole and was able to coordinate the fractional relationships within the whole. Not surprisingly, only the most advanced students (the students who scored in the 90th percentile for the entire test) scored well on

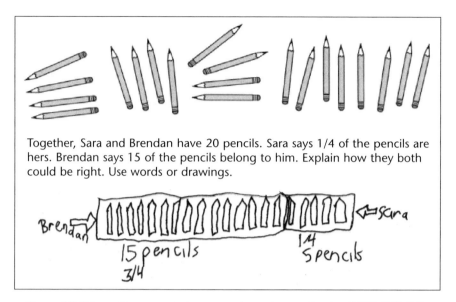

Together, Sara and Brendan have 20 pencils. Sara says 1/4 of the pencils are hers. Brendan says 15 of the pencils belong to him. Explain how they both could be right. Use words or drawings.

Figure 4.7. "Correct" response to item assessing units coordination (2003-4M7 #15).

this item. Only 11% of all responses were scored as "correct." Of course, if the majority of Grade 4 students had not conceived of fractions as relative extents, we could hardly expect much success on an item that involves the coordination of two fractional extents in a whole.

Sample responses scored as partially correct included "5 pencils are Sara's." Such a response indicates no fractional understanding because the response does not relate the 5 pencils to a fraction of the whole. However, an illustrative incorrect response—"Brandon gets 10, Sara gets 10"—does indicate a disposition among students that objects should be shared equally. We have already argued that the equal-shares idea plays a dominant (in this situation, detrimentally so) role in students' conceptions of fractions. So the relatively few Grade 4 students who answered correctly demonstrated a great deal of understanding about fractions.

Figure 4.8 includes a Grade 4 item and a sample student response scored as "incorrect." The responses to this item were scored as "extended," "satisfactory," "partial" (partially correct), "minimal," or "incorrect." The Questions Tool included a sample response for each category. An examination of student responses generated a more complete picture of students' fraction knowledge.

In four of the five responses (those not illustrated), we encountered no significant surprises. All but one of the responses included labels of Strips B and C as "1/2" and "5/10." Those responses are indicative of a part-whole conception of fractions. Such a conception relies on counting the number of pieces in a shaded part and comparing it with the number of equally sized pieces fitting into the

The shaded part of each strip below shows a fraction.

A.

This fraction strip shows 3/6.

B.

What fraction does this fraction strip show? $\frac{2}{1}$

C.

What fraction does this fraction strip show? $\frac{10}{5}$

What do the fractions shown in A, B, and C have in common?

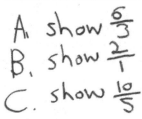

A, show $\frac{6}{3}$
B, show $\frac{2}{1}$
C. show $\frac{10}{5}$

Shade in the fraction strips below to show two different fractions that are equivalent to the ones shown in A, B and C.

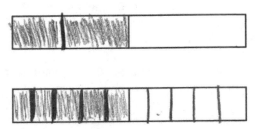

Figure 4.8. "Incorrect" response to item involving equivalent fractions (2003-4M10 #18).

whole rectangle. The student giving the fourth response had labeled Strip C as "5/5" but labeled Strip B correctly. The student may have recognized Strip B as representing the special fraction 1/2, which can be "read" from the picture, but was unable to consider part-whole relationships in general. That student's response to the question of what the strips have in common—"they are all close numbers" (presumably referring to a comparison of the numerator and denominator in each fraction)—also supports that interpretation. One of the students who had labeled Strip C in an appropriate manner reasoned similarly: "You just add two more to each number." That student had apparently understood the protocol of labeling fractions through counting pieces in the part and the whole but did not understand fractions as a relative extent of a given whole. Both students had trouble shading fractions equivalent to one-half in the two empty strips, further supporting our hypothesis that students can recognize simple fraction terms and appropriately label Strip B without a part-whole conception of fractions.

One Grade 4 student's response (Figure 4.8) illustrates a very sophisticated concept of fraction. Whereas the student's inversion of numerator and denominator was surprising to us, its consistent use throughout responses to the first three parts of the item indicates that the fractions were meaningful to the student. In fact, the fractions were otherwise correct. We also note that the student understood the importance of creating equal pieces in the whole and shading half of them as he or she did in the last fraction strip (apparently even erasing and redrawing marks to make them more evenly spaced). Perhaps most impressive was the student's use of shading and marks in the second-to-last fraction strip. The student partitioned only half of the strip into equal pieces and shaded them. That approach suggests that the student realized that the pieces in half of the strip could be projected into the other half, indicating a conception of fractions based on a multiplicative relationship between the fraction and the whole. Such a view of fraction goes beyond a part-whole relationship. The student seemed to understand that what is essential to being one-half is not a relationship between pieces in the part and pieces in the whole but a multiplicative relationship by which the whole can be reproduced by using the part so many times (in this example, two times). That relationship defines the fraction as a relative extent of the whole.

Fractions Summary

Nearly all Grade 4 and Grade 8 students have a conception of fractions that includes an image of equally partitioned pieces in a whole. The trouble is that many students' conceptions are dominated by equal-partitions image, to the point that the number of pieces in the part and whole is ambiguous and the size of the whole is irrelevant. By Grade 8, most students seem to have developed an understanding of a part-whole relationship that appropriately relates the numerator and denominator of a fraction to the pieces of the fraction and the total number of pieces in the whole. What remains lacking among the majority of Grade 8 students is the concept of a fraction as a relative extent of a whole. Without such a concept, tasks involving the use of fractions for nontrivial measurements (ones in which an object's measure cannot simply be read from a ruler) are daunting. And when challenged with tasks involving computation with fractions, students rely on rote procedures for which they have no meaningful interpretation.

Fractions had not yet become measurable items for many of the students at either grade, although our analyses indicate that students did seem to move toward such a conception between Grade 4 and Grade 8. At first, students view fractions as in-between numbers (between two whole numbers) that can be read or recognized. Students then progress to counting fractions and forming a part-whole conception of them. Finally, for the few Grade 8 students who progress further, fractions become measures of relative extent, similar to the way that whole numbers become extents relative to a defined unit.

Trends in Student Performance

Table 4.8 illustrates trends in Grade 4 students' performances on the fractions items. Note that every significant change is a positive one, with the exception of students' performance on the toothpick item (Item 4). We have previously mentioned that the toothpick item requires students to consider whole numbers and simple fractions as extents. In fact, it is the only item in Table 4.8 that requires such a conception of fractions to generate a correct response. One possible explanation for the decline in students' performance is that teachers' focus on preparing students for typical part-whole fractions items (such as Items 3, 12, and 13) interferes with their development from the part-whole conception to a conception of fractions as extents.

For Grade 8 students, we note once again that successful performance on the measuring item (Table 4.9, Item 6) has decreased over the years while successful performance on part-whole items has increased (Items 5 and 13). The trend of Grade 8 students' decreasing ability to consider fractions as extents is made further evident when we consider Item 8: recognizing equivalent fractions. Also noteworthy is the fact that student performance on items involving rote procedures, such as inverting and multiplying to divide fractions or using a formula to convert between temperature scales (Items 3 and 4), has increased. Over the same time, students' ability to form a meaningful word problem requiring division by a fraction (Item 11) has significantly decreased.

CONCLUSIONS

Our analysis of Grade 4 and 8 students' performance and responses on NAEP items illustrates that significant gains have been made on many tasks since 1996. We found evidence that Wearne and Kouba's (2000) conclusions from their analysis of the 1996 NAEP data still hold true. Our analysis also yields further insights about students' understandings of units and procedural and conceptual knowledge. These insights may suggest directions for mathematics educators as they strive to support children in their development of understanding of rational numbers.

Table 4.8
Grade 4 Student Performance on Items Involving Fractions

		Percentage Correct		
	Item Description	1996	2000	2003
1.	Determine elapsed time (3 1/2 hours). (Table 4.7)	38	41	40
2.	Divide 3/4 of a string into eighths. (Table 4.6)	23*	26	27
3.	Shade 1/3 of the rectangle.	20*	25*	28
4.	Find the length of a toothpick (2 1/2 inches). (Figure 4.5)	24	25*	20
5.	Show where 3/4 is on a number line. (Figure 4.4)	30*	33*	37
6.	Reason using fraction concepts.	15*	21	20
7.	Recognize equivalent fractions.	41*	47	49
8.	List equivalent fractions.	49*	54	53
9.	Identify the correct fraction.	61*	65*	70
10.	Justify that 1/4 of 20 is 5. (Figure 4.7)	9	11	11
11.	Solve a problem with fractions.	11*	18	18
12.	Name and shade fractions equivalent with 1/2. (Figure 4.8)	15*	13*	19
13.	Identify the picture showing 3/4. (Figure 4.3)	72*	81*	83

Note. Items 1, 2, 7, 9, and 13 were multiple-choice items. Items 3, 4, 5 and 6 were short constructed-response items. The rest were extended constructed-response items. Calculators were allowed on Items 1 and 10.

* Indicates the percentage correct is significantly different from the 2003 percentage correct.

What Constitutes the Unit?

Wearne and Kouba's (2000) conclusions from the 1996 NAEP rational number items suggested that students' notion of "the unit" appeared to be at the root of difficulties. To make sense of decimal and fraction representations, students must identify a part in relation to some whole. Success with this conceptualization comes in many forms. For both decimals and fractions, notation can be interpreted using part-whole reasoning. Students display such reasoning when they count pieces making up a whole and count pieces making up their part, developing a representation that contains the results of those counts. For instance, a student might notate 47 of 100 beans as 0.47 or as 47/100. Perhaps the difficulty with decimal notation occurs because the representation can be interpreted in many ways. Forty-seven hundredths could also be 4.7 tenths and 470 thousandths, just to name two.

Table 4.9

Grade 8 Student Performance on Items Involving Fractions

		Percentage Correct		
	Item Description	1996	2000	2003
1.	Use a pattern of fractions to determine which element is equivalent to 0.95. (2003-8M7 #12)	23*	28	27
2.	Arrange fractions in order from least to greatest.	35*	43*	46
3.	Convert Fahrenheit to Celsius.	26*	32	34
4.	Divide 3/4 of a string into eighths. (Table 4.6)	47*	54	55
5.	Shade 1/3 of the rectangle. (2005-8M3 #9)	67*	68*	73
6.	Find the length of a toothpick (2 1/2 inches). (Figure 4.5)	64*	64*	60
7.	Show where 3/4 is on a number line. (Figure 4.5)	60*	63	64
8.	Recognize equivalent fractions.	71	74*	71
9.	Read a weight from a scale with half-ounce increments. (Figure 4.6)	84	82	82
10.	Find an angle measure in a circle using an arc measure.	34	35	34
11.	Write a word problem using fractions. (2005-8M4 #18)	24*	23*	12
12.	Complete a rational number line.	64*	68	70
13.	Identify the picture showing 3/4. (Figure 4.3)	89*	92*	94

Note. Items 1, 2, 3, 4, 8, 10, and 13 were multiple-choice items; the rest were short constructed-response items. Calculators were allowed on Items 1, 2, 3, 9, and 10.

* Indicates the percentage correct is significantly different from the 2003 percentage correct.

Using students' performance on fraction items as a guide, we see that many Grade 4 students had achieved success with part-whole reasoning, and even more Grade 8 students appeared to use it. Student reasoning of that sort is more difficult to see with decimals because released items do not ask students to represent numerals as quantities. Nonetheless, part-whole reasoning is insufficient in developing a robust conception of decimals and rational number in general, because decimal notation is intended to convey a multiplicative rather than additive relationship between its parts.

Each numeral in a decimal indicates a value that is weighted by a power of 10. Moreover, the decimal point itself signifies which numeral numerates the number of whole units, from which all other numerals obtain their relative value. Therefore, the idea of numbers as extents of a specified whole is necessary to relate the numerals within a decimal, and in the fractions section, we have argued that very few Grade 8 students tested had achieved the conception of rational number as a relative extent.

Supporting student movement toward richer conceptions of decimals and fractions and connections among understandings of those representations may require further shifts in teaching. Specifically, educators who have been largely successful improving student performance on computation and representation items may want to move their emphasis to fostering understanding of rational number representations in a variety of mathematics domains. We explore that possibility next.

Rational Concepts or Rote Procedures?

Most improvement on rational number items since 1996 has focused on one-step problems that assess computation or representation of quantities with rational numbers. As in previous NAEP assessments, student scores show evidence of growth in performance from Grade 4 to Grade 8. An analysis of student responses still reveals areas that teachers may wish to target for improvement. First, performance gains may be linked with procedural proficiency; research has suggested that such an emphasis may inhibit future conceptual growth (National Research Council, 2001). Curricula designed to support the growth of conceptual understanding and link representations of rational numbers offer avenues for teachers to explore (Lappan, Fey, Fitzgerald, Friel, & Phillips 2002a, 2002b; Moss & Case, 1999).

Second, evidence shows that when fractions and decimals are used in measurement tasks, data-analysis tasks, and algebraic reasoning tasks, student performance suffers. That finding is not unusual but may indicate that students at the levels tested are still struggling with their understanding of rational numbers. Fragile or simply procedural understanding cannot be used as flexibly as conceptual understanding (Skemp, 1987). Students having difficulty interpreting either distracters or notations in a problem (examples: toothpick problem and vacation-letters problem) will perform poorly. To minimize that difficulty, students should be provided with opportunities to integrate their mathematical knowledge. NAEP tasks for Grade 8 students in strands other than number assume an understanding and proficiency with both fraction and decimal notations. In support of students' use and understanding of real numbers, they need opportunities to struggle with and discuss such notations in mathematical contexts other than numerical computation.

REFERENCES

Carpenter, T. P., Fennema, E., & Romberg, T. A. (Eds.). (1993). *Rational numbers: An integration of research.* Hillsdale, NJ: Erlbaum.

Curcio, F. (1987). Comprehension of mathematical relationships expressed in graphs. *Journal for Research in Mathematics Education, 18,* 382–393.

D'Ambrosio, B., Kastberg, S. E., McDermott, G., & Saada, N. (2004). Reading and interpreting data in disciplines other than mathematics. In P. Kloosterman & F. K. Lester Jr. (Eds.), *Results and interpretations of the 1990–2000 mathematics assessments of the National Assessment of Education Progress* (pp. 363–381). Reston, VA: National Council of Teachers of Mathematics.

Hiebert, J. (1985). Children's knowledge of common and decimal fractions. *Education and Urban Society, 17,* 427–437.

Hiebert, J., & Wearne, D. (1985). A model of students' decimal computation procedures. *Cognition and Instruction, 2,* 175–205.

Hiebert, J., & Wearne, D. (1988). Instruction and cognitive change in mathematics. *Educational Psychologist, 23,* 105–117.

Hiebert, J., Wearne, D., & Taber, S. (1991). Fourth graders' gradual construction of decimal fractions during instruction using different physical representations. *Elementary School Journal, 91,* 321–341.

Kamii, C., & Lewis, B. A. (1993). The harmful effects of algorithms in primary arithmetic. *Teaching PreK–8, 23*(4), 36–38.

Kloosterman, P., & Lester, F. K., Jr. (Eds.). (2004). *Results and interpretations of the 1990–2000 mathematics assessments of the National Assessment of Education Progress.* Reston, VA: National Council of Teachers of Mathematics.

Lappan, G., Fey, J., Fitzgerald, W., Friel, S., & Phillips, E. (2002a). *Bits and pieces I: Understanding rational numbers.* Upper Saddle River, NJ: Prentice Hall.

Lappan, G., Fey, J., Fitzgerald, W., Friel, S., & Phillips, E. (2002b). *Bits and pieces II: Using rational numbers.* Upper Saddle River, NJ: Prentice Hall.

Moss, J., & Case, R. (1999). Developing children's understanding of the rational numbers: A new model and an experimental curriculum. *Journal for Research in Mathematics Education, 30,* 122–147.

National Research Council. (2001). *Adding it up: Helping children learn mathematics.* Washington, DC: National Academy Press.

Pitkethly, A., & Hunting, R. (1996). A review of recent research in the area of initial fraction concepts. *Educational Studies in Mathematics, 30,* 5–38.

Resnick, L., Nesher, P., Leonard, F., Magone, M., Omanson, S., & Peled, I. (1989). Conceptual bases of arithmetic errors: The case of decimal fractions. *Journal for Research in Mathematics Education, 20,* 8–27.

Sharp, J., & Adams, B. (2002). Children's constructions of knowledge for fraction division after solving realistic problems. *Journal for Educational Research, 95,* 333–347.

Silver, E. A., & Kenney, P. A. (Eds.). (2000). *Results from the seventh mathematics assessment of the National Assessment of Educational Progress.* Reston, VA: National Council of Teachers of Mathematics.

Skemp, R. (1987). *The psychology of learning mathematics.* Hillsdale, NJ: Erlbaum.

Steffe, L. (2002). A new hypothesis concerning children's fractional knowledge. *Journal of Mathematical Behavior, 20,* 267–307.

Steffe, L., Cobb, P., & von Glasersfeld, E. (1988). *Construction of arithmetical meanings and strategies.* New York: Springer-Verlag.

Wearne, D., & Kouba, V. (2000). Rational numbers. In E. A. Silver & P. A. Kenney (Eds.), *Results from the seventh mathematics assessment of the National Assessment of Educational Progress* (pp. 163–191). Reston, VA: National Council of Teachers of Mathematics.

Zawojewski, J. S., & Shaughnessy, J. M. (2000). Data and chance. In E. A. Silver & P. A. Kenney (Eds.), *Results from the seventh mathematics assessment of the National Assessment of Educational Progress* (pp. 235–268). Reston, VA: National Council of Teachers of Mathematics.

5

Performance in Measurement and Geometry From the Viewpoint of *Principles and Standards for School Mathematics*

Glendon W. Blume, Enrique Galindo, and Crystal Walcott[1]

Measurement and geometry constitute two of the five Content Standards in *Principles and Standards for School Mathematics (Principles and Standards)* (National Council of Teachers of Mathematics, 2000). In school mathematics curricula and in the suggested content emphases across Grades prekindergarten (pre-K) through 8 in *Principles and Standards*, measurement and geometry constitute a substantial amount of the content—the suggested combined emphasis on measurement and geometry represents more content emphasis than what is devoted to number, algebra, or data analysis and probability (see Figure 3.1 on p. 30 of NCTM [2000]). Measurement and geometry also are particularly important mathematics content; *Principles and Standards* notes that measurement is important from Grades pre-K through 12 because of its practicality and pervasiveness in many aspects of everyday life. *Principles and Standards* also notes that geometric modeling and spatial reasoning can be important tools in mathematical problem solving. According to *Principles and Standards*, some of the essential aspects of geometry are that it entails analysis of characteristics and properties of geometric shapes, specification of locations and spatial relationships through the use of coordinate systems, use of transformations and symmetry, and visualization and spatial reasoning. Although many potential frameworks can be used to structure measurement and geometry content, we chose to use the expectations given in the *Principles and Standards* Measurement and Geometry Standards to structure this chapter, because those

---

[1] The authors are listed alphabetically; all contributed equally to this chapter.

Highlights

- Between 1996 and 2003, the Grade 4 and Grade 8 scale scores for measurement improved significantly (9 scale points at Grade 4 and 5 scale points at Grade 8). The 2003 Grade 4 and Grade 8 scale scores for geometry also improved significantly over that period (8 scale points at Grade 4 and 5 scale points at Grade 8).

- Although no significant difference occurred in performance from 2000 to 2003 for many of the items related to understanding measurable attributes, students did reasonably well in this area.

- Applying appropriate techniques, tools, and formulas to determine measurements is a measurement area in which 4th-grade students had more difficulty and in which performance decreased on a number of items from 2000 to 2003. At Grade 8, the picture is better, with stable or improving performance seen on most items. A small decline occurred in performance on measuring length, and a small improvement was seen on items related to measuring area.

- On items addressing attributes and classification of geometric figures, little change occurred from 2000 to 2003 at Grade 4 or Grade 8.

- Although only a small number of NAEP items addressed specifying locations and describing spatial relationships using coordinate geometry, performance on most of those items increased significantly at both Grade 4 and Grade 8.

- Eighth-grade students' lack of improvement on items involving geometric transformations persisted, as it did from 1990 to 2000.

- On items involving three-dimensional geometry, students at Grades 4 and 8 generally improved from 2000 to 2003 or maintained their level of performance.

expectations fairly explicitly "specify the understanding, knowledge, and skills that students should acquire" (NCTM, 2000, p. 29).

Current school mathematics curricula and national as well as state and provincial mathematics standards and assessments all include substantial amounts of emphasis on measurement and geometry. For example, measurement and geometry constituted approximately 25% of the Canadian 2001 SAIP assessment (see http://www.cmec.ca/saip/math2001/public/criteria.en.pdf). Evidence can be cited that indicates that the expectations in the *Principles and Standards* Measurement and Geometry Standards can be addressed productively at a variety of levels of school mathematics. For example, Berry and Wiggins (2001) describe how their 6th-grade students developed an understanding of angle measurement, Chappell (2001) provides examples of middle-grades students' use of spatial reasoning to solve real-world problems, Kenehan and Ambrose (2005) describe 3rd graders' investigation of properties of polyhedra, and Swindal (2000) illustrates how elementary school students can communicate about symmetry and two- and three-dimensional geometric objects. Because elementary and middle school students produce approximate measures and reason about the precision of measurements; use coordinate geometry to represent geometric objects and to examine their properties; and use spatial reasoning to solve problems, investigate symmetry, and study geometric transformations, the assessment of students' capabilities in those areas has become increasingly important. Also, because geometry software that provides dynamic capabilities (e.g., Cabri Geometry, Geometer's Sketchpad) has become more widely available in schools, the study of students' capabilities in the area of geometric transformations, visualization, and spatial reasoning is especially important.

OVERALL PERFORMANCE TRENDS IN MEASUREMENT AND GEOMETRY

This chapter discusses results from the majority of the 129 items addressing Measurement or Geometry and Spatial Sense in the 2003 NAEP Mathematics Assessment.[2] The assessment included 32 Measurement items at Grade 4 (26 multiple choice and 6 constructed response) and 30 Measurement items at Grade 8 (20 multiple choice and 10 constructed response). The assessment also included 29 Geometry items at Grade 4 (16 multiple choice and 13 constructed response) and 38 Geometry items at Grade 8 (21 multiple choice and 17 constructed response).[3] On some items students were allowed to use calculators, and on some items students had materials available (e.g., manipulable geometric shapes).

In addition to providing grade-level composite scale scores (see chapter 2), NAEP releases scale scores for each of the content strands. From 1996 to 2000, the Measurement scale score was stable (259) at Grade 4 and rose only 2 points (from 268 to 270, a gain that was not statistically significant) at Grade 8. Growth in Geometry was also minimal (and not statistically significant) over the same period, rising from 224 to 226 in Grade 4 and from 269 to 270 in Grade 8. From 2000 to 2003, the more substantial gains were statistically significant. Grade 4 students gained 9 scale points in the Measurement content strand and 8 scale points in the Geometry strand. Grade 8 students gained 5 points in both the Measurement and Geometry strands.

REPORTING OF ITEMS AND DATA IN THIS CHAPTER

As background for the interpretations that follow, we note that the item descriptions used in this chapter are consistent with descriptions used in previous monographs (Kenney & Silver, 1997; Kloosterman & Lester, 2004; Silver & Kenney, 2000). At times, descriptions contain vocabulary that does not appear

---

[2] Throughout the chapter we often use the term *Geometry* to refer to the Geometry and Spatial Sense content strand.

[3] Because their content appeared to involve both measurement and geometry, we considered some items for which the NAEP classification was Measurement to be Geometry items, and vice versa.

in the item itself. For example, a description such as "Find the length of the diagonal of a rectangle" might refer to an item in which the terms *diagonal* or *rectangle* are not used. Instead, the item might refer to a diagram of a rectangle with a drawn diagonal, indicated as segment *XY*, in which students are asked to find the length *XY*. In this example, we chose vocabulary to describe the item in the clearest, most consistent, and most efficient way possible, but not necessarily using the wording used in the item. Also, because of the nature of the items, some content spanned more than one *Principles and Standards* category or grade level. Therefore, a number of items listed in the tables appear in more than one table.

We report the item-level data in this chapter in terms of the percentage of students answering the item correctly, and, following the convention throughout this volume, the 0.05 level is used to determine statistical significance. When the percentage correct on items did not change enough from one year to the next to be statistically significant, performance on those items was considered stable. Note that although we report percentage correct on items for each of the 1996, 2000, and 2003 assessments, our primary focus is on change from 2000 to 2003.

RELATIONSHIP BETWEEN THE *PRINCIPLES AND STANDARDS* MEASUREMENT AND GEOMETRY CONTENT STANDARDS AND THE MEASUREMENT AND GEOMETRY CONTENT IN THE NAEP 2003 FRAMEWORK

Before presenting our discussion of performance on the 2003 NAEP Measurement and Geometry items, we examine the framework used to guide the content and format of NAEP items and its relationship to the Measurement and Geometry Standards in *Principles and Standards*. According to the mathematics framework for the 2003 NAEP (National Assessment Governing Board [NAGB], 2002), the Measurement strand "focuses on an understanding of measurement and the use of numbers and measures to describe and compare mathematical and real-world objects" (p. 23). It also specifies "the assessment focus at grade 4 is on time, money, temperature, length, perimeter, area, capacity, weight/mass, and angle measure," and that for Grades 8 and 12, in addition to including those measurement concepts, the focus should shift to problems that involve volume or surface area; or that require students to combine shapes, translate shapes, and apply measures; or that involve proportional thinking.

More specifically, the NAEP Measurement content strand includes the following aspects of measurement:[4] (a) estimate the size of objects or compare objects with respect to a given attribute; (b) select and use appropriate measurement instruments, units of measurement, and methods of measurement (direct or indirect); (c) estimate, calculate, or compare perimeter, area, volume, and surface

---

[4] This is an abridged description of the 2003 NAEP Measurement strand; for a complete description, see the 2003 mathematics framework (National Assessment Governing Board, 2002, p. 24).

area in meaningful contexts; (d) convert measurements within the same system; (e) determine precision, accuracy, and error; and (f) apply the concept of rate to measurement situations.

The Measurement Standard in *Principles and Standards* includes two major expectations: (a) understand measurable attributes of objects and the units, systems, and processes of measurement; and (b) apply appropriate techniques, tools, and formulas to determine measurements (NCTM, 2000, p. 44). In the Measurement Standard we also find more specific expectations for different grade bands. The statement of the measurement expectations for Grades 3–5 and Grades 6–8 can be seen in Tables 5.1 through 5.4, which appear later in this chapter. For our analysis, we tried to classify each NAEP item using one of the *Principles and Standards* expectations. By examining the number of items under each category in Tables 5.1 through 5.4, one can see that many items are listed under some *Principles and Standards* categories but none under others.

According to the Geometry and Spatial Sense strand of the mathematics framework for the 2003 NAEP (NAGB, 2002), spatial sense must be an integral component of the study and assessment of geometry; furthermore, an understanding of spatial relations allows students to connect mathematics with their world. The NAEP framework also specifies that this strand goes beyond low-level identification of geometric shapes to include transformations and combinations of geometric shapes, informal constructions and demonstrations along with their justifications, and the extension of proportional thinking to similar figures and indirect measurements. It prescribes that 4th-grade students "are expected to model properties of shapes under simple combinations and transformations and use mathematical communication skills to draw figures given a verbal description" and that 8th-grade students "are expected to understand properties of angles and polygons and apply reasoning skills to make and validate conjectures about transformations and combinations of shapes" (p. 26).

More specifically, the NAEP Geometry and Spatial Sense strand includes the following aspects: (a) describe, visualize, draw, and construct geometric figures; (b) investigate and predict results of combining, subdividing, and changing shapes; (c) identify the relationship (congruence, similarity) between a figure and its image under a transformation; (d) describe the intersection of two or more geometric figures (Grade 8); (e) classify figures in terms of congruence and similarity, and informally apply these relationships using proportional reasoning where appropriate (Grade 8); and (f) apply geometric properties and relationships in solving problems.

The Geometry Standard in *Principles and Standards* includes four major expectations: (a) analyze characteristics and properties of two- and three-dimensional geometric shapes and develop mathematical arguments about geometric relationships; (b) specify locations and describe spatial relationships using coordinate geometry and other representational systems; (c) apply transformations and use symmetry to analyze mathematical situations; and (d) use visualization, spatial reasoning, and geometric modeling to solve problems (NCTM,

2000, p. 41). In the Geometry Standard we also find more specific expectations for different grade bands. The statement of the Geometry expectations for Grades 3–5 and Grades 6–8 can be seen in Tables 5.5 to 5.12, which appear along with discussion of performance on Geometry later in the chapter. These tables give us a sense of the extent to which a match exists between the *Principles and Standards* Geometry expectations and the NAEP Geometry and Spatial Sense strand. As with the Measurement strand, we found that many items fit in some Geometry *Principles and Standards* categories but none in others. Although we have not found complete alignment between the two, an analysis of NAEP items using the *Principles and Standards* expectations can help give a sense of the extent to which *Principles and Standards* goals are being met. Our discussion in the following sections presents this analysis. We should note, however, that one of the stated goals of making revisions to the NAEP framework is "to reflect curricular emphases and objectives [and to] include what various scholars, practitioners, and interested citizens believe should be in the assessment" (NAGB, 2002, p. 4). An analysis of the extent to which NAEP strands meet *Principles and Standards* expectations lends a sense of how responsive the NAEP framework is to changes in national recommendations about mathematics learning.

UNDERSTANDING MEASURABLE ATTRIBUTES OF OBJECTS AND THE UNITS, SYSTEMS, AND PROCESSES OF MEASUREMENT

According to *Principles and Standards,* students should have many informal experiences in understanding measurable attributes of objects and situations before using tools to measure them or relying on formulas to compute measurements. Tables 5.1 and 5.2 show 2003 NAEP items related to understanding measurable attributes. Of the 11 items in this category, 9 were administered only to 4th-grade students, 1 was administered both to 4th-grade and 8th-grade students, and 1 was administered only to 8th-grade students. The only item for which a significant difference was noted was an item in which students were asked to identify a reasonable amount of time for a two-mile walk (Item 3 in Table 5.1). Performance on this item decreased significantly (from 91% to 88% correct), returning to the level of performance that had been achieved in 1996.

Although no significant difference in performance from 2000 to 2003 was found for the other nine items, performance on those items shows that, in general, students did moderately well on NAEP items related to understanding measurable attributes. For example, 68% of students correctly identified feet as a unit that is appropriate to measure the length of a car (Item 1 in Table 5.1), and 88% correctly indicated that 60 minutes is a reasonable amount of time for a two-mile nature walk (Item 3 in Table 5.1). However, students continued to have considerable difficulty with certain items in this category. Items that involve

Table 5.1

Items Related to Understanding Measurable Attributes of Objects and the Units, Systems, and Processes of Measurement (Subcategories for Grades 3–5)

Item Description	Percentage Correct: Grade 4			Percentage Correct: Grade 8		
	96	00	03	96	00	03
Understand such attributes as length, area, weight, volume, and size of angle and select the appropriate type of unit for measuring each attribute.						
1. Which of the following is usually measured in feet? (Options are coin, paperclip, car, or distance between two cities.) (2003-4M10 #1)	n.a.	70	68			
2. Identify an appropriate unit of length (English units).	78	80	80			
3. Rudy takes a two-mile walk along a nature trail. Which of the following is a reasonable amount of time for Rudy to take to walk the trail? (Options are 60 seconds, 60 minutes, 60 hours, or 60 days.) (2003-4M7 #2)	89	91*	88			
4. Recognize the best measurement unit.	38	39	41			
5. Identify an appropriate unit of length (metric units).	34	36	36			
6. Identify an appropriate unit of length (English units).	87	88	88			
7. Choose an appropriate context for a measurement situation.	n.a.	n.a.	73			
8. Choose a situation in which a meterstick would be a proper measurement tool. (2005-4M12 #5)[a]	n.a.	n.a.	76			
Understand the need for measuring with standard units and become familiar with standard units in the customary and metric systems.	*No corresponding NAEP items*					
Carry out simple unit conversions, such as from centimeters to meters, within a system of measurement.						
9. Work with units of liquid measure.	n.a.	29	30			
10. Given illustrations of four objects labeled with the weight of each, identify heaviest object. (2003-4M6 #4, 2003-8M6 #4)	75*[#]	82	82	85*[#]	88	88
Understand that measurements are approximations and how differences in units affect precision.	*No corresponding NAEP items*					
Explore what happens to measurements of a two-dimensional shape, such as its perimeter and area, when the shape is changed in some way.	*No corresponding NAEP items*					

Note. n.a. indicates that the item was not administered in this year. All items described in this table were multiple-choice items. Calculators were allowed on Items 2, 3, 4, and 9.

[a] Items for 2005 were released while this volume was in production. The 2005 block and item numbers have been added to tables so that interested readers can find these items using the online Questions Tool.

* Indicates that the percentage correct is significantly different from the 2003 percentage correct.

[#] Indicates that the percentage correct is significantly different from the 2000 percentage correct.

Table 5.2

Items Related to Understanding Measurable Attributes of Objects and the Units, Systems, and Processes of Measurement (Subcategories for Grades 6–8)

	Percentage Correct: Grade 4			Percentage Correct: Grade 8		
Item Description	96	00	03	96	00	03
Understand both metric and customary systems of measurement.	*No corresponding NAEP items*					
Understand relationships among units and convert from one unit to another within the same system.						
1. 1 mile = 5,280 feet. How many feet are in 18 miles? (2003-8M7 #1)				84*#	88	89
2. Given illustrations of four objects labeled with the weight of each, identify the heaviest object.[a] (2003-4M6 #4, 2003-8M6 #4)	75*#	82	82	85#	88	88
Understand, select, and use units of appropriate size and type to measure angles, perimeter, area, surface area, and volume.	*No corresponding NAEP items*					

Note. n.a. indicates that the item was not administered in this year. All items were multiple-choice items. Calculators were allowed on Item 1.

[a] This item also appeared as Item 10 in Table 5.1. A number of items in the remaining tables in this chapter appear in more than one table because they address multiple *PSSM* categories.

* Indicates that the percentage correct is significantly different from the 2003 percentage correct.

# Indicates that the percentage correct is significantly different from the 2000 percentage correct.

metric units were difficult for students. For example, only 41% of 4th-grade students correctly answered a question about selecting the best metric unit for a situation involving volume (Item 4 in Table 5.1), and only 36% correctly answered a question asking them to select a metric unit of length that was appropriate for the size of a given object (Item 5 in Table 5.1).

Another category of items with which students had some difficulties is carrying out simple unit conversions. Two 4th-grade measurement items involved unit conversions and produced mixed results. In one item (Item 10 in Table 5.1) students were asked to identify the heaviest object. Figures of four objects were provided, and each object had a caption with the name of the object and its weight. The first object was a metal ball shown with a weight of 8 pounds, which 82% of Grade 4 and 88% of Grade 8 students correctly identified as the heaviest object. However, less positive results occurred for an item (Item 9 in Table 5.1) in which students needed to make conversions within the same system using units of liquid measure. Only 30% of 4th-grade students answered this item correctly. One reason for the difference in performance in those two items may have been the conceptual cues provided by the pictures and objects illustrated in the first item.

Although 4th-grade students performed fairly well on the NAEP items described above, many aspects of students' understanding of measurable attributes and measuring processes that are part of the Grades 3–5 expectations in *Principles and Standards* did not seem to be represented in any NAEP items. Although we found 10 Grade 4 items that could be classified in this category, the picture we can get from those items about understanding of measurable attributes is incomplete. Eight of the NAEP items we classified in this category pertained to understanding measurable attributes and selecting the appropriate type of unit for measuring each attribute. However, 5 of them were related to appropriate length units, and only 1 item was devoted to each of the attributes of time, weight, and volume. The other 2 items related to 4th-grade students' understanding of measurable attributes were discussed previously and involved carrying out simple unit conversions within the same system of measurement. We cannot learn much about students' understanding of unit conversions from those two items, as students did fairly well on the item in which they had to identify the heaviest object but had considerable difficulty with the item that required them to work with units of liquid measure. On the basis of the released NAEP items and the descriptions used for items in the secure data base, some aspects—such as understanding the need for measuring with standard units, understanding that measurements are approximations and how differences in units affect precision, and understanding what happens to measurements of a two-dimensional shape when the shape is changed in some way—did not seem to be assessed by Grade 4 NAEP items.

Only two 8th-grade NAEP items assessed understanding of measurable attributes. Those items had to do with converting from one unit to another within the same system. Item 1 of Table 5.2 asked students to find the number of feet in 18 miles. Eighty-nine percent of 8th-grade students correctly answered that question. The second item (Item 2 in Table 5.2; Item 10 in Table 5.1), involving identification of the heaviest object, was noted previously. Performance on both of those items was good and remained at the same level as in 2000. Other aspects of 8th-grade students' understanding of measurable attributes—such as understanding metric and customary systems of measurement and understanding, selecting, and using units of appropriate size and type to measure angles, perimeter, area, surface area, and volume—did not seem to be assessed by Grade 8 NAEP items.

APPLYING APPROPRIATE TECHNIQUES, TOOLS, AND FORMULAS TO DETERMINE MEASUREMENTS

In addition to developing an understanding of measurable attributes of objects and situations, students need to develop strategies to determine measurements. Students need to learn to use tools to take measurements and to develop the general relationships or formulas that are used to produce measurements. Tables 5.3 and 5.4 focus on NAEP items related to applying appropriate techniques, tools, and formulas to determine measurements. A significant difference in performance was noted from 2000 to 2003 on 17 out of the 43 items. For the 14 items administered only to 4th-grade students, a significant decrease in performance occurred from 2000 to 2003 on 6 items and a significant increase in performance occurred on 2 items. For the 26 items administered only to 8th-grade students, a significant increase in performance was seen on 5 items and a significant decrease in performance was seen on 3 items. A significant decrease in performance was noted in 1 of the 4 items that were administered at both levels. Thus performance in 2003, compared with that in 2000, on NAEP items related to determining measurements stayed the same or decreased on the majority of items administered to 4th-grade students and stayed the same or increased on the majority of items administered to 8th-grade students.

Items 3, 6, 7, 8, 11, and 14 in Table 5.3 are related to measuring length. Performance in 2003 decreased significantly compared with that in 2000 on four of those items (3, 7, 11, and 14) and increased significantly on two of them (6 and 8). The item in which students had the greatest difficulty, and exhibited a decrease in performance, was Item 11 in Table 5.3. In this item students were asked to determine the length of a toothpick pictured above a ruler, for which neither of the ends of the toothpick was aligned with the zero on the ruler. Only 20% of 4th-grade students in 2003 answered this question correctly as compared with 25% in 2000, suggesting that students may be getting even less effective instruction about zero points (Lehrer, 2003), a measurement concept identified as being difficult (Lehrer, Jenkins, & Osana, 1998; Stephan & Clements, 2003). Fourth-grade students' performance on this item mirrors that reported by Lehrer et al. (1998) for students in Grades 1–3. Performance also decreased significantly for Item 7, in which students were asked to measure a segment using a ruler. Only 40% of 4th-grade students answered correctly in 2003, compared with 55% in 2000. Another length-related item for which performance decreased significantly was Item 3, in which students were required to understand a scale drawing. The percentage of correct responses was 51 in 2003 compared with 56 in 2000.

Looking at the measurement items in Table 5.3 as a group, we see that the greatest performance decrease was on Item 7, on which Grade 4 performance dropped from 55% correct in 2000 to 40% correct in 2003. This decline was the greatest 2000-to-2003 difference for any measurement item. This difference is more noticeable in light of performance on Item 6, on which 63% of 4th-grade students correctly used a ruler to measure length. What caused this marked decrease in performance on Item 7? Is it the result of differences in emphasis on, or experiences related to, measurement in the mathematics curriculum? The only clear conclusion is that the majority of measurement items for which performance decreased for 4th-grade students in 2003 dealt with measuring length (Items 3, 7, 11, and 14 in Table 5.3).

The other items in Table 5.3 related to other measurement attributes, such as weight (Item 1), temperature (Items 4 and 5), time (Items 2, 10, 12, and 15), area (Item 16), and speed (Item 9). In Item 1, in which students were asked to identify an instrument used to weigh an apple, performance declined from 88% correct in 2000 to 85% correct in 2003. In Item 9, which required students to interpret the reading from a commonly used measurement instrument, performance declined from 66% to 61%. On three items dealing with time (Items 2, 10, and 12), at most 40% of students answered correctly. Performance on the two items related to temperature (4 and 5) and the item related to area (13) remained the same in 2003 compared with 2000, although less than half of the students correctly answered those items.

In general, performance on the 17 Grade 4 items related to applying appropriate techniques, tools, and formulas to determine measurements indicates that 4th-grade students have considerable difficulty with this aspect of measurement, which encompasses the greatest number of items for which performance decreased from 2000 to 2003. Performance in 2003 decreased significantly for 7 items, remained the same for 7 items, and increased significantly for only 2 items. Because 1 of those 17 items was new in 2003, comparison with previous performance was not possible for that item.

We next examine performance on Grade 8 items related to applying appropriate techniques, tools, and formulas to determine measurements. Most of the items under this category correspond to the subcategory of selecting and applying techniques and tools to accurately find length, area, volume, and angle measures to appropriate levels of precision. We classified 19 of the 28 measurement items that were administered to 8th-grade students under this subcategory (see Table 5.4). A noteworthy observation is that 3 of 4 measurement items on which students exhibited a significant decrease in performance, and 4 of 5 items on which students exhibited a significant increase, fell in this subcategory. Eighth graders' performance on most items in this subcategory was below 50% correct, and their performance on only 4 items was above 70%.

Items 4, 5, 13, and 19 in this subcategory were about length. Eighth graders' performance in 2003 decreased significantly from that in 2000 for two of them (Items 4 and 13) and remained the same for the other item given in both years (5). As we discussed previously, several 4th-grade items about length asked students for direct measurements, and performance was not high. If similar items had been administered at Grade 8, we would have been able to assess whether students have effectively surmounted such difficulties by the time they complete Grade 8.

Table 5.3
Items Related to Applying Appropriate Techniques, Tools, and Formulas to Determine Measurements (Subcategories for Grades 3–5)

Item Description	Percentage Correct: Grade 4			Percentage Correct: Grade 8		
	96	00	03	96	00	03
Develop strategies for estimating the perimeters, areas, and volumes of irregular shapes.	*No corresponding NAEP items*					
Select and apply appropriate standard units and tools to measure length, area, volume, weight, time, temperature, and the size of angles.						
1. Which of the following would be used to find the weight of an apple? (Options are a measuring cup, ruler, scale, and thermometer.) (2003-4M10 #4)	87	88*	85			
2. Solve a problem involving time.	n.a.	31*	25			
3. Understand a scale drawing.	n.a.	56*	51			
4. Read a thermometer. (2003-4M10 #13)	36	37	40			
5. The Celsius temperature rose from 4 degrees above zero to the temperature shown on the thermometer above. How many degrees did the temperature rise? (Thermometer reads 16, and the options are 6, 7, 12, 20.) (2003-4M7 #13)	47	50	50			
6. Use a ruler to measure a length (metric units).	54*	57*	63			
7. Use a ruler to measure a segment (metric units).	57*	55*	40			
8. Use a ruler to find the differences in distances between given locations.	31	30*	33			
9. Interpret reading from a commonly used instrument.	64	66*	61			
10. Ted went to the beach at 10:30 a.m. and came home at 2:00 p.m. How many hours was he gone? (Options are 8½, 4½, 3½, and 2½.) (2003-4M7 #17)	38	41	40			

Table 5.3 (continued)

Item Description	Percentage Correct: Grade 4			Percentage Correct: Grade 8		
	96	00	03	96	00	03
11. Determine the length of a toothpick. (A picture of the toothpick is shown with one end at the 8-inch mark and the other end at the 10½-inch mark on a ruler.) (2003-4M6 #18, 2003-8M6 #18)	24*	25*	20	64*	64*	58
12. Solve a problem involving the conversion of one measure of time to another.	22*#	27	26	53	56	55
13. Choose the correct value for the area of a polygon depicted on a centimeter grid. (2005-4M4 #6)	41*#	46	45	77	79	78
Select and use benchmarks to estimate measurements.						
14. Find the length of a branch (shown in illustration). (2003-4M10 #12)	n.a.	50*	47			
15. Given a time in minutes, approximate the equivalent fraction of an hour. (2005-4M12 #7)	n.a.	n.a.	50			
Develop, understand, and use formulas to find the area of rectangles and related triangles and parallelograms.						
16. Determine the area of a geometric figure, given the area of an inscribed figure.	44	48	47			
Develop strategies to determine the surface areas and volumes of rectangular solids.						
17. Compare the volumes of two solids.	n.a.	52	53			

Note. n.a. indicates that the item was not administered in this year. Items 2, 4, 7, 8, and 11 were short constructed-response items, and the rest were multiple-choice items. Calculators were allowed on Items 2, 3, 5, 10, and 17.
* Indicates that the percentage correct is significantly different from the 2003 percentage correct.
# Indicates that the percentage correct is significantly different from the 2000 percentage correct.

Table 5.4
Items Related to Applying Appropriate Techniques, Tools, and Formulas to Determine Measurements (Subcategories for Grades 6–8)

Item Description	Percentage Correct: Grade 4			Percentage Correct: Grade 8		
	96	00	03	96	00	03
Use common benchmarks to select appropriate methods for estimating measurements.						
1. The cruise ship <u>Titanic</u> was 882 feet long. Which of the following is closest to that length? (Options are two moving-van lengths, fifty car lengths, one hundred skateboard lengths, five hundred school-bus lengths, one thousand bicycle lengths) (2003-8M10 #14)				n.a.	42*	39
2. Given illustrations of four angles drawn in different orientations, choose the correct ordering of their angle measures. (2005-8M3 #1)				68#	73	71
3. Choose the best estimate for an area of a region.				60*	62*	67
Select and apply techniques and tools to accurately find length, area, volume, and angle measures to appropriate levels of precision.						
4. Determine the length of a toothpick. (A picture of the toothpick is shown with one end at the 8-inch mark and the other end at the 10½-inch mark on a ruler.) (2003-4M6 #18, 2003-8M6 #18)	24*	25*	20	64*	64*	58
5. The perimeter of a square is 36 inches. What is the length of one side of the square? (Options are 4, 6, 9, and 18 inches.) (2003-4M6 #10, 2003-8M6 #10)	43*#	47	47	63*#	69	68
6. Choose the correct value for the area of a polygon depicted on a centimeter grid. (2005-4M4 #6)	41*#	46	45	77	79	78
7. 1 mile = 5,280 feet. How many feet are in 18 miles? (2003-8M7 #1)				84*#	88	89
8. Find the area of a figure shown on a geoboard grid, and then construct another figure with the same area. (2005-8M4 #17)				n.a.	4	2
9. Identify an instrument for measuring angles.				84	87*	85

Table 5.4 (*continued*)

Item Description	Percentage Correct: Grade 4			Percentage Correct: Grade 8		
	96	00	03	96	00	03
10. Compare the areas of two shapes.				n.a.	42*	46
11. Choose the correct numerical expression for the area rectangle (4 × 6 rectangle pictured). (2003-8M7 #5)				42*#	51	48
12. Draw an arrow in the direction given in degrees. (2005-8M3 #2)				22	23	22
13. Length can be measured to within 0.05 centimeter accuracy by using a certain type of measuring instrument. A reading of 3.7 centimeters on this instrument means that the actual length is at least (options are 3.20, 3.65, 3.69, 3.70, and 3.75 centimeters). (2003-8M6 #22)				24	25*	22
14. Determine the number of squares necessary to cover a region.				14*	14*	17
15. Find the measure of a central angle in a circle.				34	35	34
16. Determine the volume of a sphere, given the radius.				35*	37*	41
17. Given the dimensions, draw one rectangular region enclosed by another. (2005-8M3 #3)				36*	40*	46
18. Find the total weight of two objects.				n.a.	n.a.	49
19. Find length of a rectangle, given perimeter and width. (2005-8M12 #2)				n.a.	n.a.	39
20. Given the measure of one acute angle of a right triangle, find the measure of the other acute angle. (2005-8M12 #8)				n.a.	n.a.	46
21. Read 6.5 from a scale graduated in whole ounces. (2003-8M7 #4)				84	82	82
22. Read the temperature shown on the thermometer, and calculate an increase in temperature. (2005-8M12 #5)				n.a.	n.a.	69

(*table continues*)

Table 5.4 (continued)

Item Description	Percentage Correct: Grade 4			Percentage Correct: Grade 8		
	96	00	03	96	00	03
Develop and use formulas to determine the circumference of circles and the area of triangles, parallelograms, trapezoids, and circles and develop strategies to find the area of more complex shapes.						
23. Show three ways a region with square corners can be divided to find the area. (2003-8M6 #29)				9	11	10
24. Solve a problem involving distance.				n.a.	n.a.	18
Develop strategies to determine the surface area and volume of selected prisms, pyramids, and cylinders.						
25. Determine the surface area of a rectangular solid.				20*#	25	24
26. Compare the volume of several objects.				n.a.	n.a.	74
Solve problems involving scale factors, using ratio and proportion.						
27. Given a scale diagram of a room, determine the number of boxes of square tiles it would take to cover the region. (2005-8M3 #18)				9*	10	12
28. Draw a figure similar to a given figure on the basis of a ratio involving the areas of the figures. (2005-8M4 #14)				6	8	7
Solve simple problems involving rates and derived measurements for such attributes as velocity and density.	*No corresponding NAEP items*					

Note. n.a. indicates that the item was not administered in this year. Items 4, 8, 12, 14, 17, 18, 21, and 28 were short constructed-response items. Items 23 and 27 were extended constructed-response items, and the rest were multiple-choice items. Calculators were allowed on Items 3, 7, 9, 11, 15, 16, 21, and 25.

* Indicates that percentage correct is significantly different from the 2003 percentage correct.
# Indicates that percentage correct is significantly different from the 2000 percentage correct.

Two items required students to find one side of a quadrilateral, given its perimeter. In Item 5 students were asked for the length of the side of a square, given its perimeter. Performance was 68% correct, similar to that in 2000. Students had more difficulty finding the length of one side of a rectangle, given its perimeter and the length of the other side (see Item 19). On this new item, only 39% of students answered correctly. The most difficult length item in this subcategory was Item 13. In this item students were asked about the minimum length of an object measured at 3.7 cm when the accuracy of the measurement instrument was 0.05 cm. Performance on this item decreased from 25% correct in 2000 to 22% correct in 2003.

Seven items in the subcategory of applying appropriate techniques, tools, and formulas to determine measurements were about area (3, 6, 8, 10, 11, 14, and 17 in Table 5.4). The three items with changes in performance for 2003 were Items 10, 14, and 17, and on which performance increased significantly from the corresponding levels in 2000. Although no changes in performance in 2003 were seen for Items 8 and 11, we were interested in examining how students answered them. In Item 8 students were asked to find the area of a figure shown on a geoboard grid and then to construct another figure with the same area. In Item 11 students had to choose the correct value for the area of a polygon shown on a centimeter grid. Performance on Item 11 was relatively high, with 78% correct, but only 2% of students answered Item 8 correctly. A closer examination of the answers to Item 8 shows that 48% of responses were partially correct, that is, responses giving the correct value for the area or showing the correct figure on the geoboard, but not both. Apparently, Item 8 was particularly difficult because the grid had no squares outlined (as in Item 11), it was not a multiple-choice item, and it had an additional part asking students to construct a new figure of the same area. Assuming that performance on Item 8 can be considered an anomaly because of the difficulty of the item, we can say that 8th-grade students made progress in the topic of area measurement in 2003.

Four items about angle measurement were classified in the subcategory of applying appropriate techniques, tools, and formulas to determine measurements (9, 12, 15, and 20 in Table 5.4). In Item 9 students were asked to identify an instrument for measuring angles. Performance on this item was quite good in 2000, with 87% correct, although it dropped slightly to 85% in 2003. Performance on the other three angle items was relatively low. In Item 20, students had to find the measure of one acute angle of a right triangle, given the measure of the other acute angle. On that item only 46% of responses were correct. On Item 15, which addressed finding the measure of a central angle in a circle, 34% of Grade 8 students correctly responded. And in Item 12, which required drawing an arrow in the direction 75° south of west, 22% of the responses were correct. We should note that in 2003, 50% of the answers for Item 12 were partially correct. According to the scoring guide, answers having an arrow located at 75° with respect to the x-axis and answers having a correct arrow direction but an incorrect angle measure were considered partially correct. Since 72% of responses to Item 12 were correct or partially correct, we might hypothesize that students do not frequently encounter the language used for the direction of the arrow ("75° south of west") in the measurement portion of the school mathematics curriculum.

Of the other four items we classified in the subcategory of applying appropriate techniques, tools, and formulas to determine measurements, one had to do with volume (Item 16), two with weight (Items 18 and 21), and one with temperature (Item 22). In Item 21 students were asked to read a weight, in ounces, from an illustration of a scale, and they continued to do relatively well on this item, with 82% correct responses. Performance for Item 16, in which students had to determine the volume of a sphere when given the radius, increased to 41% correct in 2003 compared with 37% in 2000. Looking at the 19 items in the subcategory of applying appropriate techniques, tools, and formulas to determine measurements as a whole, we have the most information about area measurement and can conclude that students made progress on this measurement topic in 2003.

Another *Principles and Standards* expectation for Grades 6–8 is using common benchmarks to select appropriate methods to estimate measurements. We classified 3 of 28 measurement items administered to 8th-grade students in this subcategory. For Item 2 in Table 5.4, in which students had to order four angles according to their angle measures, performance in 2003 was 71% correct, similar to the 73% correct in 2000. On Item 3, in which students estimated the area of a region, performance increased to 67% correct in 2003 from 62% in 2000. On Item 1, however, in which students had to estimate the length of the *Titanic* using the length of other objects, performance decreased from 42% to 39% correct. Accordingly, performance was relatively high on using benchmarks to estimate angle and area, but not to estimate length.

Four other expectations of *Principles and Standards* for Grades 6–8 related to applying appropriate techniques, tools, and formulas to determine measurements are (a) develop and use formulas to determine the circumference of circles and area of triangles, parallelograms, trapezoids, and circles, and develop strategies to find the area of more complex shapes; (b) develop strategies to determine the surface area and volume of selected prisms, pyramids, and cylinders; (c) solve problems involving scale factors, using ratio and proportion; and (d) solve simple problems involving rates and derived measures for such attributes as velocity and density. We found no items for the latter subcategory and only two items for each of the other three. All of those items were fairly difficult for students to answer, with scores ranging from 7% correct to 24% correct, and only on Item 26, a new item in which students had to compare the volume of several objects, was performance as high as 74% correct.

To sum up, 8th graders' performance remained the same or increased significantly from 2000 to 2003 on most of the 28 items related to applying appropriate techniques, tools, and formulas to determine measurements. Of 9 items on which performance changed, 3 of 4 items on which performance decreased were about length and 4 of 5 items on which performance increased were about area. So 8th-grade students lost some ground on the topic of measuring length and made progress on items related to measuring area. As mentioned previously, many of the *Principles and Standards* measurement topics in Grades 5–8 are not well represented in the Grade 8 items in the NAEP Measurement strand.

PERFORMANCE ON ITEMS INVOLVING GEOMETRIC RELATIONSHIPS AND PROPERTIES OF TWO- AND THREE-DIMENSIONAL SHAPES

A substantial number of the 2003 NAEP Geometry items involved characteristics and properties of two- and three-dimensional shapes and analysis of relationships between or among geometric objects. Tables 5.5 and 5.6 summarize students' performance on 33 distinct items that entailed identification, comparison, or analysis of attributes of geometric objects, description and classification of shapes according to their properties, composition and decomposition of shapes, and understanding of relationships among attributes of similar objects.

Attributes of Geometric Figures and Classification of Two- and Three-Dimensional Shapes

Items 1–14 in Table 5.5 and Items 1–11 in Table 5.6 represent 21 distinct items—5 of which were administered only at Grade 4, 6 of which were administered at both Grades 4 and 8, and 10 of which were administered only at Grade 8. Those 21 items required students to use attributes to identify or produce geometric objects or attributes of those objects, for example, use a square's perimeter and its equilaterality to find its side length, or classify figures according to their properties.

On items that were administered in both 2000 and 2003, 4th-grade students' performance improved significantly on three items (Items 2 and 4 in Table 5.5 and Item 4 in Table 5.6), remained unchanged from 2000 to 2003 on five items (Items 5, 6, 7, 8, and 12 in Table 5.5), and declined significantly from 2000 to 2003 on one item, which required students to draw a "closed figure with five sides" that contained two right angles (Item 1 in Table 5.5). Performance on this item—one that required students to draw a figure that met three conditions and was not an often-encountered geometric object—declined substantially. More than half of the 4th-grade students drew figures that had no right angles, were not a pentagon, or were not closed, indicating that they were not able to attend to the multiple conditions.

The three items on which significant gains occurred at Grade 4 (Items 2 and 4 in Table 5.5 and Item 4 in Table 5.6) required identification of a figure with three angles, drawing an angle with measure greater than 90º, and identifying a four-sided figure that was not a rectangle, all involving relatively familiar

Table 5.5

Items Related to Analyzing Characteristics and Properties of Two- and Three-dimensional Geometric Shapes and Developing Mathematical Arguments About Geometric Relationships (Subcategories for Grades 3–5)

Item Description	Percentage Correct: Grade 4			Percentage Correct: Grade 8		
	96	00	03	96	00	03
Identify, compare, and analyze attributes of two- and three-dimensional shapes and develop vocabulary to describe the attributes.						
1. Draw a closed figure with five sides. Make two of the angles right angles. (2003-4M7 #19)	30#	34*	27			
2. Which of the following has only three angles? (Options are triangle, square, rectangle, and cube.) (2003-4M10 #2)	92*	94*	95			
3. Solve a problem involving right angles.	n.a.	n.a.	35			
4. Draw an angle that is larger than 90°. (2003-4M6 #21, 2003-8M6 #21)	12*#	24*	32	71*#	77	78
5. Identify a shape with an angle greater than a given angle.	n.a.	32	34	n.a.	64	66
6. Determine the number of faces on a cube. (2005-8M3 #7)	46*#	56	59	75*#	81*	78
7. Choose the number of angles that are smaller than a right angle in a diagram of an obtuse triangle. (2005-4M4 #4)	37*#	40	41	63*#	69	68
8. The perimeter of a square is 36 inches. What is the length of one side of the square? (Options are 4, 6, 9, and 18 inches.) (2003-4M6 #10, 2003-8M6 #10)	43*#	47	47	63*#	69	68
9. Find the measure of a central angle in a circle.				34	35	34
Classify two- and three-dimensional shapes according to their properties and develop definitions of classes of shapes such as triangles and pyramids.						
10. Solve a problem related to attributes of shape.	n.a.	n.a.	87			
11. Alan says that if a figure has four sides, it must be a rectangle. Gina does not agree. Which of the following figures shows that Gina is correct? (Options are a rectangle, a circle, a triangle, and a quadrilateral with noncongruent sides and no right angles.) (2003-4M6 #7, 2003-8M6 #15)	55*#	62*	69	80*#	84	85

Table 5.5 (continued)

Item Description	Percentage Correct: Grade 4			Percentage Correct: Grade 8		
	96	00	03	96	00	03
12. Given diagrams of four three-dimensional solids, identify the shapes that are cylinders. (2005-4M4 #2)	79*#	83	85	92#	94	93
13. Apply the Pythagorean theorem.				30*#	36	36
14. Name the shape shown in an illustration.				n.a.	n.a.	38
Investigate, describe, and reason about the results of subdividing, combining, and transforming shapes.						
15. Use manipulative tiles to make pentominoes. (2005-4M4 #14, see Figure 5.1)	16*#	18*	23			
16. Determine how many manipulative pieces are needed to cover a shape.	n.a.	75*	78			
17. Solve a problem involving the attributes of two shapes.	43	44	44			
18. Make a design using shapes.	n.a.	12*	15			
19. Assemble manipulative pieces to cover a shape.	n.a.	38	39	n.a.	59*	62
20. Make a shape with given properties.	n.a.	19	19	n.a.	28	30
21. Show how three triangles can be arranged to form a given parallelogram. (2003-8M10 #6, see Figure 5.4)				63	63	62
22. Show how three triangles can be arranged to form a given rectangle. (2003-8M10 #7)				66#	62*	65
Explore congruence and similarity.	*No corresponding NAEP items*					
Make and test conjectures about geometric properties and relationships and develop logical arguments to justify conclusions.	*No corresponding NAEP items*					

Note. n.a. indicates that the item was not administered in this year. Items 1, 4, 19, 20, 21, and 22 were short constructed-response items. Items 15 and 18 were extended constructed-response items, and the rest were multiple-choice items. Calculators were allowed on Items 1, 9, and 17.

* Indicates that the percentage correct is significantly different from the 2003 percentage correct.
# Indicates that the percentage correct is significantly different from the 2000 percentage correct.

Table 5.6
Items Related to Analyzing Characteristics and Properties of Two- and Three-dimensional Geometric Shapes and Developing Mathematical Arguments About Geometric Relationships (Subcategories for Grades 6–8)

Item Description	Percentage Correct: Grade 4			Percentage Correct: Grade 8		
	96	00	03	96	00	03
Precisely describe, classify, and understand relationships among types of two- and three-dimensional objects using their defining properties.						
1. Given a diagram of a rectangle with labeled dimensions, determine the width after the rectangle is folded. (2005-4M12 #13)	n.a.	n.a.	50			
2. The perimeter of a square is 36 inches. What is the length of one side of the square? (Options are 4, 6, 9, and 18 inches.) (2003-4M6 #10, 2003-8M6 #10)	43*#	47	47	63*#	69	68
3. Draw an angle that is larger than 90°. (2003-4M6 #21, 2003-8M6 #21)	12*#	24*	32	71*#	77	78
4. Alan says that if a figure has four sides, it must be a rectangle. Gina does not agree. Which of the following figures shows that Gina is correct? (Options are a rectangle, a circle, a triangle, and a quadrilateral with noncongruent sides and no right angles.) (2003-4M6 #7, 2003-8M6 #15)	55*#	62*	69	80*#	84	85
5. A triangle that has sides with lengths 6, 6, and 10 is called (options are acute, right, scalene, isosceles, equilateral). (2003-8M6 #23)				33*	36*	43
6. Choose a property that is not true for parallelograms. (2003-8M7 #10)				40*#	47	47
7. Given the measure of an exterior angle (135°) and one remote interior angle of a triangle (25°), find the measure of the other remote interior angle. (2003-8M10 #9)				31#	36*	33
8. Given several properties that define a quadrilateral, select a deduction that must be true. (2005-8M3 #14)				23*#	25	25
9. Determine the measure of one angle in a triangle, given the measures of the other two. (2003-8M7 #3)				44*#	53	51

Table 5.6 (continued)

Item Description	Percentage Correct: Grade 4			Percentage Correct: Grade 8		
	96	00	03	96	00	03
10. Solve a problem involving rays.				n.a.	n.a.	40
11. Solve a problem involving properties of quadrilaterals.				n.a.	n.a.	30
Understand relationships among the angles, side lengths, perimeters, areas, and volumes of similar objects.						
12. Find the length of a side of one of two similar triangles using given lengths.				52*#	56	58
13. Draw a figure similar to a given figure on the basis of a ratio involving the areas of the figures. (2005-8M4 #14)				6	8	7
Create and critique inductive and deductive arguments concerning geometric ideas and relationships, such as congruence, similarity, and the Pythagorean relationship.	*No corresponding NAEP items*					

Note. n.a. indicates that the item was not administered in this year. Items 3, 11, 12, and 13 were short constructed-response items, and the rest were multiple-choice items. Calculators were allowed on Items 6, 9, and 12.

* Indicates that the percentage correct is significantly different from the 2003 percentage correct.
# Indicates that the percentage correct is significantly different from the 2000 percentage correct.

geometric objects (triangle, right angle, and rectangle). Interestingly, on the item that required students to draw an angle with measure greater than 90 ° (Item 4 in Table 5.5), from 1996 to 2003 performance improved from 12% to 32% correct, and despite the fact that only about one-third of 4th-grade students answered correctly, about three-fourths of 8th-grade students could correctly draw such an angle, most likely reflecting greater attention in middle school curricula than in elementary curricula to identification of various types of angles.

On Item 4 in Table 5.6, 21% of 4th-grade students (but only 7% of 8th-grade students) chose a rectangle. Those students who answered incorrectly may have misunderstood what was required by the task, namely, using logic to find a counter-example that negates a given statement. Those students may simply have chosen the rectangle (it has four sides and is a rectangle) as representing a figure that met the conditions described by Alan in the task stem, that is, may have chosen an example rather than a counterexample. Eighth-grade students' more advanced logical abilities may explain the less frequent occurrence of that error at this level.

On 12 items that were administered at Grade 8 in both 2000 and 2003, performance improved significantly only on an item that assessed whether students know what *isosceles* means with respect to triangles (Item 5 in Table 5.6). Not much difference occurred in students' selection of angle-related distracters (acute and right, 18% and 12%, respectively) and side-related distracters (scalene and equilateral, 18% and 8%, respectively).

Performance remained unchanged from 2000 to 2003 on nine Grade 8 items (Items 5, 7, 8, 9, 12, and 13 in Table 5.5 and Items 6, 8, and 9 in Table 5.6). Item 6 in Table 5.6 required students to select a property that was not necessarily true of parallelograms. Less than half (47%) of 8th-grade students correctly answered that in a parallelogram, adjacent sides are not necessarily equal in length, and more than one-fourth incorrectly concluded that opposite angles need not be congruent. A small number, 5–10%, chose each of the other distracters, ones that stated more familiar properties of parallelograms (opposite sides parallel or opposite sides congruent). Low performance on this item might be attributable, at least in part, to a combination of a negatively worded item and lack of understanding of the logic of the phrase "NOT necessarily true."

Item 8 in Table 5.6 required 8th-grade students to reason about a geometric figure. They were told that a certain four-sided figure has only one pair of opposite sides that are parallel, only one pair of opposite sides equal in length, and parallel sides that are not equal in length. They were then asked whether the sides that are equal in length had to be (a) perpendicular to each other, (b) each perpendicular to an adjacent side (c) equal in length to one of the other two sides, (d) not equal in length to either of the other two sides, or (e) not parallel. Although no significant difference was seen in performance from 2000 to 2003, we note that when faced with a reasoning task of this nature, nearly as many students (18%, 13%, 23%, 20%) chose each of the four distracters as chose the correct response (25%) that the equal-length sides must be nonparallel. The near-chance level of performance on this item suggests that students not only had difficulty with the item but may have resorted to guessing instead of reasoning carefully about what the three conditions implied about the figure.

Performance at Grade 8 declined significantly from 2000 to 2003 on Item 6 in Table 5.5 and Item 7 in Table 5.6. On the first of those items, which asked students to determine the number of faces on a cube ("Amanda wants to paint each face of a cube a different color. How many colors will she need?"), despite a decline from 2000 to 2003, performance in 2003 remained significantly higher than performance in 1996. On the second, performance in 2003 declined from the 2000 level but was comparable to performance in 1996.

In general, performance was higher for items whose content included commonly encountered geometric figures, for example, right angles, triangles, squares, rectangles, cubes, and cylinders. The more difficult items—items on which approximately one-third of Grade 8 students answered correctly—typically addressed less commonly encountered geometric objects, such as rays, a central angle in a circle, or parallelograms; identification of scalene, isosceles, or equilateral triangles; and nonstraightforward applications of the Pythagorean theorem. However, by Grade 8 students have typically studied all of the content addressed in those more difficult items, suggesting that one should expect their performance on those items to be greater than what was demonstrated in the 2003 NAEP assessment. Considerably less than 50% of the students answered those items correctly, yet most middle school teachers likely would not consider the items to be particularly difficult and probably would expect their students to answer them correctly subsequent to instruction that focused on those topics.

Subdividing, Combining, and Transforming Shapes

Of the eight items that involved subdividing, combining, and transforming shapes (Items 15–22 in Table 5.5), four were administered only at Grade 4, two were administered at both grades, and two were administered only at Grade 8. In the eight items students used manipulative pieces to cover shapes or to compose a geometric shape from constituent shapes. No significant difference in performance occurred from 2000 to 2003 on three of the items administered at Grade 4, but significant improvement was made on the other three items, all of which involved arrangement of tiles or manipulative pieces to create a shape. Similarly, at Grade 8, no significant difference in performance occurred from 2000 to 2003 on two items, but a significant increase was found on two items that required students to compose geometric figures to form a particular figure. Although performance improved from 2000 to 2003 on half of the items in this category, the fact that performance in 2003 remained the same as it had been in 2000 on the other half of the items suggests that improvement was not universal on items that required visualizing and composing geometric figures.

Although less than one-fourth of Grade 4 students' responses to the two extended constructed-response items (Items 15 and 18 in Table 5.5) were at the satisfactory or extended level, performance in 2003 was significantly better than performance in 2000, and in the instance of Item 15, the significant gain realized from 1996 to 2000 continued. Item 15 (see Figure 5.1) presented three examples and two nonexamples of pentominoes and asked students to create three additional pentominoes that were distinct from those given. The improvement in 4th-grade students' performance on that item might be attributable to increased use of manipulatives or to a general increase in 4th-grade students' visualization capability—perhaps resulting from more curricular emphasis on three-dimensional geometry and visualization.

Please remove the 10 number tiles and the paper strip from your packet and put them on your desk. Turn the tiles facedown so that the blank side is showing.

It is possible to arrange 5 tiles so that at least one side of each tile completely shares one side of another tile. Here are 3 different ways to do this.

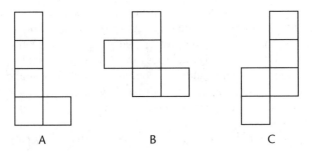

Two figures are not considered different if one figure can be turned or flipped to match the other.
The figures below are <u>not</u> examples of proper arrangements or new arrangements.

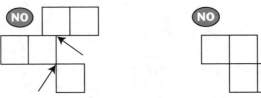

Tiles do not share <u>whole</u> sides.   This is the same as C turned.

Using 5 of your tiles, show 3 <u>other</u> different ways to arrange the tiles. Trace the tiles to show each figure. **Show the lines separating the individual squares.**

Figure 5.1. Grade 4 extended constructed-response item (Table 5.5 #15, 2005-4M4 #14).

Relationships Between Similar Objects

No NAEP items administered at Grade 4 addressed similar figures, but two Grade 8 items (Items 12 and 13 in Table 5.6) required students to use similarity to find the length of a side of a triangle or to draw a figure similar to a given figure. No significant difference occurred in performance from 2000 to 2003 on either of those items, although on Item 12 the significant gain from 1996 to 2000 was maintained. Because *Principles and Standards* suggests exploration of congruence and similarity in Grades 3–5, the existence of some Grade 4 NAEP items to address congruence and similarity would be helpful.

PERFORMANCE ON ITEMS INVOLVING SPECIFYING LOCATIONS AND DESCRIBING SPATIAL RELATIONSHIPS USING COORDINATE GEOMETRY

The value of the ability to use coordinate systems to describe locations and spatial relationships lies in the provision of a common frame of reference to actions on geometric objects. Coordinate systems, and other representational systems, act as a medium of interpersonal geometric communication in which locations and spatial relationships are described and understood. Tables 5.7 and 5.8 show the NAEP items related to describing locations and spatial relationships using coordinate systems.

Table 5.7

Items Related to Specifying Locations and Describing Spatial Relationships Using Coordinate Geometry and Other Representational Systems (Subcategories for Grades 3–5)

Item Description	Percentage Correct: Grade 4			Percentage Correct: Grade 8		
	96	00	03	96	00	03
Describe location and movement using common language and geometric vocabulary.						
1. Describe the position of a shape following a transformation.	n.a.	65*	69			
Make and use coordinate systems to specify locations and to describe paths.	*No corresponding NAEP items*					
Find the distance between points along horizontal and vertical lines of a coordinate system.	*No corresponding NAEP items*					

Note. n.a. indicates that the item was not administered in this year. Item 1 was a multiple-choice item.

* Indicates that the percentage correct is significantly different from the 2003 percentage correct.

Table 5.8

Items Related to Specifying Locations and Describing Spatial Relationships Using Coordinate Geometry and Other Representational Systems (Subcategories for Grades 6–8)

Item Description	Percentage Correct: Grade 4			Percentage Correct: Grade 8		
	96	00	03	96	00	03
Use coordinate geometry to represent and examine the properties of geometric shapes.						
1. Choose the correct coordinates of a vertex of an undrawn rectangle, given the coordinates of the other vertices.				42*#	52*	57
2. Graph points to form a shape and then find its perimeter.				n.a.	4	5
3. Given the coordinates of the endpoints of a line segment, calculate the midpoint. (2005-8M12 #8)				n.a.	n.a.	37
Use coordinate geometry to examine special geometric shapes, such as regular polygons or those with pairs of parallel or perpendicular sides.						
4. Choose the correct coordinates of a vertex of an undrawn rectangle, given the coordinates of the other vertices (same item as Item 1 in this table).				42*#	52*	57

Note. n.a. indicates that the item was not administered in this year. Item 2 was a short constructed-response item, and the rest were multiple-choice items. NAEP classified the item described in Item 1 of this table as an Algebra content strand item. Calculators were allowed on Item 2.

* Indicates that the percentage correct is significantly different from the 2003 percentage correct.

# Indicates that the percentage correct is significantly different from the 2000 percentage correct.

In the Grade 4 assessment, only one item was related to coordinate systems (see Table 5.7). On that item, which required naming the translation shown in an illustration of a figure and its transformed image presented using a grid, performance improved significantly, from 65% correct in 2000 to 69% correct in 2003. Although that item involved identifying a transformation, its setting called on the ability to read and interpret coordinates. Because one cannot generalize on the basis of just one item with respect to students' ability to describe spatial relationships, and because 3rd- and 4th-grade students encounter such relationships in a number of current curricula, the inclusion of more of such items on future NAEP assessments would be useful.

Of the two Grade 8 items administered both in 2000 and 2003 (Items 1 and 2 in Table 5.8), only performance on naming the coordinates of vertices of a rectangle improved significantly, from 52% in 2000 to 57% in 2003. Note that the percentage correct on this item in 1996 was 42%, suggesting that over a 7-year span, students have improved substantially in their ability to identify coordinates.

PERFORMANCE ON ITEMS INVOLVING GEOMETRIC TRANSFORMATIONS

An important capability for mathematical problem solving—and for everyday living as well—is understanding and using geometric transformations, particularly in dealing with such topics as symmetry and congruence. Tables 5.9 and 5.10 summarize 4th-grade and 8th-grade students' performance on 11 items related to geometric transformations, the majority of which dealt with reflections.

On two items that required students to describe the results of a reflection (Items 1 and 2 in Table 5.9), 4th-grade students' performance in 2003 was unchanged from their performance in 2000. Figure 5.2 presents one of those items, administered in both Grades 4 and 8, which required students to describe the orientation of a block letter **F** after reflection. Performance for Grades 4 and 8 was fairly comparable: more than 70% of 4th-grade students and more than 80% of 8th-grade students could correctly identify the orientation of the letter after it was "flipped over" (reflected). At both grade levels the most commonly chosen distracter, C, was the one that showed an "upside-down **F**."

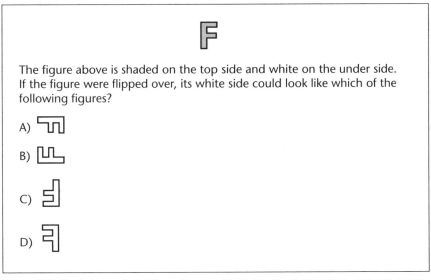

Figure 5.2. Grade 8 item involving reflection (Table 5.9 #1, 2003-4M6#5, 2003-8M6 #5).

Table 5.9

Items Related to Applying Transformations and Using Symmetry to Analyze Mathematical Situations (Subcategories of Grades 3–5)

Item Description	Percentage Correct: Grade 4			Percentage Correct: Grade 8		
	96	00	03	96	00	03
Predict and describe the results of sliding, flipping, and turning two-dimensional shapes.						
1. Choose the correct representation for a figure when it is flipped over. (2003-4M6 #5, 2003-8M6 #5, see Figure 5.2)	68	72	72	79*#	83	82
2. Indicate the location of one figure when folded over a vertical line. (2005-4M4 #13)	25	27	28	61	61	61
3. Shade five additional squares on a grid so that if the completed figure were folded along the fold line, both sides would match. (2005-8M4 #13)				59	59	59
4. Add three tiles to an illustrated design so that the design is different after being rotated 90°. (2005-8M4 #16)				32	34*	29
Describe a motion or a series of motions that will show that two shapes are congruent.						
5. Describe the position of a shape following a transformation.	n.a.	65*	69			
6. Describe a result of a transformation of a shape shown on a grid.				n.a.	62*	59
Identify and describe line and rotational symmetry in two- and three-dimensional shapes and designs.						
7. Select the figure that is not symmetrical.	91*#	94	95			
8. For each figure, draw a line of symmetry.				44*	48*	57

Note. n.a. indicates that the item was not administered in this year. Items 2, 3, 4, and 8 were short constructed-response items, and the rest were multiple-choice items. Calculators were allowed on Items 7 and 8.

* Indicates that the percentage correct is significantly different from the 2003 percentage correct.

# Indicates that the percentage correct is significantly different from the 2000 percentage correct.

Table 5.10
Items Related to Applying Transformations and Using Symmetry to Analyze Mathematical Situations (Subcategories for Grades 6–8)

	Percentage Correct: Grade 4			Percentage Correct: Grade 8		
Item Description	96	00	03	96	00	03
Describe sizes, positions, and orientations of shapes under informal transformations such as flips, turns, slides, and scaling.						
1. Choose the correct representation for a figure when it is flipped over. (2003-4M6 #5, 2003-8M6 #5, see Figure 5.2)	68	72	72	79*#	83	82
2. Identify the correct location of a point when folded over an oblique line. (2003-8M7 #7, see Figure 5.3)				46#	50*	45
3. Show how three triangles can be arranged to form a given parallelogram. (2003-8M10 #6, see Figure 5.4)				63	63	62
4. Draw the result of reflecting the image of a figure over a vertical line. (2005-8M12 #4)				n.a.	n.a.	75
Examine the congruence, similarity, and line or rotational symmetry of objects using transformations.	*No corresponding NAEP items*					

Note. n.a. indicates that the item was not administered in this year. Items 1 and 2 were multiple-choice items, and Items 3 and 4 were short constructed-response items. Calculators were allowed on Item 2.

* Indicates that percentage correct is significantly different from the 2003 percentage correct.

\# Indicates that percentage correct is significantly different from the 2000 percentage correct.

On Item 5 in Table 5.9, just over two-thirds of 4th-grade students successfully selected a transformation that mapped a given pre-image shape onto its given image shape. This result was a significant improvement from 2000. On Item 7 in Table 5.9, an item in which students were to determine whether a figure was symmetrical, 95% of 4th-grade students were correct. Performance on this item was unchanged from 2000 to 2003 but maintained a significant gain that was realized from 1996 to 2000. Given the high performance on this item in 2000, the lack of gain from 2000 to 2003 is not surprising, because a performance ceiling had likely been reached.

Eighth-grade students' performance on items involving transformations was mixed, with performance on Item 8 in Table 5.9 improving significantly from 2000 to 2003, performance on Items 4 and 6 in Table 5.9 and Item 3 in Table 5.10 declining significantly, and performance on Items 1, 2, and 3 in Table 5.9 and Item 3 in Table 5.10 unchanged over that period. The general lack of improvement on Grade 8 items involving geometric transformations is consistent with the decade-long lack of improvement on such items noted by Sowder, Wearne, Martin, and Strutchens (2004). On Item 4 in Table 5.10, administered only in 2003, three-fourths of 8th-grade students were able to correctly draw the image of a given figure after it was reflected. On Item 2 in Table 5.10, involving reflecting a point about an oblique line (see Figure 5.3), less than half of 8th-grade students answered correctly, performance that declined significantly from 2000 to 2003. More than one in five students thought that the image of a vertex of a nonsquare rectangle under reflection across its diagonal would be its opposite vertex, suggesting that some students may not be aware of the perpendicularity relationship between a line of reflection and a segment connecting a pre-image and its image under reflection.

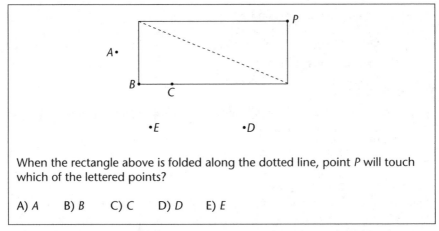

When the rectangle above is folded along the dotted line, point *P* will touch which of the lettered points?

A) *A*   B) *B*   C) *C*   D) *D*   E) *E*

Figure 5.3. Grade 8 item involving reflection about a line (Table 5.10 #2, 2003-8M7 #7).

Figure 5.4 shows Item 3 in Table 5.10, in which students were given pictures of three triangles and were asked to draw how they could be arranged to form a parallelogram. That item required students to mentally carry out the results of transformations. Sixty-two percent of the 8th-grade students illustrated an appropriate arrangement of the triangles.

Most of the items in Tables 5.9 and 5.10 require visual perception, in that students might select answers on the basis of visual cues in the item. However, Items 4 and 6 in Table 5.9 involve problem solving and require analysis rather than primarily call for visualization. Interestingly, performance in 2003 declined significantly from performance in 2000 on each of those two Grade 8 items.

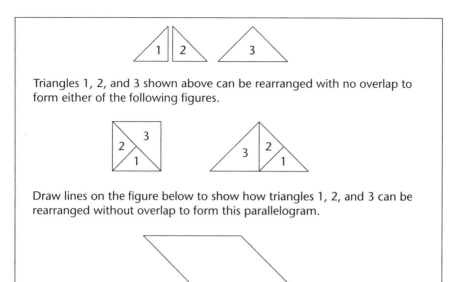

Triangles 1, 2, and 3 shown above can be rearranged with no overlap to form either of the following figures.

Draw lines on the figure below to show how triangles 1, 2, and 3 can be rearranged without overlap to form this parallelogram.

Figure 5.4. Grade 8 item involving a parallelogram (Table 5.10 #3, 2003-8M10 #6).

Principles and Standards emphasizes the importance of the use of transformations in examining congruence, similarity, and symmetry. Despite that emphasis, no NAEP items required students to examine congruence, similarity, or line symmetry using transformations, and no NAEP items involved scaling (dilations, either magnifications or contractions). Items that focus on those areas would be useful to include in future NAEP assessments.

PERFORMANCE ON ITEMS INVOLVING SPATIAL VISUALIZATION AND REASONING

Because students routinely encounter three-dimensional objects in their everyday lives, spatial visualization and reasoning about three-dimensional objects are important tools, especially with increasing use of computer graphics in the workplace (NCTM, 2000). Tables 5.11 and 5.12 summarize students' performance on 22 items related to visualization, spatial reasoning, and geometric modeling. The sections that follow describe students' performance on several subcategories related to those three topics.

Visualizing, Composing, and Drawing Geometric Shapes

Items 1–6 in Table 5.11 and Items 1–5 in Table 5.12 required students to compose or draw geometric figures with some specified properties. Several of those items involved tangram-type tasks, in which students assembled manipulative pieces to produce or cover a particular shape.

Table 5.11
Items Related to Using Visualization, Spatial Reasoning, and Geometric Modeling to Solve Problems (Subcategories for Grades 3–5)

Item Description	Percentage Correct: Grade 4			Percentage Correct: Grade 8		
	96	00	03	96	00	03
Build and draw geometric objects.						
1. Use manipulative tiles to make pentominoes. (2005-4M4 #14, see Figure 5.1)	16*#	18*	23			
2. Determine how many manipulative pieces are needed to cover a shape.	n.a.	75*	78			
3. Identify squares in a figure depicted on a grid.	41	44	43			
4. Identify triangles in a figure depicted on a grid.	36	36	36			
5. Show how a nonrectangle can be formed from drawn geometric shapes.	6*#	10	9			
6. Assemble manipulative pieces to cover a shape.	n.a.	38	39	n.a.	59*	62
Create and describe mental images of objects, patterns, and paths.						
7. A cow is tied to a post in the middle of a flat meadow. If the cow's rope is several meters long, which of the following figures shows the shape of the region where the cow can graze? (Options are a hexagon, pentagon, circle, and square.) (2003-4M10 #14)	31	31	30			
8. Determine the number of unit cubes in a three-dimensional composite object.	n.a.	n.a.	55			
9. Select the net that could not be used to form a cube. (2003-4M6 #14, see Figure 5.5)	32*	36	38	63*#	69	71
10. Determine the number of faces on a cube. (2005-8M3 #7)	46*#	56	59	75*#	81*	78

Table 5.11 (continued)

Item Description	Percentage Correct: Grade 4			Percentage Correct: Grade 8		
	96	00	03	96	00	03
11. Identify the shape formed when a paper tube is cut down the side. (2005-8M3 #4)	68*	72*	74	82*	86*	88
12. Given a triangle, rectangle, square, five-sided figure, and nine-sided figure, choose the one that cannot be formed by the overlapping parts of two square tiles. (2005-8M4 #15)				50*	52	53
13. Choose the resulting shape when another shape is folded.				n.a.	49*	42
Identify and build a three-dimensional object from two-dimensional representations of that object.				*No corresponding NAEP items*		
Identify and draw a two-dimensional representation of a three-dimensional object.						
14. Select the net that could not be used to form a cube. (2003-4M6 #14, see Figure 5.5)	32*	36	38	63*#	69	70
Use geometric models to solve problems in other areas of mathematics, such as number and measurement.	*No corresponding NAEP items*					
Recognize geometric ideas and relationships and apply them to other disciplines and to problems that arise in the classroom or in everyday life.	*No corresponding NAEP items*					

Note. n.a. indicates that the item was not administered in this year. Item 1 was an extended constructed-response item. Items 3, 4, 5, 6, and 11 were short constructed-response items, and the rest were multiple-choice items. Calculators were allowed on Item 13.
* Indicates that the percentage correct is significantly different from the 2003 percentage correct.
# Indicates that the percentage correct is significantly different from the 2000 percentage correct.

Table 5.12
Items Related to Using Visualization, Spatial Reasoning, and Geometric Modeling to Solve Problems (Subcategories for Grades 6–8)

Item Description	Percentage Correct: Grade 4			Percentage Correct: Grade 8		
	96	00	03	96	00	03
Draw geometric objects with specified properties, such as side lengths or angle measures.						
1. Draw a closed figure with five sides. Make two of the angles right angles. (2003-4M7 #19)	30#	34*	27			
2. Use a ruler to draw a figure with two sides given.	18*#	22*	27			
3. Use a ruler to draw a figure with a given perimeter.	22*	19*	26			
4. Draw a figure similar to a given figure on the basis of a ratio involving the areas of the figures. (2005-8M4 #14)				6	8	7
5. Given the dimensions, draw one rectangular region enclosed by another. (2005-8M3 #3)				36*	40*	46
Use two-dimensional representations of three-dimensional objects to visualize and solve problems such as those involving surface area and volume.						
6. Select the net that could not be used to form a cube. (2003-4M6 #14, see Figure 5.5)	32*	36	38	63*#	69	71
7. On a grid, draw two different nets that form boxes that hold eight cubic units. (2003-8M10 #16)				8*	9*	13
8. Given diagrams of five nets, choose the one that when folded will form the triangular prism shown. (2005-8M12 #16)				n.a.	n.a.	88
Use visual tools such as networks to represent and solve problems.	*No corresponding NAEP items*					
Use geometric models to represent and explain numerical and algebraic relationships.	*No corresponding NAEP items*					
Recognize and apply geometric ideas and relationships in areas outside the mathematics classroom, such as art, science, and everyday life.						
9. Solve a problem involving three-dimensional objects.				13*	13*	17

Note. n.a. indicates that the item was not administered in this year. Items 6 and 8 were multiple-choice items. Item 7 was an extended constructed-response item, and the rest were short constructed-response items. Calculators were allowed on Item 1.

* Indicates that the percentage correct is significantly different from the 2003 percentage correct.

# Indicates that the percentage correct is significantly different from the 2000 percentage correct.

Fourth-grade students' performance improved significantly from 2000 to 2003 on four items (Items 1 and 2 in Table 5.11 and Items 2 and 3 in Table 5.12), remained unchanged from 2000 to 2003 on four items (Items 3, 4, 5, and 6 in Table 5.11), and declined significantly on Item 1 in Table 5.12—the released item, discussed previously, in which students were asked to draw a closed figure having five sides and containing two right angles. The four items on which 4th-grade students' performance improved significantly from 2000 to 2003 involved creating arrangements of two-dimensional figures or using a ruler to draw a figure.

On the three items involving composing or drawing geometric figures with certain properties, 8th-grade students' performance was stable from 2000 to 2003 on Item 4 in Table 5.12 and improved significantly on Item 6 in Table 5.11 and Item 5 in Table 5.12. Item 6 was a tangram-type task that required students to draw how a certain collection of manipulative pieces could be arranged to cover a given shape; Item 5 required students to use a ruler to draw two rectangles that met certain conditions.

Creating Mental Images of Geometric Objects and Relating Three-Dimensional Objects and Their Two-Dimensional Representations

Items 7–14 in Table 5.11 and Items 6–8 in Table 5.12 involved either creating mental images of objects or identifying two-dimensional representations of three-dimensional geometric objects. Fourth-grade students' performance remained unchanged from 2000 to 2003 on Items 7, 9, 10, and 11 in Table 5.11. We note, however, that on Items 9, 10, and 11, the 2003 level of performance represented a significant gain from the 1996 level.

On Item 9, the released item shown in Figure 5.5, students were asked to determine which of four nets could not be folded into a cube. Less than 40% of 4th-grade students identified the correct net, and almost as many students chose distracter C. As Clements (2003) notes, "Learning only plane figures in textbooks during the early primary grades may cause some initial difficulty in learning solids. Construction activities involving nets (foldout shapes of solids) may be valuable because they require children to switch between more-analytic 2D and synthetic 3D situations" (p. 161). Eighth-grade students performed much better (71% correct) on this item, perhaps as a result of greater attention to three-dimensional geometry in middle school mathematics curricula than in elementary mathematics curricula.

Item 7 in Table 5.11 involved a cow tied to a post in the middle of a meadow. This multiple-choice item required students to visualize a locus of points representing the region in which a cow could graze. The choices included a regular hexagon, a regular pentagon, a circle, and a square. To complete this item successfully, students had to understand several things about the context (e.g., how

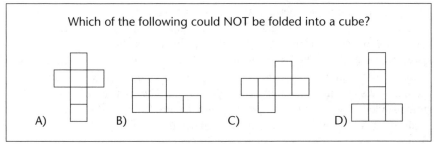

Figure 5.5. Grade 4 item involving nets to make a cube (Table 5.11 #9, 2003-4M6 #14).

a cow can move when tied, the meaning of "graze") and know that the locus of points equidistant from a given point is a circle. Of the incorrect distracters, the square was the most popular choice, selected by 42% of the 4th-grade students. This error likely is due to young children's commonly held image of a cow in a "field" that is rectangular. For those students, and for the 27% of students who chose the hexagon or the pentagon, various aspects of the context (e.g., fenced fields are polygonal, enclosed by straight lines of fencing strung between posts, some of which form the vertices of the polygon) seem to have overwhelmed the mathematical necessity for the locus of points equidistant from a given point to be a circle. Most children are not likely to have an image of a farm pasture as being circular.

Eighth-grade students' performance improved significantly from 2000 to 2003 on Item 11 in Table 5.11 and Item 7 in Table 5.12, remained unchanged on Items 9 and 12 in Table 5.11, and declined significantly on Items 10 and 13 in Table 5.11. The two significant declines occurred on items that required students to identify and apply a property of a three-dimensional figure and describe the result of folding a two-dimensional figure in a certain way. The significant improvements in performance occurred on items that involved identifying a two-dimensional decomposition of a three-dimensional shape and producing two-dimensional nets that would form a solid with a given volume. The variety among those items causes difficulty in attempting to use them to identify areas of geometry in which performance improved or declined.

Using Geometric Models in Other Areas of Mathematics or in Everyday Life

Several additional areas of visualization, spatial reasoning, and geometric modeling are identified by *Principles and Standards* as important in Grades 3–5 and 6–8 but were assessed minimally or not at all by NAEP in 2003. *Principles and Standards* calls for Grade 3–5 students to be proficient in building a three-dimensional object from its two-dimensional representation; no NAEP items fell into this subcategory. Similarly, no Grade 4 NAEP items related to using geometric models to solve problems in other areas of mathematics or ones that arise in everyday life (see Table 5.11). At Grade 8 only one NAEP item (Item 9 in Table 5.12) addressed the application of geometric ideas to an everyday-life situation (i.e., visualizing an arrangement of three-dimensional objects). Although a significant increase occurred in 8th-grade students' performance on this item from 2000 to 2003, less than 20% of the students were able to complete it correctly. That poor performance suggests that curricula should place more emphasis on geometric modeling—creating or describing geometric figures that meet certain conditions of a real situation.

The two items, Item 11 in Table 5.11 and Item 8 in Table 5.12, on which 8th-grade students performed exceptionally well required decomposition of a three-dimensional object to its two-dimensional representation. Item 11 required students to realize that when a paper tube is cut down the side, the resulting paper is a square, whereas Item 8 required students to select the appropriate net for constructing a triangular prism. Students' performance on those items suggests that they have had productive experiences with visualization and that they can do well on items that require conceptual understanding.

COMMON 4TH- AND 8TH-GRADE ITEMS

The 2003 assessment contained a total of 16 Geometry and Measurement items that were administered at Grades 4 and 8. Just as with scale-score achievement, one would expect 8th-grade students to score higher on an item than do their 4th-grade counterparts. Figure 5.6 depicts the performance of 4th- and 8th-

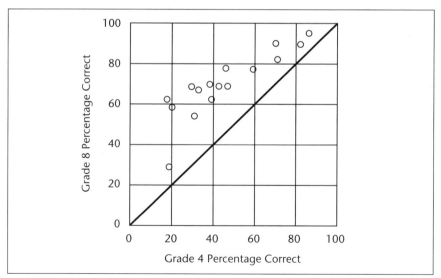

Figure 5.6. Performance on NAEP Measurement and Geometry items common to Grade 4 and Grade 8.

Table 5.13
Normalized Gains for Items Common to Grades 4 and 8

Item Description	Percentage Correct: Grade 4	Percentage Correct: Grade 8	Normalized Gain
1. Make a shape with given properties.	19	29	12%
2. Given illustrations of four objects labeled with the weight of each, identify the heaviest object. (2003-4M6 #4, 2003-8M6 #4)	82	88	33%
3. Choose the correct representation for a figure when it is flipped over. (2003-4M6 #5, 2003-8M6 #5, see Figure 5.2)	72	82	36%
4. Assemble manipulative pieces to cover a shape.	39	62	38%
5. Solve a problem involving the conversion of one time measure to another.	26	55	39%
6. The perimeter of a square is 36 inches. What is the length of one side of the square? (Options are 4, 6, 9, and 18 inches.) (2003-4M6 #10, 2003-8M6 #10)	47	68	40%
7. Determine the number of faces on a cube. (2005-8M3 #7)	59	78	46%
8. Choose the number of angles that are smaller than a right angle in a diagram of an obtuse triangle. (2005-4M4 #4)	41	68	46%
9. Indicate the location of one figure when folded over a vertical line. (2005-4M4 #13)	28	61	46%
10. Select a figure that has an angle greater than 90°.	34	66	48%
11. Determine the length of a toothpick. (A picture of the toothpick is shown with one end at the 8-inch mark and the other end at the 10½-inch mark on a ruler.) (2003-4M6 #18, 2003-8M6 #18)	20	58	48%
12. Select the net that could not be used to form a cube. (2003-4M6 #14, see Figure 5.5)	38	70	52%

Table 5.13 (*continued*)

Item Description	Percentage Correct: Grade 4	Percentage Correct: Grade 8	Normalized Gain
13. Alan says that if a figure has four sides, it must be a rectangle. Gina does not agree. Which of the following figures shows that Gina is correct? (Options are a rectangle, a circle, a triangle, and a quadrilateral with noncongruent sides and no right angles.) (2003-4M6 #7, 2003-8M6 #15)	69	85	52%
14. Given diagrams of four three-dimensional solids, identify the shapes that are cylinders. (2005-4M4 #2)	85	93	53%
15. Choose the correct value for the area of a polygon depicted on a centimeter grid. (2005-4M4 #6)	45	78	60%
16. Draw an angle that is larger than 90°. (2003-4M6 #21)	32	78	68%

grade students on the common items. Each circle corresponds to a single item appearing on both the Grade 4 and Grade 8 assessments in 2003. For instance, the circle plotted at (19, 29) represents an item that 19% of 4th-grade and 29% of 8th-grade students answered correctly. The percentage correct on common items ranged from 19% to 85% at Grade 4 and from 29% to 93% at Grade 8. The circles all fall above the line $y = x$, indicating that Grade 8 students scored higher than Grade 4 students on all common items.

Table 5.13 lists the Measurement and Geometry items common to the Grade 4 and Grade 8 assessments. The greatest gain on any one common item was 46 percentage points, and the least gain was 6 percentage points. However, Grade 4 achievement on some items results in more potential for growth than for others. For instance, the Grade 4 percentage correct for Item 13 was 85%, leaving potential for a gain of 15 percentage points. In contrast, 19% of 4th-grade students answered Item 1 correctly, leaving room for 81 percentage points of growth. To consider the 4th-grade-to-8th-grade gain relative to the possible gain, we consider the normalized gain. This type of gain describes improvement from one grade level to another in relation to potential for growth (Hake, 1998; Kehle, Wearne, Martin, Strutchens, & Warfield, 2004). Normalized gains are especially helpful in discussing gains on items for which performance is already high. For example, if 95% of Grade 4 students correctly answered an item, the largest possible gain for Grade 8 students would be 5 percentage points. If performance on the same item was 97% for Grade 8, then the realized gain would be 2 points of the potential 5 points. The normalized gain for this item is 40%, or the ratio of realized gain to potential gain (2:5). Contrast this normalized gain with that for another item on which 45% of Grade 4 students answered correctly but performance increased to 47% for Grade 8. In that item, the growth in raw percentage points is the same as in the previous example, that is, 2 percentage points. However, the normalized gain is a mere 4%, that is, students realized a gain of only 2 points out of a potential 55-point gain. Table 5.13 shows item-level performance and normalized gains for items common to the Grade 4 and Grade 8 assessments.

A closer look at released items helps us understand the types of assessment questions for which the least and greatest normalized gains occurred from Grade 4 to Grade 8. Items 2 and 3 illustrate two released items on which the normalized gains were less than 40% (33% and 36%, respectively). Fourth-grade students realized high performance on those items, but the growth from Grade 4 to Grade 8 resulted in some of the lowest normalized gains in Table 5.13. Items 15 and 16 have the highest normalized gains at 60% and 68%. Grade 4 performance was relatively low on one item and moderate on the other, but performance at Grade 8 was identical for the two items. In Item 16, a constructed-response item, students were asked to draw an angle that is larger than 90°. Fourth-grade students' performance on this item was low (32%), perhaps highlighting a curricular emphasis in Grade 4 on identifying angles versus constructing them. In contrast, Item 15 asks students to select the correct area of a concave hexagonal region displayed on a centimeter grid. Fourth-grade students' performance on Item 15 was somewhat better than their performance on Item 16, likely because they could simply count nine whole squares and two additional ones that resulted from the four half squares to obtain their answer.

CONCLUSION

We believe that the scale-score increases from 2000 to 2003 for both Measurement and Geometry at both Grade 4 and Grade 8 indicate that students' learning in those areas has improved recently. For some measurement and geometry topics (e.g., identifying coordinates) students have made great strides during the past decade, whereas for others (e.g., transformations) performance has been stable at a much-lower-than-desired level. The significant decline in performance for some items, coupled with the general level of performance being less than what is desired, suggests that much work remains to be done to improve students' learning of measurement and geometry. Preston and Thompson (2004) call for integration of measurement topics across the curriculum. Perhaps their suggestions and greater use of integrated mathematics curricula in which algebra, measurement, and geometry topics are interwoven or addressed concurrently can result in more emphasis on measurement and geometry in the school mathematics curriculum and corresponding improvement in students' learning in those content areas. Finally, NAEP needs to expand its items to address a broader variety of topics in the Measurement and Geometry strands, namely, those *Principles and Standards* categories that no NAEP items currently address.

REFERENCES

Berry, R. Q., III, & Wiggins, J. (2001). Measurement in the middle grades. *Mathematics Teaching in the Middle School, 7,* 154–156.

Chappell, M. F. (2001). Geometry in the middle grades: From its past to the present. *Mathematics Teaching in the Middle School, 6,* 516–519.

Clements, D. H. (2003). Teaching and learning geometry. In J. Kilpatrick, W. G. Martin, & D. Schifter (Eds.), *A research companion to "Principles and Standards for School Mathematics"* (pp. 151–178). Reston, VA: National Council of Teachers of Mathematics.

Hake, R. R. (1998). Interactive engagement versus traditional methods: A six thousand–student survey of mechanics test data for introductory physics courses. *American Journal of Physics, 66,* 64–74.

Kehle, P., Wearne, D., Martin, W. G., Strutchens, M., & Warfield, J. (2004). What do 12th-grade students know about mathematics? In P. Kloosterman & F. K. Lester Jr. (Eds.), *Results and interpretations of the 1990–2000 mathematics assessments of the National Assessment of Educational Progress* (pp. 145–174). Reston, VA: National Council of Teachers of Mathematics.

Kenehan, G., & Ambrose, R. (2005, Spring). 3D geometry in the 3rd grade: Sorting and describing polyhedra. *On-Math, 3*(3). Retrieved November 28, 2005, from http://my.nctm.org/eresources/view_article.asp?article_id=7076#

Kenney, P. A., & Silver, E. A. (Eds.). (1997). *Results from the sixth mathematics assessment of the National Assessment of Educational Progress.* Reston, VA: National Council of Teachers of Mathematics.

Kloosterman, P., & Lester, F. K., Jr. (Eds.). (2004). *Results and interpretations of the 1990–2000 mathematics assessments of the National Assessment of Educational Progress.* Reston, VA: National Council of Teachers of Mathematics.

Lehrer, R. (2003). Developing understanding of measurement. In J. Kilpatrick, W. G. Martin, & D. Schifter (Eds.), *A research companion to "Principles and Standards for School Mathematics"* (pp. 179–192). Reston, VA: National Council of Teachers of Mathematics.

Lehrer, R., Jenkins, M., & Osana, H. (1998). Longitudinal study of children's reasoning about space and geometry. In R. Lehrer & D. Chazan (Eds.), *Designing learning environments for developing understanding of geometry and space* (pp. 137–167). Mahwah, NJ: Erlbaum.

National Assessment Governing Board (NAGB). (2002). *Mathematics framework for the 2003 National Assessment of Educational Progress.* Washington, DC: Author. Retrieved August 27, 2005, from www.nagb.org/pubs/math_fw_03.pdf

National Council of Teachers of Mathematics. (2000). *Principles and standards for school mathematics.* Reston, VA: Author.

Preston, R., & Thompson, T. (2004). Integrating measurement across the curriculum. *Mathematics Teaching in the Middle School, 9,* 436–441.

Silver, E. A., & Kenney, P. A. (Eds.). (2000). *Results from the seventh mathematics assessment of the National Assessment of Educational Progress.* Reston, VA: National Council of Teachers of Mathematics.

Sowder, J. T., Wearne, D., Martin, W. G., & Strutchens, M. (2004). What do 8th-grade students know about mathematics? Changes over a decade. In P. Kloosterman & F. K. Lester Jr. (Eds.), *Results and interpretations of the 1990–2000 mathematics assessments of the National Assessment of Educational Progress* (pp. 105–143). Reston, VA: National Council of Teachers of Mathematics.

Stephan, M., & Clements, D. H. (2003). Linear measurement in prekindergarten to grade 2. In D. H. Clements & G. Bright (Eds.), *Learning and teaching measurement: 2003 Yearbook.* Reston, VA: National Council of Teachers of Mathematics.

Swindal, D. N. (2000). Learning geometry and a new language. *Teaching Children Mathematics, 7,* 246–250.

Student Performance in Data Analysis, Statistics, and Probability

James E. Tarr and J. Michael Shaughnessy

UNTIL recently, the study of data analysis, statistics, and probability in the United States was largely restricted to the postsecondary level (Konold & Pollatsek, 2002; Friel, in press). In the wake of recommendations of the National Council of Teachers of Mathematics' *Curriculum and Evaluation Standards for School Mathematics* (1989) and *Principles and Standards for School Mathematics* (2000), probability and statistics are now featured prominently in most school mathematics curricular materials. Moreover, of the 44 U.S. states with published curriculum frameworks for mathematics, nearly all offer grade-level learning expectations for data analysis and probability, spanning primary through secondary school and even beginning in kindergarten (Center for the Study of Mathematics Curriculum, 2005).

The emergence of probability and statistics as essential components of the school mathematics curriculum is further manifested in the composition of the National Assessment of Educational Progress (NAEP) for mathematics. More specifically, at Grade 8, items devoted to data analysis, statistics, and probability doubled from 8% in 1986 to 15% in 1996 but have remained stable since then, with 31 (or 15%) of 203 items focused on that content in the most recent assessment. At Grade 4, slightly more than 10% of the 183 items focused on such content, and that percentage has remained stable across the six most recent administrations of NAEP, dating back to 1986.

Despite a recent assertion that teachers in middle schools "are least prepared to teach statistics and probability" (Conference Board of the Mathematical Sciences, 2001, p. 114), teachers report placing a marked increase in emphasis on that content. In particular, the percentage of 4th-grade teachers indicating "little or no emphasis" on data analysis and probability has dramatically declined,

Highlights

- Significant growth occurred from 1996 to 2003 in 8th-grade students' performance on NAEP items that required them to determine the mean and median of given data sets. However, when asked to select the most appropriate summary statistic, most students selected the mean regardless of the distribution of the data; only about one in five students were able to justify their choice of the median.

- Although about four in seven 8th-grade students could identify a general formula for the mean, only about one in four students could determine the mean from a grouped frequency distribution, and even fewer demonstrated an understanding of the mean as representative of the entire data set.

- Less than half the students assessed in Grade 8 considered the potential for bias in sampling, but more than half recognized limitations associated with drawing inferences from small samples.

- Student performance on creating data displays was strong and may have reached ceiling levels in Grade 8 on bar graphs, pictographs, and circle graphs.

- Student performance was poor on complex items that involved interpretation or application of information in tables and graphs. Small or no gains were made from 2000 to 2003, and performance on such items may in fact have slightly eroded from previous levels.

- Approximately four in nine 4th-grade students could construct a complete sample space by applying counting strategies. Eighth-grade students, however, struggled to generate a complete sample space, often misinterpreting the sampling conditions or failing to consider reversed-pairs as distinctive elements.

- Students in Grades 4 and 8 were generally successful in identifying the probability of an event in "one out of N" situations and could make appropriate predictions on the basis of stated probabilities. However, students at both grade levels were less successful in determining probabilities in "several out of N" situations, and they struggled to apply probability concepts and justify their probabilistic reasoning.

from 72% in 1990 to 54% in 1992, 19% in 2000, and 13% in 2003, while "heavy emphasis" increased from 3% in 1990 to 24% in 2003. Similarly, 8th-grade teachers indicating "little or no emphasis" on that content declined markedly, from 53% in 1990 to 30% in 1992 and to 15% in 2000; the question was not asked of 8th-grade teachers in 2003.

Concomitant to the emergence of probability and statistics in written and enacted school mathematics curricula, student performance was relatively high in that content area. In particular, the scale scores of students in Grade 4 and 8 were higher in Data Analysis, Statistics, and Probability than any other content strand. For example, the scale scores of 237 (Grade 4) and 280 (Grade 8) are both significantly higher than the mathematics composite scale score.[1] Moreover, students in Grade 4 have made significant improvement in that content strand since 1992, as have students in Grade 8 since 1990, with an average 17-point increase in scale scores for both groups. Although record-high achievement was attained in Data Analysis, Statistics, and Probability, a small but significant achievement gap between males and females continued to exist, with males slightly outperforming females.

One might reasonably conclude that the increased emphasis on data analysis explains the increase in student achievement on that content strand. Interestingly, however, only 4th-grade students of teachers indicating "moderate emphasis" on data analysis scored significantly higher than other students; that is, 4th graders whose teachers reported "heavy" or "little or no" emphasis on data analysis scored significantly lower in Data Analysis, Statistics, and Probability than teachers who indicated "moderate emphasis." Among 8th-grade students in 2000, no significant differences in achievement were observed in the scale scores for Data Analysis, Statistics, and Probability when disaggregated by teacher emphasis on that content.

In 2003, the relative emphases that NAEP placed on content areas within mathematics was largely consistent with the recommendations in *Principles and Standards for School Mathematics* (NCTM, 2000); for data analysis and probability, three Standards deal with data analysis but only one Standard addresses probability. In particular, among the 31 NAEP items used at Grade 8 in 2003, 15 (48%) assessed students' ability to construct or reason about data displays, 6 (19%) focused on measures of central tendency, 3 (10%) dealt with reasoning with data (including collecting and analyzing samples), and 7 (23%) were related to probability and chance (including combinatorics). At Grade 4, descriptive statistics were not assessed, and thus probability and chance formed a greater portion (47%) of the total items, approximately double the percentage at Grade 8. The remaining 10 (or 53%) of 19 items focused on creating or reasoning about data displays.

Several important concepts and skills related to statistical literacy were not assessed at either the 4th- or 8th-grade level by the 2003 NAEP, including (a) box-and-whisker plots, (b) histograms, (c) scatterplots, (d) measures of dispersion, including variation, (e) linear regression, (f) conditional probability, and (g) the relationship between experimental and theoretical probabilities. The absence of those topics is notable for two reasons: they were included on the 2000

---

[1] Although it is true that scale scores in Data Analysis, Statistics, and Probability were higher than scale scores in the other four mathematics strands, one cannot say with certainty that this outcome means that students performed "better" in Data Analysis, Statistics, and Probability than the other areas.

NAEP for Grade 12, and many are considered appropriate for middle school students (see Friel, Curcio, & Bright, 2001) and appear in popular middle-grades mathematics curricular materials (e.g., Connected Mathematics Project [Lappan, Fey, Fitzgerald, Friel, & Phillips, 1998], Mathematics: Applications and Connections [Bailey, Day, Frey, Howard, Hutchens, & McClain, 2004]). However, none of those topics was assessed in 2003. Notwithstanding limitations related to content focus and question format, the results of the 2003 NAEP do foster insights about what 4th- and 8th-grade students know about data analysis, statistics, and probability. This chapter is organized around the four primary content foci: central tendency, reasoning about data, constructing and interpreting data displays, and probability and chance.

CENTRAL TENDENCY

Measures of central tendency—*mean, median,* and *mode*—are efficient ways of characterizing a data set or comparing two or more data sets. Although six NAEP items addressed measures of central tendency (all at Grade 8), those items focused on mean and median only. None directly assessed students' use of mode. Moreover, the items generally assessed procedural knowledge related to measures of central tendency, without addressing fundamental properties of the arithmetic mean, such as that the sum of the deviations from the mean is zero, and that when calculating the mean, a value of zero, if it appears, must be taken into account (see Strauss & Bichler, 1988). Irrespective of those limitations, the 2003 results are somewhat encouraging in relation to past performance, as shown, for example, in Table 6.1.

Although previous NAEP results indicated relatively low achievement on items involving the mean and median (Zawojewski & Heckman, 1997; Zawojewski & Shaughnessy, 2000), student achievement on those items improved in 2003. Longitudinal performance results from 2003 for the mean and median items appear in Table 6.1. Item 1 involved identifying a symbolic expression for the average number of miles traveled per day. Options for that multiple-choice item were $x + y + z$, xyz, $3(x + y + z)$, $3(xyz)$, and $(x + y + z)/3$. The performance level for 2003 was relatively high (58% in Grade 8) and was significantly higher than performance on the same item in 1996, in which only 50% of students in Grade 8 answered correctly; no significant differences in performance were detected in relation to 2000 data for the same item.

Student performance on Item 1 was consistent with previous studies (e.g., Mokros & Russell, 1995) that suggest that most 8th graders know the proce-dure for finding the mean of a set of values. However, when the set of values is presented as a grouped frequency distribution, as it is in Item 2 (see Table 6.2), performance was markedly lower. On Item 2, students must determine the mean score *to the nearest whole number.* An important point to note is that use of a scientific calculator was permitted while working on this item; thus an exact

Table 6.1

Grade 8 Performance on Items Involving Mean and Median

	Percentage Correct		
Item Description	1996	2000	2003
1. Tetsu rides his bicycle x miles the first day, y miles the second day, and z miles the third day. Which expression represents the average number of miles per day that Tetsu travels? (2003-8M7 #17)	50[*]	57	58
2. Determine the mean from a grouped frequency distribution. (See Table 6.2, 2003-8M7 #13.)	22[*a]	24[a]	24[a]
3. What is the median of 4, 8, 3, 2, 5, 8, 12? (2003-8M6 #28)	32[*]	46[*]	57
4. Determine the median of an even set of numbers given nonsequentially.	n.a.	n.a.	45
5. Select the summary statistic that best describes a given data situation (mean, median, mode are among the choices).	20	19	19
6. Select and explain the statistic that best represents the typical value of a data set.	4	4	5

Note. n.a. indicates that the item was not administered in this year. Items 2 and 6 were short constructed-response items; the rest were multiple-choice items. Calculators were allowed on Items 1, 2, 5, and 6.
[*] Indicates that the percentage correct is significantly different from the 2003 percentage correct.
[a] Includes the percentage of students who gave an unrounded answer, which was considered incorrect according to the NAEP scoring guide.

determination of the mean (69.090909…) was scored as "incorrect" despite sound student reasoning about the mean. For purposes of this analysis, "correct" and "unrounded but correct calculation" were collapsed to reflect student proficiency for finding the grouped mean. Although the performance level for 2003 was low on this item (24% for Grade 8), it was significantly higher than performance on the same item in 1996, in which 22% answered correctly or provided unrounded responses, and in 1990, when only 16% did so; no significant differences in performance were detected in relation to 2000 data for the same item. Notwithstanding recent improvements, more than 75% of students were not able to determine the mean from a grouped frequency distribution; 31% determined the median or mode value, and 41% offered other responses.

Robust improvements in performance were found on Item 3 in Table 6.1, which assessed student ability to determine the median of a set of seven ungrouped data values. In particular, the percentage of Grade 8 students answering correctly rose from 20% in 1990, to 32% in 1996, to 46% in 2000, and to 57% in 2003. Moreover, the fact that only 33% of Grade 12 students responded correctly in

1996 further underscores improved performance on that item by Grade 8 students and may reflect the infusion of statistical topics into middle school mathematics curricula during the 1990s. Girls outperformed boys on the item, 59% to 55%, although reasons for the observed discrepancies are not clear. Developed for 2003, Item 4 (Table 6.1) assessed student ability to determine the median of a set containing an even number of elements. After arranging the data sequentially, two distinct data values emerge as "in the middle," requiring students to calculate the mean of those values to determine the median of the data set. The additional required step likely explains the drop in student performance, from 57% correct when an odd number of elements composed the data set (Item 3 in Table 6.1) to 45% when an even number of elements were in the data set.

Table 6.2
Item Requiring Calculation of a Mean From a Grouped Frequency Distribution (2003-8M7 #13)

Score	Number of Students
90	1
80	3
70	4
60	0
50	3

The table above shows the scores of a group of 11 students on a history test. What is the average (mean) score of the group to the nearest whole number?

Answer:	Percentage Responding
Correct: 69	19
Incorrect #3: 69 and any decimal	5
Incorrect #2: 70 (median or mode)	31
Incorrect #1: Any incorrect response other than those above	41
Omitted	3

Note. Calculators were allowed.

Items 5 and 6 of Table 6.1 required students to select the appropriate summary statistic to represent a data set. Making the correct selection usually requires complex reasoning and involves both an analysis of the distribution of data and an understanding of the problem context (Zawojewski & Shaughnessy, 2000). Because the mean is representative of the *entire* data set, one could argue that the mean is the best choice among all measures of central tendency. Nevertheless, on both items, the presence of at least one outlier in the data set presumably necessitated the selection of median as most appropriate. Student preference for the mean was evident in performance data on those items. Performance was even more disappointing when a short constructed-response format was used, as in Item 6, which involves comparing the mean and median and determining which more appropriately represents a "typical" data value. A similar item was administered on the 1996 NAEP, in which the mean and median daily attendance at two movie theaters were given for five days, and students had to explain which statistic would be used to describe the typical daily attendance (see Zawojewski & Shaughnessy, 2000, p. 240). Remarkably low performance was observed on Item 6 in 2003, on which 4% of Grade 8 students responded correctly and 22% of responses were scored partially correct. On that item no significant differences in performance were detected between 1996 and either of 2000 or 2003.

REASONING WITH DATA

Principles and Standards for School Mathematics states that instructional programs should enable all students to "develop and evaluate inferences and predictions that are based on data" (NCTM, 2000, p. 48) and that "a key element in developing ideas associated with statistical inference involves developing concepts of sampling" (Watson & Moritz, 2000, p. 44). Ideally, random sampling from a target population is the most desirable method for determining a sample, but such samples are often impractical (or impossible) to generate. When nonrandom samples are used, attention needs to be paid to how well the sample selected reflects the target population and whether an adequate number of data points have been collected.

Collecting and Analyzing Samples

Until recently, little research has been done into students' understanding of samples and sampling, but two items in the 2003 NAEP indicated relatively strong performance by Grade 8 students. The released item in Table 6.3 assessed students' knowledge of the importance of the qualitative features of the sample by asking them to decide whether a baseball game would be a good place to survey opinions about the most popular sport in a city. The question format (short constructed response) meant that students needed to provide an answer (yes or no) as well as a written justification for their choice. Forty-five percent of 8th-grade students correctly realized that surveying those attending a baseball game would likely represent a biased sample and yield faulty inferences, but that performance was significantly lower than performance in 2000 and 1996, when 55% and 52% of students, respectively, responded correctly and provided sound justifications. On the 2000 NAEP, performance on the bias item was significantly lower among students who indicated they "'never or hardly ever' talk with other students about how they solved mathematics problems" by comparison with all other categories of responses.

Table 6.3
Explain Sampling Bias Item: Sample Grade 8 Student Responses (2003-8M7 #15)

A survey is to be taken in a city to determine the most popular sport. Would sampling opinions at a baseball game be a good way to collect this data? Explain your answer.

	Percentage Responding
Correct response: "No" with correct explanation	
Answer: *Most people at a baseball game would be fans of baseball, and so the survey would likely be inaccurate and skewed towards baseball.*	45
Incorrect #1: "Yes" with incorrect or no explanation	
Answer: *Yes because baseball's a sport and why would their be people at a game if they didn't like sports.*	33
Incorrect #2: "No" but with incorrect or no explanation	
Answer: *No, that would only be refering to baseball, and no other information can be collected.*	17
Omitted	5

Note. Calculators were allowed.

A second, but unreleased, short constructed-response item was used on the 2003 NAEP to assess students' attention to the aspect of sample size and was also administered on the 2000 NAEP. In general, larger samples are more likely to reflect the parent population from which they are drawn, enabling the formulation of valid inferences, yet research indicates that many students lack an understanding of the importance of sample size (Shaughnessy, Garfield, & Greer, 1996). Thus an encouraging outcome in 2003 was that 57% of 8th-grade students attended to sample size when identifying the best survey; their performance was significantly higher than the 53% correct response rate of students on the 1996 NAEP but not significantly different from performance in 2000, in which 59% responded correctly.

UNDERSTANDING AND USING GRAPHICAL DATA DISPLAYS

The 2003 NAEP contained 24 items that asked students to create, interpret, or reason about data displays in graphical or tabular form. Two of the three items that assessed aspects of Grade 8 students' statistical reasoning were discussed above.

The data on those two relatively straightforward items suggest that more than half of Grade 8 students were aware of the importance of sample size, and more than half could also identify clear sources of bias in a sample. Watson (1997) has developed a three-tier scale of statistical literacy. The ability to recognize the role of sample size in context is a Tier 2 literacy skill in Watson's scheme ("use of statistical terms in context"), and identifying bias in a sample is a Tier 3 skill that involves "critiquing the use of statistics in context." NAEP's use of questions that potentially require higher levels of statistical literacy is encouraging, as is Grade 8 students' reasonably high performance on them. The remaining 21 of the 24 items fall into two principal categories: creating data displays, and reading and interpreting data displays.

Creating Data Displays

At Grade 4, six items asked students to create or modify displays of data. At Grade 8, four such items were administered, including three that were given at both grade levels. Longitudinal performance data for the items on creating data displays are summarized in Table 6.4 and Table 6.5 for Grades 4 and 8, respectively. Only two of the items on creating displays were released in 2003: a Grade 8 item on creating pictographs (Item 1, Table 6.5) and an item on creating bar graphs that was administered at both grade levels (Item 3, Table 6.4 and Item 3, Table 6.5).

Table 6.4

Grade 4 Performance on Items Involving the Creation of Pictographs and Bar Graphs

	Percentage Correct		
Item Description	1996	2000	2003
1. Create a pictograph from data presented in a table.	45*	50	53
2. Create a pictograph based on given data.	65*	71*	75
3. Complete a bar graph by drawing in two bars for the frequencies of two scores given in a data table. (2003-4M6 #6)	57*	63*	73
4. Create a bar graph based on given data.	69*	75	76
5. Complete a bar graph based on stated numerical relationships. (2005-4M4 #7)[a]	37*	43	43
6. Modify a bar graph to include one additional data element.	n.a.	n.a.	37

Note. n.a. indicates that the item was not administered in this year. All items were short constructed response. Calculators were available on Item 1.

[a] 2005 items were released while this volume was in production. Block and item numbers have been added so that interested readers can find the 2005 items using the online Questions Tool.

* Indicates that the percentage correct is significantly different from the 2003 percentage correct.

Table 6.5

Grade 8 Performance on Items Involving the Creation of Pictographs and Bar Graphs

Item Description	Percentage Correct		
	1996	2000	2003
1. Determine the number of symbols to use in a pictograph from data presented in a table. (2003-8M10 #4)	80*	83*	78
2. Create a pictograph based on given data. (2005-8M3 #6)	89*	93*	92
3. Complete a bar graph by drawing in two bars for the frequencies of two scores given in a data table. (2003-8M6 #6)	85*	89	89
4. Complete a bar graph based on stated numerical relationships. (2005-8M4 #7)	78	81*	79

Note: Item 1 was multiple choice, and the rest were short constructed response.
* Indicates that the percentage correct is significantly different from the 2003 percentage correct.

The overall trend across the three most recent administrations of NAEP suggests that student performance on creating data displays is strong but has perhaps reached ceiling levels in Grade 8 on bar graphs, pictographs, and circle graphs. Consistently strong performance is evident on such items, as shown in Table 6.5, with student success ranging between 78% and 93%, with the exception of a pictograph task (Item 1, Table 6.5) on which 2003 performance slipped below even 1996 levels. Given that Grade 8 students have clearly performed strongly on items involving the creation of pictographs and circle graphs, the inclusion of NAEP items to assess their abilities to create other types of data displays, such as dot plots, stem plots, box-and-whisker plots, and even histograms, would seem appropriate. All of those types of data displays are included in most state mathematics curriculum frameworks for Grade 8, as well as in recent NCTM recommendations (NCTM, 2000) and in documents written by the American Statistical Association (2005).

Reading and Interpreting Data Displays

Fourteen items on the 2003 NAEP asked students to read or interpret data represented in graphs or in tables: 4 items were administered at Grade 4, 11 were administered at Grade 8, and only 1 was administered at both grade levels. Longitudinal performance data on those items are summarized in Table 6.6 and Table 6.7 for Grades 4 and 8. Some of those items also required students to perform additional calculations or to make decisions about information conveyed in tables and graphical displays. Seven of the 14 items involved either circle graphs

Table 6.6

Grade 4 Performance on Items Involving the Reading or Interpretation of Graphs

Item Description	Percentage Correct		
	1996	2000	2003
Circle Graphs			
1. In a circle graph, if ¼ of the circle represents 2, what amount does the whole circle represent? (2003-4M6 #3)	44*	51	51
Data Tables			
2. A table shows amount of rain each day for a week (0, 0, 6.3, 0, 1.4, 0.5, and 0.4 cm). What is the total rainfall for the week? (2003-4M7 #3)	n.a.	79	79
Bar Graphs			
3. Determine an appropriate title for bar graph. (2005-4M12 #11)	n.a.	n.a.	51
Pictographs and Stem-and-Leaf Plots			
4. Interpret a pictograph.	n.a.	n.a.	82

Note. n.a. indicates that the item was not administered in this year. All items were multiple choice. Calculators were allowed on Item 2.

* Indicates that the percentage correct is significantly different from the 2003 percentage correct.

or bar graphs. Two of the 14 items were short constructed-response questions (Item 4, Table 6.6 and Item 6, Table 6.7), and two were extended constructed-response tasks (Items 7 and 9 in Table 6.7).

As depicted in Table 6.7, significant increases were seen in Grade 8 performance over time on several items involving the reading and interpretation of data displays: Items 1, 3, 8, and 11 showed significant gains from 1996 to 2000. Performance levels on Items 1 (interpreting a circle graph) and 11 (reading values on a stem plot) were maintained from 2000 through 2003. In comparison, 2003 performance on Item 8 (reading a line graph) showed a significant decrease from 2000, falling to the 1996 performance level. Performance trends were observed for Item 3 (Table 6.7), on making a computation from information in a circle graph, with a significant increase from 1996 to 2000, followed by a significant drop in 2003. With those two exceptions, the trend in student performance on items involving reading and interpreting data displays was essentially flat from the 2000 to the 2003 administration. Performance on interpretation of graphs has not made any progress since 2000 and may in fact be eroding.

Two low-level released items (Items 1 and 11, Table 6.7) ask students simply to read information from a graph. Performance on those items was high but appears to have stabilized between 70% and 80% over the past two NAEP

Table 6.7

Grade 8 Performance on Items Involving the Reading or Interpretation of Graphs

Item Description	Percentage Correct		
	1996	2000	2003
Circle Graphs			
1. In a circle graph, if ¼ of the circle represents 2, what amount does the whole circle represent? (2003-8M6 #3)	72*	80	79
2. Read a circle graph.	n.a.	n.a.	87
3. There are 1,200 students enrolled in Adams Middle School. According to the circle graph shown, how many of these students participate in sports? (Graph indicates 38% participate in sports.) (2003-8M7 #14)	48*	57*	54
4. Evaluate the correctness of four statements about a circle graph.	26*	29	29
Data Tables			
5. Use data displayed in a table, and compute.	n.a.	n.a.	80
Bar Graphs			
6. Read a bar graph, and compute.	n.a.	11	9
7. Read a complex bar graph.	n.a.	37	35
Line Graphs			
8. Interpret data from a line graph. (See Table 4.5, 2003-8M7 #8.)	46	50*	46
9. Interpret a piecewise line graph. (See Table 6.8, 2003-8M10 #19.)	n.a.	9	8
10. Compare consumer price indices.	n.a.	50	49
Pictographs and Stem-and-Leaf Plots			
11. Read a value from a stem-and-leaf plot. Example of how to read is provided. (2003-8M10 #8)	61*	71	73

Note. n.a. indicates that the item was not administered in this year. Item 6 was short constructed response; Items 7 and 9 were extended constructed response; the rest were multiple choice. Calculators were allowed on Items 3, 4, 6, 7, 8, and 10.

* Indicates that the percentage correct is significantly different from the 2003 percentage correct.

administrations. The remaining items in Table 6.7 involve interpreting information from tables and graphs or using the information to make additional computations or comparisons. Performance on those more complex items that involve interpretation or application of information was considerably lower than on items requiring low levels of cognitive demand. For example, two unreleased items on which students have maintained low performance levels involve multistep computational processes combined with the interpretation of multiple bar graphs (Items 6 and 7 in Table 6.7).

A third item (Item 9 from Table 6.7) revealing seemingly low performance levels across three administrations of NAEP is a released item in which students were asked to interpret a graph of a bicycle trip over time (Table 6.8). Whether this graph should be classified as a statistics item or whether it has more to do with the behavior of variables in algebra is arguable. Regardless, the task requires reflection, coordination, interpretation, and written communication of graphical information, and therefore it involves multiple high-level reasoning processes.

Table 6.8
Item 9 From Table 6.7 About Interpreting a Trip Graph (2003-8M10 #19)

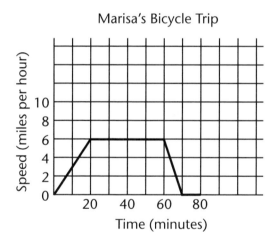

The graph above represents Marisa's riding speed throughout her 80-minute bicycle trip. Use the information in the graph to describe what could have happened on the trip, including her speed throughout the trip.

During the first 20 minutes, Marisa

_____

From 20 minutes to 60 minutes, she

_____

From 60 minutes to 80 minutes, she

_____

(table continues)

Table 6.8 (*continued*)

Item	Percentage Responding
Extended	4
Satisfactory	4
Partial	1
Minimal	31
Incorrect	49
Omitted	11
Off Task	1

Although only 8% of Grade 8 students merited a satisfactory or extended score on their response to this item, 40% of the students achieved at least a minimally correct response. The sample student responses to Marisa's trip provided in Figure 6.1 indicate that quite a few students understood the basic situation described in Marisa's graph, as even the minimal response describes Marisa's activity fairly well.

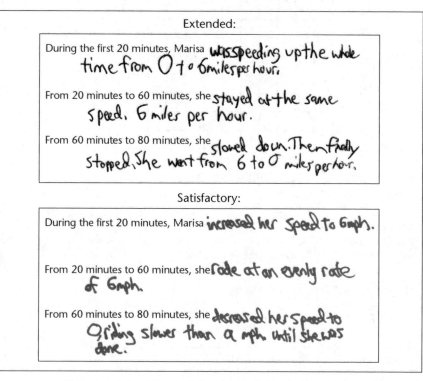

Figure 6.1. Selected responses to Marisa's Bike Trip problem.

Partial:

During the first 20 minutes, Marisa *went down a hill, so she sped up*

From 20 minutes to 60 minutes, she *rode at a steady pace on flat land*

From 60 minutes to 80 minutes, she *went up a hill, slowed down, and finally stopped*

Minimal:

During the first 20 minutes, Marisa *was speeding up slowly.*

From 20 minutes to 60 minutes, she *kept the same speed.*

From 60 minutes to 80 minutes, she *slowed to a stop.*

Incorrect:

During the first 20 minutes, Marisa *went 6 miles per hour.*

From 20 minutes to 60 minutes, she *went the same speed 6 miles per hour*

From 60 minutes to 80 minutes, she *went 6 miles per hour to 0 miles per hour.*

Figure 6.1. (continued)

Performance on Marisa's trip might actually be better than the percentage of satisfactory responses indicates. In particular, the fact that students offered relatively few satisfactory "stories" may be related to time. Requiring students to write an explanation in a timed-test situation is not conducive to the production of optimal writing samples—although to their credit most Grade 8 students did at least attempt the item (only 11% omitted it). Items such as Marisa's trip are important types of tasks to include in assessments because they tap multiple reasoning processes. Furthermore, what initially may appear to be low performance on an item actually may be quite good upon careful examination of samples of student work.

Overall, the longitudinal performance of Grades 4 and 8 students on items that involve interpretation or application of information in graphs and tables ranges from mediocre to poor. Those results suggest that teachers and teacher educators need to provide many more opportunities for their students and preservice and in-service teachers to analyze and interpret data from tables and graphs. Two indicators in Table 6.7 suggest ways to help improve student performance on short constructed-response or extended constructed-response items involving the interpretation and application of data: technology and teacher preparation. On 5 of the 14 items, students who used or had access to a calculator every day performed significantly better than those who did not use calculators regularly in their mathematics class. In addition, on three other items students whose teachers had an undergraduate or graduate major in mathematics or mathematics education performed significantly better than those students whose teachers did not have such a major. Those significant results suggest that student access to appropriate technology and teachers who are highly qualified in mathematics education can improve student performance in mathematics.

PROBABILITY AND CHANCE

Probability has emerged as a "mainstream area in the school mathematics curriculum" (Jones, 2005, p. 1), and that new emphasis is particularly evident in the fact that at Grade 4, more than 40% of items on the 2003 NAEP focused on probability or chance concepts—a stark contrast with the mere handful of probability items in previous NAEP administrations. Numerous studies support the appropriateness of including probability in the school mathematics curriculum (Fischbein & Schnarch, 1997; Jones, Langrall, Thornton, & Mogill, 1999; Metz, 1998; Pratt, 2000; Shaughnessy, Canada, & Ciancetta, 2003; Stohl & Tarr, 2002; Tarr & Jones, 1997). Those studies document elementary and middle school students' capacity to learn skills and concepts related to probability and chance. When considered in view of the results of such studies, the results of the 2003 NAEP lend insights into students' judgments under uncertainty.

Combinatorics

An understanding of sample space "is fundamental to all aspects of probabilistic reasoning" (Langrall & Mooney, 2005, p. 106), and two released items focused primarily on the fundamental counting principle. Longitudinal performance results for sample-space items appear in Tables 6.9 and 6.10 for Grades 4 and 8, respectively. On two items (Item 1 of Table 6.9 and Item 1 of Table 6.10), students were required to list the complete sample space for a given problem context. Although nine elements form the sample space in each problem,

Table 6.9
Grade 4 Performance on Item Involving Sample Space

	Percentage Correct		
Item Description	1996	2000	2003
Jan's Snack Shop has 3 flavors of ice cream: vanilla, chocolate, and strawberry. The ice cream can be served in a dish, a sugar cone, or a regular cone. There are 9 people who choose 1 dip of ice cream in a dish, or in a sugar cone, or in a regular cone, and all of their choices are different. List or show the 9 different choices. Could another person have a choice that is different from one of these 9 choices? Why or why not? (Table 9.8, 2003-4M10 #17)	30^{a*}	37^{a*}	45^{a}

Note. Item is extended constructed response.

* Indicates that the percentage correct is significantly different from the 2003 percentage correct.

[a] Includes percentage of students who gave satisfactory or extended responses according to the NAEP scoring guide.

performance data are markedly different, with higher scores observed on the item administered at Grade 4. The 4th-grade item states that nine people chose one of three flavors of ice cream in a dish, sugar cone, or regular cone; students are required to list or show the nine possible choices and then explain whether another person could have a choice different from one of those nine choices. In all, 34% of responses in Grade 4 were classified as "extended" because students correctly showed all nine ways and answered "yes" or "no" with appropriate explanation. An additional 11% of responses were classified as "satisfactory" because students showed nine ways without an explanation or with an inappropriate or incorrect explanation, or they showed seven or eight ways with or without

Table 6.10
Grade 8 Performance on Items Involving Sample Space

	Percentage Correct		
Item Description	1996	2000	2003
1. List the complete sample space associated with a two-stage experiment, sampling with replacement. (See Table 6.11, 2003-8M6 #25.)	14*	17	18
2. List the complete sample space to satisfy stated selection criteria.	n.a.	n.a.	18

Note. n.a. indicates that the item was not administered in this year. Item 1 is short constructed response. Item 2 is multiple choice.
* Indicates that the percentage correct is significantly different from the 2003 percentage correct.

an explanation. Such high and markedly improved performance over time is consistent with the research of English (2005), who reported that elementary school children, using child-appropriate materials and meaningful task contexts (and without instructional intervention), are able to list the complete sample space by employing a variety of solution strategies.

By way of contrast, Item 1 in Table 6.10 (and depicted in Table 6.11) proved to be perplexing for Grade 8 students. Specifically, only 18% of responses were classified as "correct," with all 9 ordered pairs correct, and that figure remained stable even when considering responses that included all 9 ordered pairs and additional erroneous pairs. An additional 18% of students were able to list 6–8 ordered pairs (including correctly listing reversed pairs), and NAEP's scoring guide classified such responses as "correct" even though such a response clearly does not constitute a complete listing. Although the performance level for 2003 was low on the ordered-pairs item (18%), it was significantly higher than performance on that same item in 1996, in which 14% listed enough ordered pairs to be

Table 6.11
Item 1 From Table 6.10 Involving Listing of All Possible Pairs (2003-8M6 #25)

Item	Percentage Responding
A box contains 3 chips numbered 1 through 3. One chip will be taken at random from the box and then put back into the box. Then a second chip will be taken from the box.	
In the space provided below, list all possible pairs of chips.	
Number on First Chip | **Number on Second Chip**	
Correct response: Answer has all 9 ordered pairs correct	18
Incorrect #5: 9 correct pairs and at least one erroneous pair	0
Incorrect #4: 6–8 correct pairs other than those noted in Incorrect #3	18
Incorrect #3: The 6 correct pairs that do not take the order of draw into account, i.e., no reversed pairs	4
Incorrect #2: 1–5 correct pairs	27
Incorrect #1: No correct pairs	17
Omitted	14
Off Task	2

considered a correct response. No significant differences in performance were detected in relation to the 2000 data for the same item.

An examination of sample student responses helps explain why 8th-grade performance was substantially lower on Item 1 (Table 6.10). As depicted in Figure 6.2, Response 1 reflects a systematic strategy for listing the sample space and is consistent with the "odometer strategy" (English, 1993), which involves repeating the selection of an item until all possible combinations with that item have been formed. Specifically, the student appears to have held constant chip numbered 1 while exhausting all possible outcomes of the second draw. Upon exhaustion of the possibilities for the first chip (chip numbered 1), the student chose a new "constant" item (chip numbered 2) and repeated the systematic matching process. Response 2 might reflect student confusion of the sampling conditions. In particular, the student appears to have misinterpreted the experiment as not involving replacement of the first chip after it is drawn. Consequently, identical outcomes—(1, 1), (2, 2), and (3, 3)—are not listed. Response 3 fails to consider reversed pairs in generation of the sample space; therefore, events (1, 2) and (2, 1) are not distinguished from each other. That error is largely analogous to the belief that when rolling two dice, the events "1 on the first die, 2 on the second die" and "2 on the first die, 1 on the second die" represent the same event. Response 4, in which the student lists only identical outcomes of the first and second draws, is essentially the complement to Response 2. Finally, Response 5 lists the sample space of each individual draw but fails to generate ordered pairs.

Similar disappointing performance was observed on Item 2 in Table 6.10, developed for 2003, which assessed ability to determine the complete sample space according to stated selection criteria. In particular, the sample space associated with Item 3 varies in size, from one to three elements; by way of contrast, in both Item 1 (Table 6.9) and Item 1 (Table 6.10), the elements of the sample space are essentially ordered pairs. Only 18% of 8th-grade students answered correctly, a remarkably poor performance given the multiple-choice format of five responses. Stated differently, the correct response rate of 18% is *lower* than would be expected from randomly selecting one of the five choices. The lack of a clear-cut algorithm for solving the problem might explain the low performance, although the question format precludes a more rigorous analysis of students' reasoning.

Simple Probability

Despite the relatively large number of items related to probability and chance, only two items involving simple probability were released, thereby limiting in-depth discussion of student performance in that area. Longitudinal performance data for 2003 are depicted in Table 6.12 (Grade 4) and Table 6.13 (Grade 8). The items are discussed by content focus, including "one out of *N*," "several out of *N*," "predicting outcomes," and "applying probability concepts."

Response 1:
9 correct pairs, no additional erroneous pairs

Number on First Chip	Number on Second Chip
1	1
1	2
1	3
2	1
2	2
2	3
3	1
3	2
3	3

Response 2:
6 correct pairs but no identical pairs for first and second draws

Number on First Chip	Number on Second Chip
1	2
1	3
2	1
2	3
3	1
3	2

Response 3:
6 correct pairs but no reversed pairs

Number on First Chip	Number on Second Chip
1	1
1	2
1	3
2	2
2	3
3	3

Response 4:
1–5 correct pairs

Number on First Chip	Number on Second Chip
1	1
2	2
3	3

Response 5:
No correct pairs

Number on First Chip	Number on Second Chip
1,2,3	1,2,3

Figure 6.2. Selected responses to all-possible-pairs problem in Table 6.11.

Table 6.12
Grade 4 Performance on Items Involving Probability

Item Description	Percentage Correct		
	1996	2000	2003
Probabilities: "One out of *N*"			
1. Given a sample space of *N* equally likely outcomes, determine the simple probability of "one out of *N*" occurring. (discrete model, Table 6.14, 2003-4M7 #10)	58*	65	66
2. Given a sample space of *N* equally likely outcomes, determine the simple probability of "one out of *N*" occurring. (area model)	51*	58	59
3. Given bags with 10, 100, or 1,000 marbles, in which each contains one red and the remainder yellow marbles, identify the bag giving the greatest chance of picking a red marble. (discrete model, Table 9.8, 2003-4M10 #16)	57*	65	65
Probabilities: "Several out of *N*"			
4. Choose the correct probability in a "several out of *N*" situation.	26*	27*	31
Predicting Outcomes			
5. Identify most likely outcome in a single-trial experiment. (2005-4M12 #10)	n.a.	n.a.	90
6. Identify most likely distribution of outcomes in a repeated experiment.	61*	71*	75
7. Identify most likely outcome in a single-trial experiment, and determine the probability of "several out of *N*" occurring.	n.a.	n.a.	15
Applying Probability Concepts			
8. Label a spinner game to reflect stated probabilities. Explain.	n.a.	18*	14

Note. n.a. indicates that the item was not administered in this year. Items 1 and 7 were short constructed response; Item 8 was extended constructed response; the rest were multiple choice. Calculators were allowed on Items 1 and 6.

* Indicates that the percentage correct is significantly different from the 2003 percentage correct.

Table 6.13

Grade 8 Performance on Items Involving Probability

	Percentage Correct		
Item Description	1996	2000	2003
Probabilities: "Several out of *N*"			
1. Choose the correct probability in a "several out of *N*" situation.	60*	72	72
2. Determine the probability of "several out of *N*" occurring in a sampling-without-replacement situation. (2005-8M4 #19)	37	41	40
3. Determine the probability of "several out of *N*" occurring in another sampling-without-replacement situation.	22*	27*	30
Predicting Outcomes			
4. Identify expected number of outcomes in a repeated experiment.	n.a.	n.a.	56
Applying Probability Concepts			
5. Determine the probability of "several out of *N*" occurring with stated selection criteria[a].	20*	8*	6
6. Distinguish between independent and dependent events. (2005-8M12 #7)	n.a.	n.a.	16

Note. n.a. indicates that the item was not administered in this year. Items 3 and 6 were short constructed response; Item 5 was extended constructed response; the rest were multiple choice. Calculators were allowed on Item 3.

[a] The scoring system for this item appears to have changed between 1996 and 2000. Such a change could account for part or all of the drop in performance between 1996 and 2000.

* Indicates that the percentage correct is significantly different from the 2003 percentage correct.

"One out of *N*"

The ability to assign numerical probabilities to describe the likelihood of an event is a rudimentary skill. Two items measured Grade 4 students' ability to determine the probability of an event. More specifically, in both items students are required to determine the probability in situations in which exactly one outcome is compared with the total number of possible equally likely outcomes. The context of Item 1 in Table 6.14 involves sampling discrete items from a box; 66% of Grade 4 students responded correctly, and that outcome is significantly higher than the 58% correct observed in 1996 but not significantly different from the 65% performance in 2000. Approximately one in three students did not correctly compare the number of ways the target event can occur with the total number of elements in the sample space. The choice of "1 out of 3" by 14% of the students

Table 6.14
Grade 4 Performance on a Simple Probability Problem (2003-4M7 #10)

Item	Percentage Responding
The balls in this picture are placed in a box, and a child picks one without looking. What is the probability that the ball picked will be the one with dots?	

A. 1 out of 4	66
B. 1 out of 3	14
C. 1 out of 2	11
D. 3 out of 4	8

Note: Percentages do not sum to 100 because 1% of students omitted the item. Calculators were allowed on the item.

assessed perhaps reflects their misapplication of odds instead of numerical probabilities. Similarly, the 11% who chose "1 out of 2" might have been considering the fact that two outcomes are possible—namely, the ball with dots *will be selected* or *will not be selected*—and thus have erroneously concluded that those events are equally likely.

Item 2 (Table 6.12) is similar but involves determining the probability of "one out of N" occurring within the context of an area (continuous) model, and performance was similar, with 59% of Grade 4 students responding correctly, a significant increase from 1996, when 51% responded correctly, but not markedly different from the 58% answering correctly in 2000. A released item (Item 3, Table 6.12) administered on each NAEP assessment dating back to 1990 revealed that Grade 4 students were generally capable of successfully applying subjective probabilities, that is, describing likelihood in relative terms, such as "more likely" and "less likely."

In Item 3, students were asked to identify which of three bags of marbles—containing 10, 100, or 1,000 marbles including one red marble in each—gives the greatest chance of a target event. In all, 65% responded correctly, and that outcome is significantly higher than in 1996, when 57% did so. The item does not require the determination of (formal) numerical probabilities but rather affords students a variety of strategies (e.g., subjective probabilities, odds) in identifying the sample space that is associated with the greatest chance.

"Several out of *N*"

Notwithstanding the generally high performance of Grade 4 students on simple probability items, performance dropped precipitously on items requiring the determination of numerical probabilities in "several out of *N*" situations. One particular item that illustrates the performance decline was administered to Grade 4 students (Item 4, Table 6.12) and Grade 8 students (Item 1, Table 6.13). The item is generally equivalent to the following task: "Suppose Ramya has 7 cherry, 8 grape, and 5 lemon candies in a bag. If she picks one candy without looking, what is the probability that the candy she picks will be cherry?" The item requires students to compare the several ways the target event can happen with the total number of elements in the sample space, a number that is not explicitly provided. Although the 31% correct performance of Grade 4 students may seem relatively low, it nevertheless represents marked growth from 2000, when 27% responded correctly, and from 1996, when 26% did so (see Table 6.12). On the same item, 72% of Grade 8 students answered correctly, a figure significantly higher than in 1996, when only 60% provided the correct answer, but almost identical to performance in 2000 (see Table 6.13). Grade 4 males outperformed females on the item, but the gender difference in the Grade 8 population was not significant.

Two additional items assessed Grade 8 students' performance on "several out of *N*" situations. Both items were situated within the context of drawing two elements at random from a sample space. Neither item explicitly states *how* the two items are sampled: *simultaneously* (two at a time) or *without replacement* (one after another). Although counterintuitive to most students (Falk, 1988), those sampling techniques are mathematically equivalent in that they yield the same outcomes. Perhaps that reason explains the relatively poor performance of Grade 8 students on the two items. Specifically, on Item 2 (Table 6.13) only 40% of Grade 8 students correctly determined the probability, but that result is significantly higher than the 37% answering correctly in 1996; males outperformed females 43% to 36%, a significant difference in 2003. On Item 3 (Table 6.13), performance significantly improved from 1996 (22% correct) to 2000 (27% correct) to 2003 (30% correct). The relatively low scores on Item 3 might be attributed, in part, to the question format (short constructed response on Item 3, multiple choice on Item 2).

Predicting Outcomes

Three items assessed Grade 4 students' ability to predict the outcomes of an experiment. On Item 5 (Table 6.12), Grade 4 students were required to identify the most likely outcome in a single-trial experiment. The item is tantamount to determining the most likely outcome from a set of four events and can be answered *without* the use of formal numerical reasoning (i.e., without determining the probability). Perhaps for that reason, performance was quite robust, with 90% of Grade 4 students responding correctly. Items 6 and 7 (Table 6.12) are related to each other but differ in two important ways. First, Item 6 requires students to identify the most likely *distribution* of outcomes rather than a *single* outcome (Item 7). Second, in Item 6 the experiment is said to be carried out *repeatedly* rather than *exactly once* (in Item 7), and that scenario requires students to consider the long-run behavior of a random device. Despite those differences, performance remained relatively high on Item 6, with 75% answering correctly in 2003, a significantly higher percentage than in 2000 (71%) and 1996 (61%).

The strong performance of Grade 4 students on Item 6 was tempered by performance data on Item 7, which requires students to identify the most likely outcome in a single-trial experiment and determine the associated probability of the target event. In particular, although 90% of students were successful in a multiple-choice format (Item 5), only 15% of Grade 4 students responded correctly in the short constructed-response format, and males (17%) were significantly more likely to answer correctly than females (13%). The dramatic differences in performance on Items 5 and 7 can apparently be attributed to students' inability to state numerical probabilities. Grade 4 students have likely not yet learned how probabilities are formally expressed: using part-whole reasoning, as a ratio of two quantities.

Developed for 2003, Item 4 in Table 6.13 involves the application of expected value, or the long-run average value of a random variable. On that item, 56% of Grade 8 students correctly determined the expected value, in part through the application of multiplicative or proportional reasoning. Perhaps the straightforward computational nature of Item 4 might explain the relatively high performance on it.

Applying Probability Concepts

Two extended constructed-response items—one each at Grades 4 and 8–proved to be perplexing to the vast majority of students. Item 8 (Table 6.12) requires students to design a two-player spinner game to reflect stated parameters for winning and to justify their choices. Only 14% of Grade 4 students successfully completed the task, and that result represents a significant decrease in performance from 2000, when 18% of students did so. Item 5 (Table 6.13) requires students to determine the probability of a given event and justify their reasoning. Only 6% of Grade 8 students successfully responded, a significant decrease in performance from 2000 (8%). Those declines in performance raise questions that might not be answerable given that Item 5 (Table 6.13) and the student responses on it have not been released. An important point to note is that poor performance on extended constructed-response items was not unique to Data Analysis, Statistics, and Probability. Indeed, Arbaugh, Brown, Lynch, and McGraw (2004) report that performance on ECR items has remained remarkably low for students at Grades 4, 8, and 12 across all administrations of NAEP since 1990.

Developed for 2003, Item 6 (Table 6.13) assessed 8th-grade students' ability to distinguish between independent and dependent events. In particular, the question requires students to determine whether the probabilities of events change in a without-replacement situation. Only 16% of Grade 8 students could correctly justify their reasoning, and that performance was lower than reported in other studies of middle school students (Fischbein & Gazit, 1984; Tarr & Lannin, 2005). The relatively low performance is likely attributed to students' inability to monitor the composition of the sample space, realize that it is changed in with-replacement situations, and conclude that the probability of all events is likewise changed.

The results of student performance on items involving application of probability concepts should not be surprising given the low level of cognitive demand required for mathematical tasks implemented by classroom teachers (see Stein, Smith, Henningsen, & Silver, 2000). In particular, in a recent analysis of two popular middle school mathematics textbooks series—Connected Mathematics Project (Lappan et al., 1998) and Mathematics: Applications and Connections (Bailey et al., 2004)—Jones (2004) found that the majority of probability tasks required lower levels of cognitive demand, with most focusing on the development of "procedures without connections." Those findings might explain the generally poor performance on tasks requiring the justification of students' probabilistic reasoning, in that many students are not likely to have been regularly expected to do so.

CONCLUSION

Student performance on Data Analysis, Statistics, and Probability has improved steadily since 1990. The improvement may be due in part to the fact that probability and statistics have been given a more prominent place in national and state curriculum frameworks and school mathematics curricular materials, and teachers consequently report placing significantly more emphasis on that content than they did a decade ago.

Improvement in student performance is evident on items successively administered in 1996, 2000, and 2003. In particular, of the 14 probability and statistics items that were common to the 2000 and 2003 NAEP examinations at Grade 4, students performed significantly higher in 2003 on 5 items and lower on only 1. More impressively, among the 12 items common to the 1996 and 2003 NAEP examinations, Grade 4 students scored significantly higher in 2003 on 11. In contrast, of the 25 8th-grade items common to the 2000 and 2003 NAEP examinations, students scored significantly higher on 2 but lower on 7. More positive trends are evident across 19 items common to the 1996 and 2003 NAEP examinations, with 8th graders scoring significantly higher on 10 items in 2003 and lower on only 2. Their performance on the remaining items was stable.

Improvement was observed across the content subdomains, with particular gains made in performance on measures of central tendency and probability. The average 17-point increase in scale scores on Data Analysis, Statistics, and Probability since 1990—although impressive—cannot obscure the profound difficulties students continued to demonstrate on constructed-response items, including items requiring justification of statistical or probabilistic reasoning. Because such items provide a clearer picture of what students know and understand, in that regard the results of the 2003 assessment are disappointing. Indeed, the highest performance was demonstrated on items requiring only procedural skills, such as identifying the probability of an event in a "one out of N" situation, predicting the most likely outcome of a single-trial experiment, and reading circle graphs and pictographs. Items requiring more sophisticated skills associated with statistical literacy were largely coupled with woefully low performance levels, clearly an indication of the challenges still facing mathematics teachers and teacher educators.

Given the interrelatedness of concepts in data and chance, analysis would be aided by the addition of clusters of items that assess student ability to design studies, collect and analyze data, and draw appropriate inferences as well as evaluate the reasonableness of data-based claims. Moreover, additional items need to be added to gauge student ability to construct and interpret box-and-whisker plots, histograms, and scatterplots, as well as measure the extent to which students attend to variation in comparing data sets. Likewise, items are needed to assess students' reasoning about the interplay between experimental and theoretical probabilities, and such items could simultaneously integrate probability and statistical concepts rather than treat data analysis, statistics, and probability as discrete units of the school mathematics curriculum. Finally, a format in which more NAEP items are administered to all three grade-level populations would be desirable to provide a clearer picture of the conceptual development in data and chance across Grades 4, 8, and 12.

Many of the aforementioned suggestions for improving the NAEP may be implemented on future assessments. In particular, the Mathematics Framework for the 2005 National Assessment of Educational Progress (National Assessment Governing Board [NAGB], 2004) indicates that box-and-whisker plots, scatterplots, and linear regression will be assessed in Grades 8 and 12 on the 2005 NAEP. Moreover, the NAGB also has proposed that the Data Analysis, Statistics, and Probability strand comprise 25% of the Grade 12 assessment, an astonishing portion given that data and chance have only recently emerged as important elements of the school mathematics curriculum.

REFERENCES

American Statistical Association. (2005). *A curriculum framework for preK–12 statistics education.* Retrieved October 4, 2005, from www.amstat.org/education/gaise/GAISEpreK–12.htm

Arbaugh, F., Brown, C., Lynch, K., & McGraw, R. (2004). Students' ability to construct responses (1992–2000): Findings from short and extended constructed-response items. In P. Kloosterman & F. K. Lester, Jr. (Eds.), *Results and interpretations of the 1990– 2000 mathematics assessments of the National Assessment of Educational Progress* (pp. 337–362). Reston, VA: National Council of Teachers of Mathematics.

Bailey, R., Day, R., Frey, P., Howard, A. C., Hutchens, D. T., & McClain, K. (2004). *Glencoe mathematics.* Applications and connections series. New York: Glencoe/ McGraw-Hill.

Center for the Study of Mathematics Curriculum. (2005). *State mathematics content standards.* Columbia: University of Missouri. Retrieved November 7, 2005, from matheddb. missouri.edu/states.php

Conference Board of the Mathematical Sciences. (2001). *The mathematical preparation of teachers.* Washington, DC: Mathematical Association of America.

English, L. D. (1993). Children's strategies in solving two- and three-dimensional combinatorial problems. *Journal for Research in Mathematics Education, 24,* 255–273.

English, L. D. (2005). Combinatorics and the development of children's combinatorial reasoning. In G. A. Jones (Ed.), *Exploring probability in school: Challenges for teaching and learning* (pp. 121–141). New York: Springer-Verlag.

Falk, R. (1988). Conditional probabilities: Insights and difficulties. In R. Davidson & J. Swift (Eds.), *The Second International Conference on Teaching Statistics* (pp. 292– 297). Victoria, British Columbia: University of Victoria.

Fischbein, E., & Gazit, A. (1984). Does the teaching of probability improve probabilistic intuitions? *Educational Studies in Mathematics, 15,* 1–24.

Fischbein, E., & Schnarch, D. (1997). The evolution with age of probabilistic, intuitively based misconceptions. *Journal for Research in Mathematics Education, 28,* 96–105.

Friel, S. N. (in press). The research frontier: Where technology interacts with the teaching and learning of data analysis and statistics. In M. K. Heid & G. W. Blume (Eds.), *Research on technology and the teaching and learning of mathematics: Syntheses and perspectives,* vol. 1. Greenwich, CT: Information Age.

Friel, S. N., Curcio, F. R., & Bright, G. W. (2001). Making sense of graphs: Critical factors influencing comprehension and instructional implications. *Journal for Research in Mathematics Education, 32,* 124–158.

Jones, D. L. (2004). Probability in middle grades mathematics textbooks: An examination of historical trends, 1957–2004. Unpublished doctoral dissertation, University of Missouri, Columbia.

Jones, G. A. (Ed.). (2005). *Exploring probability in schools: Challenges for teaching and learning.* New York: Springer-Verlag.

Jones, G. A., Langrall, C., Thornton, C., & Mogill, A. T. (1999). Students' probabilistic thinking in instruction. *Journal for Research in Mathematics Education, 30,* 487–519.

Konold, C., & Pollatsek, A. (2002). Data analysis as the search for signals in noisy processes. *Journal for Research in Mathematics Education, 33,* 259–289.

Langrall, C. A., & Mooney, E. S. (2005). Characteristics of elementary school students' probabilistic reasoning. In G. A. Jones (Ed.), *Exploring probability in school: Challenges for teaching and learning* (pp. 95–119). New York: Springer-Verlag.

Lappan, G., Fey, J. T., Fitzgerald, W., Friel, S., & Phillips, E. D. (1998). Connected Mathematics Project series. Boston, MA: Pearson Prentice Hall.

Metz, K. E. (1998). Emergent ideas of chance and probability in primary-grade children. In S. P. Lajoie (Ed.), *Reflections on statistics: Learning, teaching, and assessment in grades K–12* (pp. 149–174). Mahwah, NJ: Erlbaum.

Mokros, J., & Russell, S. J. (1995). Children's concepts of average and representativeness. *Journal for Research in Mathematics Education, 26,* 20–39.

National Assessment Governing Board [NAGB]. (2004). *Mathematics framework for the 2005 National Assessment of Educational Progress.* Retrieved November 1, 2005, from www.nagb.org/pubs/m_framework_05/toc.html

National Council of Teachers of Mathematics. (1989). *Curriculum and evaluation standards for school mathematics.* Reston, VA: Author.

National Council of Teachers of Mathematics. (2000). *Principles and standards for school mathematics.* Reston, VA: Author.

Pratt, D. (2000). Making sense of the total of two dice. *Journal for Research in Mathematics Education, 31,* 602–625.

Shaughnessy, J. M., Canada, D., & Ciancetta, M. (2003). Middle school students' thinking about variability in repeated trials: A cross-task comparison. In N. A. Pateman, B. J. Dougherty, & J. T. Zilliox (Eds.), *Proceedings of the 27th conference of the International Group for the Psychology of Mathematics Education held jointly with the 25th conference of PME-NA* (pp. 159–165). Honolulu: Center for Research and Development Group, University of Hawaii.

Shaughnessy, J. M., Garfield, J., & Greer, B. (1996). Data handling. In A. J. Bishop, K. Clements, C. Keitel, J. Kilpatrick, & C. Laborde (Eds.), *International handbook of mathematics education* (Part 1) (pp. 205–237). Dordrecht, Netherlands: Kluwer.

Stein, M. K., Smith, M. S., Henningsen, M. A., & Silver, E. A. (2000). *Implementing standards-based mathematics instruction: A casebook for professional development.* New York: Teachers College Press.

Stohl, H., & Tarr, J. E. (2002). Developing notions of statistical inference with probability simulation tools. *Journal of Mathematical Behavior, 21,* 319–337.

Strauss, S., & Bichler, E. (1988). The development of children's concepts of the arithmetic average. *Journal for Research in Mathematics Education, 19,* 64–80.

Tarr, J. E., & Jones, G. A. (1997). A framework for assessing middle school students' thinking in conditional probability and independence. *Mathematics Education Research Journal, 9,* 39–59

Tarr, J. E., & Lannin, J. K. (2005). How do teachers build notions of conditional probability and independence? In G. A. Jones (Ed.), *Exploring probability in school: Challenges for teaching and learning* (pp. 148–169). New York: Springer-Verlag.

Watson, J. D., & Moritz, J. B. (2000). Developing concepts of sampling. *Journal for Research in Mathematics Education, 30,* 44–70.

Watson, J. M. (1997). Assessing statistical thinking using the media. In I. Gal & J. Garfield (Eds.), *The assessment challenge in statistics education* (pp. 107–121). Amsterdam: IOS Press.

Zawojewski, J. S., & Heckman, D. (1997). What do students know about data analysis, statistics, and probability? In P. A. Kenney & E. A. Silver (Eds.), *Results from the sixth mathematics assessment of the National Assessment of Educational Progress* (pp. 195–223). Reston, VA: National Council of Teachers of Mathematics.

Zawojewski, J. S., & Shaughnessy, J. M. (2000). Data and chance. In E. A. Silver & P. A. Kenney (Eds.), *Results from the seventh mathematics assessment of the National Assessment of Educational Progress* (pp. 235–268). Reston, VA: National Council of Teachers of Mathematics.

## 7

What NAEP Can (and Cannot) Tell Us About Performance in Algebra

*Daniel Chazan, Aisling M. Leavy, Geoffrey Birky, Kathleen M. Clark,
H. Michael Lueke, Wanda McCoy, and Farhaana Nyamekye*

A S WE turn our attention to what NAEP can tell us about algebra in the U.S. curriculum, a useful approach is to take stock of recent trends in school algebra. Those trends suggest questions to which one might want NAEP to speak. However, as we outline subsequently, although NAEP can provide some useful information, the process cannot yet provide evidence that will speak to some important questions one might want to answer about trends in school algebra.

Over the previous decade, a movement has been underway in secondary schools to increase standards and to hold students, teachers, and schools accountable for student learning. Algebra 1, as a course, has become a requirement for graduation in many school districts. That requirement has brought much public attention and scrutiny to algebra as a part of the mathematics curriculum. Increasingly, for some students, algebra is no longer a 9th-grade course but rather an 8th-grade (as advocated by Usiskin, 1987) or even a 7th-grade course. Thus a good deal of instruction in algebra happens in junior high school or middle school, and given the nature of teacher certification in many states, it is orchestrated by teachers with elementary school, rather than secondary school, certification. As a result, an investigation of what is happening to achievement in algebra seems reasonable.

In the context of the course called Algebra 1, over the previous decade debates over what should be taught have been shaped by the widespread availability of graphing calculators that support alternative methods to those traditionally taught in school algebra. Textbooks now commonly suggest that students can solve an equation numerically by graphing both sides of an equation and using information about the expressions on both sides of the equals sign to identify the

Highlights

- An examination of trend data from 1990 to 2003 indicates that at both the 4th- and 8th-grade levels, Algebra and Functions, relative to other mathematics content areas, has shown the largest improvement in mean scale scores, but the gap between racial and ethnic groups on the Algebra and Functions subscale has not narrowed.

- At the 4th-grade level, we found a pattern of slowly increasing difference in male and female Algebra and Functions scale scores, although the difference was statistically significant only in 2003. No clear pattern was evident in results by gender data at the 8th-grade level.

- The released Grade 4 items place a heavy emphasis on problems involving pattern completion at the expense of other types of algebraic reasoning.

- At the 8th-grade level, student performance on a set of five procedural tasks was stronger than their performance on other algebra items.

- Students performed less well on extended constructed-response items than the other two question types.

- Students who used graphing calculators regularly for schoolwork scored substantially better than those who did not, although those who used symbol manipulators did more poorly than their peers.

x values of intersection points of the two graphs. Many graphing calculators now also have the capacity to do symbolic manipulation. Such technological advances have challenged educators to rethink what algebra should be offered in school. And, again, they call for an examination of how such changes might be linked with achievement in algebra.

With the vision presented in the NCTM (2000) *Principles and Standards for School Mathematics,* algebra is a strand of the curriculum that begins in the elementary grades. That vision entails providing students with a set of experiences that is integrated into their mathematical experience at every grade rather than confined to longer, separate courses at the high school level. Although the number of secondary schools that have adopted an "integrated" vision of school mathematics seems to be comparatively small, curricula based on the NCTM vision are more widely adopted at the elementary and middle school levels, and thus many more students are having experiences with algebraic ideas earlier in the curriculum. One might like to know whether the performance on algebra items of elementary and middle school students reflects a greater emphasis on algebra. For secondary students, one might be interested in trends in performance on algebra items of students in integrated programs.

At the same time that algebra as a school subject is in flux, NAEP is also changing. NAEP is becoming the states' report card as well as the nation's report card. The data from NAEP, through the evolving NAEP online tool (see chapter 1), are now more readily available to the public. With that accessibility in mind, as well as larger calls for evidence-based decision making in education (Mosteller & Boruch, 2002), we seek in this chapter to explore and illustrate the kinds of questions about algebra in U.S. schools that can be explored with the data generated by the NAEP process. The results of our exploration are more limited than we would like. In the 2003 NAEP administration, only 4th- and 8th-grade cohorts were assessed, and thus the majority of students who have taken a course named algebra are not represented in the sample. On the positive side, with the availability of the online Data Explorer, we can illustrate the sorts of analyses that might be done with the Data Explorer in the future with NAEP algebra items by schools, districts, and states. We also comment on aspects of the NAEP process that could be improved to make such analyses feasible.

In this chapter we provide a short overview of student performance on the 2003 NAEP Algebra and Functions items. We then explore the ways in which the NAEP items represent the nature of algebraic activity. In the next section we look at student performance on two groups of released items—one group involving graphing points on number lines and coordinate planes and a second group that, following Usiskin (1988), might be labeled as a view of algebra as a collection of procedures for solving problems. Next, we examine student performance by item type and then look at two pairs of similar items with differential student performance, exploring the potential pedagogical ramifications of those differences. Finally, we consider uses of student questionnaire data in relation to specific items to explore the impact of the use of graphing calculators on student performance. In our closing, we indicate ways in which the mathematics education community can seek over time to use the NAEP process to our advantage.

OVERVIEW OF STUDENT PERFORMANCE ON NAEP ALGEBRA ITEMS

The 2003 NAEP mathematics assessment contained 65 Algebra and Functions strand items, down from 77 items in 2000. Sixteen of those items were administered at the 4th-grade level and 39 at the 8th-grade level. Ten additional items were administered at both grades and thus allow comparison of performance across the two grades. Of those 65 items, 22 were released in 2003: 5 items used only in 4th grade, 14 items used only in 8th grade, and 3 items used in both grades.

Without revealing the wording of the items not released, we can use performance on the set of items identified by NAEP as algebra items to track achievement over the years on algebra and compare trends in performance in algebra with trends in other mathematics content strands. Table 7.1 presents a summary of student performance on the Algebra and Functions strand in the previous five administrations of the NAEP assessment, broken down by gender and race/ethnicity. Overall achievement for 4th and 8th graders in Algebra and Functions increased between each consecutive pair of NAEP administrations between 1990 and 2003. In fact, the gains of 27 scale points by Grade 4 students and 19 points by Grade 8 students were the largest in any of the five NAEP mathematics content areas. The particularly visible improvement in performance at the 4th-grade level may be a reflection of the NCTM emphasis on integrating attention to algebra into the elementary school curriculum. The improvement at the 8th-grade level may reflect an increase in the number of students completing algebra in middle and junior high schools.

Table 7.1

Performance on the Algebra and Functions Strand by Year of Administration, Gender, and Race/Ethnicity

Year	Mean	Male	Female	Asian American/ Pacific Islander	White	American Indian	Hispanic	Black
				Average Scale Scores for 4th-Grade Students				
2003	241	242	239	253	248	232	230	224
2000	230	231	229	—	237	—	215	210
1996	227	227	226	231	234	—	216	204
1992	219	218	219	232	226	—	201	192
1990	214	214	214	—	220	—	200	190
				Average Scale Scores for 8th-Grade Students				
2003	280	280	280	295	289	267	263	257
2000	275	276	275	292	285	—	255	250
1996	271	272	270	—	280	—	253	244
1992	268	267	270	292	276	—	248	238
1990	261	261	262	—	268	—	245	238

Note. Data from 1990 and 1992 are for samples for which accommodations were not permitted.

The structure of the NAEP data set also allows one to analyze achievement on framework strands by selected groups. For example, differential achievement is evident when performance across race/ethnicity is examined. In the 4th- and 8th-grade cohorts for the 2003 administration, a similar pattern of differential performance by racial/ethnic group is evident (see Table 7.1). Specifically, although performance improved by approximately 30 scale points for 4th graders and 20 scale points for 8th graders over the previous decade, the sizeable gap between racial or ethnic groups persists. Patterns in achievement across SES groups (as measured by eligibility for free and reduced-price lunches) are similar to those based on race/ethnicity, with higher SES groups gaining higher scores. That pattern persists across the five NAEP mathematics content areas.

Similarly, in the Grade 4 data, gender differences in algebraic performance became more evident from 1990 to 2003. Examination of Table 7.1 shows a pattern of slowly increasing difference in male and female scale scores—no achievement difference was seen in 1990, a difference of 1 point occurred in 1992 and 1996, and a difference of 2 points occurred in 2000. None of these differences, however, were statistically significant. The 3-point disparity in achievement in 2003 represents the largest and only statistically significant gender difference in more than a decade. Gender data for Grade 8 do not follow a straightforward trend. Males and females achieved equally well in Algebra and Functions in 2003, whereas in 1996 and 2000 males had higher achievement and in 1990 and 1992 females had higher achievement. None of those gender differences, however, were statistically significant.

Looking at the 10 items in the 2003 NAEP assessment that were administered to both 4th- and 8th-grade students, one might assume that older students would do better. That outcome was true for all the items, although for an item involving completion of a letter pattern (Item 4, Table 7.2), a relatively small difference of 13 percentage points was observed between 4th and 8th graders. An examination of the item reveals that it requires little more than completion of a repeating pattern—an item that should be easily solved by an 8th grader. Perhaps a lack of familiarity with patterns accounts for 8th graders' low performance. The NCTM (2000) *Principles and Standards* document places greater emphasis on the importance of patterns at the elementary level than at higher levels, perhaps accounting for the strong performance of Grade 4 students in relation to their Grade 8 counterparts.

ALGEBRA AS REPRESENTED IN THE NAEP FRAMEWORK AND ALGEBRA ITEMS

Performance on NAEP algebra items as indicators of national or state curricular trends in algebra assumes validity of the assessment. Specifically, an important question to ask is what the 65 Algebra and Functions items on NAEP actually measure. Meaningful exploration of that question is hampered by the secrecy that surrounds such tests as NAEP (see Schwartz & Viator, 1990, for discussion of that issue). NAEP provides three resources, each having its own limitations, that help one review the nature of the Algebra and Functions strand: (a) the components of the 2003 NAEP framework (National Assessment Governing Board, 2002) (the framework was changed for the 2005 administration), (b) the item descriptors (which are unconstrained, not indexed to the framework, and not intended for wide distribution), and (c) the small number of items released after an administration of the NAEP. (As noted in chapter 1, items are sometimes released because they are deemed ineffective). After looking at those three indicators at Grade 4, three conclusions became evident. First, the NAEP and

Table 7.2

Performance of 4th- and 8th-Grade Students on Items Administered at Both Levels

Item Description	Percentage Correct	
	4th	8th
1. Use algebraic reasoning to determine a relationship between two quantities. (2003-4M6 #13, 2003-8M6 #13)	39	75
2. What are all the whole numbers that make $8 - x > 3$ true? (2003-4M6 #20, 2003-8M6 #20)	24	63
3. Determine the solution of a simple linear equation, presented in number sentence format.	67	86
4. Peter wrote down a pattern of A's and B's that repeats in groups of 3. Here is the beginning of his pattern with some of the letters erased. Fill in the missing letters. A, B, _ , A, _, B, _, _, _. (2003-4M6 #8, 2003-8M6 #8)	52	65
5. Identify correct order. (2005-8M3 #5)[a]	66	86
6. List different possibilities (coins).	57	81
7. Find the next several numbers in a given growing pattern, and write the rule used.	32	64
8. Given a rule for creating the path of an object in a coordinate plane, draw the path. (2005-8M4 #10)	21	53
9. Choose the nth term in a repeating pattern consisting of orientations of a geometric figure. (2005-4M4 #3)	73	89
10. Supply the missing coordinates on a number line.	39	70

Note. Items 1, 2, 5, and 9 were multiple choice; the rest were short constructed response.

[a]2005 items were released while this volume was in production. Block and item numbers have been added so that interested readers can find the 2005 items using the online Questions Tool.

NCTM views of algebra are not identical. Second, the language used by NCTM to describe Algebra and Functions Standards is more specific than that found in the NAEP framework. Third, released items that connect algebra with completion of patterns are heavily represented, perhaps overrepresented.

At the 8th-grade level, one can analyze items in terms of the NAEP framework and also in terms of Usiskin's (1988) four conceptions of algebra related to the different uses of variables: (a) generalized arithmetic, (b) a study of procedures for solving certain problems, (c) a study of relationships, and (d) a study of structures (Usiskin suggests that conception [d] is prevalent mostly at the university level). Three NAEP objectives were the focus of the lion's share of the

17 released Grade 8 items. Six items involved using patterns, 4 focused on using number lines and coordinate systems as representational tools, and 4 others involved representing or describing solutions to linear equations or inequalities with whole-number solution sets. Ten items fit into Usiskin's framework: 2 as generalized arithmetic, 5 as the study of procedures for solving certain problems, and 3 as the study of relationships. None of the remaining 7 items could be placed in Usiskin's framework because they did not use variables. Item 4 in Table 7.2, which focuses on patterns, is an example of one of those items. Additionally, 6 of those items do not seem like algebra at all; rather, they might better be described as involving number sense and operations, geometry, or thinking logically.

In brief, our analysis of the content of the NAEP algebra items raises questions about the utility of the NAEP item bank for tracking curricular progress with respect to school algebra. Taken together, our comments about the 4th- and 8th-grade items suggest that conclusions drawn on the basis of the set of NAEP Algebra and Functions items should be considered quite tentatively.

DATA ON SUBTOPICS IN ALGEBRA

In addition to examining scores on the algebra items as a set, we can look at achievement on individual items or groups of items. In this section, we examine student performance on topics that were addressed by six or more items—enough to form generalizations. Our analysis builds on work of interpretive studies of earlier NAEP administrations (Blume & Heckman, 1997, 2000) and makes use of scores for both released and nonreleased items.

The largest category—containing eight items, two of which were given at both 4th- and 8th-grade levels (see Table 7.3)—was the category labeled graphing points on the number line and in the coordinate plane (Blume & Heckman, 2000). A comparison of performance between 2000 and 2003 on the three items in that category administered at 4th grade shows an insignificant increase in performance for two items and a large increase for one item. Specifically, performance on Item 3 in Table 7.3, which involved missing coordinates on a number line, increased from 28% correct in 2000 to 39% correct in 2003. The increase of 11 percentage points is encouraging with respect to students' abilities on number lines involving fractional quantities.

Eighth graders' performance over time on Items 4–10 varied considerably, with some items showing stability in performance, some revealing an increase in performance, and others demonstrating a decrease in performance. As compared with performance in 2000, the percentage of students presenting correct solutions remained relatively stable for two items that involved working with the number line. Item 5 (Table 7.3) required supplying a missing coordinate on a number line, and Item 10 required that the student graph all numbers greater than or equal to –1 and less than or equal to 3 on a number line (see Figure 7.1). The first item was answered correctly by 70% of students, and the second item, by 45%. An

Table 7.3
Graphing Points on Number Lines and Coordinate Planes

Item Description	Percentage Correct	
	2000	2003
4th-grade items		
1. Choose the correct sum involving several terms in a growing pattern.	65	67
2. Given a rule for creating the path of an object in a coordinate plane, draw the path. (2005-4M4 #10)	20	21
3. Supply the missing coordinates on a number line.	28*	39
8th-grade items		
4. Given a rule for creating the path of an object in a coordinate plane, draw the path. (2005-8M4 #10)	60*	53
5. Supply the missing coordinates on a number line.	68	70
6. Given a rule for creating a path of an object in a coordinate plane, determine whether a particular point would be on that path; explain. (2005-8M4 #11)	25	24
7. Choose the correct coordinates of a vertex of an undrawn rectangle, given the coordinates of the other vertices. (2005-8M3 #13)	52*	57
8. Determine the location of a particular point in the coordinate plane. (2003-8M10 #15)	45*	41
9. Choose the correct coordinates of a vertex of a polygon when the polygon's other vertices are given. (Figure 7.2, 2003-8M6 #26)	59*	62
10. Shade the part of a number line that shows all numbers ≥ –1 and ≤ 3. (Figure 7.1, 2003-8M6 #24)	44	45

Note. Items 1, 7, 9 were multiple choice, and the rest were short constructed response. Calculators were allowed on Item 1.

* Indicates that the percentage correct is significantly different from the 2003 percentage correct.

interesting aspect of student performance on the item in Figure 7.1 is the categorization of incorrect responses. We might imagine that incorrect responses would identify the values as falling between –1 and 3 but would involve some inaccuracy in terms of the upper and lower limits of the interval, leading to three plausibly incorrect solutions as seen below. However, only 2% of the incorrect responses were of that form, with the remaining 47% identifying a different interval or solution. An example of one such incorrect response—incorrect solution 2 in Figure 7.1—shows a focus on individual points rather than on an interval.

On the number line below, shade the part of the line that shows the set of all numbers greater than or equal to –1 and less than or equal to 3.

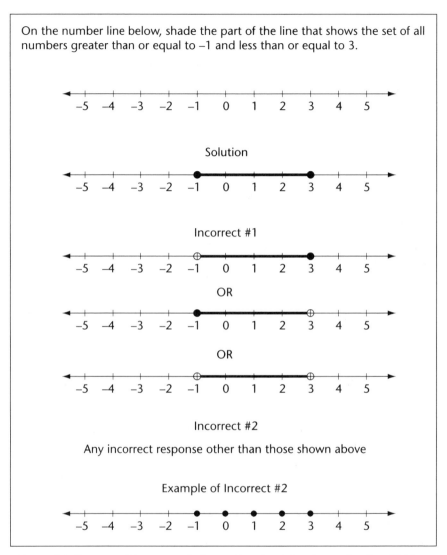

Figure 7.1. Correct and incorrect solutions to item involving the number line (2003-8M6 #24).

Items 7 and 9 in Table 7.3 showed an increase of 3 or more percentage points in performance. Both of those items required that the correct coordinates of a vertex of a polygon be provided when the polygon's other vertices were given. Item 9, which is shown in Figure 7.2, was correctly solved by 59% of 8th-grade students in 2000 and by 62% in 2003. Little difference was observed in the popularity of distracters A, B, and C. Distracter E was selected half as often as the others.

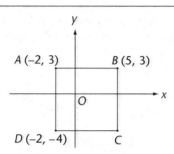

In the figure above, if *ABCD* is a square, then the coordinates of vertex *C* are

A)   (4, 5)
B)   (3, –4)
C)   (3, –2)
D)   (5, –4)
E)   (5, –2)

Figure 7.2. Item requiring identification of a point in the coordinate plane (2003-8M6 #26).

On the remaining three items in Table 7.3, performance decreased from 2000 to 2003, although the decrease was statistically significant only on Items 4 and 8. Items 4 and 6 are similar in that they focus on a path or points in a coordinate plane. When given a rule for creating a path on a coordinate plane, Item 4 requires that the student draw the path and Item 6 requires a reason for whether a particular point in the plane would be on that path. Item 8, presented in Figure 7.3, involves determination of the location of a particular point in the coordinate plane. That item demonstrated a modest decrease in performance, dropping from 45% correct in 2000 to 41% correct in 2003. That decrease is unexpected given the greater emphasis on graphical representations proposed in NCTM *Standards* documents.

Another set of five items can be categorized using Usiskin's (1988) system as reflecting algebra as the study of procedures to solve problems. We can compare performance on the five procedural items identified by Usiskin against the complete set of 8th-grade Algebra and Functions items. An examination of data from the 2003 and 2000 administrations reveals that the mean performance on the procedural items was more than 8 percentage points higher than performance on the entire set of Algebra and Functions items. Taken together with the results on the graphing items above, those results may reflect limited implementation by teachers of NCTM's vision for algebra instruction. An examination of Table 7.4 indicates stability or improvement in achievement in procedural items between 1996 and 2003. That outcome suggests that any changes in practice that may

On the map below, the rock is located 2 miles west and 1 mile north of the tree. A treasure chest (not shown) is located 8 miles east and 4 miles north of the rock. Mark the location of the treasure chest on the map with an X.

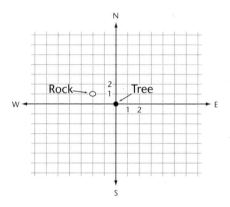

What is the position of the treasure chest with respect to the <u>tree</u>?

Answer: _____ miles east and _____ miles north of the tree

Figure 7.3. Graphing item on which performance declined significantly from 2000 to 2003.

Table 7.4
Items Identified as a Study of Procedures for Solving Certain Problems (Usiskin, 1988)

| | Percentage Correct | | |
Item Description	1996	2000	2003
1. If the value of the expression $x + 2$ is less than 12, which of the following could be a value of x? (2003-8M10 #3)	75	77	77
2. What are all the whole numbers that make $8 - x > 3$ true? (2003-8M6 #20)	56*	63	63
3. If $3 + w = b$, then $w = $? (2003-8M7 #18)	50	54*	48
4. Use algebraic reasoning to determine a relationship between two quantities. (2003-8M6 #13)	68*	76	75
5. On a number line, shade the part that shows all numbers ≥ -1 and ≤ 3. (Figure 7.1, 2003-8M6 #24)	44	44	45

Note. Item 5 is a short constructed-response item, and the remaining are multiple-choice items. Calculators were allowed on Item 3.

* Indicates that the percentage correct is significantly different from the 2003 percentage correct.

have taken place in school algebra instruction have not resulted in a decrease in student performance on traditional algebra exercises.

PERFORMANCE BY NAEP CLASSIFICATION SCHEMES

The analyses presented in Tables 7.3 and 7.4 provide a sense of student performance on both graphing and procedural algebra items. However, to maximize what can be learned from the NAEP assessment with respect to instruction (Wilcox & Lanier, 2000), we need additional ways to classify items to make sense of the differential performance. We next turn to the sorts of classifications that are available through NAEP and examine student performance on those groups of items. Doing so complicates slightly the picture we drew in the previous section. Differences in performance may be due to aspects other than the topics ostensibly tested by the items.

NAEP provides two item classifications schemes[1] that can be used to aggregate performance on subsets of algebra items and examine patterns in performance without direct knowledge of the wording of the problems. One of those categorizations regards format, and the other regards what NAEP calls "mathematical ability" (and which is available only for released items).

NAEP items are categorized into three question types: multiple choice, short constructed response, and extended constructed response (see chapter 1). One might like to understand how student performance is linked with those formats of the tasks. With respect to the 75 Algebra and Functions items administered in 2003 (counting twice the 10 items that were given to both 4th- and 8th-grade students), 48 were multiple choice, 17 were short constructed response, and 10 were extended constructed response. Multiple-choice questions were represented to a greater extent on the 8th-grade assessment than on the 4th-grade assessment, whereas extended constructed response constituted a greater proportion of 4th-grade items. An examination of achievement on 4th-grade items indicates that students performed less well on extended constructed-response items than on the other two question types. (That result is supported by the analysis in Arbaugh, Brown, Lynch, & McGraw, 2004.) A similar pattern can be seen in the 8th-grade data (Table 7.5).

The results in Table 7.5 could be interpreted as natural and expected outcomes of increased difficulty of extended constructed-response items. Alternatively, one might imagine that achievement should not differ by the format of the problem and thus interpret the differential achievement as an indication of problematic instruction.

---

[1] NAEP uses a third classification scheme but provides no description of it, so we do not describe it here.

Table 7.5
Performance on Items Classified by Question Type

	Grade 4		Grade 8	
Question Type	Proportion Represented	Mean Score	Proportion Represented	Mean Score
Multiple choice	50%	51%	71%	55%
Short constructed response	19%	64%	25%	56%
Extended constructed response	31%	29%	4%	8%

NAEP also categorizes all mathematics items under three levels of mathematical ability: procedural, conceptual, and problem solving (see chapter 1). Those three categorizations are descriptions of the ways in which the item developers expect students to approach the items: by using a previously taught procedure, applying a concept, or crafting a novel solution process. However, an examination of those levels is possible only for the released items.

The NAEP categorization scheme seems problematic because it involves assumptions about what students have learned prior to the administration of the NAEP—assumptions that are questionable because different students will have learned different material. For example, even though the item shown in Figure 7.4 concerning the numbers of letters Tara sends while on vacation is listed as problem solving, for a student who learned to solve systems of equations in Algebra 1, it should more accurately be classified as a procedural item.

Nonetheless, performance does differ by the foregoing mathematical ability categories. Of the released items at the 4th-grade level, performance was lowest on those categorized as problem solving. Of all released Grade 4 Algebra and Functions items, performance was lowest on an extended constructed-response item (2003-4M7 #20) that read as follows: "The table below shows how the chirping of a cricket is related to the temperature outside. For example, a cricket chirps 144 times each minute when the temperature is 76°. What would be the number of chirps per minute when the temperature outside is 90° if this pattern stays the same? Explain how you figured out your answer." Only

---

Description: Solve problem using informal algebra

Item:
While she was on vacation, Tara sent 14 friends either a letter or a postcard. She spent $3.84 on postage. If it costs $0.20 to mail a postcard and $0.33 to mail a letter, how many letters did Tara send? Show what you did to get your answer.

Figure 7.4. An 8th-grade item that can be solved using a variety of approaches.

3% of Grade 8 students received full credit on this item, although another 46% received partial credit.

Another extended constructed problem-solving item (2003-4M7 #6) was also very difficult for Grade 4 students:

> A school yard contains only bicycles and wagons. On Monday there were 3 bicycles and 2 wagons in the school yard. How many wheels were in the school yard?

Twenty-five percent of Grade 4 students correctly answered the bicycles-and-wagons problem in 1996 and 2000. That proportion increased to 29% in 2003. Similarly, at the 8th-grade level, the lowest percentage correct for an algebra item was on the postage problem shown in Figure 7.4. That problem was also an extended constructed-response problem-solving item for which only 11% of students received full credit in 2000 and 2003.

COMPARING ACHIEVEMENT ON ALGEBRA ITEMS: TWO PAIRS OF RELEASED ITEMS

One can also gain understanding of student achievement by examining differential achievement on items deemed similar on some dimension. Such comparisons might be useful for generating recommendations for practice; poor performance on some particular type of problem might suggest a weakness in current approaches that might be remediated through curricular change or instructional innovation. In this section we explore the possibility of identifying areas of weakness in performance.

To explore such a possibility, we present comparisons of student achievement on two pairs of released items. The pairings were created by choosing the released problems for which achievement was low and pairing them with problems that were similar along some dimensions but for which achievement was different. Released Items 2003-4M7 #5 (referred to hereafter as "Bicycles and wagons: simple problem") and 2003-4M7 #6 ("Bicycles and wagons: complex problem") are paired because they are Grade 4 problems that use the same context, and were given to students together, but reflect a disparity in student performance. That disparity matches previous findings in the literature on student learning of algebra (e.g., Koedinger & Nathan, 2004). Released Items 2003-8M7 #19 (postage problem) and 2003-8M10 #13 (water loss and gain) are two 8th-grade rate problems in context, but in the second problem, students are supported by the presentation of a graph.

Performance on Two Problems in the Same Context

Item 2003-4M7 #5 (Bicycles and wagons: simple problem) is shown in Figure 7.5. Administered to 4th graders, it is a short constructed-response item that is categorized as procedural. It is described in the NAEP Questions Tool as "Solve problem involving multiples of 2 and 4." Sixty-nine percent of students answered the item correctly, 29% provided an incorrect solution, 1% provided a partial solution, and 1% omitted the item. Sixty-three percent of students provided a correct solution in the 1996 assessment, and 70% did so in the 2000 assessment.

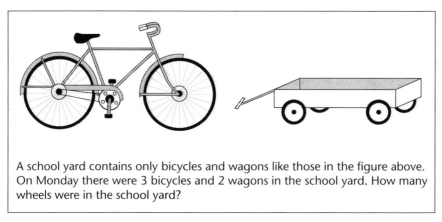

A school yard contains only bicycles and wagons like those in the figure above. On Monday there were 3 bicycles and 2 wagons in the school yard. How many wheels were in the school yard?

Figure 7.5. An example of an item that shares context with another item ("bicycles and wagons: simple problem") (2003-4M7 #5).

The companion item, 2003-4M7 #6 (bicycles and wagons: complex problem), is a short constructed-response item that is categorized as problem solving. Shown in Figure 7.6, it is described in the Questions Tool as "Find two possible correct solutions for problem." In 2003, 29% of students got this item correct, 51% provided an incorrect solution, 17% provided a partial solution, 2% omitted the item, and 1% were off task. A partial solution was considered to be one correct response or the same correct response twice. The fact that 17% of students received partial credit indicates that they could identify one correct combination. Not enough information is available to assess whether the students gave an incorrect second combination or whether they did not present a second combination. The 29% of students giving a correct response was a slight increase from 1996 and 2000, when 25% of students provided a correct solution.

How do we account for differences in performance between two items that are both short constructed-response items and are couched in the same context? What different aspect accounts for the differing levels of performance? The disparity in achievement fits with Koedinger and Nathan's (2004) finding about the difference in directionality of algebra problems. In the context of problems involving a single linear relationship, they distinguish between "result unknown" problems, which are easier for students, and "start unknown" problems, which are harder. In this example, the start-unknown problem that requires working backward did result in lower student performance.

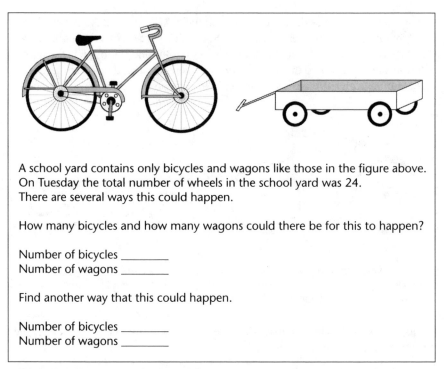

A school yard contains only bicycles and wagons like those in the figure above.
On Tuesday the total number of wheels in the school yard was 24.
There are several ways this could happen.

How many bicycles and how many wagons could there be for this to happen?

Number of bicycles _____
Number of wagons _____

Find another way that this could happen.

Number of bicycles _____
Number of wagons _____

Figure 7.6. An example of an item that shares context with another item ("bicycles and wagons: complex problem") (2003-4M7 #6).

Performance on Two Contextualized Items

Eighth-grade Item 2003-8M7 #19 (postage problem, Figure 7.4) is an extended constructed-response item that is categorized as problem solving. It is described in the NAEP Questions Tool as "solve [a] problem using informal algebra." Student performance on that item was poor, with 11% of students presenting an extended response and 4% presenting a satisfactory response. Thirteen percent of students not eligible for free lunch presented a correct response, compared with 5% of students eligible for free lunch. In terms of the remaining students, 7% presented a partial response, 20% gave a minimal response, 41% produced an incorrect response, 13% omitted the item, and 4% were deemed off task. In 2000, the item was answered correctly by 11% of students.

Figure 7.7 shows Item 2003-8M10 #13 (water loss and gain), a short constructed-response item that is categorized as conceptual. It is described as "solve [a] problem involving two linear relationships." Performance data on that item indicated that 19% of students presented a correct solution, 31% offered a partial response, 41% gave an incorrect response, 7% omitted the item, and 2% were off task. Twenty-two percent of males presented a correct solution, as compared with 16% of females. Twenty-three percent of white students and 29% of Asian/Pacific

Islander students presented a correct solution, as compared with 7% of black students. In 2000, the task was answered correctly by 19% of students.

Two large storage tanks, T and W, contain water. T starts losing water at the same time additional water starts flowing into W. The graph below shows the amount of water in each tank over a period of hours.

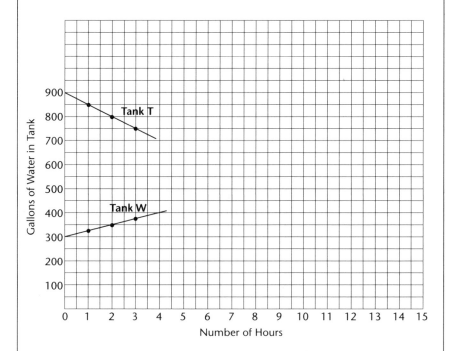

Assume that the rates of water loss and water gain continue as shown. At what number of hours will the amount of water in T be equal to the amount of water in W? Show or explain how you found your answer.

Figure 7.7. Example of a problem-solving item ("water loss and gain") (2003-8M10 #13).

Incorrect responses were given by the same percentage of students to both problems. However, a larger percentage of students gave a correct response to the second item, whereas a lower percentage omitted the task or were off task. Since both problems are released items, we know that both items involve linear processes in a context and a solution that involves only one variable. How do we account for the differential performance on the two items? One possible explanation is that the presence of the graph supports students' responses, offering them both a place to start and a way to check the validity of their answer. Alternatively, if extended response items are indeed more difficult, then the difference in difficulty here may be in part due to that aspect of the problem.

CALCULATOR USE AND ACHIEVEMENT

NAEP provides opportunities for examining relationships between contextual and instructional variables as identified by the student, teacher, and school questionnaires as independent variables and aggregated achievement on the Algebra and Functions strand as a dependent variable. A wealth of questions might be asked, for example, What are the trends in performance of those students who have had a course in algebra or an integrated course with an algebra strand? Unfortunately, such a question cannot be addressed without including an item on the student questionnaire that establishes the names of the courses that students have taken. Instead, since questions are asked about calculator use, one might want to ask how graphing calculator use at the 8th-grade level correlates with achievement. One important limitation to note is that questionnaire items have changed over time. As a result, the opportunity for trend analyses that involve background data is limited. To illustrate the potential of analyses that use student questionnaire and achievement data, in this section we focus on one trend relevant to school algebra: calculator use, more specifically, graphing calculator use.

A variety of questions are asked of students and teachers regarding their individual backgrounds and the practices in which they engage in classrooms. Among the questions in the 2003 administration were items regarding the extent to which calculators were used in classroom activity, homework assignments, and quizzes or examinations. Some items asked specifically about particular types of calculators (scientific, graphing, symbol manipulators), whereas others dealt with computing devices in general. Using the NAEP online Data Explorer, one can look at algebra scores in relation to responses to those questions. Although that level of analysis is rather perfunctory, it reveals a trend: 8th-grade students who responded that they used calculators on a regular basis scored higher on Algebra and Functions items than those who reported little use of calculators. That trend is by no means uniform, but in some instances, the gap between the two groups is noteworthy (as seen in Table 7.6).

In 2003, the sample size was large enough that gaps between groups were statistically significant even when they were much smaller than in Table 7.6 (see chapter 1). A rough conclusion from that quick data inspection is that students who use graphing calculators regularly for schoolwork score substantially better than those who do not. For many mathematics educators and teachers, that result is not surprising; the reform movement begun by the NCTM with the release of

Table 7.6

Average Grade 8 Algebra and Functions Scale Scores in Relation to Student-Reported Use of a Graphing Calculator

		Yes		No	
Year	N	Average scale score	Standard error	Average scale score	Standard error
2003	149,218	288	(0.5)	277	(0.3)
2000	15,798	287	(2.0)	273	(0.9)
1996	6,932	271	(3.1)	272	(1.0)

Note. The question was worded "Do you use a graphing calculator for your mathematics schoolwork?"

the first *Standards* document in 1989 advocated strongly for the use of technology. The rationale for that advocacy continues to be that such tools facilitate students' ability to make important connections between mathematical ideas, especially when calculations are sizeable or tedious enough to obscure such links. Since that time, many new technological advances have been made, making the technology more user-friendly and versatile. In addition, calculators—especially graphing calculators—have become a typical feature of the landscape in school mathematics, and the release of the more recent *Principles and Standards for School Mathematics* (NCTM, 2000) has strengthened the call for use of technology. Finally, a broad range of examples of effective teaching strategies employ calculators; these examples are arising in an ever-widening diversity of contexts. In short, on the one hand, the data above suggest that technology is having the effect on achievement for which many had hoped. On the other hand, the superficial nature of the data may conceal important information.

Arguably, the students who have access to sophisticated computational devices are in more affluent school districts and have access to more qualified teachers, in addition to other factors that have potential to skew the data. If that argument were so, then one would expect to see different results for students within different socioeconomic strata. Do all students benefit from increased technology use? Analyses to explore such questions are not possible with the online Data Explorer but were possible for the authors of this volume because they had access to the secure data set. To investigate the question, we divided the sample students into three groups on the basis of their eligibility for free or reduced-price lunch at school (the most commonly used measure of socioeconomic status from the NAEP questionnaire): not eligible, eligible for reduced-price lunch, and eligible for free lunch. We then ran a multiple regression analysis of achievement on the questionnaire responses for multiple items regarding calculators. The model examines the degree to which variables associated with calculator use (use calculator for mathematics, use scientific calculator, use graphing calculator, use symbol manipulator for mathematics, use calculator for classwork, use calculator for homework, and use calculator for tests) explain a substantial proportion of the variance in achievement. The model generated a statistically significant overall relationship between the responses to those items and achievement. Although some individual relationships between calculator use and achievement were not significant, others were significant and remarkable.

Among 8th graders across all SES strata, the average scale scores of students who responded affirmatively to the use of a graphing calculator was 6 to 11 points higher than those who responded negatively. Scientific calculator use was also positively correlated with achievement in that model, although its influence was smaller. All students who reported regular use of calculators for tests and quizzes were predicted by the model to score 6–9 points higher than those who did not.

In contrast, through all socioeconomic strata, student use of symbol manipulators (e.g., the Derive package installed on TI-89 calculators) was related to poorer performance on algebra items than by students who did not report using such tools. We hypothesize that teaching practices that help make the use of such tools effective are not yet widespread, and their use in such a vacuum may actually be detrimental to student learning. The same trend was present in the data for graphing calculators in the early and mid-1990s, although that trend has reversed in recent years, perhaps as graphing calculators have become ubiquitous and effective strategies for using them have become a greater part of mainstream school algebra instruction.

CONCLUSION

The results from the 2003 NAEP mathematics assessment reveal that achievement in the Algebra and Functions strand has increased more than in other mathematics strands, but important and continuing performance gaps were evident between racial and ethnic groups. In light of the gender differences in performance evident at Grade 4, the equal achievement of males and females at Grade 8 indicates the dissipation of gender differences in performance on algebra items as students get older. Not surprisingly, an analysis of results on items given at both grade levels reveals that performance of 8th graders was superior to that of 4th graders. Regardless of grade level, students performed significantly better on multiple-choice problems than on extended constructed-response items. In part that finding may be attributable to the relationship between problem structure and the nature of mathematical thinking required to solve problems. The extended constructed-response format allows more latitude for the construction of items that require students to draw on problem-solving or conceptual skills, both of which have higher cognitive demand than problems that draw on procedural understanding. Achievement on one pair of released items fell into a pattern that closely aligned with predictions based on the Nathan and Koedinger (2004) framework, with start-unknown verbal word-equation formats and start-unknown symbolic formats presenting the most challenge to students.

As the foregoing analyses suggest, for educators interested in understanding school algebra, the NAEP process has much potential, but it also has room for substantial growth. On the positive side, the concern for representativeness and the sample size make NAEP the only nationally representative, regularly repeated assessment of achievement on Algebra and Functions in the United States. In addition to achievement data, a wealth of information is attainable from the questionnaire data to support the exploration of a multitude of factors that may influence the development of algebraic understanding. The availability of the NAEP data in a user-friendly online format opens access to all parties interested in education and allows for wider dissemination of knowledge.

But NAEP cannot yet help us answer some of the important questions about school algebra in the United States raised at the beginning of our chapter. We hope that the continued evolution of the NAEP will allow that limitation to change. For example, we hope that the process of creating item descriptors will change. We suggest that this process use constructs (such as "start unknown" and "result unknown") from the mathematics education literature and that it connect items explicitly with the NAEP framework and NAEP's "mathematical ability" categories. Poor descriptors of the content of the items together with the secrecy surrounding the items allow little opportunity to interpret the meaning of many results. Further, we hope that the potential of the questionnaire items is realized and that care is taken to maintain a core of items that will provide information about trends in beliefs and classroom practices that potentially affect algebra performance. Finally, to gain further information on secondary algebra instruction, we hope that assessment of high school students continues more frequently in the future.

REFERENCES

Arbaugh, F., Brown, C., Lynch, K., & McGraw, R. (2004). Students' ability to construct responses (1992–2000): Findings from short and extended constructed-response items. In P. Kloosterman & F. K. Lester Jr. (Eds.), *Results and interpretations of the 1990–2000 mathematics assessments of the National Assessment of Educational Progress* (pp. 337–362). Reston, VA: National Council of Teachers of Mathematics.

Blume, G. W., & Heckman, D. S. (1997). Algebra and functions. In P. A. Kenney & E. A. Silver (Eds.), *Results from the sixth mathematics assessment of the National Assessment of Educational Progress* (pp. 225–277). Reston, VA: National Council of Teachers of Mathematics.

Blume, G. W., & Heckman, D. S. (2000). Algebra and functions. In E. A. Silver & P. A. Kenney (Eds.), *Results from the seventh mathematics assessment of the National Assessment of Educational Progress* (pp. 269–300). Reston, VA: National Council of Teachers of Mathematics.

Koedinger, K. R., & Nathan, M. J. (2004). The real story behind story problems: Effects of representations on quantitative reasoning. *Journal of the Learning Sciences, 13,* 129–164.

Mosteller, F., & Boruch, R. (2002). *Evidence matters: Randomized trials in education research.* Washington, DC: Brookings Institution Press.

National Assessment Governing Board (2002). *Mathematics framework for the 2003 National Assessment of Educational Progress.* Washington, DC: Author. Retrieved October 31, 2005, from www.nagb.org/pubs/math_framework/toc.html

National Council of Teachers of Mathematics (2000). *Principles and standards for school mathematics.* Reston, VA: Author.

Schwartz, J. L., & Viator, K. A. (Eds.). (1990). *The prices of secrecy: The social, intellectual, and psychological costs of current assessment practice.* Cambridge, MA: Educational Technology Center, Harvard University.

Usiskin, Z. (1987). Why elementary algebra can, should, and must be an eighth-grade course for average students. *Mathematics Teacher, 80,* 428–438.

Usiskin, Z. (1988). Conceptions of school algebra and uses of variables. In A. F. Coxford & A. P. Schulte (Eds.), *The ideas of algebra* (pp. 8–19). Reston, VA: National Council of Teachers of Mathematics.

Wilcox, S. K., & Lanier, P. E. (Eds.). (2000). *Using assessment to reshape mathematics teaching: A casebook for teachers and teacher educators, curriculum and staff development specialists.* Mahwah, NJ: Erlbaum.

## 8

Teachers, the School Environment, and Students: Influences on Students' Opportunities to Learn Mathematics in Grades 4 and 8

Margaret Schwan Smith, Fran Arbaugh, and Cos Fi

A CCORDING to the National Council of Teachers of Mathematics (NCTM, 2000), all students should have access to high-quality instructional programs in mathematics and to learning opportunities that challenge them at an appropriate level. Such opportunities are shaped in large measure by teachers who make decisions about what students need to learn and the optimal way of supporting student learning, by the nature and organization of the school environment, and by students' motivations and beliefs. "Achieving equity [in mathematics education] requires a significant allocation of human and material resources in schools and classrooms" (NCTM, 2000, p. 14).

In this chapter we present a portrait of United States teachers, the schools in which they work, and the students who attend them. We also identify, to the extent possible, teacher, school, and student characteristics and practices that appear to be connected with differential levels of student performance. The portrait is based on responses to a set of questionnaires that were completed by teachers, principals, and students during the 2003 NAEP administration. The chapter is organized into three parts that correspond to each of the questionnaires: Our Nation's Teachers, School Environment, and Our Nation's Students.

OUR NATION'S TEACHERS

In this section, we offer insight into the experiences, education, and instructional practices that characterize our nation's teachers, drawing on data from

Highlights

- More that 50% of students at Grades 4 and 8 had teachers with 10 or more years of teaching experience, and less than 25% of students at both grade levels had teachers with less than 5 years of experience.

- Years of teaching experience appeared to be linked with student performance at Grades 4 and 8. In general, students who had teachers with more experience had significantly higher scale scores than students with less experienced teachers.

- Teachers' undergraduate major appeared to be linked with student performance at Grade 8 but not at Grade 4. Specifically, Grade 8 students whose teachers had undergraduate degrees in mathematics or mathematics education had significantly higher average scale scores than students who had teachers with degrees in other disciplines.

- Teachers at Grade 4 participated in (or led) few mathematics-related professional development opportunities during a 2-year period. Teachers at Grade 8 participated in a wider range of professional development activities and in greater numbers than their Grade 4 counterparts.

- At Grade 4, about 80% of students had teachers who used multiple-choice tests for assessment purposes no more than twice a month. Students who completed multiple-choice tests less often had significantly higher scale scores than students who completed such tests on a more frequent basis.

- More than 40% of students at Grade 4 received less than 3 hours of mathematics instruction a week. Students with 3 or more hours of mathematics instruction had significantly higher average scale scores than students who received less instruction.

- A large percentage of students at Grades 4 and 8 (45% and 35%, respectively) responded that they see mathematics as mostly memorizing facts.

the teacher background questionnaire. The teacher background questionnaire was administered to teachers at Grades 4 and 8 who had one or more students participating in the 2003 NAEP. No teacher questionnaire data are available for Grade 12 because no NAEP assessment was conducted at that grade in 2003. The data are reported in terms of the percentage of students who have teachers who fall into a particular category. That wording is necessary because NAEP data are based on representative samples of *students,* not teachers.

In previous analyses of NAEP teacher questionnaire data (Grouws & Smith, 2000; Grouws, Smith, & Sztajn, 2004), we made an effort to compare results of previous NAEP questionnaire analyses to observe patterns of change over time. Such comparisons were all but impossible in 2003 because the questionnaire was changed substantially that year. Questions that had appeared previously were eliminated, answer choices were modified, and new questions were added.

Experience and Education of Grade 4 and Grade 8 Teachers

What teachers know has a substantial impact on what students learn. In a meta-analysis of studies on the effect of school resources on students' achievement, Greenwald, Hedges, and Laine (1996) found a strong relationship between teacher-quality variables (e.g., teacher education and experience) and student achievement. In this section we report on six teacher variables: years of teaching experience, race or ethnicity, certification, academic preparation, professional development, and leadership responsibilities.

Years of Teaching Experience

In the NAEP 2003 questionnaire, teachers were asked to indicate the number of years they had taught in elementary or secondary schools, including part-time assignments. As shown in Table 8.1, about 45% of students at Grades 4 and 8 had teachers with less than 10 years of experience. By contrast, nearly 30% had teachers with 20 years or more experience. Significant differences were evident in the percentage of students with teachers at varying levels of experience on the basis of the school location (i.e., central city, urban fringe/large town, rural/small town). Specifically, rural and small town students were more apt than central city and urban fringe students to have teachers with 10 or more years of experience.

The data in Table 8.1 also show that the greater the number of years of teaching, the higher the average scale scores. Eighth graders who had teachers with 20 or more years of experience had higher average scale scores than students with less experienced teachers. However, at Grade 4, no significant difference existed in the average scale scores of students whose teachers had 10–19 years of experience and those whose teachers had 20 years or more.

Table 8.1
Student Scores and Their Teachers' Years of Experience

Years of Teaching	Grade 4		Grade 8	
	Percentage of students	Average scale score	Percentage of students	Average scale score
0–4	23	232	22	274
5–9	22	235*	22	278*
10–19	26	237*#	26	280*#
20+	29	237*#	29	284*#^

Note. Column percentages may not add to 100, because of rounding.

* Indicates that the value is significantly higher than the value for 0–4 years.

# Indicates that the value is significantly higher than the value for 5–9 years.

^ Indicates that the value is significantly higher than the value for 10–19 years.

The data in Table 8.1 relate to years of teaching experience, not specifically to experience in teaching *mathematics*. Unlike in previous administrations of the NAEP questionnaire, teachers at Grade 4 were not asked to report the number of years they had taught mathematics. The number of years of teaching mathematics may be less than the number of years of overall teaching, since some elementary teachers handle a narrower range of subjects. At Grade 8, however, teachers were asked to indicate the number of years they had taught mathematics in Grades 6 through 12, in addition to the total years of teaching.

The data in Table 8.2 show that the relationship between years of teaching mathematics and student performance is the same as that between teaching in general and student performance—teachers with many years of mathematics teaching experience have students who perform higher than teachers with only a few years of mathematics teaching experience. Some of the differences between the percentages in Tables 8.1 and 8.2 are not easy to explain, for example, how 28% of students have teachers with 0–4 years of mathematics teaching experience but only 22% of students have teachers with 0–4 years of teaching experience. The percentage of students who have teachers with 4 years or less of mathematics teaching experience should be less than or equal to the percentage of students who have teachers with 4 years or less of teaching experience. One explanation is that some teachers did not include middle school teaching in their response to the general question regarding teaching experience, because the question specifies "as an elementary or secondary teacher," but did include middle school in their response to the second question, because 6–12 was given as the grade span. As noted in the analysis of NAEP data from 1992 (Lindquist, 1997), 1996 (Grouws & Smith, 2000), and 2000 (Grouws, Smith, & Sztajn, 2004), the relationship between student performance and years of teaching experience may, in part, be accounted for by the fact that more experienced teachers are often assigned the better students, whereas new teachers are often assigned classes designed for low-achieving students.

Table 8.2
Grade 8 Students' Scores and Teachers' Years of Teaching Mathematics

Years of Teaching	Percentage of Students	Average Scale Score
0–4	28	273
5–9	24	278*
10–19	26	282*#
20+	22	285*#^

* Indicates that the value is significantly higher than the value for 0–4 years.

\# Indicates that the value is significantly higher than the value for 5–9 years.

^ Indicates that the value is significantly higher than the value for 10–19 years.

Race/Ethnicity

The NAEP questionnaire asked teachers to report on their race/ethnicity. Although teachers were asked to indicate which option "best describes you," they were able to select more than one category for race/ethnicity (e.g., white, black, Asian) and to identify one or more categories to describe their Hispanic origins (e.g., Mexican or Mexican American, Puerto Rican or Puerto Rican American, Cuban or Cuban American). Hence the categories, unlike in previous years, are not mutually exclusive.

As shown in Table 8.3, about 85% of students at both Grades 4 and 8 were taught by white teachers. Those data make salient the lack of diversity in our nation's teachers and the fact that the majority of all students, regardless of race or ethnicity, are taught by white teachers. Specifically, as shown in Table 8.4, whereas more than 90% of white students at Grades 4 and 8 have white teachers, only one-third of black students are taught by black teachers and less than 25% of Hispanic students are taught by Hispanic teachers. Although teachers do not need to be of the same race or ethnicity as their students to understand them, understanding students' culture is an important characteristic of effective teaching (Ladson-Billings, 1994). The data suggest the importance of providing teachers, especially white teachers, with opportunities to understand the cultures of all students.

Table 8.3
Teachers' Race/Ethnicity

Race/Ethnicity	Grade 4	Grade 8
White	86	85
Black	8	9
Hispanic or Latino	8	5
Asian	2	2
American Indian or Alaska Native	1	1
Native Hawaiian or other Pacific Islander	0	0

Note. Numbers are percentages of students who had teachers who fell into a particular category. Column percentages exceed 100 because the categories are not mutually exclusive.

Type of Teacher Certification

Teachers were asked to report on the type of certification they hold. At least 85% of students at Grades 4 and 8 have teachers who report holding a regular or standard state certificate or advanced professional certificate. Because most teachers attain a regular certificate after teaching a minimum number of years (e.g., 3–5), and most report teaching 5 years or more (see Table 8.1), the large percentage of teachers in this category is not surprising.

Table 8.4
Percentage of Students Who Have White, Black, and Hispanic Teachers

Students'	Teacher's Race/Ethnicity		
Ethnicity	White	Black	Hispanic
	Grade 4		
White	95	2	2
Black	62	32	4
Hispanic	78	7	24
	Grade 8		
White	93	3	2
Black	61	34	4
Hispanic	77	9	17

Note. Row percentages do not add up to 100, because only three racial/ethnic sub-groups are reported. The percentages for the column labeled Hispanic represent the sum of the percentages for each of the four Hispanic subgroups. Because a teacher could select more than one subgroup, the actual percentage of students who have teachers who are Hispanic may be less than the percentage that is reported.

The data in Table 8.5 show that type of certificate is related to student performance at both Grades 4 and 8. In general, students who had teachers who held regular or advanced certification had significantly higher average scale scores than students who had teachers with probationary (the initial certificate issued after satisfying all requirements except the completion of the probationary period), provisional (given to those who are still participating in alternative certification programs), temporary (requires additional college coursework or student teaching), or emergency (must complete a regular certification program to continue teaching) certification. Disaggregating data by school location (central city, urban fringe/large town, rural/small town) reveals a relationship between school location and the likelihood that teachers will have regular certification. Specifically, students in central city schools are less likely than those in urban fringe and rural areas to have teachers with regular certification. Furthermore, students in urban fringe areas are less likely than those in rural areas to have teachers with this level of qualification.

Students at Grades 4 and 8 whose teachers reported that they had no teaching certification had higher average scale scores than those who had teachers with temporary or emergency certification. In addition, Grade 8 students who had teachers with no certification had average scale scores equal to those of students who had teachers with regular certification. Disaggregating the data by school type (public, Catholic, other nonpublic) provides a possible explanation for this phenomenon. The percentage of Catholic and nonpublic school students at both

Table 8.5
Teachers' Certification

Certification Type	Grade 4		Grade 8	
	Percentage of students	Average scale score	Percentage of students	Average scale score
Regular or advanced	88	236*#+	85	281*#
Probationary	4	234*	4	276*^
Provisional	4	231*	4	273*
Temporary	1	219	2	264
Emergency or waiver	1	221	2	257
None	2	231*	3	280*^

Note. Column percentages may not add to 100, because of rounding.

* Indicates that the value is significantly higher than the value for temporary or emergency.

# Indicates that the value is significantly higher than the value for probationary and provisional.

^ Indicates that the value is significantly higher than the value for provisional.

+ Indicates that the value is significantly higher than the value for none.

Grades 4 and 8 who had teachers with no certification is significantly greater that the percentage of public school students who had uncertified teachers. This outcome is not surprising given the fact that most nonpublic schools do not require certification to teach, yet students in those schools generally outperform students in urban schools.

Since 1995, teachers who have a baccalaureate degree and have taught for a minimum of 3 years have also been able to apply for certification from the National Board for Professional Teaching Standards (NBPTS), a nonprofit, nonpartisan organization created to "advance the quality of teaching and learning by maintaining high and rigorous standards for what accomplished teachers should know and be able to do" (www.nbpts.org). As of November 2004, a total of 40,200 teachers had been certified nationwide.

Teachers completing the NAEP questionnaire in 2003 were, for the first time, asked whether they were working toward or had received National Board Certification (NBC). As shown in Table 8.6, only about 10% of students at Grades 4 and 8 had teachers who reported that either they had received NBC or they were working toward it. Although NBPTS is grounded in the belief that quality teachers are necessary for student learning, no positive relationship appears to exist between NBC and student performance. In fact, the average scale scores for students at both Grades 4 and 8 who had teachers who were working toward NBC were significantly lower than the average scale scores of students with teachers in each of the other groups. In addition, students who had teachers who were not familiar with NBC had average scale scores that were equal to (Grade 8) or significantly greater than (Grade 4) the average scale scores of students who had teachers who received NBC.

Table 8.6
Teachers' Reports on National Board Certification (NBC)

Have Received NBC		Currently Working Toward NBC		Do Not Have NBC/Not Working Toward NBC		Not Familiar With NBC	
Percentage of students	Average scale score	Percentage of students	Average scale score	Percentage of students	Average scale score	Percentage of students	Average scale score
Grade 4							
6	234*	4	228	67	235*	23	237*^
Grade 8							
4	282*	4	268	64	280*	27	280*

* Indicates that the value is significantly higher than the value for "currently working on NBC."

^ Indicates that the value is significantly higher than the value for "have received NBC."

An important point to note, however, is that NAEP data provide no information about the *area* in which a teacher has received or is seeking NBC. Twenty-four different certificates are available, including generalist certificates (e.g., early or middle childhood generalist) and specialist certificates (e.g., early adolescence or adolescence and young adulthood mathematics). Additional research is needed to determine whether teachers who have NBC in mathematics produce higher average scale scores than teachers without NBC or with NBC in an area other than mathematics.

Focus of Academic Preparation

In the NAEP 2003 questionnaire, teachers were given a list of subjects and asked to indicate whether they had a major or minor (or special emphasis) in each area at the undergraduate or graduate level. Data on a subset of relevant undergraduate majors are reported in Table 8.7. Because teachers can major in more than one field, the data do not represent mutually exclusive categories.

Three-fourths of students at Grades 4 and 8 had teachers with a major or minor in education. The existence of a link between student performance and having a major or minor in education at both grade levels is interesting to note. The average scale scores for students at Grades 4 and 8 who had teachers with a major or minor in education were significantly higher than the average scale scores for students who had teachers who majored or minored in some other field.

Having a teacher with an undergraduate major in mathematics or mathematics education appears to be positively correlated with student performance at Grade 8 but not at Grade 4. As shown in Table 8.7, Grade 8 students whose teachers majored in mathematics or mathematics education had significantly higher average scale scores than those whose teachers pursued degrees in other fields. Because teachers could major in both mathematics and mathematics education, some subset of the mathematics majors may also have majored in mathematics education; therefore, the same teachers and their students may have been counted in both subgroups. By contrast, 4th graders who had teachers with a minor in mathematics or no mathematics specialty had significantly higher average scale scores than students whose teachers held degrees in mathematics. No differences occurred in average scale scores between students with teachers who did or did not major or minor in mathematics education.

Table 8.7
Teachers' Reports on Their Undergraduate Major

Undergraduate major	Education		Mathematics		Mathematics Education	
	Percentage of students	Average scale score	Percentage of students	Average scale score	Percentage of students	Average scale score
Grade 4						
Major	67	236*	2	230	2	231
Minor	11	235*	8	234^	8	235
No	23	232	90	236^	90	236
Grade 8						
Major	54	280*	30	284*!	26	284*!
Minor	20	282*^	35	281*	28	281*
No	27	276	35	274	46	275

* Indicates that the value is significantly higher than for "no major."

^ Indicates that the value is significantly higher than for "major."

! Indicates that the value is significantly higher than for "minor."

A similar pattern emerges from the examination of teachers' graduate majors and minors as shown in Table 8.8. Eighth graders who had teachers with a graduate major or minor in mathematics education had significantly higher scale scores than students whose teachers did not. Fourth graders who had teachers with a graduate major in mathematics or mathematics education had significantly lower average scale scores than those whose teachers did not.

The data on teachers' academic preparation highlight the importance of Grade 8 teachers' having at least an undergraduate minor in mathematics or

Table 8.8
Teachers' Reports on Their Graduate Major

Graduate Major	Education		Mathematics		Mathematics Education	
	Percentage of students	Average scale score	Percentage of students	Average scale score	Percentage of students	Average scale score
Grade 4						
Major	43	235	1	223	2	228
Minor	9	234	4	232^	7	235^
No	48	235	96	236^!	92	236^
Grade 8						
Major	43	280*	8	280	16	283*
Minor	12	279	15	281*	15	281*
No	45	278	76	279	69	278

* Indicates that the value is significantly higher than that for "no major."

^ Indicates that the value is significantly higher than that for "major."

! Indicates that the value is significantly higher than that for "minor."

mathematics education. What remains unknown from those data are the number of mathematics content and pedagogy courses actually taken by teachers, as well as the focus of the courses. Such information is crucial in determining the types of experiences that lead to improved student learning outcomes.

Professional Development Activities

The professional development of teachers is seen as a crucial ingredient in improving our nation's schools (Darling-Hammond & Sykes, 1999). The perceived importance of professional development is directly related to the ambitious nature of reform goals, state standards, and federal mandates that have been put into place over the past decade.

Teachers responding to the NAEP questionnaire in 2003 were asked about their involvement (as participants or leaders) in the previous 2 years in a wide range of professional development activities related to the teaching of mathematics. A striking feature of those data, shown in Table 8.9, is the relatively small percentage of students at Grade 4 with teachers who indicated that they participated in *any* mathematics-related professional development during the previous 2 years. Less than one third of fourth-grade students had teachers who were involved in any professional development activities outside of workshops, training sessions, or independent reading, and less than 60% of 4th graders had teachers who reported participating in those forms of professional development.

Table 8.9
Teachers' Professional Development Activities Related to Teaching Mathematics

Activity	Grade 4				Grade 8			
	Yes		No Response		Yes		No Response	
	Percentage of students	Average scale score	Percentage of students	Average scale score	Percentage of students	Average scale score	Percentage of students	Average scale score
College course after first certification	16	236	84	235	36	280	64	279
Workshop or training session	59	236*	41	234	89	280*	11	277
Conference or professional association meeting	28	237*	72	235	66	281*	34	276
Observational visit to another school	15	234	85	235	28	278	72	280
Mentoring and/or peer observation and coaching	26	236	74	235	47	280	53	279
Committee on curriculum, instruction, or assessment	33	236*	67	235	63	281*	37	276
Discussion or study group	24	235	76	235	43	278	57	280^
Teacher collaborative or network	11	234	89	235	22	278	78	280^
Individual or collaborative research	17	235	83	235	32	279	68	279
Independent reading	40	236*	60	235	69	280	31	278
Co-teaching/team teaching	27	236*	73	235	42	279	58	279
Consultation with math specialist	27	235	73	235	46	277	54	281^

Note. At Grade 4, teachers were given three choices for each type of activity (yes, related to language arts; yes, related to mathematics; or no) and were instructed to select one or more. No response indicates that the response "yes, related to mathematics" was not selected.

* Indicates that the value for "yes" is significantly higher than that for "no."

^ Indicates that the value for "no" is significantly higher than that for "yes."

Although workshops have long been the staple of professional development, in the past several years increased emphasis has been placed on alternative forms of professional development, such as professional networks, coaching and mentoring, and action research. As noted by Loucks-Horsely and her colleagues, the combination of activities in which teachers engage enriches their professional learning (Loucks-Horsely, Hewson, Love & Stiles 1998; Loucks-Horsley, Love, Stiles, Mundry & Hewson, 2003). The NAEP data suggest that the majority of Grade 4 teachers participated in a narrow range of activities, if at all. The data do not clarify whether teachers had opportunities to participate in activities and elected not to do so or whether opportunities were limited or nonexistent.

Eighth-grade teachers reported greater participation than their 4th-grade colleagues in every type of professional development activity. That finding is not surprising, because many 8th-grade teachers are content specialists and therefore can focus on professional development in a single content area. In particular, almost 90% of 8th graders had teachers who reported being involved in workshops or training sessions, and more than 60% of students had teachers who reported they had attended conferences or professional meetings; served on committees focused on curriculum, instruction, or assessment; or engaged in independent reading on a regular basis. Also interesting to note is the connection between professional development and student performance. As shown in Table 8.9, the average scale scores for 4th- and 8th-grade students with teachers who reported that they were involved in workshops or training sessions; conferences or professional association meetings; and committees on curriculum, instruction, or assessment were significantly greater that the average scale scores of students with teachers who did not participate in those activities. Furthermore, disaggregating the data by eligibility in the National School Lunch Program, an indicator of socioeconomic status (SES), reveals that the differences in average scale scores between students with teachers who were involved in professional development activities versus students with teachers who were not involved are not associated with SES. The data seem to suggest that teachers' involvement in those types of professional development activities has a positive impact on student performance that transcends SES. Not clear, however, is whether professional development activities attract teachers who are already effective or whether such activities facilitate the development of effective teachers. In the former instance, the nature of the professional development is less crucial, because the teachers are already effective.

For three activities at Grade 8, a negative relationship appears to exist between teachers' participation in professional development and student performance. Eighth-grade students with teachers who reported participating in discussion or study groups, teacher collaboratives or networks, or consultation with a mathematics specialist had significantly lower average scale scores than students whose teachers did not engage in those activities. Disaggregating those data by major subgroups (race/ethnicity and National School Lunch Program) revealed no significant differences between the performance of students with teachers who did or did not participate in teacher collaboratives or networks and discussion or study groups. However, the percentage of students eligible for the National School Lunch Program who had teachers who consulted with math specialists was significantly greater (and the scale scores significantly lower) than the percentage and average scale scores of students not eligible for the National School Lunch Program with teachers who consulted with math specialists.

Leadership Responsibilities

In 2003, 4th- and 8th-grade teachers completing the NAEP questionnaire were asked for the first time whether they had any special leadership responsibilities for mathematics education at their school, such as mentor teacher, lead teacher, resource specialist, department chair, or master teacher. As shown in Table 8.10, 19% of 4th graders and 38% of 8th graders had teachers who reported that they had special leadership responsibilities.

Table 8.10
Teachers' Reports on Special Leadership Responsibilities

Yes		No	
Percentage of students	Average scale score	Percentage of students	Average scale score
Grade 4			
19	236	81	235
Grade 8			
38	282*	62	277

* Indicates that the value is significantly higher than the value for no leadership responsibilities.

Although having a teacher with leadership responsibilities does not appear to be an advantage at Grade 4, the data suggest that it does at Grade 8. The average scale scores for 8th graders who had teachers who indicated that they had special leadership responsibilities were significantly higher than the average scale scores of students whose teachers did not. Disaggregating the data by achievement level reveals that those differences could be due to the fact that a significantly higher percentage of 8th-grade students scoring at the advanced level had teachers who reported having special leadership responsibilities.

Instructional Practices of Grade 4 Teachers

Teachers' instructional practices have an impact on students' opportunities to learn mathematics. The 2003 NAEP questionnaire results lend some insight into the instructional practices of Grade 4 teachers. Unlike on the questionnaires for

1992, 1996, and 2000, only one question on the 2003 questionnaire pertained to the instructional practices of Grade 8 teachers. Hence in this section we report on the instructional practices of 4th-grade teachers only. Specifically, we discuss the mathematical topics that the teachers emphasized, the assessment techniques that they employed, and the ways in which they implemented technology.

Attention to Mathematical Topics

Students' opportunity to engage in learning a broad range of mathematics is affected by teachers' choices of mathematical topics to emphasize. Over the past decade increased attention has been paid to broadening the content of the elementary curriculum to include topics beyond number, operations, and measurement. In the 2003 administration of the NAEP questionnaire, teachers were asked to indicate the amount of emphasis they gave to each of the five NAEP mathematical content strands: Number and Operations; Measurement; Geometry; Data Analysis, Statistics, and Probability; and Algebra and Functions.

As shown in Table 8.11, nearly 90% of 4th graders had teachers who reported placing a heavy emphasis on Number and Operations, more than three times the percentage of students with teachers who placed a heavy emphasis on any other topic. This heavy emphasis has remained virtually unchanged since 2000. A significant increase has occurred from 2000 to 2003 in the percentage of students with teachers who reported placing a heavy emphasis on Data Analysis, Statistics, and Probability as well as on Algebra and Functions. Possibly the inclusion of those topics in the pre-K–2 and 3–5 grades bands in the most recent NCTM *Standards* document (NCTM, 2000) as well as in state and local standards is having an impact on the content that is being taught.

Table 8.11
Grade 4 Teachers' Reported Attention to Mathematical Topics

Topic	Little/No		Moderate		Heavy	
	2000	2003	2000	2003	2000	2003
Numbers and Operations	<1	<1	13	12	87	88
Measurement	3	6*	72	70	25	25
Geometry	8	7	71	70	21	24
Data Analysis, Statistics, and Probability	20	13*	61	63	19	24*
Algebra and Functions	28	16*	55	58	17	26*

* Indicates significant differences from 2000.

Assessment

No Child Left Behind (NLCB) has focused considerable attention on standardized assessments in the United States to measure students' progress in mathematics, with NAEP playing a major role in accountability assessments. At the same time, increased emphasis has been placed on alternative forms of assessment for measuring student understanding of mathematics (NCTM, 2000). Some teachers may feel a tension between the perceived requirements of NCLB and recommendations from learned societies such as NCTM. As a result, the assessment practices of teachers may lend insights into how teachers are reacting to accountability pressures as well as to calls for using new forms of assessment.

Teachers were asked to report the frequency of their use of four types of assessments: multiple-choice tests, problem sets, short or long written responses, and individual or group projects or presentations. As shown in Table 8.12, 96% of students in Grade 4 had teachers who reported using problem sets for assessment purposes on a frequent basis, either once or twice a month or once or twice a week. In addition, 71% of 4th-grade students had teachers who reported that they used short or long written responses as a method of assessment. The data seem to indicate that students are being asked to provide answers for mathematical tasks rather than only to select answers from a set of predetermined options. We do not know from those data, however, whether teachers focus on correctness of answers, mathematical processes (e.g., communication, reasoning), completeness of assignment, or a combination of the three when they use problem sets and short written responses for assessment purposes.

Table 8.12
Grade 4 Teachers' Reports on the Frequency and Type of Assessments

Assessment Type	Never or Hardly Ever	Once or Twice a Year	Once or Twice a Month	Once or Twice a Week
Multiple-choice tests	19	14	48	19
Problem sets	2	2	29	67
Short or long written responses	16	14	39	32
Individual/group projects or presentations	37	32	25	6

The data in Table 8.12 show that teachers are also using multiple-choice tests for assessment purposes. As indicated in the table, almost 70% of students in Grade 4 had teachers who reported using multiple-choice tests at least once or twice a month. Of particular interest is the relationship between the frequency of administration of multiple-choice tests and student performance. Specifically, as shown in Table 8.13, students who had teachers who reported using multiple-choice tests never or on a very limited basis (e.g., hardly ever or once or twice a year) had significantly higher average scale scores than those whose teachers reported more frequent use. Furthermore, students who had teachers who reported that they used a multiple-choice test once or twice a month had significantly higher average scale scores than those whose teachers reported even more frequent use of this type of assessment. Those data raise an interesting question regarding the impact of the frequent use of multiple-choice items on student performance on such assessments as NAEP, which often involve a broader range of item types. For example, students who participated in the 2003 administration of the mathematics portion of NAEP had to respond not only to multiple-choice items but also to short constructed-response and extended constructed-response items. (See chapter 1 of this volume for a description of those item types.) Frequent use of multiple-choice tests as a means of assessing student performance in mathematics may result in students' having difficulty answering more open-ended questions on local, state, and national assessments.

Table 8.13
Grade 4 Teachers' Use of Multiple-Choice Assessments and Associated Scale Scores

Never or Hardly Ever		Once or Twice a Year		Once or Twice a Month		Once or Twice a Week	
Percentage	Scale score	Percentage	Scale score	Percentage	Scale score	Percentage	Scale score
19	238*	14	238*	48	236&	19	230

* Scale scores are significantly higher than that for "once or twice a month" and that for "once or twice a week."

& Scale score significantly higher than that for "once or twice a week."

Technology Use

Research indicates that students benefit from having access to technology when learning mathematics (e.g., Ellington, 2003; Heid, Blume, Hollebrands, & Piez, 2002). As calculators and computers become more affordable for schools, and as mathematics textbooks incorporate more technology-based lessons, teachers' use of such technologies is important to consider.

Computer use

Teachers chose among five options in reporting their primary use of computers for mathematics instruction. As shown in Table 8.14, 30% of 4th graders had teachers who reported that they do not use computers for mathematics instruction, and 39% had teachers who reported using computers for playing mathematical games. In addition, 23% of students had teachers who reported using computers for drill and practice. Fewer students had teachers who reported using computers to demonstrate new topics (2%) or for simulations and applications (6%).

Those data indicate that students who had teachers who reported using computers for demonstrating new topics, playing games, or for simulations and applications had significantly higher scale scores, on average, than those students whose teachers reported using computers for drill and practice or not using computers at all. However, a disaggregation of the data on the basis of eligibility in the National School Lunch Program (NSLP) reveals that students who were eligible for the NSLP and those who were not may benefit from different types of computer use. For example, as evidenced by significantly higher average scale scores, students not eligible for NSLP seem to have been advantaged by having opportunities to engage in computer applications and simulations, whereas students who were eligible for NSLP appear to have benefited from using computers to demonstrate new topics.

Table 8.14
Grade 4 Teachers' Reported Use of Computers in Instruction

NSLP Eligibility	Do Not Use Computers		Drill and Practice		Demo New Topics		Playing Math Learning Games		Simulations/ Applications	
	%	Average scale score	%	Average scale score	%	Average scale score	%	Average scale score	%	Average scale score
Overall	30	234	23	234	2	239*	39	236*	6	238*^
Eligible for the NSLP	29	221	23	222	2	226$	38	222	6	223
Not eligible for the NSLP	28	244	23	243	2	246	40	245#	6	249&

* Indicates significant difference from values for "do not use computers" and "drill and practice."

^ Indicates significant difference from value for "playing math games."

$ Indicates significant difference from value for "do not use computers."

& Indicates significant difference from values for "do not use computers," "drill and practice," and playing math games."

# Indicates significant difference from value for "drill and practice."

Calculator use

Teachers were asked four questions regarding their instructional practices related to calculator use. The questions and results are shown in Table 8.15. Whereas nearly 80% of Grade 4 students had access to calculators, less than 10% of students had teachers who permitted the use of calculators on tests or permitted unrestricted use of calculators in class. However, a relationship does appear to exist between access to calculators owned by the school and instruction in the use of calculators. Specifically, students with teachers who permitted access to school-owned calculators and who provided instruction in calculator use had significantly higher average scale scores than students whose teachers answered "no" to each of those questions.

Table 8.15
Grade 4 Teacher-Reported Practices With Calculator Use

Teacher Practice	Yes		No	
	%	Average scale score	%	Average scale score
Do you permit students in this class unrestricted use of calculators?	6	233*	94	235
Do you permit students in this class to use calculators for tests?	9	235	91	235
Do students in this class have access to calculators owned by the school?	79	236*	21	231
Do you provide instruction to students in this class in the use of calculators?	70	237*	30	232

* Indicates significant difference from those who responded "no."

Further investigation of the data indicates that the significant difference between average scale scores of students who had access to school-owned calculators and students who did not have access did not change when examined by racial or ethnic subgroups. The data appear to show that all students, regardless of race or ethnicity, had significantly higher average scale scores when the answer to the calculator-access question was yes rather than no. However, when considering NAEP achievement level, student scores at the advanced and proficient levels showed no difference between a yes or no answer to that question (the advanced average scale score was 291 for both answers; the proficient average scale score was 262 for both answers). The differences came for students who scored in the basic and below-basic achievement levels. Students at the basic level who attended schools where they had access to school-owned calculators had an average scale score of 233, which is significantly higher than the average scale score of students in the basic level who attended schools where they did not have access to school-owned calculators (232). A similar relationship occurs at the below-basic level, with students who had access to school-owned calculators having average scale scores that were significantly higher than the scores of students who did not (196 vs. 195).

SCHOOL ENVIRONMENT

Educators have long known that school environment affects students' opportunity to learn (Edmonds, 1979). The types of schools that 4th- and 8th graders attend, the number enrolled in those schools, and the ways in which those schools are organized vary widely across the United States. Additionally, the amount of instructional time dedicated to mathematics is a school-based decision that can affect students' opportunity to learn. In this section, we report on characteristics that define the instructional environment. Those results originate from questions asked on the school background questionnaire, which was completed by principals or heads of schools.

Type of School

Principals were asked to select, from a list of ten descriptors, all those that characterized the type of school attended by students who participated in the 2003 administration of NAEP. Those results for 4th and 8th grades are shown in Table 8.16. As would be expected, most students (87% of 4th graders and 84% of 8th graders) attended "regular" elementary, middle, or secondary schools. A much smaller percentage attended either independent private schools (1% of

Table 8.16
Principals' Reports on the Type of Schools

	Grade 4		Grade 8	
Type of School	Percentage of students	Average scale score	Percentage of students	Average scale score
1. Regular elementary, middle, or secondary	87	235	84	277
2. Regular school with a magnet program	4	231	4	264
3. Magnet school or a school with a special program emphasis	3	232	3	273
4. Primarily serves students with disabilities	1	229	1	265
5. Alternative	1	239	1	257
6. Private (independent)	1	249	2	303
7. Private (religiously affiliated)	8	243	7	289
8. Charter	1	228	1	271
9. Privately run public school	—	—	—	—
10. Other	3	233	3	275

4th graders, 2% of 8th graders) or religiously affiliated private schools (8% of 4th graders, 7% of 8th graders). Only 1% of 4th and 8th graders attended charter schools. These data give evidence that public schools in the U. S. continue to educate a large majority of students in Grades 4 and 8.

Although the average scale scores reported in Table 8.16 seem to suggest that students who attended independent private schools performed at a higher level than students who attended other types of schools, those data can be a bit deceiving. (See Table 8.17 for significant differences for data shown in Table 8.16.) For example, when considered on the basis of schools that were eligible for Title 1 funding, the average scale scores of 4th graders in independent private schools were not significantly different from average scale scores of 4th graders in regular elementary schools. However, when schools that were not eligible for Title 1 funding are considered, the average scale scores of 4th graders in independent private schools were significantly higher ($p < .01$) than the average scale scores of students who attended regular elementary schools. At the 8th-grade level, average scale scores of students who attended private schools were significantly higher than the average scale scores of students who attended regular middle or high schools, regardless of the school's eligibility for Title 1 funds.

Given the growth of charter schools over the past 5 years, perhaps the most interesting comparisons to examine here are the differences in average scale scores between students who attended regular elementary, middle, or high schools and those students who attended charter schools. At the 4th-grade level, and regardless of eligibility for Title 1 funding, students who attended regular elementary schools had significantly higher average scale scores than students who attended charter schools. At the 8th-grade level, no significant difference occurred between the average scale scores of students who attended regular schools and the average scale scores of students who attended charter schools. However, among students who were eligible for Title 1 funding, those attending regular schools had significantly higher average scores. No significant difference in average scale scores was found for students who were not eligible for Title 1 funding and attended regular or charter schools. Those results appear to suggest that eligibility for Title 1 funding was a greater predictor of achievement for 8th graders than enrollment in a regular or charter school.

Student Enrollment

Principals provided student enrollment data for total school population in response to an open-ended question. The data were then categorized and reported as falling into a range, as represented in Table 8.18 for schools that included 4th grade and in Table 8.19 for schools that included 8th grade.

The 4th-grade data indicate that students who attended smaller schools (1–299, 300–499, 500–699) had, on average, significantly higher scale scores than those students who attended larger schools (700+). However, when considering eligibility for the NSLP, the results show interesting patterns. The average scale

Table 8.17
Significant Difference Results for Data Shown in Table 8.16

Type of School	Students' Average Scale Score Significantly Higher Than Students Who Attended ...
	Grade 4
Regular	Charter ($p < .01$)
Private (independent)	Regular with magnet ($p < .05$)
	Magnet or school with a special program interest ($p < .05$)
	Primarily serves students with disabilities ($p < .05$)
	Charter ($p < .05$)
	Other ($p < .05$)
Private (religious)	Regular with magnet ($p < .05$)
	Magnet or school with a special program interest ($p < .05$)
	Primarily serves students with disabilities ($p < .05$)
	Charter ($p < .01$)
	Other ($p < .05$)
	Grade 8
Regular	Regular with magnet ($p < .05$)
	Primarily serves students with disabilities ($p < .05$)
	Alternative ($p < .01$)
Regular with magnet	Alternative ($p < .01$)
Magnet or school with a special program of interest	Primarily serves students with disabilities ($p < .05$)
	Alternative ($p < .01$)
	Charter ($p < .01$)
Private (independent)	Regular ($p < .01$)
	Regular with magnet ($p < .01$)
	Magnet ($p < .01$)
	Private (religious) ($p < .05$)
	Charter ($p < .01$)
	Other ($p < .01$)
Private (religious)	Regular ($p < .01$)
	Regular with magnet ($p < .01$)
	Magnet ($p < .01$)
	Charter ($p < .01$)
	Other ($p < .01$)
Other	Primarily serves students with disabilities ($p < .01$)
	Alternative ($p < .01$)

Table 8.18
Principals' Reports on the Current Enrollment of Schools Housing Grade 4

	1–299		300–499		500–699		700+	
NSLP Eligibility	%	Average scale score	%	Average scale score	%	Average scale score	%	Average scale score
Total students	15	236*	31	237*&	29	235*	25	233
Eligible	12	224#	29	223#	30	221	30	220
Not eligible	13	242	34	245$	30	245$	22	244$

* Indicates significant difference from value for 700+.

& Indicates significant difference from value for 500 to 699.

# Indicates significant difference from value for 500 to 699 and 700+.

$ Indicates significant difference from value for 1 to 299.

scores for students who were eligible for the NSLP appear to have followed the overall trend; that is, students who attended smaller schools had significantly higher average scale scores than those who attended larger schools. In contrast, for those students who were not eligible for the NSLP, students who attended the larger schools (300–499, 500–699, and 700+) had, on average, significantly higher scale scores than those students who attended schools with the smallest enrollment (1–299). The size of school may be less of a factor in the achievement of students from higher SES families (who are not eligible for the NSLP).

Similarly, the 8th-grade data, as shown in Table 8.19, indicate that students who attended schools with less than 1,000 students had, on average, significantly higher average scale scores than those students who attended schools with more than 1,000 students. An analysis of data based on eligibility for NSLP shows that school size had no impact on average scale scores of students who were not eligible for NSLP. By contrast, NSLP-eligible students who attended schools with an enrollment of 1,000+ had lower average scale scores than students attending schools with fewer than 600 students.

Table 8.19
Principals' Reports on the Current Enrollment of Schools Housing Grade 8

	1–399		400–599		600–799		800–999		1,000+	
NSLP Eligibility	%	Average scale score	%	Average scale score	%	Average scale score	%	Average scale score	%	Average scale score
Total	16	280^	18	279^	21	278^	18	278^	27	275
Eligible	15	263^$	17	260^	21	259	18	261	30	256
Not eligible	14	287	17	286	22	288	20	287	26	287

^ Indicates significant difference from value for 1,000+.

$ Indicates significant difference from value for 600 to 799.

An analysis of the data with a focus on location of school indicates a some-what different result. When examining only schools identified as "central city," 4th-grade students who attended schools with enrollments of 1 to 299 had significantly higher scale scores than students who attended schools with enrollments of 500 to 699 or 700 or more. In schools identified as being in "urban fringe/large town" areas, 4th-grade students who attended schools with enrollment of 300 to 499 had significantly higher average scale scores than students in those areas who attended schools with enrollments of 500 to 699 or of 700 or more. However, when considering data from 4th-grade students who attended schools in "rural/small town" areas, where 39% of students attended schools with enrollment of 500 or more, no significant differences between sizes of schools were indicated.

A similar pattern of significant differences occurs at the 8th-grade level. When considering students at schools identified as "central city," 8th-grade students who attended schools with enrollment of 1 to 399 had significantly higher average scale scores than students who attended schools with enrollments of 600 to 799 and of 1,000 or more. Furthermore, 8th-grade students who attended "central city" schools with enrollment of 400 to 599 had significantly higher scale scores when compared with students who attended schools with enrollment of 600 to 799 (although no significant difference existed between the average scale scores of students who attended schools with enrollments of 400 to 599 and of 1,000 or more). When considering schools located in areas classified as "urban fringe/large town," students attending schools with enrollments exceeding 1,000, had significantly lower scale scores than students who attended schools with smaller enrollments. No significant differences existed between average scale scores of students in schools with different enrollments in "rural/small town" areas. These results suggest that students attending schools in urban and fringe areas with enrollment exceeding 1000 may be better served by smaller schools. Small enrollment is one of three features of exemplary schools "that serve ordinary and extraordinary children well" that have been identified by research (Meier, 1998, p. 359).

How Students Are Organized for Instruction

Principals of schools that included Grade 4 were asked to choose among three options for reporting how their students were organized for classroom instruction (see Table 8.20). Those data suggest that most students in the 4th grade were either in "self-contained" classrooms (50%) (defined as "students stay with the same teacher for all academic subjects") or were "regrouped" for instruction (40%) (defined as "students stay with the same teacher for most subjects but may have another teacher for one or two subjects"), and a small percentage of students (10%) attended schools that were organized departmentally. Additionally, those 4th graders who attended schools that self-reported "regrouping" for instruction had significantly higher average scale scores than students in the other two groups. Those differences could not be attributed to achievement level or to race or ethnicity but were associated with eligibility for the NSLP. Those students who were not eligible for the NSLP and were regrouped for instruction had significantly higher scale scores than those students who were not eligible for NSLP and were in self-contained classrooms. Possibly the higher-performing ineligible students are regrouped for accelerated or gifted programs in mathematics. The data seem to suggest that regrouping for instruction is not equally beneficial for all students.

Table 8.20
Principals' Reports on How Grade 4 Students Are Organized for Instruction

	Self-Contained		Departmentalized		Regrouped	
NSLP Eligibility	%	Average scale score	%	Average scale score	%	Average scale score
Total	50	234	10	234	40	237*
Eligible	52	221	12	223	36	222
Not eligible	50	244	9	243	41	246&

* Indicates significant difference from value for "self-contained" and "departmentalized" in same row.

& Indicates significant difference from value for "self-contained" in same row.

At the 8th-grade level, principals were also asked to report on how their students were organized for instruction. As shown in Table 8.21, 90% of principals reported that their schools are departmentalized (defined as "students have different teachers for most or all academic subjects") for instruction at the 8th-grade level. Further, the data suggest that 8th-grade students who attended schools that are organized by department had average scale scores that were significantly different from the scale scores of students who attended schools where 8th grade is self-contained. Additionally, students who attended schools that reported semidepartmentalization (defined as "students are taught by different teachers in some of their subjects") had significantly higher average scale scores than those students who attended schools where they "stay with the same teacher all day." Those results held across all achievement levels; in other words,

Table 8.21
Principals' Reports on How Grade 8 Students Are Organized for Instruction

Self-Contained		Semidepartmentalized		Departmentalized	
%	Average scale score	%	Average scale score	%	Average scale score
1	268	9	277*	90	278*

* Indicates significant difference from value for "self-contained."

the significant differences held across students scoring at every achievement level: below basic, basic, proficient, and advanced. No significant differences were found across categories when the data were examined on the basis of race or ethnicity or of eligibility for the NSLP. Perhaps factors outside of the available NAEP data would help explain the differences in average scale scores as indicated in Table 8.21. One possible explanation is that teachers at Grade 8 who teach only mathematics (as is typical in a departmentalized school) are better prepared to do so than teachers who teach mathematics in schools that have self-contained 8th-grade classes.

Principals were also asked to report whether 4th and 8th graders in their schools were typically assigned to classes on the basis of ability or achievement levels. Table 8.22 shows the 4th-grade results; Table 8.23 shows the 8th-grade results.

Table 8.22

Principals' Reports on Whether Grade 4 Students Are Typically Assigned to Classes by Ability and/or Achievement

Yes, by Math Ability		Yes, by Reading Ability		Yes, by General Ability		No	
%	Average scale score	%	Average scale score	%	Average scale score	%	Average scale score
2	245*	4	227	7	231$^{&}$	87	236$^{\$}$

* Indicates significant difference from values for "yes, by reading ability," "yes, by general ability," and "no."

$^{&}$ Indicates significant difference from value for "yes, by reading ability."

$^{\$}$ Indicates significant difference from values for "yes, by reading ability" and "yes, by general ability."

The data show that 87% of 4th graders attended schools where they were not typically assigned to classes by ability or achievement. However, those results also indicate that students who did attend schools where they were assigned to classes by mathematics ability had significantly higher average scale scores than students who were assigned to classes by reading ability, by general ability, or not at all. Those significant differences held when the analysis focused on public

Table 8.23

Principals' Reports on Whether Grade 8 Students Are Assigned to Mathematics Classes by Ability

Yes		No	
%	Average scale score	%	Average scale score
73	280*	27	271

* Indicates significant difference from value for "no."

and private schools and when student eligibility for the NSLP was considered. In other words, assignment to classes by mathematics ability appears to affect performance on NAEP regardless of type of school or SES. However, when considered by race or ethnicity, only white and black students appear to benefit from being assigned to classes on the basis of ability. For Hispanics, Asians/Pacific Islanders, and American Indians, no significant differences in average scale scores existed between students assigned to classes by mathematics ability and those who were not. Clearly, those results show that ability grouping does not benefit all students.

At the 8th-grade level, the data indicate that a majority of students (73%) attended schools where they were assigned to mathematics classes by ability. The results further indicate that those students who attended schools where they were assigned to mathematics classes by ability had significantly higher average scale scores than those students who attended schools where they were not assigned to mathematics classes by ability. The significant differences hold for students attending public and nonpublic schools, as well as for students attending central city schools, suburban and large-town schools, and rural schools. When the race and ethnicity data are considered, average scale scores were *not* significantly different between Hispanic students who were grouped by mathematics ability for instruction and those who were not. In all other subcategories based on race or ethnicity (white, black, Asian/Pacific Islander, and American Indian), students who attended schools where they were assigned to mathematics classes on the basis of ability had significantly higher scale scores than students who were not.

Instructional Time in Mathematics

Principals were asked how much time each week a typical student in 4th (or 8th) grade received instruction in mathematics. The results are shown in Table 8.24.

A not particularly surprising outcome is that at the 4th-grade level, students who received 3 or more hours of mathematics instruction a week had, on average, significantly higher scale scores than students who had less instructional time each week. Of somewhat more concern is the fact that 41% of the 4th-grade students who participated in the 2003 administration of NAEP attended schools where they received less than 3 hours of mathematics instruction a week. This lack of time dedicated to mathematics at the 4th-grade level appears to have had the most effect on those students who scored at the basic and below-basic NAEP achievement levels. Specifically, students at those levels who attended schools where they received 3 hours or more of mathematics instruction had significantly higher average scale scores than their peers who attended schools where the principals indicated they received "at least 1 hour" of mathematics instruction a week.

At the 8th-grade level, the percentages appear to be of less concern. However, 12% of the 8th-grade students who participated in the 2003 administration of

Table 8.24
Principals' Reports on the Amount of Instructional Time Devoted to Mathematics Each Week

	Less Than 1 Hour		At Least 1 Hour		At Least 2 Hours		3 Hours or More
%	Average scale score	%	Average scale score	%	Average scale score	%	Average scale score
				Grade 4			
3	232	36	232	3	232	59	237*
				Grade 8			
5	272^	5	267	2	277^	88	278^

* Indicates significant difference from values for "less than 1 hour," "at least 1 hour," and "at least 2 hours."

^ Indicates significant difference from value for "at least 1 hour."

NAEP attended schools where they received weekly mathematics instruction of less than 3 hours, which converts to less than 36 minutes per day. A comparison of those findings with the results from the TIMSS video study (National Center for Education Statistics, 2003) produces interesting observations. When the TIMSS researchers examined the amount of time each day that students in different countries received instruction in mathematics, they found that the median amount of time per day across countries was 36 to 50 minutes. The United States reported an average of 46 minutes a day of mathematics instruction for 8th graders. The six countries that outperformed the United States did not necessarily have mathematics classes that were longer than the U.S. reported median. The data suggest that although time matters, at Grade 8 the nature of instruction—what students get a chance to do during the instructional time—is an essential factor in student achievement.

OUR NATION'S STUDENTS

The importance of the teacher in creating learning opportunities in the classroom cannot be overemphasized. However, examining students' perceptions of mathematics, including how they think of the subject itself and how they think of themselves as learners of mathematics, is important for our overall understanding of students' motivation to learn mathematics (Dweck, 1986). Furthermore, examining students' activities outside of school can help us identify those factors outside the teacher's or school's control that influence students' opportunities to learn mathematics.

The analysis presented in this section is based on students' responses to a subset of items that appeared on the NAEP 2003 student background questionnaire.

The questionnaire was completed by 190,147 Grade 4 students and 153,189 Grade 8 students.

Perceptions of Mathematics

Grade 4 students were given three statements (see Table 8.25) and asked to mark the answer that best describes themselves. Nearly 50% of 4th-grade students indicated that they like mathematics, 50% indicated that they are good at mathematics, and 57% indicated that they understand most of what goes on in mathematics class. The data suggest that holding a positive self-view of mathematical ability has a positive relationship with performance. Specifically, students who responded to the statements by indicating "this is a lot like me" had significantly higher average scale scores than students who did not identify as strongly with the statements. In addition, students who responded to the statement by indicating "this is a little like me" had significantly higher average scale scores than students who indicated that the statements were "not like me."

Table 8.25
Grade 4 Students' Reports on Views of Themselves as Mathematics Learners

	Not Like Me		A Little Like Me		A Lot Like Me	
Students' View	%	Average scale score	%	Average scale score	%	Average scale score
I like mathematics.	16	226	37	234^	47	239*
I am good at mathematics.	10	216	40	229^	50	244*
I understand most of what goes on in mathematics class.	8	215	35	227^	57	243*

* Indicates significant difference from value for "not like me" and for "a little like me."
^ Indicates significant difference from value for "not like me."

Students were also asked to respond to a series of statements about the nature of mathematics activity by marking the answer that conveyed how much they agreed with the statement. As shown in Table 8.26, 66% of 4th-grade students saw mathematics as useful in solving everyday problems, and 57% thought problems could be solved in more than one way. The shaded entries in the table represent a view of mathematics that is consistent with the perspective that mathematics is a problem-solving activity that can be approached in different ways and that all students can do it. Students who selected responses that aligned with that view of mathematics (i.e., disagree with the first two statements and agree with the last two statements in Table 8.26) had significantly higher average scale scores than students who responded in some other way.

Table 8.26
Grade 4 Students' Reports on Their Views of Mathematics

	Disagree		Not Sure		Agree	
Students' View	%	Average scale score	%	Average scale score	%	Average scale score
There is only one way to solve a mathematics problem.	57	243*	28	229^	15	216
Learning mathematics is mostly memorizing facts.	25	244*	31	234^	45	231
Mathematics is useful for solving everyday problems.	13	224	22	227^	66	240*
All students can do well in mathematics if they try.	5	220	12	231^	83	237*

* Indicates significantly higher than values for the other response options.
^ Indicates significantly different from values for the other response options.

Although Grade 8 students were asked to respond to the same set of statements, they were given five answer choices and asked to indicate how much they agreed with the statement. At least half of the 8th-grade students indicated that they agreed or strongly agreed with each of the first three statements in Table 8.27. That result suggests that students who have positive views of mathematics have significantly higher average scale scores. In fact, as the response becomes increasingly more positive, the average scale score also increases. For example, the average scale for students who strongly disagreed with the statement "I like math" was significantly lower than for any other response. However, as the response became more positive (disagree, undecided, agree, strongly agree), the average scale scores increased. All the differences are statistically significant.

The shaded entries in Table 8.27, which correspond to the last four statements, represent a view of mathematics that is consistent with the perspective that mathematics is a problem-solving activity that can be approached in different ways and that all students can do it. More than 70% of 8th-grade students indicated that they agreed with that perspective (disagreed that there is only one correct way to solve a mathematics problem and agreed that math is useful and that all students can learn it). Only 38% of 8th-grade students disagreed at some level with the statement that learning mathematics is mostly memorizing facts. A relationship also exists between perspective on mathematics and performance at Grade 8. Students who disagreed or strongly disagreed with statements that there is one way to solve a problem and that learning math is mostly memorizing had significantly higher scale scores than students who responded in other ways. In addition, students who agreed or strongly agreed that mathematics is useful for solving everyday problems had significantly higher scale scores than

Table 8.27
Grade 8 Students' Reports on Their Views of Mathematics and Themselves

Students' View	Strongly Disagree		Disagree		Undecided		Agree		Strongly Agree	
	%	Scale score	%	Scale score	%	Scale score	%	Scale score	%	Scale score
I like mathematics.	15	263	15	273	21	277	35	283	14	288
I am good at mathematics.	7	252	11	257	22	270	44	285	16	297
I understand most of what goes on in mathematics class.	4	254	7	260	15	265	54	280	20	294
There is only one correct way to solve a mathematics problem.	39	284	38	280	14	270	6	254	2	252
Learning mathematics is mostly memorizing facts.	12	285	26	288	28	278	27	270	8	263
Mathematics is useful for solving everyday problems.	5	264	7	273	15	279	40	281	32	278
All students can do well in mathematics if they try.	5	270	8	288	16	288	34	281	37	271

students who disagreed or were undecided. By contrast, however, no significant difference was observed in performance between students who strongly agreed or strongly disagreed that all students can do well in mathematics if they try.

Activities Outside of School

Students spend their time outside of school in a variety of activities that can affect their performance in school in both positive and negative ways. For example, Bransford, Brown, and Cocking (2000) reported that in a year, students spend more time watching TV than they spend in school. Here we examine three factors that appear to have an impact on student performance: time spent on homework, discussions with family members about schoolwork, and hours spent watching TV programs or videos.

Homework

The amount of time students spent on homework appears to be related to their performance. Specifically, as shown in Table 8.28, Grade 8 students who reported spending 30 or 45 minutes a day on mathematics homework had significantly higher average scale scores than students who reported spending less time (i.e., no time, 15 minutes) or more time (i.e., 1 hour, or more than 1 hour). The data also show that Grade 4 students who reported spending 15 or 30 minutes a day on mathematics homework had significantly higher average scale scores than students who reported that they spent no time or more than 30 minutes (i.e., 45 minutes, 1 hour, or more than 1 hour) a day on homework. In addition, students who spent 15 minutes a day on mathematics homework had significantly higher average scale scores than students who spent 30 minutes.

Table 8.28
Students' Reports on Minutes Spent on Mathematics Homework

	None	15	30	45	60	More Than 60
	Grade 4					
Percentage	5	45	24	11	9	5
Average scale score	228	239*^	236*	232	229	225
	Grade 8					
Percentage	8	34	33	14	7	4
Average scale score	266	278	281#	280#	277	274

Note. The table does not highlight all significant differences.

* Indicates significant difference from values for none, 45, 60, and more than 60.

^ Indicates significant difference from value for 30.

# Indicates significant difference from values for none, 15, 60, and more than 60.

The data could be interpreted as suggesting that 15 to 30 minutes a day of homework at Grade 4 and 30 to 45 minutes a day of homework at Grade 8 are optimal amounts in terms of student achievement. However, a possible explanation may be that many Grade 8 students who spend more than 45 minutes a day on homework are those who have mathematics deficiencies, forcing them to devote more time to their studies.

When the data are disaggregated by race or ethnicity, the same general pattern holds for white, black, and Hispanic students at Grade 4. At Grade 8, white students who spent 30 to 45 minutes had higher average scale scores than all other white students; black students who spent 15 to 45 minutes had higher average scale scores than all other black students; Hispanic students who spent any amount of time on homework outperformed Hispanic students who did not do homework at all. Those data also suggest that although homework appears to play an important role in student achievement, too much homework may have a negative impact. A recent report suggests that the way to improve students' learning outcomes is by focusing not on homework but on issues of instructional quality and equity of access to opportunities to learn (Baker & LeTendre, 2005). Whatever the positive influences turn out to be, the role of homework requires more study.

Discussions about schoolwork

Nearly 70% of 4th graders and 60% of 8th graders reported talking with family members about things they have studied in school at least once a week (see Table 8.29). Family support for schoolwork appears to be linked with student achievement. Students in Grades 4 and 8 who reported talking with someone in their family about things they have studied in school two or three times a

Table 8.29
Students' Reports on Time Spent Talking With Family About Things Studied in School

	Never or Hardly Ever	1–2 Times a Month	1 Time a Week	2–3 Times a Week	Every Day
			Grade 4		
Percentage	19	13	11	19	38
Average scale score	231	233	239^	244*	232
			Grade 8		
Percentage	23	19	18	21	20
Average scale score	270	275	282^	284*	278

Note. Not all significant differences are noted.

* Indicates significant difference from values for all other categories.

^ Indicates significant difference from values for all categories except 2–3 times a week.

week had significantly higher average scale scores than students who reported talking with a family member less frequently (never or hardly ever, once every few weeks, about once a week) or more frequently (every day). In addition, students who reported talking with a family member once a week had significantly higher average scale scores than students who reported talking with a family member less frequently or every day. Talking with a family member one to three times a week had a positive impact on student performance regardless of the school's location (i.e., central city, urban fringe/large town, rural/small town) or the student's race or ethnicity.

Television and video viewing

As shown in Table 8.30, about one-third of students at Grades 4 and 8 spent 4 or more hours watching TV or videos outside school each day. An interesting observation is the fact that the relationship between TV-and-video viewing and student performance appears to be different depending on grade level. Fourth graders who watched 2 to 3 hours of TV and videos a day had significantly higher scale scores than those who watched TV more or less frequently. No difference was seen in the performance of students who watched no TV and those who watched 6 or more hours. The same general patterns were found when the data were disaggregated by race or ethnicity and school location.

Eighth graders who watched 1 hour or less of TV and videos had significantly higher average scale scores than students who did so either more frequently or less frequently. Students who watched TV and videos 6 or more hours a day had

Table 8.30
Students' Reports on Time Spent Watching TV and Videos Outside of School per Day

	None	1 Hour or Less	2–3 Hours	4–5 Hours	6 Hours or More
			Grade 4		
Percentage	11	27	30	13	20
Average scale score	225	237	242*	239^	226
			Grade 8		
Percentage	4	23	41	17	14
Average scale score	273	285*	282!	275	260#

Note. To alleviate complexity in this table, some significant differences are not noted.

* Indicates significantly higher value than those for all other categories.

^ Indicates significantly higher value than those for all categories except 2–3 hours a night.

! Indicates significantly higher value than those for all categories except 1 hour or less.

# Indicates significantly lower value than those for all other categories.

significantly lower average scale scores than students who did so less frequently. No difference was noted in the average scale scores of students who watched no TV and videos and those who did so 4 to 5 hours a night.

Disaggregating data by school location indicates several differences. Grade 8 students who attended schools in the central city and watched TV and videos 1 hour or less a day had significantly higher average scale scores than students who did so more frequently or not at all. Students who attended schools in urban fringe and large towns or in rural and small towns and watched 1 to 3 hours of TV and videos a day had significantly higher scale scores than students who watched more or less. Moreover, although white students who watched TV and videos for 1 hour or less had higher average scale scores than all other students, black and Hispanic students who watched TV and videos for 2 to 5 hours a day had higher average scale scores than all other black and Hispanic students.

CONCLUSION

Our review of the background questionnaire data has led to some insight into our nations' classrooms—the teachers who determine what students will learn and how, the school contexts in which teachers and students work, and the students who participate in the instructional opportunities provided. In particular, we have described the qualifications and experiences of teachers at Grades 4 and 8, the instructional practices of teachers at Grade 4, the school environments (school type, enrollment, organization), and students' perceptions of mathematics and the activities in which they engage outside the school day. In addition, we have examined relationships between teacher, school, and student factors and student performance to generate hypotheses about the factors that appear to influence student performance.

Although many factors influence students' learning of mathematics, many argue that teachers—what they know and how they use their knowledge to design and enact instructional opportunities for students—are paramount. Several reports in the past decade make salient the vital role of teachers in improving student achievement (e.g., Glenn Commission, 2000) and creating better schools (e.g., National Commission on Teaching and America's Future, 1997). An important caveat to note, however, is that the insights garnered by the questionnaires are limited given their form and substance. For example, a recent study by Hill, Rowan, and Ball (2005) makes salient the relationship between teachers' mathematical knowledge for teaching (i.e., knowledge of how to represent quantities in different representational forms, how to construct an explanation of a mathematical idea that is accessible to students, the range of ways in which a particular problem can be solved) and student achievement in the early primary grades. Although NAEP questionnaire data provide some information regarding years of mathematics teaching experience (at Grade 8) and graduate and undergraduate major, the questionnaire lends no insights into teachers' knowledge of the content they teach and of the ways in which the content can best be understood by children.

Therefore, although the data reported herein present a general description of what goes on in U.S. classrooms and suggest some connections between teacher, school, and student characteristics and student performance, additional research is needed to better understand those relationships. In particular, we need to investigate linkages among teachers' characteristics, teaching practices, and differential levels of student performance. Such research will provide a basis for designing new professional learning opportunities that have the potential to enhance teachers' knowledge base for teaching and, ultimately, improve student learning outcomes.

REFERENCES

Baker, D. P., & LeTendre, G. K. (2005). *National differences, global similarities: World culture and the future of schooling.* Stanford, CA: Stanford University Press.

Bransford, J., Brown, A. L., & Cocking, R. R. (2000). *How people learn: Brain, mind, experience, and school.* Washington, DC: National Research Council.

Darling-Hammond, L., & Sykes, G. (Eds.). (1999). *Teaching as the learning profession: Handbook of policy and practice.* San Francisco: Jossey-Bass.

Dweck, C. S. (1986). Motivational processes affecting learning. *American Psychologist, 41,* 1040–1048.

Edmonds, R. (1979). Effective schools for the urban poor. *Educational Leadership, 37,* 15–24.

Ellington, A. J. (2003). A meta-analysis of the effects of calculators on students' achievement and attitude levels in precollege mathematics classes. *Journal for Research in Mathematics Education, 34,* 431–463.

Glenn Commission (National Commission on Mathematics and Science Teaching for the Twenty-first Century). (2000, September). *Before it's too late.* Washington, DC: U.S. Department of Education.

Greenwald, R., Hedges, L. V., & Laine, R. D. (1996). The effect of school resources on student achievement. *Review of Educational Research, 66,* 361–396.

Grouws, D. A., & Smith, M. S. (2000). NAEP findings on the preparation and practices of mathematics teachers. In E. A. Silver & P. A. Kenney (Eds.), *Results from the seventh mathematics assessment of the National Assessment of Educational Progress* (pp. 107–141). Reston, VA: National Council of Teachers of Mathematics.

Grouws, D. A., Smith, M. S., & Sztajn, P. (2004). The preparation and teaching practices of U.S. mathematics teachers: Grades 4 and 8. In P. Kloosterman & F. K. Lester, Jr. (Eds.), *Results and interpretations of the 1990–2000 mathematics assessments of the National Assessment of Educational Progress* (pp. 221–269). Reston, VA: National Council of Teachers of Mathematics.

Heid, M. K., Blume, G. W., Hollebrands, K., & Piez, C. (2002). Computer algebra systems in mathematics instruction: Implications from research. *Mathematics Teacher, 95,* 586–591.

Hill, H. C., Rowan, B., & Ball, D. L. (2005). Effects of teachers' mathematical knowledge for teaching on student achievement. *American Educational Research Journal, 42,* 371–406.

Ladson-Billings, G. (1994). *The dreamkeepers.* San Francisco: Jossey-Bass.

Lindquist, M. M. (1997). NAEP findings regarding the preparation and classroom practices of mathematics teachers. In P. A. Kenney & E. A. Silver (Eds.), *Results from the sixth mathematics assessment of the National Assessment of Educational Progress* (pp. 61–86). Reston, VA: National Council of Teachers of Mathematics.

Loucks-Horsley, S., Hewson, P. W., Love, N., & Stiles, K. E. (1998). *Designing professional development for teachers of science and mathematics.* Thousand Oaks, CA: Corwin Press.

Loucks-Horsley, S., Love, N., Stiles, K. E., Mundry, S., & Hewson, P. W. (2003). *Designing professional development for teachers of science and mathematics* (2nd ed.). Thousand Oaks, CA: Corwin Press.

Meier, D. (1998). Can the odds be changed? *Phi Delta Kappan, 79,* 358–362.

National Center for Education Statistics. (2003). *Teaching mathematics in seven countries: Results from the TIMSS 1999 video study.* Washington, DC: U.S. Department of Education.

National Commission on Teaching and America's Future. (1997). *Doing what matters most: Investing in quality teaching.* New York: Author.

National Council of Teachers of Mathematics. (2000). *Principles and standards for school mathematics.* Reston, VA: Author.

## 9

NAEP Findings Regarding Race and Ethnicity: Mathematics Achievement, Student Affect, and School-Home Experiences

Sarah Theule Lubienski and Michele D. Crockett

THIS chapter examines NAEP data on students' mathematics achievement, attitudes toward mathematics, beliefs about mathematics, and experiences in their schools and homes. The primary focus is on race- and ethnicity-related patterns, with some attention given to SES interactions with race and ethnicity in overall achievement. Interactions with gender are discussed in chapter 10.

The year 2003 was the first in which the NAEP national samples encompassed individual state samples, making possible an examination of data on the relatively small Asian/Pacific Islander (PI) and American Indian/Alaskan Native populations. In contrast with the NAEP samples of 5,000 to 15,000 students at each grade level of years past, the 2003 samples contained more than 150,000 students at each of 4th and 8th grades (see chapter 1).

Largely because of sample-size limitations, most prior large-scale studies of race/ethnicity-related differences in achievement have focused only on white, African-American, and (sometimes) Hispanic students. Because of the persistence and severity of disparities between white and African-American students, several publications focusing on that topic have been produced in the past decade. Perhaps the most famous is Jencks and Phillips's (1998) *Black-White Test Score Gap,* which, in response to Herrnstein and Murray's (1994) assertions about genetic bases of achievement disparities, argued that achievement gaps can be closed with proper attention to school (e.g., class size, teacher competency requirements) and family supports. Recent studies have also focused on the extent to which gaps are due to differential school opportunities versus differences in students' experiences outside of school (e.g., during preschool years and summers) (Alexander, Entwisle, & Olson, 2001; Farkas, 2003).

This chapter does not attempt to enter debates about the various reasons for underlying achievement gaps. Instead, it focuses on race/ethnicity–related similarities and differences in students' achievement, attitudes and beliefs, school experiences, and home environments. We give attention to all five racial/ethnic categories used by NAEP: white, black, Hispanic, American Indian/Alaskan Native, and Asian/PI.[1] Given that American Indian and Asian/PI students, until now, have been largely unexamined in studies of nationally representative data sets (e.g., Strutchens, Lubienski, McGraw, & Westbrook, 2004; Strutchens & Silver, 2000), this chapter lends new insights into the mathematics learning experiences of those groups.

We begin this chapter with a look at students' mathematics achievement, followed by examinations of NAEP survey data regarding students' attitudes and beliefs about mathematics. Finally, we discuss the school and home experiences that could contribute to the race/ethnicity patterns in students' achievement and affect.

Given 10 possible pairings of the 5 racial/ethnic groups, we sometimes had difficulty determining the best way to make comparisons. Although Asian/PI students were the highest-scoring subgroup, we did not want to downplay the advantages white students receive by shifting focus to Asian/PI students as the "advantaged group," particularly since the U.S. population of Asian/PI students is less than 5%, and schooling occurs in a larger social and political context in which white people tend to be privileged (McIntosh, 1990; Oliver & Shapiro, 1995; Zeus, 2004). In this chapter we report differences in a variety of ways, often letting the pattern of each particular disparity drive the types of comparisons made. However, we sometimes treat white students as the primary comparison group. While doing so, we are mindful of dangers inherent in this approach, such as conveying that white students are the "gold standard" that other groups should emulate. Moreover, highlighting disparities between groups tends to detract attention from both the many similarities across the groups as well as the great diversity within groups. We make comparisons with the hope that they will draw attention to inequities and illuminate their nature in potentially helpful ways. Still, we acknowledge the limitations of such an analysis to fully illuminate the complex factors underlying inequities within and beyond the mathematics class-

---

[1] Students are assigned to one of these categories on the basis of school records. This method is a departure from previous years, in which race/ethnicity was self-reported by students and then supplemented by school records when needed. Although not all scholars would agree that the NAEP *racial/ethnic* categories are the most appropriate, we use them to be consistent with the NAEP survey data. We use the term *racial/ethnic* to convey that some of the terminology refers to categories traditionally conceived of as "racial differences" (e.g., black versus Asian), whereas others refer to categories more related to ethnicity (e.g., "Hispanic" students would traditionally be considered to be of the same race as "white" students but having differences in ethnicity). We use the term *subgroup* in this chapter to indicate that we are discussing subgroups who differ in race/ethnicity, as defined by the NAEP variable. For the sake of brevity, we refer to the American Indian/Alaskan Native category as "American Indian."

Highlights

- White, black, and Hispanic students' mean scores were significantly higher in 2003 than in any assessment year since 1990. The 2003 scores for Asian/Pacific Islander and American Indian/Alaskan Native students also showed improvement over prior assessment years.

- White-black and white-Hispanic mathematics achievement gaps, although still large, significantly decreased between 2000 and 2003.

- Average scores for Asian/PI 4th and 8th graders were 3 points higher than those of white students. At Grade 4, white students scored 20 points higher than American Indian students, 21 points higher than Hispanic students, and 27 points higher than black students. At Grade 8 those differences were 25, 29, and 36 points, respectively. The white-black gaps were roughly a full standard deviation at each grade level.

- The mean scores of white and Asian/PI students eligible for free/reduced-price lunch were roughly equal to, or higher than, the scores of the black and Hispanic students not eligible for free/reduced lunch.

- Measurement and data analysis were the two strands exhibiting the largest disparities between white students' scores and those of their black, Hispanic, and American Indian peers.

- An analysis of individual item responses indicated some ways in which more black, Hispanic, and American Indian students approached nonroutine problems in a relatively rote, rather than conceptual, manner.

- Asian/PI students most consistently reported liking mathematics and feeling confident in their abilities. Hispanic and American Indian students expressed relatively little confidence in their mathematical abilities. White and Asian/PI students were less likely than others to agree that "Learning mathematics is mostly memorizing facts" and "There is only one way to solve a math problem."

- Asian/PI students were less likely than other subgroups to be classified as having a disability, whereas American Indian students were the most likely to be categorized in that way.

- White students were far more likely than others to have a teacher who shared their race/ethnicity.

- Black, Hispanic, and Asian/PI students were more likely than others to have a teacher with a limited or no teaching credential. Black and Hispanic students were the most likely to have inexperienced teachers. More white and Asian/PI 8th graders than others had a teacher who majored in mathematics.

- Black students reported watching more TV than other subgroups, with about one-third reporting 6 or more hours daily. However, black students were more likely than others to report regularly discussing their school studies with a family member.

rooms. Large-scale descriptive studies such as NAEP can identify patterns that must be further examined with qualitative and longitudinal studies designed to examine both the reasons for, and the effects of, those patterns.

STUDENT ACHIEVEMENT DATA

NAEP measures mathematics performance in a variety of ways, including overall scale scores ranging from 0 to 500, achievement levels (basic, proficient, and advanced), and scale scores within each of five mathematics strands: Number Sense, Properties, and Operations; Algebra and Functions, Geometry and Spatial Sense; Measurement; and Data Analysis, Statistics, and Probability. (See chapter 1 for additional information about NAEP scales and scoring.) In this section, we first discuss trends in 1990–2003 mathematics achievement, then present comparisons of the distribution of the 2003 achievement scores within each racial/ethnic subgroup. We consider interactions between race/ethnicity and SES in overall achievement before discussing subgroup differences in achievement levels. We then examine achievement gaps within the five mathematics strands before concluding this section with an examination of student performance on particular NAEP mathematics items.

Mathematics Achievement, 1990–2003

Despite the concerns about equity raised in this chapter, the good news in the 2003 data is important to note. Specifically, at Grades 4 and 8, white, black, and Hispanic students' average scores were significantly higher in 2003 than in any previous assessment year. Average scores for Asian/PI 4th and 8th graders were higher in 2003 than in the baseline year of 1990. American Indian students scored higher in 2003 than in 2000 at Grade 4, but the increase at Grade 8 was not statistically significant[2] (see Figures 9.1 and 9.2).

Between 1990 and 2000, black-white and Hispanic-white achievement disparities did not improve (Lubienski, 2002; Strutchens et. al., 2004). However, between 2000 and 2003, black 4th graders gained 13 points and Hispanic 4th graders gained 14 points, causing a statistically significant decrease in the score disparities between those groups and white 4th graders, whose mean increased by 9 points. Similarly, at Grade 8, black students gained an average of 8 points and Hispanic students gained 6 points, compared with white students' 4-point increase, causing a gap decrease between 2000 and 2003 (significant for black students but not for Hispanic students). Gaps between American Indian and white students decreased

---

[2] NCES has warned that American Indian sample sizes were not sufficient to create reliable estimates at Grades 4 and 8 in 1990 and 1992, nor at Grade 8 in 1996. Additionally, the Asian/PI samples were considered unreliable at Grade 4 in 2000 and at Grade 8 in 1996 (Braswell, Daane & Grigg, 2004). Figures 9.1 and 9.2 contain the data available through the online Data Explorer (see chapter 1), but here we do not report on comparisons and significance tests involving those limited samples.

at 4th grade (where American Indian students gained 15 points) but did not change significantly at 8th grade. (Despite the 6-point reduction, the 4th-grade decrease was not statistically significant owing to the large standard error connected with the small American Indian sample size in 2000). Gaps between white and Asian/ PI students were similar in 2000 and 2003 at Grade 8 but cannot be compared at Grade 4 because of limitations of the 2000 Asian/PI sample.

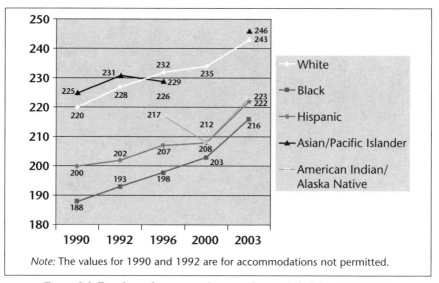

Figure 9.1. Fourth-grade mean scale scores by race/ethnicity, 1990–2003.

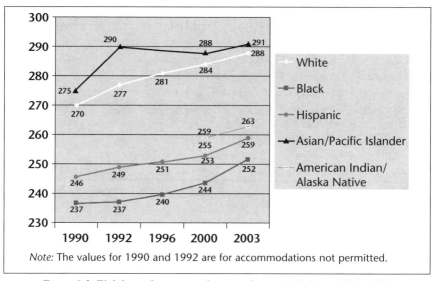

Figure 9.2. Eighth-grade mean scale scores by race/ethnicity, 1990–2003.

Despite decreases in gaps, severe race/ethnicity disparities remain. At both 4th and 8th grades, Asian/PI students had higher average scores than any other subgroup, scoring a statistically significant 3 points higher than white students. However, gaps between white and Asian/PI students pale in comparison to the gaps between those two subgroups and the other three subgroups. At Grade 4, white students scored 20 points higher than American Indian students, 21 points higher than Hispanic students, and 27 points higher than black students. At Grade 8 those differences were 25, 29, and 36 points, respectively.

One way to interpret the magnitude of those disparities is in terms of effect sizes. Standard deviations for overall achievement means were 28 at Grade 4 and 36 at Grade 8. Hence, black-white gaps were roughly a full standard deviation at each grade level, or an effect size of 1, which is considered a very large effect. In contrast, as reported in chapter 10, gender-related disparities tend to have an effect size of roughly 0.1, or one-tenth the size of black-white gaps.

Achievement by Student SES and Race/Ethnicity

One important issue to consider is the extent to which the lower scoring racial/ethnic subgroups are disproportionately of low socioeconomic status (SES), and the extent to which such disproportionate representation might account for race/ethnicity–related achievement gaps. One rough SES proxy often used in educational research is students' eligibility for free or reduced-price school lunches.

The race/ethnicity–related differences in lunch eligibility (school-reported) are striking. Whereas only 23% of white 4th graders were eligible for subsidized lunch, more than one-third of Asian/PI (35%) students and most American Indian (65%), black (70%), and Hispanic (71%) students were eligible (see Table 9.1). The patterns were similar at Grade 8, at which less than 20% of white students were eligible, in contrast with 34% of Asian/PI students, 56% of American Indian students, and more than 60% of black and Hispanic students.

Given the strong correlation between race/ethnicity and free/reduced-price lunch eligibility, an important consideration is the extent to which the race/ethnicity disparities in achievement persist after taking socioeconomic differences into account. Overall, the score gap between students eligible for free/reduced lunch and those ineligible was 22 points at Grade 4 (a significant 5 points smaller than the gap in 2000) and 28 points at Grade 8 (an insignificant 4 points smaller than in 2000). However, severe race/ethnicity–related disparities within each lunch category persisted. Most alarming is that the scores of the poorer, lunch-eligible white and Asian/PI students were roughly equal to, or higher than, the scores of the wealthier, ineligible black and Hispanic students at both Grade 4 and Grade 8. Lubienski and Shelley (2003) found similar results in examining the 2000 data.[3] (Readers interested in race-SES-gender interactions should see chapter 10.)

---

[3] However, using a stronger, multifaceted SES variable, Lubienski & Shelley (2003) found that this pattern weakened considerably, yet substantial (13–20 points) black-white and Hispanic-white gaps remained.

Table 9.1
Achievement by Free/Reduced-Price Lunch Eligibility and Race/Ethnicity

| | 4th Grade | | | | 8th Grade | | | |
| | Eligible | | Ineligible | | Eligible | | Ineligible | |
Race/Ethnicity	Row %	Mean scale score	Row %	Mean scale score	Row %	Mean scale score	Row %	Mean scale score
White	23%	231	65%	247	19%	272	69%	291
Black	70%	212	24%	226	61%	247	31%	262
Hispanic	71%	219	22%	232	64%	254	27%	269
Asian/Pacific Islander	35%	234	53%	254	34%	274	51%	300
American Indian	65%	218	28%	237	56%	255	36%	276

Note. Percentages of "eligible" and "ineligible" students within each subgroup do not sum to 100, because information was unavailable for some students.

2003 Achievement Score Distributions

Figure 9.3 shows 8th-grade mathematics scale scores by percentile for each racial/ethnic group. The 4th-grade distributions were similar. Figure 9.3 highlights the large amount of overlap in the score distributions of all five racial/ethnic groups. Examining the data in this way reminds us that strong similarities are evident across the subgroups, as well as great diversity within each group.

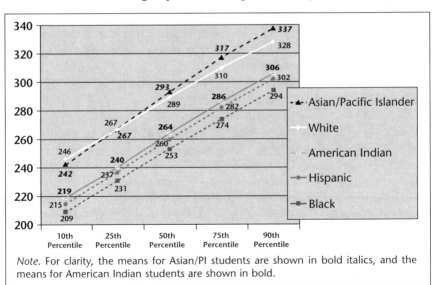

Note. For clarity, the means for Asian/PI students are shown in bold italics, and the means for American Indian students are shown in bold.

Figure 9.3. Average 2003 mathematics scores by percentile and race/ethnicity, Grade 8.

The score distributions also shed light on the nature of the achievement differences between subgroups. At both 4th and 8th grades, the gap between Asian/PI and white students' scores was largest at the upper ends of the achievement spectrum and reversed at the lowest end. For example, at the 10th percentile a 4-point difference favored white 8th graders, but at the 90th percentile a 9-point difference favored Asian/PI 8th graders. The pattern was similar at Grade 4, although not quite as pronounced. Still, overall, the extent to which the lines for black, Hispanic, and American Indian students are parallel to each other and to those for white and Asian/PI students indicates strong similarities in the nature of their score distributions.

Achievement-Level Results by Race/Ethnicity

On the basis of scale scores, NAEP assigns students to one of four achievement levels: advanced, proficient, basic, and below basic (see chapter 1 for discussion of achievement levels). The percentages of students assigned to the various levels by subgroup are presented in Figures 9.4 and 9.5. The results again indicate severe disparities among subgroups. Whereas only 13% of white and Asian/PI 4th graders scored below the basic level in 2003, more than one-third of American Indian and Hispanic students and almost half (46%) of black students scored at that level. Similarly, although 48% of Asian/PI and 43% of white 4th graders scored at the proficient or advanced levels, only 10% of black students and less than 20% of Hispanic and American Indian students scored at those levels.

The disparities were even more striking at the 8th-grade level, at which 48% of American Indian, 52% of Hispanic, and 61% of black students scored below basic, in comparison with 22% of Asian/PI and 20% of white students. And although 43% of Asian/PI and 37% of white students scored at or above the proficient level, only 7% of black students, 12% of Hispanic students, and 15% of American Indian students did so.

Given the improvements in scale scores that occurred for most subgroups between 2000 and 2003, we wondered whether a movement toward higher achievement levels would be uniform across all subgroups. Hence Figures 9.4 and 9.5 also include data from 2000. At both Grade 4 and Grade 8, we see a decrease in the percentage of every subgroup considered below basic, but subgroup differences are evident in the ways in which the growth in other categories was distributed. For white students, growth tended to occur in the proficient and advanced categories. Some growth occurred at those levels for other groups as well, but greater percentage-point gains occurred at the basic level for black, Hispanic, and American Indian students, particularly at Grade 4. Because of a lack of data on Asian/PI 4th graders, the 2000–2003 comparison cannot be made. For Asian/PI 8th graders, the modest gains that occurred in the top three categories were similar.

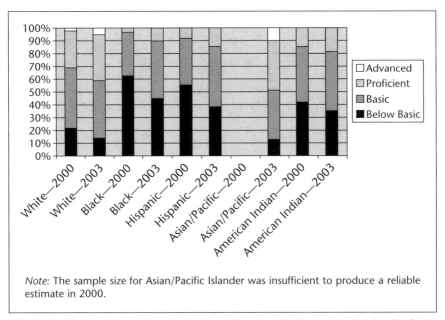

Note: The sample size for Asian/Pacific Islander was insufficient to produce a reliable estimate in 2000.

Figure 9.4. Percentage of students at each achievement level by race/ethnicity, Grade 4.

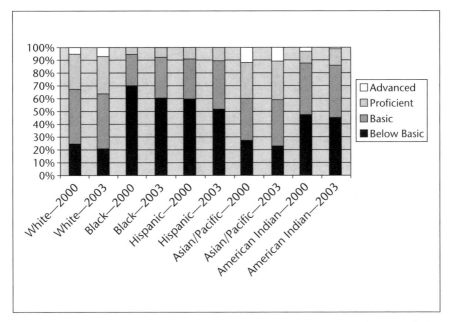

Figure 9.5. Percentage of students at each achievement level by race/ethnicity, Grade 8.

Gaps by Mathematical Strand, 2003

NAEP creates scale scores within each of the five mathematics strands. The mean scale scores did not differ drastically across the strands. At Grade 4, those scores ranged from a low of 233 (Number Sense, Properties, and Operations) to a high of 241 (Algebra and Functions), and at Grade 8 they ranged from 275 (Measurement; Geometry and Spatial Sense) to 280 (Data Analysis, Statistics, and Probability; Algebra and Functions). However, of interest for the purposes of this chapter are the disparities between subgroups across the strands. For the sake of brevity, gaps between white students and others are given primary consideration.

Figures 9.6 and 9.7 display the scale-score gaps between white students and the other four subgroups for each of the five mathematics strands. Consistent with NAEP results from past years (e.g., Strutchens et al., 2004), the measurement and data analysis strands revealed the largest disparities between white students and their black, Hispanic, and American Indian peers. Those were also the only strands for which the mean scale score for white students was higher than Asian/PA students' scores (this outcome occurred for measurement at Grade 4 and for data analysis at Grade 8). At both Grade 4 and Grade 8, the black-white measurement gap stood out from the others as particularly large—33 points at Grade 4 and a full 50 points at Grade 8.

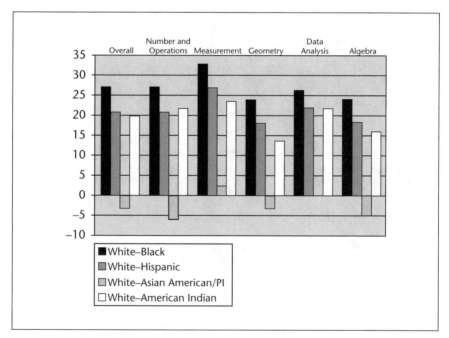

Figure 9.6. Mean scale score gaps between white 4th graders and those of other racial/ethnic groups, by mathematics strand.

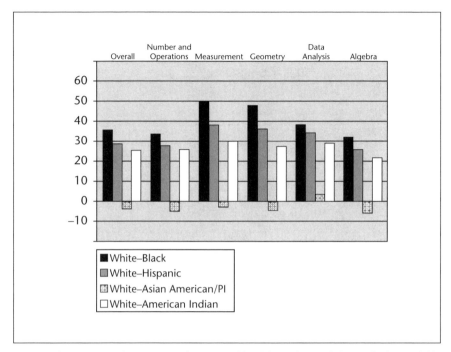

Figure 9.7. Mean scale score gaps between white 8th graders and those of other racial/ethnic groups, by mathematics strand.

Again, given our interest in understanding the nature of the score gains that occurred between 2000 and 2003, we investigated whether the gains for the various subgroups were concentrated among particular mathematics strands. That investigation revealed no significant patterns at Grade 4. For example, scale score gains were between 11 and 14 points on each strand for both black and Hispanic students, whereas gains for white 4th graders were between 6 and 10 points for the various strands (see Table 9.2). However, one statistic did stand out at Grade 8: black students' measurement score gain of 13 points was particularly large.

Given the forementioned pattern, we investigated the gains for black 8th graders on each of the measurement items administered in both 2000 and 2003. Of the 30 measurement items administered in 2003, 24 were also administered in 2000. We compared the 2000 and 2003 mean percentage correct for black students on each of the 24 items. However, none of the items showed a statistically significant gain. Three multiple-choice items reflected the largest gain—about 5 percentage points—but many other items showed losses. The mean gain across the 24 items was less than 1 percentage point (0.7). Hence, whether the 13-point gain for black students' measurement scale score represents a meaningful gain in measurement understanding is not clear.

Table 9.2
Scale Score Gains by Strand and Race/Ethnicity, 2000–2003

	White		Black		Hispanic		Asian		Am. Indian	
	4th	8th	4th	8th	4th	8th	4th	8th	4th	8th
Number and Operations	8	3	11	6	13	4		4	2	3
Measurement	8	4	11	13	11	8		3	4	8
Geometry	6	4	12	7	12	5		1	6	3
Data Analysis	8	4	14	9	12	7		2	2	6
Algebra	10	4	13	7	13	8		3	8	7
Composite (Overall)	8	4	12	8	12	6		3	4	4

Note. Fourth-grade Asian/PI samples were considered unreliable in 2000 (Braswell et al., 2003).

A Closer Look: An Examination of Individual Items

In an attempt to portray more richly the ways in which mathematics achievement varies by race/ethnicity, we present an in-depth look at a few of the many items administered in 2003. General performance data were available on each administered item; however, only those items that were released by NCES can be discussed in detail (see chapter 1). Again, with five subgroups to be considered, we had difficulty deciding which items to discuss. Ultimately, we decided to focus on the released items for which a large gap (in terms of percentage-point differences) occurred between white students' performance and that of all three of the lowest scoring groups. We identified a set of 30 items with the largest black-white gaps and then identified corresponding sets of items for Hispanic and American Indian students. Each set of 30 items contained approximately 10 released items. We then identified the released items in the intersection of those three sets. This process resulted in four items at Grade 4 and three items at Grade 8. We also examined performance data from a few additional relevant items that stood out in some important ways.

Before discussing details of the selected items, we need to consider whether achievement gaps on items represent true differences in mathematical performance or whether such differences are due largely to incompletion of the task by students from some subgroups, either because, in NAEP terms, students were "off task" or because the item was "omitted" or "not reached." An examination of data pertaining to the released items revealed that few students from any subgroup (generally 2% or less) were coded as being "off task" on items, regardless of item type: multiple choice, short constructed response (SCR), or extended constructed response (ECR). Additionally, few of the students (2% or less) from any subgroup omitted multiple-choice items. However, omit rates differed by subgroup on the SCR and ECR items. The patterns were consistent but most striking on 8th-grade

ECR items, on which omit rates averaged more than 20% for black and Hispanic students, 14% for American Indian students, and only 11% for white and Asian/PI students. The percentage of students coded as not having reached a particular item varied greatly, depending on where in the block (test book) the item was placed. For the items with particularly large gaps, subgroup differences in reaching the item were considered but determined to be at most a minor factor in shaping the performance differences.

Before focusing on those items for which disparities were particularly large, we want to note that some items had very small differences between white students and their black, Hispanic, and American Indian peers. On a few items, Hispanic and American Indian students slightly outperformed white students. On most of the items with small gaps, all subgroups did either very poorly or very well. For example, at Grade 8, 91% of both white and black students correctly answered a multiple-choice item in which they had to add 238 and 462. And less than 4% of 8th graders from any subgroup correctly found the area of a pentagon on an SCR item, resulting in small percentage-point differences among subgroups.

Fourth-Grade Items With Large Disparities

The four released items with the largest disparities between white 4th graders and their black, Hispanic, and American Indian peers included three multiple-choice items (two number and operations items and one data analysis item) and one ECR data analysis item (see Figure 9.8). The two multiple-choice number and operations items were computation problems that required a bit more than routine procedures with the given numbers. First, on a multistep word problem asking the number of additional eggs needed to fill three egg cartons (if 34 eggs were already obtained), 54% of white students and 53% of Asian/PI students answered correctly, far greater than the percentage of black (30%), Hispanic (33%), and American Indian students (35%) who answered correctly.

The second problem involved an extraneous number. About two-thirds of white (64%) and Asian/PI (66%) 4th graders correctly responded that 3×5 would produce the total number of fish, whereas only 37% of black students, 43% of American Indian students, and 45% of Hispanic students answered correctly. Although only 22% of white students and 26% of Asian/PI students chose the option involving adding the three given numbers (option D), 43% of black students and just slightly more than one-third of Hispanic (34%) and American Indian (35%) students chose that option.

The results of the foregoing items stand in contrast with a more traditional computation item (2003-4M6 #1), on which the vast majority of students from every subgroup answered correctly. When asked to add 238 and 462, between 84% and 93% of each group answered correctly at Grade 4 (and, as noted previously, roughly 90% of each subgroup responded correctly to this same item at Grade 8). Taken together, the evidence suggests that issues other than computational skill led to performance disparities.

Carl has 3 empty egg cartons and 34 eggs. If each carton holds 12 eggs, how many more eggs are needed to fill all 3 cartons?

A)   2
B)   3
C)   4
D)   6

Pat has 3 fish bowls. There are 4 plants and 5 fish in each bowl. Which gives the total number of fish?

A)   3 + 5
B)   3 × 4
C)   3 × 5
D)   3 + 4 + 5

There is only one red marble in each of the bags shown below. Without looking, you are to pick a marble out of one of the bags. Which bag would give you the greatest chance of picking the red marble?

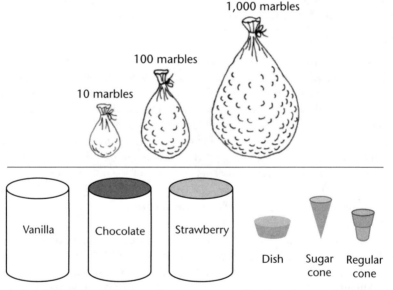

Jan's Snack Shop has 3 flavors of ice cream—vanilla, chocolate, and strawberry. The ice cream can be served in a dish, a sugar cone, or a regular cone.

There are 9 people who choose 1 dip of ice cream in a dish, or in a sugar cone, or in a regular cone, and all of their choices are different. List or show the 9 different choices.

Could another person have a choice that is different from one of these 9 choices? Why or why not?

Figure 9.8. Fourth-grade items with largest performance differences by racial/ethnic group (2003-4M6 #12; 2003-4M7 #11; 2003-4M10 #16; 2003-4M10 #17).

The third item with large disparities at Grade 4 was a multiple-choice probability problem asking students to choose the bag that provides the best chance of drawing a red marble (bags with 10, 100, and 1,000 marbles but each having just 1 red marble). Whereas 73% of white students and 66% of Asian/PI students correctly chose the bag with only 10 marbles, only about half of black (49%), Hispanic (52%), and American Indian (52%) students answered correctly. The most popular incorrect answer was the largest bag, an option selected by twice as many black students (28%) as white (14%) or Asian/PI (15%) students (and chosen by 24% of Hispanic students and 22% of American Indian students).

Finally, an extended constructed-response item asked students to list the nine possible combinations resulting from three ice-cream flavors and three serving containers. Although more than half of white (55%) and Asian/PI (54%) students gave a "satisfactory" or "extended" response, less than one-fourth of black students (24%) and less than one-third of Hispanic (29%) and American Indian (32%) students gave such a response. Significantly more black (11%), American Indian (11%), and Hispanic (9%) students omitted the item than Asian/PI and white students (5%).

Consistent with the strand disparities discussed previously, several measurement items showed large disparities, yet many of those items were not released. The released 4th-grade measurement item (2003-4M10 #1) with the largest disparities asked students to identify the object that would typically be measured in feet. (The item was among the 30 items with the largest black-white and Hispanic-white gaps and among the 32 items with the largest American Indian–white gaps.) The options given were "thickness of a coin," "length of a paperclip," "length of a car," and "distance between New York City and Chicago." Although 76% of white students and 72% of Asian/PI students correctly chose "car," those percentages were only 52, 56, and 59 for black, Hispanic, and American Indian students, respectively. The most popular incorrect answer for each group was "paper clip," chosen by significantly more black (23%) and Hispanic students (22%) than white (13%) or Asian/PI students (14%).

Eighth-Grade Items With Large Disparities

The three items identified as having large race/ethnicity–related disparities at Grade 8 included an SCR algebra item, an SCR data analysis and probability item, and a multiple-choice geometry item (see Figure 9.9). The SCR algebra item asked students to shade an inequality on a number line. Slightly more than half of white (53%) and Asian/PI (51%) students answered correctly, whereas only 30% of Hispanic and American Indian students and 22% of black students answered correctly.

In another problem involving a number line (2003-8M6 #16), students were asked to place a dot where 3/4 would be, given the points 0, 1/2, and 1. That item was among the 30 released items having the largest black-white and Hispanic-white gaps (but not American Indian–white gaps), with 72% of white

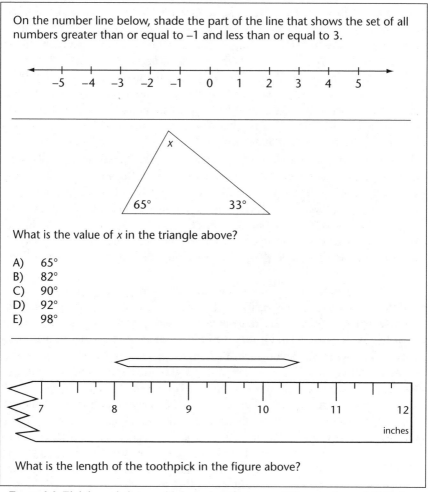

On the number line below, shade the part of the line that shows the set of all numbers greater than or equal to –1 and less than or equal to 3.

What is the value of x in the triangle above?

A)   65°
B)   82°
C)   90°
D)   92°
E)   98°

What is the length of the toothpick in the figure above?

Figure 9.9. Eighth-grade items with largest performance differences by racial/ethnic group (2003-8M6 #24, 2003-8M7 #3, 2003-8M6 #18).

8th graders responding correctly but only 45% of black and 50% of Hispanic students responding correctly. However, on a multiple-choice item that also pertained to fractions (2003-8M6 #2), at least 90% of black and Hispanic students could correctly choose the shaded rectangular region representing 3/4. Taken together, the evidence suggests that black and Hispanic students (and American Indian students to a lesser extent) get less experience with number-line representations than do white and Asian/PI students.

The second item revealing large disparity asked students whether surveying attendants at a baseball game would be a good strategy for collecting data about favorite sports. A response was considered correct if it noted that the sample would be biased toward baseball fans. A much larger percentage of white (54%) and Asian/PI (47%) students answered correctly, as compared with black (25%), Hispanic (28%), and American Indian (31%) students. Omit rates were highest for black (9%) and Hispanic (10%) students, and more black (10%) and Hispanic (7%) students than others did not reach this problem. Still, almost half of black and Hispanic students (compared with only 27% of white students) responded that sampling opinions at a baseball game would be a good way to collect the data (e.g., "Because people there like sports" or other reasons).

Finally, a multiple-choice geometry item (Figure 9.9) asked 8th graders to find the measure of a missing angle in a triangle. A much higher percentage of white (58%) and Asian/PI (62%) students than black (33%), Hispanic (36%), or American Indian (34%) students correctly identified that the third angle of the triangle is 82 degrees. Although no large differences were seen in the numbers of students from each subgroup choosing the incorrect answers A, C, and D, black (39%), Hispanic (34%), and American Indian (39%) students were roughly twice as likely as white (17%) and Asian/PI (19%) students to choose option E, which is the sum of the two given numbers in the problem. Again, the approach of "combine the given numbers" is consistent with performance patterns in the fish-bowl item previously, suggesting disparities in students' experiences with reasoning through problems that call for more than simple computations with given numbers.

The item with the largest black-white gap of all items at Grade 8 (and the largest Hispanic-white gap of any released item) was an SCR measurement item regarding the length of a toothpick (Figure 9.9 [ruler not shown full size on p. 242]). Although the American Indian–white gaps were not among the largest on this item, the magnitude of the black-white and Hispanic-white gaps on this item is cause to include attention to it here. Whereas 69% of white 8th graders correctly answered that the length of the toothpick is 2.5 inches, only 26% of black and 43% of Hispanic 8th graders answered correctly. About one-fourth of black and Hispanic students responded "3.5 inches," indicating a focus on the numbers on the ruler and not the spaces as units of measurement. More than twice as many black students (18%) as students in other subgroups responded "10.5 inches," perhaps indicating an orientation toward a rote measurement process rather than an understanding of the concept. The toothpick item was also given at Grade 4, at which 27% of white 4th graders responded correctly—much more than the 5% of black and 10% of Hispanic 4th graders (and even more than the 26% of black 8th graders) responding correctly.

Taken together, the 4th- and 8th-grade items reflecting the largest disparities point toward differences in students' knowledge of underlying mathematical processes, as well as differences in exposure to nonroutine problems. The evidence suggests that black, Hispanic, and American Indian students could be exposed to relatively less of the curricular shift toward conceptual understanding and complex problem solving called for by NCTM (1989, 2000). In the next section, we consider survey data collected from students, teachers, and schools as a means of shedding additional light on the foregoing and other instruction-related disparities in students' experiences.

STUDENT, TEACHER, AND SCHOOL SURVEY DATA

NAEP data are not designed for making cause-and-effect inferences about instructional methods and student outcomes. However, analyses of NAEP student, teacher, and school questionnaires can reveal similarities and differences in students' backgrounds, beliefs, and experiences, thereby illuminating factors that could shape the achievement differences noted in this chapter.

Student Beliefs and Attitudes

Data on students' mathematical attitudes and beliefs are important to consider. Although shaped by a variety of factors, such beliefs are likely linked with both students' mathematics achievement and the instruction they receive. The beliefs and attitudes of students could be considered both an outcome of their instructional opportunities and a potential factor in shaping the achievement differences outlined previously.

NAEP survey questions (see chapter 1) ask students to indicate their level of agreement with various statements about themselves and mathematics. For most of those variables, more similarities than differences were apparent in students' responses when compared across subgroups. Still, some differences were large enough to merit discussion.

Attitudes Toward Mathematics

Between 45% and 56% of 4th graders from each subgroup reported liking mathematics (see Table 9.3). Although the differences were relatively small, Asian/PI 4th graders were significantly more likely than other groups to report that they like mathematics, whereas white 4th graders were significantly less likely than their peers to report liking mathematics. Between 45% and 58% of 8th graders reported liking mathematics, with more Asian/PI and black 8th graders reporting that view than their American Indian, white, and Hispanic peers.[4]

---

[4] The scales for reporting this and many other survey variables differed in 2003 from previous years. The responses "agree," "unsure," and "disagree" were replaced with "a lot like me," "a little like me," and "not like me" for some questions at Grade 4 (see table note). For other survey items at Grade 4 and 8, the order in which the response options were presented was reversed, impeding our ability to draw conclusions about slight changes in percentages of students responding in various ways. Because of those issues, as well as space limitations, comparisons between 2003 results and those of previous years are not focal in this chapter. However, we noted with interest that although in previous years, student attitudes toward mathematics appeared more positive at Grade 4 than at Grade 8, the 2003 data do not convey that pattern. Again, that outcome could be due to changes in response options between 2000 and 2003. Interested readers can refer to Strutchens et al. (2004) for more information about 1990–2000 race/ethnicity–related trends in NAEP data.

Table 9.3
Student Agreement With Statements About Themselves and Mathematics by Race/ Ethnicity, 2003

Statement	Grade	Percentage Agreeing[a]				
		White	Black	Hispanic	Asian/ PI	Am. Indian
I like mathematics.[b]	4	45	50	49	56	48
	8	47	55	47	58	45
I am good at mathematics.[b]	4	52	49	43	56	41
	8	62	61	48	64	51
I understand most of what goes on in mathematics class.[b]	4	61	51	49	63	46
	8	75	74	68	81	68
All students can do well in mathematics if they try.	4	84	82	82	87	80
	8	65	80	81	78	75
Learning mathematics is mostly memorizing facts.	4	41	52	52	45	48
	8	29	50	44	34	46
There is only one correct way to solve a mathematics problem.	4	11	22	25	12	26
	8	7	10	13	8	15
Mathematics is useful for solving everyday problems.	4	70	58	59	66	57
	8	71	78	73	75	69

[a] In Grade 8, the response options were "strongly agree," "agree," "undecided," "disagree," and "strongly disagree." In this table, the "percentage agreeing" represents the sum of the percentages selecting "agree" and "strongly agree."

[b] In Grade 4, the response options for these first three questions were "a lot like me," "a little like me," and "not like me." The percentage reported here is that of students responding, "A lot like me." For the remaining questions, the response options were "agree," "unsure," and "disagree."

At both 4th and 8th grades, Hispanic and American Indian students were significantly less likely than all other groups to agree with the statement "I am good at mathematics." Also at both grades, the frequency of agreement was highest for Asian/PI students (although differences between Asian/PI students and white and black students were small and not significant at Grade 8).

The disparities in mathematical confidence continue with students' responses to the statement "I understand most of what goes on in mathematics class." At Grade 4, white and Asian/PI students were significantly more likely than their peers to agree, whereas Hispanic and American Indian students were significantly less likely to agree. At Grade 8, the patterns were similar, with more Asian/PI students agreeing that they understand most of what goes on in mathematics class, and relatively few Hispanic and American Indian students agreeing.

Beliefs About Mathematics

The level of agreement with the statement "All students can do well in mathematics if they try" was strikingly similar across all subgroups at Grade 4, with between 82% and 87% of each group agreeing with the statement. Much consistency was also apparent across the subgroups at Grade 8, with the exception of white students, who were significantly less likely than the others to agree with the statement (only 65% versus roughly 80%). That outcome is consistent with the findings of Strutchens et al. (2004) regarding the 2000 data—white 8th graders were less likely than their black and Hispanic peers to agree with that statement. One hypothesis made by Strutchens and her colleagues for this disparity is course-taking differences that might be emerging in 8th grade. However, the fact that Asian/PI students also tend to agree with the statement raises further questions about the reasons underlying that pattern.

Previous examinations of 2000 NAEP data revealed that white students were less likely than black or Hispanic students to agree with the statements "Learning mathematics is mostly memorizing facts" and "There is only one correct way to solve a mathematics problem" (Strutchens et al., 2004). Moreover, a more in-depth analysis revealed that the level of disagreement with those statements correlated positively with achievement and that the correlation persisted even after controlling for demographic differences among students (Lubienski, 2006). Hence, again, the disparities in students' level of agreement with those statements are important to examine.

According to the 2003 data, white 4th graders (41%) were significantly less likely than their peers to agree with the statement "Learning mathematics is mostly memorizing facts," whereas black and Hispanic 4th graders (52% each) were significantly more likely than other subgroups to agree. At 8th grade, a significantly smaller percentage of white (29%) and Asian/PI (34%) students agreed that mathematics learning is fact memorization, in contrast with half of black students, 46% of American Indian students, and 44% of Hispanic students.

Relatively few students expressed agreement with the statement "There is only one correct way to solve a mathematics problem." Still, whereas roughly one-quarter of American Indian, black, and Hispanic 4th graders agreed with the statement, significantly fewer Asian/PI (12%) and white (11%) 4th graders expressed agreement. Even fewer 8th graders agreed that there is a single correct solution path for mathematics problems, but still the pattern persisted that white and Asian/PI students expressed the least amount of agreement.

At both 4th and 8th grades, the majority of students in each subgroup indicated agreement with the statement "Mathematics is useful for solving everyday problems." White 4th graders (70%) were significantly more likely than Asian/PI 4th graders (66%), who were significantly more likely than other subgroups (57–59%), to agree that mathematics is useful for solving everyday problems. However, those race/ethnicity–related patterns did not persist at Grade 8.

School Classifications and Experiences

School administrators, teachers, and students were asked a variety of survey questions regarding students' experiences in schools—experiences that could potentially shape the achievement and affective disparities discussed above. School administrators were asked whether each participating student was categorized as learning disabled or limited English proficient (LEP). Teachers were asked about their backgrounds and teaching practices. Students were asked how often they participated in particular instructional activities, as well as the frequency with which they used various instructional tools. Many questions asked of teachers and students in 2003 were inconsistent between 4th and 8th grades, and many questions asked of teachers in 2000 were not asked in 2003 (such as questions about curricular emphases, familiarity with the NCTM *Standards*, and frequency of some instructional practices). Here we report on the data that were available in 2003, focusing on similarities and differences across subgroups.

Disability and LEP Status

Striking race/ethnicity–related disparities were found in the percentage of students categorized by the school as having a learning disability (see Table 9.4). Specifically, at each grade level Asian/PI students (6%–7%) were significantly less likely than all other groups to be categorized as having a disability, whereas American Indian students (15%–17%) were significantly more likely—more than twice as likely as Asian/PI students at Grade 4 and almost three times as likely at Grade 8. At Grade 4, black students (12%) were significantly more likely than white and Hispanic students (10%) to be classified as having a disability, whereas at Grade 8, both black and Hispanic students (12%) were significantly more likely than white students (10%) to be so classified.

More than one-third of Hispanic 4th graders and almost one-quarter of Hispanic 8th graders were classified by their school as being LEP, signifi-

Table 9.4

Percentage of Students From Each Subgroup Classified by School as Having Disability or Limited English Proficiency (LEP)

Racial/Ethnic Subgroup	Classified as Having Disability		Classified as LEP	
	4th	8th	4th	8th
White	10%	10%	1%	1%
Black	12%	12%	1%	1%
Hispanic	10%	12%	38%	24%
Asian/Pacific Islander	7%	6%	20%	14%
American Indian	15%	17%	25%	11%

cantly more than the percentages for other groups. Still, a substantial number of American Indian students (25% and 11% at Grades 4 and 8, respectively) and Asian/PI (20% and 14% at Grades 4 and 8, respectively) students were classified as LEP. In contrast, only 1% of white and black students in both 4th and 8th grades were classified as LEP.

Course Taking

NAEP's 8th-grade student survey included the question "What mathematics class are you taking this year?" As Table 9.5 reveals, Asian/PI students (40%) were significantly more likely than white (31%), Hispanic (24%), black (17%), and American Indian (16%) students to report taking first-year algebra in Grade 8. Similarly, significantly more Asian/PI 8th graders (6%) reported taking geometry than did the other subgroups (2%–3%). Whereas roughly 40% of black, Hispanic, and American Indian students reported taking 8th-grade mathematics, that percentage was significantly less for Asian/PI (24%) and white (31%) students. Few students (roughly 2%) reported taking "Integrated Mathematics," but significantly more white and Asian/PI students than black or Hispanic students reported taking that course.

In general, the patterns in achievement across courses were not surprising— geometry students scored higher than first-year algebra students, who, in turn, scored higher than prealgebra and 8th-grade mathematics students. That pattern was consistent across each racial/ethnic group. Achievement in second-year algebra did not follow the expected pattern, thereby raising questions about the validity of that variable (i.e., students might have diverse understandings of the meaning of that course title).

The achievement of black, Hispanic, and American Indian students within most courses was significantly lower than that of white and Asian/PI students reportedly taking the same courses. Moreover, the black and Hispanic students taking first-year algebra scored roughly equal to, or slightly lower than, Asian/PI and white students in 8th-grade mathematics, raising questions about the rigor of algebra courses in high-minority middle schools.

Teachers and Teaching

The data concerning the background characteristics, teacher preparation, and teaching practices of Grade 4 and Grade 8 mathematics teachers are elaborated in chapter 8. In the following section we highlight the most striking data regarding those aspects as they relate to racial/ethnic differences and disparities. We encourage interested readers to examine the online Data Explorer for statistics concerning the survey items reported in this section.

Teacher race/ethnicity. Numerous reports already document an increasingly diverse student population and homogenous teaching force (e.g., Current Population Survey).[5] The NAEP data provide further evidence for that trend,

---

[5] See http://nces.ed.gov/programs/coe/2006/section1/indicator05.asp

Table 9.5
Mean Achievement and Percentage of Students From Each Subgroup by 8th-Grade Course

| | 8th-Grade Math | | Prealgebra | | 1st-Year Algebra | | Geometry | | 2nd-Year Algebra | | Integrated Math | |
	Mean scale score	Row %	Mean scale score	Row %	Mean scale score	Row %	Mean scale score	Row %	Mean scale score	Row %	Mean scale score	Row %
White	276	31%	280	29%	306	31%	313	2%	304	2%	304	2%
Black	247	41%	252	33%	270	17%	254	3%	254	2%	261	1%
Hispanic	255	38%	257	26%	273	24%	269	2%	257	3%	274	1%
Asian/PI	272	24%	274	21%	306	40%	330	6%	292	4%	315	2%
American Indian	256	42%	266	32%	284	16%	—	3%	—	1%	—	1%

indicating that black and Hispanic teachers are underrepresented when compared with the U.S. population. One way of viewing that disparity is to consider
that although about 94% of white students have teachers who share their race/
ethnicity, only a small percentage (ranging from 8% to 34%) of students from
other subgroups share their teacher's race/ethnicity.

Teachers' educational background. Overall, NAEP measures reveal remarkably little variation in teachers' educational backgrounds across student subgroups. However, the reader should note that those data are self-reported and do
not provide information about the quality of teachers' learning.[6] One small but
potentially important difference at Grade 8 is that a higher percentage of white
(32%) and Asian/PI (33%) students had teachers who were mathematics majors,
when compared with black (26%), Hispanic (27%), and American Indian (25%)
students (the differences between the percentages for white students and those
for black and Hispanic students were significant). Consistently across groups,
students with teachers who were undergraduate mathematics majors scored a
significant 7–15 points higher than those students who had a teacher with no
mathematics emphasis. Although the causal order is unclear (i.e., do teachers
with mathematics majors produce higher achievement, or do high achieving
students tend to be placed with more mathematically knowledgeable teachers, or
both?), differential access to teachers with mathematics degrees is one possible
contributing factor to race/ethnicity–related achievement disparities.

Teacher certification and experience. Grade 4 black (85%) and Hispanic
(83%) students were significantly less likely to have a teacher with regular
teacher certification than were white (91%) and American Indian (91%) students.
Black (25%), Hispanic (20%), and Asian/PI (27%) students were the least likely
to have teachers with 20 or more years of experience, whereas more white (32%)
and American Indian (36%) students had such teachers. At the 8th grade, black
(80%), Hispanic (83%), and Asian/PI students (86%) were significantly less
likely to have a teacher who held a regular credential than were white (88%) and
American Indian (91%) students. Grade 8 white students (32%) were the most
likely to have teachers with 20 years of experience—significantly more so than
black (26%) and Hispanic (23%) students but not statistically different from
American Indian (27%) and Asian/PI (29%) students.

---

[6] Some aspects of the teacher-reported survey items suggest that caution is warranted when drawing
conclusions from the resulting data. Survey data from teachers of American Indian 4th graders tended
to "stand out" in unexpected ways. For example, those teachers reported having significantly more
undergraduate and graduate education in mathematics, mathematics education, and mathematics-
related subjects than did teachers of other subgroups. Those findings might be due to the relatively
small sample size of that group. Additionally, the certification data regarding the National Board for
Professional Teaching Standards were peculiar because across both grades and all subgroups, the percentage of teachers who reported possessing that certification (3% to 15%) was markedly higher than
the 1.3% of the approximately 3 million public and private school teachers who hold such certification (D. Lussier, personal communication, May 23, 2005). One explanation might be that the teachers
who participated in the NAEP survey confused "National Board Certification" with the certifications
granted to them by their state boards of education.

Professional development. In 2003, for the first time, 4th- and 8th-grade teachers were asked about the mathematics professional development formats[7] that they participated in or led during the previous two years. Teachers of white students participated significantly less often than teachers of black and Hispanic students in a variety of professional development formats, including workshops and study groups. That disparity could be due to the extra efforts to raise student performance in high poverty schools serving disproportionate numbers of black and Hispanic students.

Instructional practices. NAEP asked teachers and students about a variety of instructional practices, including how often they use collaborative group work, manipulatives, textbooks, various forms of assessment (including problem sets, projects, and multiple-choice tests), and computers and calculators in the classroom. Few clear race-related patterns emerged for most of those variables. For those factors for which patterns were noted, the evidence was mixed in terms of which subgroups appeared to have access to instruction aligned with current reforms (e.g., NCTM, 2000). For example, on the one hand, black students in both grades seemed to engage in more discourse-oriented instruction than other subgroups. On the other hand, 4th-grade black (30%) students were twice as likely to have a teacher who reported weekly use of multiple-choice assessments than white (14%) or Asian/PI (15%) students. Additionally, black students reported more regular use of calculators than other subgroups at Grade 4, whereas white students reported more use than others at Grade 8.

Administrator-Reported Parent Involvement

School administrators were asked a variety of questions about parent involvement in the schools. Significantly more Asian/PI and white students had administrators who reported that schoolwide parental support for student achievement was "very positive." Similarly, at both 4th and 8th grades, Asian/PI and white students were much more likely than black and American Indian students to have their administrator report high rates of parent-teacher conference attendance. The differences were most marked at Grade 4, in which roughly 80% of white and Asian/PI students attended schools with high (at least 75%) parent attendance at conferences, compared with 47% for black, 58% for American Indian, and 67% for Hispanic students. Patterns in participation for PTA involvement, parent volunteerism, and attendance at school open houses were similar, with substantially more white and Asian/PI students attending schools in which parents were reported to regularly participate in those activities.

---

[7] Teachers were asked about the following professional development formats: college courses; professional conferences; consultation with mathematics specialists; team teaching; study groups; individual or collaborative research; formal mentoring and/or peer observation; off-site visits; teacher collaboratives or networks; workshops or training sessions; and membership on curriculum, instruction, or assessment committees.

Lareau's (1987) work on parent-school relationships cautions us against concluding that parents who are less involved in schools do not "care" about their children. Differences in parents' work schedules, transportation availability, and childcare needs, as well as parents' comfort levels within schools, can contribute to some parents' being better positioned to participate in school functions than others. NAEP data can help us understand some of the differences in parent involvement, as perceived by school administrators. However, we caution readers against placing "blame" on parents for those disparities, especially given that schooling practices may delimit the ways in which parents can contribute. We hope that such data can inform decision makers in schools' efforts to equitably involve parents in school activities.

Student-Reported Home Environment

NAEP surveyed students about a variety of factors that relate directly or indirectly to the environment and academic support that students experience at home. More similarities than differences were observed in many of those variables, including the amount of time students reported spending on homework and the percentage of students who reported having daily discussions about school with a family member, although the frequency of such discussions for black students was slightly higher than that of other subgroups. More striking race/ethnicity–related differences were found for other variables, including the frequency of students' school attendance and television viewing.

School Absences

Consistent across 4th and 8th grades, Asian/PI students (11%–14%) were significantly less likely than other subgroups to report missing three or more days of school in the prior month, whereas American Indian students (31–33%) were significantly more likely than their peers to report doing so (the percentages for other subgroups ranged from 21% to 25%). Our examinations of the relationship between student-reported school attendance and mathematics achievement revealed a consistent, positive relationship for each subgroup. Although causal conclusions cannot be drawn from those data, school attendance is one possible factor in the gaps between American Indian students and their white and Asian/PI peers.

Television Viewing

The hours of daily TV watching reported by students are disturbingly high, with black students reporting much higher rates of TV viewing than other subgroups (see Table 9.6). Almost half of black 4th graders and more than half of black 8th graders reported watching 4 or more hours of TV on school days. Moreover, roughly one-third of black 4th and 8th graders reported watching 6 or more hours daily—roughly double the percentage for non-Hispanic subgroups at Grade 4 and more than double the percentage of all other subgroups at Grade 8.

Table 9.6

Mean Achievement and Percentage of Students in Each Subgroup by Response to the Question "On a School Day, About How Many Hours Do You Usually Watch TV or Videotapes Outside of School?"

	None		1 Hour or Less		2–3 Hours		4–5 Hours		6 Hours or More	
	Mean scale score	Row %	Mean scale score	Row %	Mean scale score	Row %	Mean scale score	Row %	Mean scale score	Row %
4th Grade										
White	235	9%	244	29%	248	33%	246	13%	235	16%
Black	208	13%	214	19%	222	21%	223	13%	214	34%
Hispanic	213	12%	220	27%	227	27%	229	13%	219	22%
Asian/ Pacific Islander	248	14%	249	32%	251	28%	245	11%	234	15%
American Indian	211	17%	223	27%	232	25%	230	13%	220	18%
8th Grade										
White	285	4%	293	27%	290	43%	285	15%	272	10%
Black	239	4%	250	12%	257	30%	258	23%	248	31%
Hispanic	248	4%	257	20%	262	41%	263	20%	253	15%
Asian/ Pacific Islander	296	7%	298	27%	291	40%	289	16%	276	10%
American Indian	245	6%	265	23%	266	41%	265	19%	257	12%

However, a second pattern of interest is that TV viewing did not correlate with achievement consistently across subgroups, especially at Grade 8. For example, the mean achievement of white and Asian/PI 8th graders who watched 1 hour or less of TV was significantly higher than the mean for those watching more, whereas the mean achievement among black and Hispanic 8th graders was highest for those who watched 4 to 5 hours of TV daily. Those findings are correlations only—not evidence of causal relationships. The differences in the correlations across the various subgroups suggests that TV watching may be serving for a proxy of something else, such as SES, and that the relationship between TV permissiveness and those factors might vary by culture. In fact, Lareau's (2002) study of child-rearing practices suggests that social class is likely an underlying factor in the patterns in TV viewing. She found that both black and white middle-class families were more likely to involve their children in organized activities after school, whereas working-class families were more likely to allow their children to play with nearby family/friends and to watch TV. Lareau's conclusion that middle-class parents may tend to overschedule their busy children cautions us against inferring from those data that white, middle-class child-rearing practices are necessarily "better." Still, a consistency across all groups was that the students who reported watching 6 hours or more of TV daily scored lower than peers with more moderate viewing habits. Hence, across all subgroups, an intense degree of television watching seems to correspond in some way with less support for student learning.[8]

DISCUSSION

For more than a decade, NCTM (1989, 1991, 2000) has promoted curricular and pedagogical reform intended to increase mathematics achievement and reduce inequities. According to the results presented in this chapter, significant progress has been made, but much work remains. NAEP data indicate that mathematics achievement has increased for every racial/ethnic subgroup. Black-white and Hispanic-white achievement gaps narrowed slightly between 2000 and 2003. Still, gaps between white or Asian/PI students and the other three subgroups are very large, with the black-white gap being a full standard deviation in size.

Our analysis of item types and mathematical strands revealed that race/ethnicity–related disparities were particularly striking within the measurement and data analysis strands. Our examination of the specific mathematics items with the largest race/ethnicity–related disparities suggested that black, Hispanic, and American Indian students had more of a tendency than white and Asian/PI students to apply rote procedures to the given numbers instead of attending to what the problem called for.

Race/ethnicity–related disparities in mathematics achievement were found to persist even after accounting for differences in economic background (as approximated by eligibility for school lunch subsidy). Specifically, the relatively poor, lunch-eligible white and Asian/PI students scored roughly equal to, or higher than, the lunch-ineligible black and Hispanic students.

Those results raise the question of how such gaps in performance can be explained. We should note that even when gaps appear to be rooted in "SES" differences, such differences do not actually "explain" the gaps (Secada, 1992).[9] But black-white gaps that persist after considering SES raise further questions about explanatory factors. In recent years, many researchers have struggled to

---

[8] Another consistency across subgroups on the other end of the TV viewing spectrum was that the mean achievement of students who reported that they never or hardly ever watch TV was lower than that of students reporting that they watch 1 hour or less. Extreme poverty may be an underlying cause of that pattern, as students whose families cannot afford a television set would be included in the "never or hardly ever" category.

[9] Secada raises the important point that researchers tend to "control" for SES and then seek no further explanations for SES-based differences. Additional research is needed to understand the many home- and school-related factors that underlie SES-related achievement differences.

understand underlying causes of race-related achievement gaps. Clearly, SES differences do account for substantial portions of the gaps (Jencks & Phillips, 1998; Lubienski, 2002; Peng, Wright, & Hill, 1995). Other scholars have considered the role of teacher expectations, school structure, school funding, student motivation, and student resistance (e.g., Banks, 1988; Cook & Ludwig, 1998; Ferguson, 1998a, 1998b; Ogbu, 1994; Payne & Biddle, 1999; Steele & Aronson, 1998). Most large-scale studies have tended to focus on the overall academic performance and experiences of students, as opposed to an examination of achievement and instructional practices in a particular subject area. The analyses of the 2003 NAEP mathematics data presented in this chapter shed additional light on disparities in students' mathematics learning experiences. Although NAEP is not designed to determine causal relationships, differences in students' experiences and beliefs can shed light on potentially important factors related to school mathematics achievement.

Several aspects of students' beliefs and experiences did not correlate with achievement disparities. For example, black and Hispanic students were at least as likely as white students to report liking mathematics and talking with peers about their solutions to mathematics problems. Also, few consistent race/ethnicity-related disparities were noted in the frequency of manipulative use, computer use, and most forms of assessment, such as problem sets or projects. Additionally, black and Hispanic students were at least as likely as white students to have teachers who reported having regular professional development.

However, this study identified several differences in students' beliefs and experiences that could relate to achievement disparities. White and Asian/PI students were more likely than others to hold beliefs aligned with current reforms, including the beliefs that mathematics learning is not simply fact memorization and that there is more than one way to solve a mathematics problem. Lubienski (2006) found that belief to correlate positively with achievement even after controlling for student race and SES. Asian/PI students were the most likely subgroup to express mathematical confidence, whereas Hispanic and American Indian students were least likely. Hispanic and American Indian 4th graders were about twice as likely as white and Asian/PI 4th graders to be assessed weekly with multiple-choice tests. White and Asian/PI 8th graders also had more access to calculators on quizzes and tests.

The course-taking data revealed that Asian/PI 8th graders were more likely than students in other subgroups to report taking algebra or geometry. Black and American Indian students were least likely to report taking algebra in Grade 8. The fact that the black and Hispanic students who reported taking 8th-grade algebra scored similarly to Asian/PI and white students who reported taking "8th-grade math" also raises questions about the rigor of "algebra" in high-minority schools.

Differences in teacher background indicate some ways in which black and Hispanic students had less access to highly qualified teachers. Black and

Hispanic students were the most likely to have inexperienced teachers and to have a teacher with a limited teaching credential or none at all. Additionally, more white and Asian/PI 8th graders than others had a mathematics teacher who majored in mathematics. Furthermore, despite increasingly diverse classrooms, the teaching force remains overwhelmingly white. Hence, another way in which white students may be advantaged is by having a mathematics teacher who shares their race/ethnicity; such a teacher provides vivid, daily evidence to students that someone of their own race/ethnicity can succeed in mathematics.

School administrator–reported data shed light on other aspects of students' school experiences. American Indian students were more likely than others to be classified as having a disability, whereas Asian/PI students were the least likely to be classified in that way. Administrators of Asian/PI and white students were much more likely than administrators of black and American Indian students to report that parents were actively involved in school activities.

Finally, data from students' surveys illuminated some similarities and differences in students' home environments and support for schooling. Black students were more likely than their peers to report watching several hours of TV on school days, with about half watching 4 or more hours and one-third watching 6 or more hours. Still, black students were slightly more likely than students of other subgroups to report having conversations about their school studies with a family member on a daily basis. Another indicator of family support for schooling is the regularity with which students attend school. American Indian students were the most likely group to report missing school 3 or more days in the preceding month, whereas Asian/PI students were the least likely.

In summary, the patterns in the NAEP data reveal many areas in which students appear to be differentially supported in their mathematics learning, including within their schools, classrooms, and homes. Those patterns were often very different for black, Hispanic, and American Indian groups, suggesting that no single set of variables has uniformly shaped the achievement disadvantages between each of these subgroups and white and Asian/PI students. Closing achievement gaps will require in-depth attention to the strengths and needs of each underrepresented subgroup.

Clearly, the factors underlying race/ethnicity–related achievement disparities are complex, and many are beyond the scope of NAEP data. Examples include school funding, class size, tracking, teachers' expectations of students, teachers' involvement with students outside the classroom, summer academic gains or losses, and the many more subtle aspects of students' opportunities to learn mathematics (see Farkas, 2003; Tate, 1995).

Several of the school-related disparities identified here are beyond the traditional scope of mathematics educators, including differential rates of disability identification and eligibility for free or reduced-price lunch, as well as disparities in the qualifications of teachers. Moreover, it is difficult to know how—and even in some instances whether—mathematics educators should address home-related issues, such as race/ethnicity–related differences in students' school attendance, students' television viewing, and parents' involvement in schools. In an effort to highlight institutional and societal causes of inequities and to avoid placing "blame" on underserved families, educators have avoided emphasizing differences in students' home environments in recent decades (Lubienski, 2003; Wilson, 1987). However, the NAEP data do indicate several areas of home-related differences that might relate in some ways to students' differential school performance. Again, caution is necessary when interpreting those differences, being mindful of both socioeconomic disparities (that align with race/ethnicity) that can differentially position parents to participate in schools in ways that school administrators expect and value (e.g., Lareau, 1987, 2002), as well as historical differences in various racial/ethnic groups' experiences in the United States (e.g., Ogbu, 1994).

Differences in students' mathematics classroom experiences are likely of most interest to mathematics educators, as they are best positioned to address those aspects. Although the instruction-related differences identified here might appear minor when compared with the many similarities, some differences in students' experiences—such as the disparities in 4th-grade multiple-choice assessment use and 8th-grade calculator use—suggest a consistent tendency to teach and assess black, Hispanic, and American Indian children with a relatively greater emphasis on low-level skills. Perhaps more important, differences in students' performance on nonroutine mathematics problems combined with the disproportionate numbers of black, Hispanic, and American Indian students who view mathematics learning as memorization suggest that those students are less likely to experience mathematics learning as envisioned by the NCTM *Standards.*

Our findings are consistent with previous NAEP analyses, in which race/ethnicity–related differences in students' beliefs and classroom experiences were found to persist even after controlling for SES differences (Lubienski, 2002; Lubienski & Shelley, 2003). Those differences are reminiscent of those revealed in Anyon's (1981) study, in which lower SES students were found to receive more drill-based instruction, whereas higher SES students were taught problem-solving and reasoning skills. Other scholars (Ladson-Billings, 1997; Means & Knapp, 1991) have made similar observations about the tendency for African-American children to receive more drill-based instruction focusing on basic computational skills. This chapter provides similar evidence regarding Hispanic and American Indian students as well. Overall, the evidence suggests that, 50 years after *Brown v. Board* (1954), schools continue to employ some unequal educational practices with students on the basis of race in addition to SES. The differences in teacher qualifications and student disability identification identified in this chapter further emphasize that point.

Still, one cannot conclude that the race/ethnicity–related differences identified in this chapter are the *cause* of achievement disparities. For example, the instructional practices reported for each student are only those the student is encountering at the time the NAEP assessment is administered; students' experiences in previous years with other teachers are not reflected in the NAEP classroom practice data. Additionally, differences in student achievement might precede differential access to instructional resources and practices. Hence, readers are cautioned against leaping to causal conclusions based on the findings reported here.

CONCLUSION

NAEP data continue to reveal large race/ethnicity–related disparities in mathematics achievement, as well as both similarities and differences in students' attitudes and beliefs and experiences at both school and home. This study raises but does not answer questions regarding the reasons for the disparities identified here. More in-depth studies about the mathematics learning of particular racial/ethnic groups are necessary to complement large-scale, descriptive studies such as NAEP. Such work has already begun. For example, readers interested in learning more about the mathematics education of particular racial/ethnic groups should refer to the recent NCTM series Changing the Faces of Mathematics, which contains one volume each on African American students (Strutchens, Johnson, & Tate, 2000), Latino/a students (Ortiz-Franco, Hernandez, & De La Cruz, 1999), and Native American students (Hankes & Fast, 2002), as well as a volume on Asian American and Pacific Islanders students (Edwards, 1999).

In accordance with NCTM's (2000) vision of mathematical power for *all*, researchers must continue to monitor and seek to address inequities in both outcomes and instructional practices that relate to such outcomes. The NAEP offers one avenue for examining disparities in achievement, student/teacher attitudes, school experiences, and home environments. The patterns identified in this study set the stage for additional studies to determine the complex factors at work in shaping those differences and suggest avenues for reducing inequities.

REFERENCES

Alexander, K., Entwisle, D., & Olson, L. (2001). Schools, achievement, and inequality: A seasonal perspective. *Educational Evaluation and Policy Analysis, 23,* 171–191.

Anyon, J. (1981). Social class and school knowledge. *Curriculum Inquiry, 11,* 3–42.

Banks, J. A. (1988). Ethnicity, class, cognitive, and motivational styles: Research and teaching implications. *Journal of Negro Education, 57,* 452–466.

Braswell, J. S., Doane, M. C., & Grigg, W. S. (2004). *The nation's report card: Mathematics highlights 2003.* Washington, DC: National Center for Education Statistics. Retrieved November 6, 2005, from http://nces.ed.gov/nationsreportcard/pdf/main2003/2004451.pdf

Cook, P. J., & Ludwig, J. (1998). The burden of "acting white": Do black adolescents disparage academic achievement? In C. Jencks & M. Phillips (Eds.), *The black-white test score gap* (pp. 375–400). Washington, DC: Brookings Institution Press.

Edwards, C. (Ed.). (1999). *Changing the faces of mathematics: Perspectives on Asian Americans and Pacific Islanders.* Reston, VA: National Council of Teachers of Mathematics.

Farkas, G. (2003). Racial disparities and discrimination in education: What do we know, how do we know it, and what do we need to know? *Teachers College Record, 105,* 1119–1146.

Ferguson, R. F. (1998a). Teachers' perceptions and expectations and the black-white test score gap. In C. Jencks & M. Phillips (Eds.), *The black-white test score gap* (pp. 273–317). Washington, DC: Brookings Institution Press.

Ferguson, R. F. (1998b). Comment by Ronald F. Ferguson [Comment on "The burden of "acting white": Do black adolescents disparage academic achievement?" by J. P. Cook & J. Ludwig]. In C. Jencks & M. Phillips (Eds.), *The black-white test score gap* (pp. 394–397). Washington, DC: Brookings Institution Press.

Hankes, J. E., & Fast, G. R. (Eds.). (2002). *Changing the faces of mathematics: Perspectives on indigenous people of North America.* Reston, VA: National Council of Teachers of Mathematics.

Herrnstein, R. J., & Murray, C. (1994). *The bell curve: Intelligence and class structure in American life.* New York: Free Press.

Jencks, C., & Phillips, M. (Eds.). (1998). *The black-white test score gap.* Washington, DC: Brookings Institution Press.

Ladson-Billings, G. (1997). It doesn't add up: African American students' mathematics achievement. *Journal for Research in Mathematics Education, 28,* 697–708.

Lareau, A. (1987). Social class and family-school relationships: The importance of cultural capital. *Sociology of Education, 56,* 73–85.

Lareau, A. (2002). Invisible inequality: Social class and childrearing in black families and white families. *American Sociological Review, 67,* 747–776.

Lubienski, S. T. (2002). A closer look at black-white mathematics gaps: Intersections of race and SES in NAEP achievement and instructional practices data. *Journal of Negro Education, 71,* 269–287.

Lubienski, S. T. (2003). Celebrating diversity or denying disparities: A critical assessment. *Educational Researcher, 32*(8), 30–38.

Lubienski, S. T. (2006). Examining instruction, achievement, and equity with NAEP mathematics data. *Education Policy Analysis Archives, 14*(14). http://epaa.asu.edu/epaa/v14n14/

Lubienski, S. T., & Shelley, M. C. (2003). *A closer look at U.S. mathematics instruction and achievement: Examinations of race and SES in a decade of NAEP data.* Paper presented at the American Educational Research Association, Chicago. (ERIC Document Reproduction Service No. ED476468)

McIntosh, P. (1990). White privilege: Unpacking the invisible knapsack. *Independent School, 49,* 31–36.

Means, B., & Knapp, M. S. (1991). Cognitive approaches to teaching advanced skills to educationally disadvantaged students. *Phi Delta Kappan, 73,* 282–289.

National Council of Teachers of Mathematics. (1989). *Curriculum and evaluation standards for school mathematics.* Reston, VA: Author.

National Council of Teachers of Mathematics. (1991). *Professional standards for teaching mathematics.* Reston, VA: Author.

National Council of Teachers of Mathematics. (2000). *Principles and standards for school mathematics.* Reston, VA: Author.

Ogbu, J. U. (1994). Racial stratification and education in the United States: Why inequality persists. *Teachers College Record, 96,* 264–298.

Oliver, M. L., & Shapiro, T. M. (1995). *Black wealth/white wealth: A new perspective on racial inequality.* New York: Routledge.

Ortiz-Franco, L., Hernandez, N. G., & De La Cruz, Y. (Eds.). (1999). *Changing the faces of mathematics: Perspectives on Latinos.* Reston, VA: National Council of Teachers of Mathematics.

Payne, K. J., & Biddle, B. J. (1999). Poor school funding, child poverty, and mathematics achievement. *Educational Researcher, 28*(6), 4–13.

Peng, S. S., Wright, D., & Hill, S. T. (1995). *Understanding racial-ethnic differences in secondary school science and mathematics achievement.* Washington, DC: National Center for Education Statistics.

Secada, W. G. (1992). Race, ethnicity, social class, language, and achievement in mathematics. In D. A. Grouws (Ed.), *Handbook of research on mathematics teaching and learning* (pp. 623–660). New York: Macmillan.

Steele, C. M., & Aronson, J. (1998). Stereotype threat and the test performance of academically successful African Americans. In C. Jencks & M. Phillips (Eds.), *The black-white test score gap* (pp. 401–428). Washington, DC: Brookings Institution Press.

Strutchens, M., Johnson, M. L., & Tate, W. F. (Eds.). (2000). *Changing the faces of mathematics: Perspectives on African Americans.* Reston, VA: National Council of Teachers of Mathematics.

Strutchens, M., Lubienski, S. T., McGraw, R., & Westbrook, S. K. (2004). NAEP findings regarding race/ethnicity: Students' performance, school experiences, attitudes and beliefs, and family influences. In P. Kloosterman & F. K. Lester Jr. (Eds.), *Results and interpretations of the 1990–2000 mathematics assessments of the National Assessment of Educational Progress* (pp. 269–304). Reston, VA: National Council of Teachers of Mathematics.

Strutchens, M. E., & Silver, E. A. (2000). NAEP findings regarding race/ethnicity: Students' performance, school experiences, and attitudes and beliefs. In E. A. Silver & P. A. Kenney (Eds.), *Results from the seventh mathematics assessment of the National Assessment of Educational Progress* (pp. 45–72). Reston, VA: National Council of Teachers of Mathematics.

Tate, W. F. (1995). School mathematics and African American students: Thinking seriously about opportunity-to-learn standards. *Educational Administration Quarterly, 31,* 424–448.

Wilson, W. J. (1987). *The truly disadvantaged: The inner city, the underclass, and public policy.* Chicago: University of Chicago Press.

Zeus, L. (2004). The color of supremacy: Beyond the discourse of "white privilege." *Educational Philosophy and Theory, 36,* 137–152.

NAEP Findings Related to Gender: Achievement, Student Affect, and Learning Experiences

Rebecca McGraw and Sarah Theule Lubienski

R ESEARCHERS have found small but fairly consistent gender differences in performance on tasks involving computation (Frost, Hyde, & Fennema, 1994), rational numbers (Seegers & Boekaerts, 1996), measurement (Ansell & Doerr, 2000; Lubienski, McGraw, & Strutchens, 2004), and spatial visualization (Ansell & Doerr, 2000; Battista, 1990), as well as differences in the methods boys and girls employ to solve problems (Fennema, Carpenter, Jacobs, Franke, & Levi, 1998a). When gaps in performance exist, they typically, although not always, favor males, except on performance on computational tasks. Analyses of interactions among gender, race or ethnicity, and socioeconomic status (SES) suggest that gender gaps in mathematics achievement, at least as measured by the 2000 NAEP, (a) generally favor males and (b) generally are larger for high SES white students than for low SES students or for black students (Lubienski et al., 2004; McGraw, Lubienski, & Strutchens, 2006).

In this chapter, we report on gender-related differences in students' performance on the mathematics portion of the 2003 NAEP assessment. We begin by reporting overall trends in scale scores, then follow with a description of gender differences within content strands and a discussion of gender and student affect data taken from the NAEP student survey. Although we focus in this chapter on analyses of 2003 NAEP data, we also include some discussion of previous NAEP results. Unless otherwise indicated, the results reported for 2000 and 2003 are based on accommodations-permitted data (see chapter 1).

Highlights

- The mean mathematics scale scores for both females and males increased significantly between 2000 and 2003. In 4th and 8th grades, males scored significantly higher than females in 2003; however, the effect sizes for those differences were quite small (0.1 or less).

- The gaps in performance by gender in 2003 tended to favor males and were most pronounced at the upper end of the percentile range and for the Measurement and the Number Sense, Properties, and Operations content strands.

- Measurement items that exhibited large gender gaps (i.e., at least 5 percentage point difference in number of students responding correctly) favored males and required reading instruments, using indirect calculation methods, and choosing the best or most reasonable unit of measure.

- Number content strand items for which gender gaps were noted tended to involve fractions, rational numbers, percents, and some computational tasks (favoring males) or computational and pattern-analyzing tasks (favoring females).

- Male and female students performed similarly on most of the items administered in 2003, and overall gaps in performance by gender were minor when compared with differences related to race/ethnicity and SES.

- The number of items for which females outperformed males in 2003 was small compared with the number of items for which males outperformed females. When females outperformed males, they were more likely to do so on constructed-response items than on multiple-choice items.

- An analysis of NAEP 2003 student questionnaire data suggests that female students are less likely than males to indicate that they like or are good at mathematics; however, male and female students seem to be similar in their beliefs about their level of understanding of what goes on in mathematics classes.

MAIN NAEP ACHIEVEMENT TRENDS

Our examination of scale scores by gender suggests that gaps are generally small, but persistent, across recent reporting years (see Figure 10.1). Both male and female students' overall scale scores have improved significantly since 1990, with female students at the 4th- and 8th-grade levels scoring higher in 2003 than their male counterparts did in 2000. In 2003, the average scale score of male 4th-grade students (236) was significantly higher than that of female 4th-grade students (233); however, the overall average scale score of male 8th-grade students (278) was only 1 point higher than that of female 8th-grade students (277). Twelfth-grade students were not assessed in 2003. In 2000, the overall average scale score of male 12th-grade students (302) was significantly higher than that of female 12th-grade students (299). Note that the effect sizes for those score differences are quite small (0.1 or less), thus raising questions about the meaningfulness of those differences.

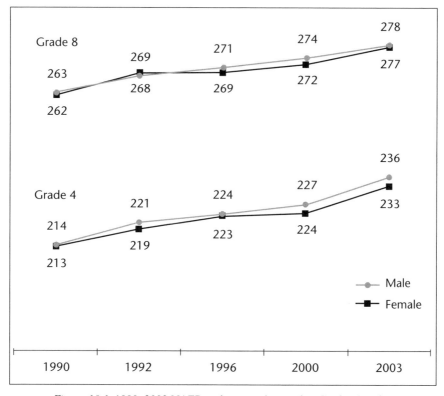

Figure 10.1. 1990–2003 NAEP scale scores by gender, Grades 4 and 8.

Although analyses of overall scale scores provide some information about differences between genders, they do not show how the gaps are distributed within male and female groups or across mathematical content areas. An analysis of gender differences in average scale scores *by percentile* (see Figure 10.2) revealed a consistent pattern across 4th and 8th grades. In 2003, no significant difference occurred by gender for 4th-grade students scoring at the 10th percentile; however, significant differences favoring males were found at the 25th, 50th, 75th, and 90th percentiles. The gap between males' and females' scores tended to increase as scores increased—from 1 point at the 10th percentile to 5 points at the 90th percentile.

Similarly, at the 8th-grade level, significant differences in males' and females' 2003 average scale scores occurred at the 50th, 75th, and 90th percentiles but not at the 10th and 25th percentiles. The largest gap in overall scale scores favoring males occurred at the 75th percentile and the 90th percentile (4 points each). That

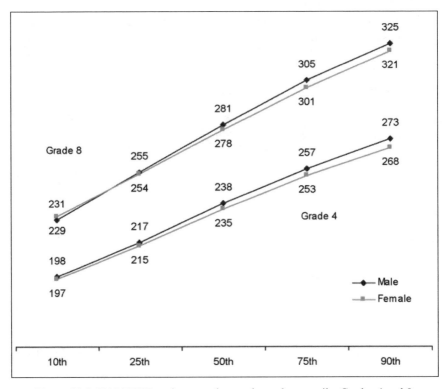

Figure 10.2. 2003 NAEP scale scores by gender and percentile, Grades 4 and 8.

pattern in score gaps is consistent with previous NAEP findings (Lubienski et al., 2004), in which similar trends were found at the 4th-, 8th-, and 12th-grade levels in 2000. For example, score differences for Grade 12 students at the 75th and 90th percentiles favored males and were 5 and 9 points, respectively (Lubienski et al., 2004). Still, as Figure 10.1 indicates, much more overlap than difference was observed in the distributions of male and female scores, with variation within the gender groups much larger than differences between them.

CONTENT STRANDS

Previous analyses of NAEP data (Ansell & Doerr, 2000) and the work of other researchers (Frost et al., 1994; Seegers & Boekaerts, 1996) suggest that differences in performance by gender are not equally distributed across mathematical content strands. In this section, we describe relationships between content foci of NAEP items and differences in performance by gender. A variety of NAEP items administered in 2003 have been released to the public, so we are able to examine this subset of items more closely and analyze patterns in correct and incorrect responses by gender. A portion of this section is devoted to the discussion of several specific items for which the difference in performance by gender was pronounced.

Analyzing 2003 NAEP data by content strand, we found significant differences favoring males in four of the five content strands (Number Sense, Properties, and Operations; Data Analysis, Statistics, and Probability; Algebra and Functions; and Measurement) at the 4th-grade level (see Table 10.1). At Grade 8, significant gaps in number and operations, data analysis, and measurement favored males. The distribution of gaps across content strands in the NAEP 2003 data is similar to that reported for the 2000 NAEP data (Lubienski et al., 2004). In both years, gaps favoring males were largest and most consistent across grade levels for measurement, a significant gap in algebra at Grade 4 was not found in Grade 8 (or at Grade 12 for the 2000 data), and gaps in number and operations appeared to increase slightly with grade level.

Table 10.1
2003 NAEP Scale Scores by Gender and Content Strand, Grades 4 and 8

	Number Sense, Properties and Operations	Data Analysis, Statistics, and Probability	Algebra and Functions	Geometry and Spatial Sense	Measure-ment	Overall Composite
			Grade 4			
Male	234	238	242	234	237	236
Female	231	237	239	234	232	233
Gap	3*	1*	3*	0	5*	3*
			Grade 8			
Male	279	281	280	275	278	278
Female	275	280	280	274	273	277
Gap	4*	1*	0	1	5*	1*

* Indicates significant difference at the 0.05 level; effect sizes of significant differences ranged from 0.02 to 0.2 with a median of 0.1.

Analyses of percentiles in conjunction with content strands revealed that gaps favoring males were most pronounced at the upper end of the percentile range for the measurement and number strands. At 4th grade in the number strand, the gap in scores was 5 points at the 75th and 90th percentiles; in the measurement strand, the gap was 7 points at the 75th and 90th percentiles. At 8th grade in the number strand, the gap in scores was 5 points at the 75th percentile and 6 points at the 90th percentile; in the measurement strand, the gap was 6 points for both percentiles. In contrast, at the lower end of the percentile range (i.e., the 10th percentile), 4th-grade girls outperformed boys by 1 and 2 points for the data analysis and geometry strands, respectively. In 8th grade, at the 10th percentile level, girls outperformed boys by 1 point in the number strand and by 3 points in the geometry, data analysis, and algebra strands. Researchers have found that male students tend to exhibit a wider range in performance than female students (Friedman, 1995), and our analysis of gender differences in NAEP content strands and by percentiles supports that finding. Males' average scores were lower than females' at the 10th percentile and higher than females' at the 90th percentile.

Table 10.2 shows item-level NAEP performance data organized by content strand. Because of the large number of students assessed in 2003, even a 1 percentage point difference in the number of correct responses by gender was statistically significant in that year (see chapter 1). Therefore, we include in Table 10.2 items for which the gender difference was at least 5 percentage points. A difference of 5 points or more was always significant in 2000; in only a few instances was a difference of fewer than 5 points significant in that year.

Table 10.2

Distribution of Items by Content Strand and Gender Difference in Performance, Grades 4 and 8, 2000 and 2003

Content Strand and Total No. of Items (2000, 2003)	No. of Items for Which Gender Difference in % Correct Was at Least 5 Points		No. of Items for Which Difference Favored Males		No. of Items for Which Difference Favored Females	
	2000	2003	2000	2003	2000	2003
Number Sense, Properties, and Operations						
Grade 4 (58, 76)	17	17	15	15	2	2
Grade 8 (43, 52)	11	16	9	12	2	4
Measurement						
Grade 4 (27, 32)	14	12	14	12	0	0
Grade 8 (24, 30)	7	4	7	4	0	0
Geometry and Spatial Sense						
Grade 4 (25, 29)	2	3	1	2	1	1
Grade 8 (32, 38)	6	5	4	3	2	2
Data Analysis, Statistics, and Probability						
Grade 4 (14, 19)	2	2	2	1	0	1
Grade 8 (24, 30)	6	3	6	3	0	0
Algebra and Functions						
Grade 4 (21, 26)	7	5	7	5	0	0
Grade 8 (39, 49)	10	4	9	3	1	1

According to the 2003 data, a substantial (i.e., 5 or more points) gender difference occurred in performance on 39 items at Grade 4 (21% of all items administered) and on 32 items at Grade 8 (16% of all items administered). The vast majority of those items—35 at Grade 4 and 25 at Grade 8—favored males. In 2003, the strands in which the highest percentages of items had at least a 5-point gender difference were Grade 4 measurement (12 of 32 items) and Grade 4 and Grade 8 number (17 of 76 items and 16 of 52 items). Gender differences for those measurement and number items generally favored males, and males significantly outperformed females overall in both the measurement and number strands (Table 10.1). Five of 26 Grade 4 algebra items and 4 of 30 Grade 8 measurement items had at least a 5-point gender difference; all those differences favored males. Comparing the number of items favoring males and the number of items favoring females for each grade and content strand, we can see that in almost every instance, males outperformed females more often than females outperformed males. The exceptions were Grade 4 geometry in 2000 and Grade 4 data analysis in 2003, for which the numbers were equal.

Comparing the 2003 and 2000 data in Table 10.2, we find that in both years in Grade 4, most of the items with differences in student performance by gender were located in the number and measurement strands. An analysis of the 27 measurement and 58 number items administered in both years at Grade 4 revealed that males outperformed females by at least 5 percentage points in both years on 8 of the measurement items and 10 of the number items. In Grade 8, marked decreases were seen from 2000 to 2003 in the numbers of items with gender differences favoring males in the measurement, data, and algebra strands. In the number strand, the number of items exhibiting a difference in performance by gender increased from 11 (26% of items administered) in 2000 to 16 (32% of items administered) in 2003.

Because of persistent gender gaps in the measurement and number strands, we next turn to a discussion of gender-related patterns in students' responses to items from those strands. Because clear gender patterns were less apparent in the geometry, data, and algebra strands, we comment on those areas more briefly in one section. Three criteria were used to select specific items for inclusion in each section. First, the items were among those released to the public, which constituted a relatively small subset of all items administered. Second, the items exhibited gender-related differences in student performance. Third, our examination of patterns in students' incorrect responses revealed differences in performance by gender.

Measurement

As discussed previously, the measurement strand average scale score was 5 points higher for males at both the 4th- and 8th-grade levels in 2003. In addition, all items exhibiting at least a 5 percentage point gender difference in correct responses favored males. Our analysis of individual measurement items suggests that differences in performance favored males and tended to occur on items that required reading instruments (e.g., thermometers, speedometers, and rulers) or using indirect calculation methods. Examples include measuring temperature and change in temperature on a thermometer, measuring the length of an item placed in the middle of a ruler, and measuring the length of an event given its beginning and ending times. Gender differences favoring males were also found for items that asked students to choose the best or most reasonable unit of measure.

The measurement item with the largest gender gap was given only at Grade 4 and involved reading change in temperature on a thermometer (Figure 10.3); 56% of males and 44% of females answered this problem correctly. The 12-point difference in performance by gender was closely related to the greater likelihood of female students' choosing the incorrect answer of "6." Students likely derived that answer from counting one rather than two degrees for each tick mark.

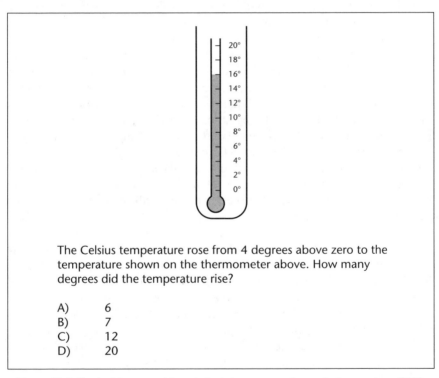

The Celsius temperature rose from 4 degrees above zero to the temperature shown on the thermometer above. How many degrees did the temperature rise?

A)   6
B)   7
C)   12
D)   20

Figure 10.3. Grade 4 item requiring students to measure change in temperature (2003-4M7 #13).

An item given at both Grade 4 and Grade 8 for which the gender gap was relatively large at both grades (6 and 8 points, respectively) required students to correctly read a ruler (Figure 10.4 [ruler not shown full size]). Overall, students of both genders were more likely to answer this question correctly at Grade 8 than

Grade 4; however, the distributions of incorrect responses varied across grade levels. At Grade 4, male students were more likely than female students to give the incorrect answer of 3.5 inches, a response consistent with counting the numbered lines instead of spaces on the ruler. Female students were more likely to give some other incorrect answer (e.g., 10.5 inches or 8 inches). At Grade 8, male and female students were equally likely to answer 3.5 inches, whereas female students were more likely than males to give a different incorrect answer.

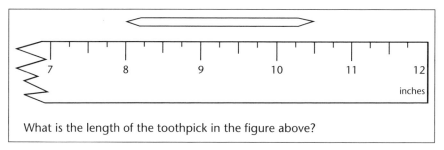

Figure 10.4. NAEP measurement item requiring students to read an interval of length (2003-4M6 #18, 2003-8M6 #18). Note: Ruler image not shown full size.

We found a substantial decrease from Grade 4 to Grade 8 in the proportion of measurement items for which males outperformed females in both 2000 and 2003. However, in Grade 8 the items with large gender differences tended to test the same content as those for which the gaps were largest at Grade 4. Again, those items involved measuring intervals of time, reading measurements from scales (e.g., rulers), identifying appropriate units of measure for a given situation, and approximating lengths using familiar but nonstandard units. Ansell and Doerr (2000) reported gender differences on similar types of measurement items in their analysis of the 1996 NAEP assessment. Drawing on the work of Leder (1992), Ansell and Doerr hypothesized—and we would agree—that differences in boys' and girls' leisure activities could contribute to the gender gaps in measurement proficiency.

Number Sense, Properties, and Operations

In 2003, the number strand average scale scores were 3 and 4 percentage points higher for males in Grades 4 and 8, respectively. Most of the items for which gender differences in performance were noted favored males (15 of 17 items at Grade 4 and 12 of 16 items at Grade 8). The items favoring males tended to involve fractions, rational numbers, and some computational tasks; the items favoring females included computational tasks and tasks that required students to analyze and create rules for number or letter patterns. Specific examples of items for which males responded correctly more often than females included finding and using ratios (Grades 4 and 8), showing the location of a fraction on a number line (Grade 4 and 8), and finding percentages and percentage change (Grade 8). Items for which females outperformed males were mainly multistep addition and subtraction problems (Grade 4 and 8).

An item administered at both Grade 4 and Grade 8 for which males responded correctly more often than females focused on finding the distance between two points on a number line (Figure 10.5). In 2003, only 27% of boys and 20% of girls answered this item correctly at Grade 4; the percentages of Grade 8 students answering correctly were 44% of boys and 33% of girls. At Grade 4, both boys and girls were most likely to choose incorrect answer "C" and least likely to choose "B." At Grade 8, girls who responded incorrectly were equally likely to choose "A" or "C" and unlikely to choose "B." Boys who responded incorrectly exhibited a similar pattern. Interestingly, at Grade 4, girls chose "B" at a higher rate than boys (22% and 17%, respectively), and at Grade 8 very few students of either gender chose "B" (8% each), yet the gender gap on this item increased from Grade 4 to Grade 8 (from 7% to 10%).

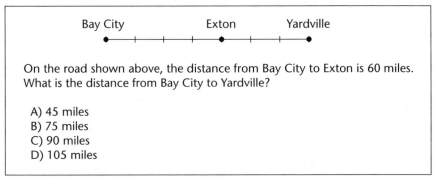

Figure 10.5. Number strand item involving finding distance on a number line (2003-4M6 #19, 2003-8M6 #19).

A second 2003 NAEP number strand item with a gender gap favoring males involved translating from a pictorial to a numerical representation of number (Figure 10.6). This item was administered only at Grade 4, with 85% of boys and 80% of girls correctly choosing "C." Girls who responded incorrectly were most likely to choose "D." An answer of "D" can be obtained in at least two ways—by reading the picture left to right and counting "2," "4," and "9" objects, or by counting the number of visible whole small squares, which is 237, and adding fractional parts to account for the partial squares. Thought of in the latter way, 249 is a more reasonable estimate of the number "shown" than 429.

Examples of two items on which girls outperformed boys are shown in Figure 10.7. For the notebook-purchasing problem, the 2003 gender gaps at Grades 4 and 8 were 4 points and 7 points, respectively. Boys who responded incorrectly were most likely to choose "B" (thinking the change from $5.00 for a $3.60 pur-

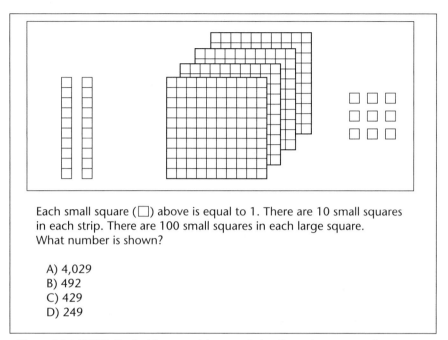

Each small square (□) above is equal to 1. There are 10 small squares in each strip. There are 100 small squares in each large square. What number is shown?

A) 4,029
B) 492
C) 429
D) 249

Figure 10.6. NAEP Grade 4 item requiring translation from picture to number (2003-4M10 #6).

1. How much change will John get back from $5.00 if he buys 2 notebooks that cost $1.80 each?

   A) $1.40
   B) $2.40
   C) $3.20
   D) $3.60

2. The band members have a goal to sell 625 candy bars. If they have sold 264 so far, how many more candy bars do they have to sell to reach their goal?

Figure 10.7. Examples of number strand items for which the gender gap favored females (2003-4M6 #15; 2003-8M6 #7; 2003-4M10 #9).

chase is $2.40, a common change-making error); girls were most likely to choose "C" (the correct change if only one notebook was purchased). At Grade 8, boys who responded incorrectly were again most likely to choose "B," but boys and girls were nearly equally likely to choose "C." The selling-candy problem was administered at Grade 4 only; the gender gap for that item in 2003 was between 4 and 5 points.

Because only a subset of 2003 NAEP items were released to the public, we cannot generalize from the relatively small number of items available to us for detailed analysis. The problems in Figure 10.7 seem typical of the overall pattern found in the number strand; the items on which female students outperformed males tended to be computational and involved addition and subtraction. Many of the number strand items on which males performed better than females involved percentages (at Grade 8) and fractions (at Grades 4 and 8); however, we do not find many examples of those items in the released item set. In addition, an important outcome to note is that male and female students performed similarly on the majority of number strand items (78% of Grade 4 items and 69% of Grade 8 items in 2003), so the differences reported here were the exception rather than the rule.

Other Findings Related to Content Strands and Performance by Gender

We found no meaningful difference in performance by gender on 90% of the geometry items at Grade 4 and 87% of the items at Grade 8 in 2003 (those percentages were 92% at Grade 4 and 81% at Grade 8 in 2000). Analyses of those items for which a gender difference was noted did not reveal consistent gender-related patterns.

Past research has indicated that spatial visualization may be a factor in gender-related differences in mathematics (Battista, 1990; Tartre, 1990), and previous analysis of NAEP data revealed that males outperformed females on more difficult problems involving spatial visualization at Grade 4 (Ansell & Doerr, 2000). Because of this prior work, we examined the 2003 released items pertaining to spatial visualization and found mixed evidence on the relationship between spatial visualization and performance by gender. For example, more 4th-grade girls (74%) than boys (70%) correctly answered a multiple-choice item about visualizing a flipped figure (see Figure 10.8). At Grade 8, gender differences in correct responses to the same item were again relatively small and favored females (84% to 81%). However, on an item asking students to visualize the result of folding a rectangle, more 8th-grade boys (49%) than girls (42%) responded correctly that point P would touch point D (see Figure 10.9). Girls (24%) were more likely than boys (18%) to choose the opposite corner of the rectangle, point B. (This item was not administered at Grade 4.) Finally, gender differences were small on a third item asking students to determine which of four given patterns could not be folded to form a cube (question 2003-8M6 #14). At Grade 4, 39% of boys and 36% of girls answered this item correctly, and at Grade 8, 71% of boys and 70% of girls answered correctly.

In the data analysis and probability strand, male and female students performed similarly on 89% of items at Grade 4 and 90% of items at Grade 8 in 2003 (percentages were 86% and 75% in 2000). Of the nine items for which we found at least a 5 percentage point difference in performance by gender at Grade 4 or

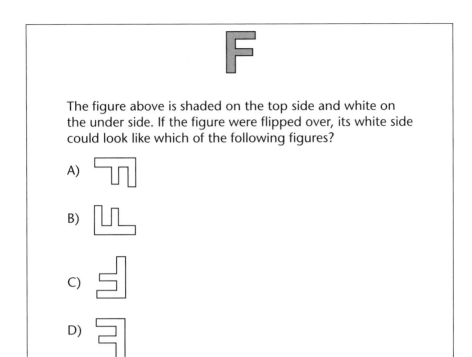

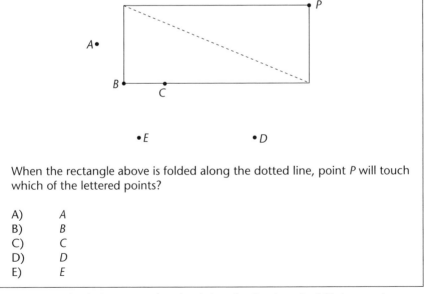

When the rectangle above is folded along the dotted line, point *P* will touch which of the lettered points?

A)   A
B)   B
C)   C
D)   D
E)   E

Grade 8 in either 2000 or 2003, six involved creating or interpreting information represented in a graph or picture (e.g., pie chart). Boys performed better than girls on all six of those items. The item exhibiting the largest and most consistent gender gap (12 percentage points in 2000 and 10 points in 2003) favored males and was given only at Grade 8 (Figure 10.10). Girls were more likely than boys to choose answer A (25% to 18%) and also more likely to choose answer C (16% to 13%). Answer A may reasonably be obtained by incorrectly reading the interval size on the vertical axis.

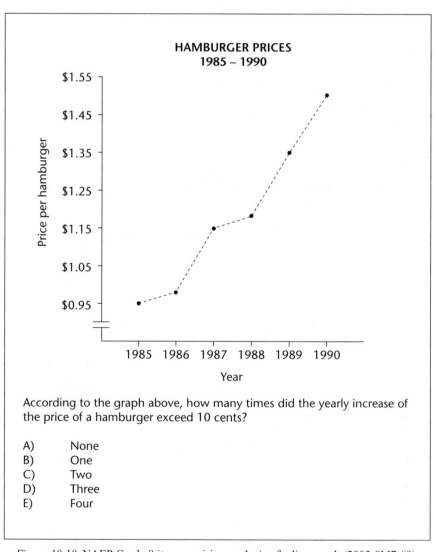

According to the graph above, how many times did the yearly increase of the price of a hamburger exceed 10 cents?

A)   None
B)   One
C)   Two
D)   Three
E)   Four

Figure 10.10. NAEP Grade 8 item requiring analysis of a line graph (2003-8M7 #8).

Differences in male and female students' performance were less than 5 percentage points on 67% (Grade 4) and 74% (Grade 8) of algebra and functions items in 2000, and differences in male and female performance were less than 5 points on 81% (Grade 4) and 90% (Grade 8) of items in that strand in 2003. Our analysis of items for which a gender difference of 5 or more points was noted did not reveal consistent gender-related patterns. Looking across content strands, we noticed one interesting pattern. Several of the items in multiple content strands for which we found large differences in performance by gender favoring males involved analyzing information presented on intervals (see Figures 10.3, 10.4, 10.5, and 10.10). On those items, female students appeared to be more likely than male students to misinterpret the meaning of the intervals. We conjecture, on the basis of a small number of items, that a relationship might exist between gender and interval analysis, but further research would be needed to explore that possibility.

ITEM TYPE AND ITEM DIFFICULTY

In 2003, a total of 39 Grade 4 items had at least a 5 percentage point gender difference, with only 4 of those 39 favoring females. At Grade 8, slightly fewer items (32) had 5 point gender differences, and more items (7) favored females at Grade 8 than at Grade 4. This decrease from Grade 4 to Grade 8 is consistent with the fact that the scale score gender gap was smaller at Grade 8 than at Grade 4. Those items for which at least 5 point differences occurred were examined by item type and item difficulty.

Data regarding NAEP item type in conjunction with gender are shown in Table 10.3. Constructed-response items are those for which students must write down an answer of their own creation (a number, a drawing, or a brief statement), and some of those items (called extended constructed-response as opposed to short constructed-response items) require that students show detailed work or write extended explanations (see chapter 1). A majority of the items administered as part of the NAEP mathematics assessment are of the multiple-choice type, so the majority of items exhibiting differences in performance by gender are, not surprisingly, multiple-choice items. We should also note that for most items, no gender differences were found. However, an analysis of the distribution of items for which males outperformed females, and vice versa, does produce some evidence of a relationship between item type and performance by gender.

In Grades 4 and 8, the items favoring males were disproportionately of the multiple-choice and short (i.e., little if any work or explanation required) constructed-response types. For example, in Grade 4, boys outperformed girls by 5 percentage points or more on approximately 20% of all multiple-choice items (23 of 114) and on 20% (12 of 60) of all short constructed-response items. That percentage drops to 0 for extended constructed-response items. The four 4th-grade items favoring girls were all constructed-response items, and one of those

Table 10.3

Distribution of 2003 NAEP Items by Item Type and Gender Difference in Performance

	Grade 4			Grade 8		
	Multiple Choice	Constructed Response		Multiple Choice	Constructed Response	
		Short	Extended		Short	Extended
Total no. of items	114	60	8	129	61	9
Items with ≥5 point gender difference in % correct	23	15	1	19	13	0
No. favoring males	23	12	0	17	8	0
No. favoring females	0	3	1	2	5	0

four was an extended constructed-response item. Patterns in the items favoring boys were similar at Grade 8; equal proportions of items favoring boys were of the multiple-choice and short constructed-response types. Most of the items (5 of 7) that favored females involved short constructed responses. None of the extended constructed-response items favored females or males at Grade 8.

Overall, the total number of items for which girls outperformed boys is quite small compared with the number of items for which boys outperformed girls. Still, a consistent pattern in gender disparities emerged at both 4th and 8th grades. Despite the fact that the majority of the items administered were multiple choice (63% in Grade 4 and 65% in Grade 8), when girls outperformed boys, they were more likely to do so on constructed-response than multiple-choice items. Those findings are consistent with the analysis of 1996 NAEP data conducted by Ansell and Doerr (2000), who found that 4th- and 8th-grade boys were more likely to outperform girls on items that did not require an explanation, whereas girls were equally likely to outperform boys on items that required an explanation.

To analyze possible relationships between item difficulty and performance by gender, we followed a convention used by Ansell and Doerr (2000) and Lubienski et al. (2004) whereby we divided the 2003 NAEP items into categories by item difficulty. The three categories used were labeled "least difficult," "moderately difficult," and "most difficult" (Table 10.4) and defined as items for which the percentages of students responding correctly were between 0 and 33, 34 and 67, and 68 and 100, respectively.

Examining the distribution of the items with gender gaps, we see that a higher proportion of the items were in the "moderately difficult" and "most difficult" categories. Relatively few items on which males outperformed females were found in the "least difficult" category. Particularly striking was the fact that males outperformed females on approximately one-fourth of the most difficult

Table 10.4
*Distribution of 2003 NAEP Items According to the Percentage of Students
Responding Correctly and Gender Difference in Performance*

	Grade 4			Grade 8		
	Least Difficult	Moderately Difficult	Most Difficult	Least Difficult	Moderately Difficult	Most Difficult
Total no. of items	49	91	42	59	93	47
Items with ≥5 point gender difference in % correct	4	23	10	4	23	4
No. favoring males	4	19	10	2	19	3
No. favoring females	0	4	0	2	4	1

items administered at Grade 4, but that pattern appeared considerably weaker at
Grade 8. Items for which females outperformed males fell mainly in the "moderately difficult" category at both grades. Overall, the patterns identified in the
2003 data related to item difficulty and performance by gender were consistent
with patterns found in previous NAEP analyses (Ansell & Doerr, 2000; Lubienski
et al., 2004); specifically, the distribution of items favoring males tended to be
skewed toward the most difficult category, and the distribution of items favoring
females tended to be skewed toward the moderately difficult level.

GENDER GAPS IN ACHIEVEMENT
BY RACE/ETHNICITY AND SES

Scholars have encouraged examinations of race/ethnicity and socioeconomic
status (SES) in conjunction with gender (Campbell, 1991; Leder, 1992). For
example, Campbell (1991) argued that studying gender, race/ethnicity, and SES
separately "causes research to be incomplete at best, and at worst, to be just plain
wrong" (p. 96). Table 10.5 compares the gender gap in scale scores across racial/
ethnic groups for 4th- and 8th-grade students from the 2003 NAEP assessment.
The table clearly shows that the differences in scale scores were much greater
between racial/ethnic groups than between males and females within the same
racial/ethnic group. Still, gender gaps were larger and more consistent for some
racial/ethnic groups than others. The only statistically significant gender differences involved white and Hispanic students,[1] with males outscoring females by
3 points at Grade 4 and by 2 points at Grade 8. Significant gender gaps were
not found for black students, a finding consistent with our previous 2000 NAEP

[1] Although we acknowledge that different opinions exist with respect to the appropriateness of the
racial/ethnic categories utilized here, we use them to be consistent with the NAEP data.

data analysis (Lubienski et al., 2004). Because of the relatively small samples of American Indian and Asian/Pacific Islander students, conclusions regarding the gender gaps within those two groups are difficult to draw.

Table 10.5
Gender Disparities in Scale Scores by Race/Ethnicity for Grades 4 and 8

	White	Hispanic	Black	American Indian	Asian/ Pacific Islander
4th grade	$N = 117210$	$N = 24720$	$N = 34683$	$N = 3873$	$N = 8055$
Males	245	223	216	224	248
Females	242	220	216	222	245
Gap (males/ females)	3*	3*	0	2	3
8th grade	$N = 100315$	$N = 16799$	$N = 25516$	$N = 3050$	$N = 6501$
Males	289	260	252	264	291
Females	287	258	253	262	291
Gap (males/ females)	2*	2*	–1	2	1

* Indicates significant difference at the .05 level; effect sizes of significant differences ranged from 0.06 to 0.1 with a median of 0.09.

An analysis of gender gaps in conjunction with both race/ethnicity and SES can reveal the extent to which race/ethnicity–related gender differences in performance persist across SES groups. Our previous analysis of the 2000 NAEP data revealed that gender gaps favoring males tended to be more prevalent among higher SES students than other groups, with the most consistent gaps occurring for high SES white students (Lubienski et al., 2004). That finding was consistent with the fact that gender gaps tend to be larger for high-achieving students, who tend to be disproportionately white and of high SES.

However, our 2003 analysis of gender gaps by race and SES (on the basis of school lunch eligibility as SES proxy) did not reveal similar patterns. In fact, no consistent relationship appeared to exist between SES and the size of the gender gap, either overall or within particular ethnic groups. Possibly the use of a more sensitive, multifaceted SES variable, as was used in 2000, would reveal more consistent patterns.

Overall, our analyses indicate that gender gaps favoring males are significant for white and Hispanic students but not for black students. However, the fact that no gender disparities were found among black students should not be taken to mean that black females are being educated equitably. On the contrary, the data indicate that race/ethnicity–related disparities (as well as SES-related disparities) are much larger and more consistent than gender-related gaps (Lubienski et al., 2004).

PATTERNS IN STUDENT AFFECT

Researchers who have examined the relationships among affective factors, mathematics achievement, and gender (Ai, 2002; Elliott, 1990; Hacket & Betz, 1989; Hembree, 1990; Ma, 1999; Ma & Kishor, 1997) have found that affective factors, such as attitude, self-concept, and self-confidence, are positively correlated with achievement for both boys and girls. Research on student affect and gender also suggests that boys have a more positive self-concept with respect to mathematics than girls (Ansell & Doerr, 2000; Lubienski et al., 2004; Meyer & Koehler, 1990; Seegers & Boekaerts, 1996). In addition, examinations of course-taking patterns reveal that girls do not persist in the study of mathematics to the same extent as boys (Ansell & Doerr, 2000; Gaffney & Gill, 1996; Lubienski et al., 2004; National Science Foundation, 2000; Smart, 1996). Reform efforts in mathematics education (NCTM, 2000) emphasize the need for students to develop self-confidence in mathematics and an appreciation for the usefulness of mathematics in careers and everyday life. As part of NAEP, surveys are administered that ask students the extent to which they agree with the statements "I like mathematics," "I am good at mathematics," and "Mathematics is useful for solving everyday problems." In this section we report findings from analyses of NAEP survey items that relate to students' self-image in mathematics and beliefs about the nature of mathematics.

Table 10.6 shows the extent to which male and female students agree with statements related to students' self-concept in mathematics. Fourth-grade girls were less likely than boys to report that the statements "I like mathematics" and "I am good at mathematics" were "a lot like me" (the gaps were 7 and 13 percentage points, respectively). Correspondingly, 4th-grade girls were more likely than boys to report that these statements were "a little like me." With respect to the statement "I am good at mathematics," 4th-grade girls were slightly, but significantly, more likely than boys to report that the statement was "not like me." Fourth-grade girls were less likely than boys to indicate that the statement "I understand most of what goes on in mathematics class" was "a lot like" them, but they were more likely to indicate that the statement was "a little like" them.

If we total the "a lot like me" and "a little like me" percentages for each of the three affect statements at the 4th-grade level, overall percentages for male and female students become very similar. That outcome leads us to conjecture that female students may be more likely than males to choose the less affirmative statement. In previous years, when 4th-grade students' choices were "agree," "undecided," and "disagree," the percentages of female students responding positively to those statements (i.e., the percentage choosing "agree") were much higher than the percentages choosing "a lot like me" in 2003, although not as high as the percentages that would be created by combining the "a lot like me" and "a little like me" responses for 2003.

Table 10.6

Student Responses Regarding Self-Concept in Mathematics for Grades 4 and 8

		Response Categories and % Responding		
	Grade 4	Not like me	A little like me	A lot like me
I like mathematics.	Male	16	33*	50*
	Female	16	41	43
I am good at mathematics.	Male	9*	35*	56*
	Female	11	45	43
I understand most of what goes	Male	8*	34*	58*
on in mathematics class.	Female	7	37	55
		Response Categories and % Responding[a]		
	Grade 8	Disagree	Undecided	Agree
I like mathematics.	Male	29*	20*	51
	Female	31	22	47
I am good at mathematics.	Male	16*	20*	65*
	Female	21	24	55
I understand most of what goes	Male	11	14*	75
on in mathematics class.	Female	12	15	73

* Indicates significant difference between female and male percentages.

[a] "Agree" represents the sum of the percentage of students who selected "Agree" and the percentage who selected "Strongly Agree." "Disagree" represents the sum of the percentage of students who selected "Disagree" and the percentage of students who selected "Strongly Disagree." In some instances, this collapsing of response categories affected the authors' ability to determine whether a significant difference existed. In those cases, no significant difference was reported.

At the 8th-grade level, male and female students' tendency to agree with the statement "I like mathematics" appeared more similar (a 4 percentage point gap) than at the 4th-grade level; slightly more girls than boys disagreed with, or were not sure about, the statement. Gender gaps in 8th- grade students' responses to the statement "I am good at mathematics" were in the same direction as those found at the 4th-grade level. Eighth-grade girls were less likely than boys to agree with the statement and more likely to disagree or indicate uncertainty. Male and female 8th-grade students were similar in their responses to the statement "I understand most of what goes on in mathematics class." Girls were slightly more likely than boys to respond that they were "not sure" whether they agreed or disagreed with the statement. In general, female and male students' responses to this statement were more similar to each other than to the other two statements, at both the 4th- and 8th-grade levels. Overall, students' responses to the three self-concept questions suggest that girls are less likely than boys to like or believe they are good at mathematics; however, they are similar to boys in their beliefs about their level of understanding of what goes on in mathematics class.

Students' levels of agreement with statements related to the nature of mathematics are shown in Table 10.7. Fourth-grade boys were slightly more likely than girls (46% and 44%) to agree with the statement "Learning mathematics is mostly memorizing facts," and yet they were also slightly more likely to disagree. For both genders, agreement with the statement had decreased by Grade 8 (to 36% and 33% for boys and girls, respectively). That statement was first included in the student survey in 1992 when the percentages of boys and girls agreeing

Table 10.7
Student Responses Regarding the Nature of Mathematics for Grades 4 and 8

	Grade 4	Response Categories and % Responding		
		Disagree	Not sure	Agree
Learning mathematics is mostly	Male	26*	28*	46*
memorizing facts.	Female	24	33	44
There is only one correct way to	Male	58*	26*	17*
solve a mathematics problem.	Female	56	30	14
Mathematics is useful for solving	Male	13*	21*	66*
everyday problems.	Female	12	23	65
All students can do well in	Male	6*	12*	82*
mathematics if they try.	Female	4	11	85
	Grade 8	Response Categories and % Responding[a]		
		Disagree	Undecided	Agree
Learning mathematics is mostly	Male	38	26*	36
memorizing facts.	Female	38	29	33
There is only one correct way to	Male	76	14	10*
solve a mathematics problem.	Female	80	14	7
Mathematics is useful for solving	Male	13	15*	73
everyday problems.	Female	11	17	73
All students can do well in	Male	14	15*	70
mathematics if they try.	Female	12	17	71

* Indicates significant difference between female and male percentages.

[a] "Agree" represents the sum of the percentage of students who selected "Agree" and the percentage who selected "Strongly Agree." "Disagree" represents the sum of the percentage of students who selected "Disagree" and the percentage of students who selected "Strongly Disagree." In some instances, this collapsing of response categories affected the authors' ability to determine whether a significant difference existed. In those cases, no significant difference was reported.

were 57% and 56% for Grade 4 and 46% and 42% for Grade 8. Agreement with the statement has decreased steadily across reporting years for both genders. Although the data suggest that many students do believe that learning mathematics is mostly memorizing facts, both male and female students were unlikely to agree that "There is only one way to solve a mathematics problem," and the percentage of students agreeing decreased from Grade 4 to Grade 8. That statement was included on NAEP student surveys in 1996 and 2000, and percentages of students agreeing have remained consistent, as has the small gender difference of 2 to 3 points in responses.

In 2003 and in previous reporting years, male and female students were very similar in their responses to the statement "Mathematics is useful for solving everyday problems." Although the percentages of 4th-grade students who agree with the statement had increased steadily from 1990 (63% overall) to 2000 (70%), the 2003 percentages of students agreeing dropped back to 1992 levels (66% overall).[2] At 8th grade, the levels of agreement for both male and female students increased slightly from 1990 (76% overall) to 1992 (80%), remained essentially stable from 1992 to 1996, and then showed decreases in both 2000 (76%) and 2003 (73%). Hence smaller percentages of male and female students agreed that "mathematics is useful for solving everyday problems" in 2003 than in 1990 (the previous low point for percentage of students agreeing). Male and female students were also similar in the extent to which they agreed that "All students can do well in mathematics if they try," with slightly higher percentages of females than males agreeing with the statement in both 4th and 8th grades.

In summary, males and females generally held similar beliefs about the nature of mathematics as measured by NAEP student survey items. They tended *not* to believe that there is only one correct way to solve a mathematics problem, and they tended to believe that all students can do well in mathematics if they try, although that belief seemed to diminish somewhat as students got older. Both genders were divided as to whether mathematics is mostly memorizing facts, but the majority believed that mathematics is useful for solving everyday problems, a belief that increased from Grade 4 to 8. With respect to students' self-concept related to mathematics, females and males were similar in their levels of agreement with the statement "I understand most of what goes on in mathematics class." However, males were more likely than females to indicate that they liked mathematics and thought that they were good at mathematics. Looking at students' responses across reporting years (1990, 1992, 1996, 2000, and 2003), we note that a downward trend continues to be evident in the per-

---

[2] The order of the response options ("agree," "unsure," "disagree") for this and other questions was reversed on the 2003 student surveys from what they were on the 1990–2000 surveys, so that this reversal was possibly a factor in this pattern. However, we did not see similar patterns in all the 2000–2003 survey response comparisons, so what role, if any, the response option reversal may have played is not clear.

centages of students indicating that they like mathematics. In their analysis of gender differences in NAEP 1990–2000 data, Lubienski et al. (2004) found an upward trend in the percentages of male and female students agreeing with the statement "I am good at mathematics." Comparing 2000 and 2003 data related to that statement, we find that levels of agreement have dropped to pre-1996 levels for both male and female students—from 71% to 65% and from 60% to 55%, respectively. Analyzing NAEP data is not particularly helpful in terms of determining the reason for such a drop, but should the downward trend continue, it would certainly warrant further investigation.

Previous NAEP monographs have reported on a variety of areas in which gender differences may occur—for example, the amount of time spent on homework or the frequency of calculator/computer use. Our analysis of 2003 NAEP data did not uncover major shifts in trends reported elsewhere. Therefore, we refer readers to other NAEP publications for information on gender differences in those areas (Lubienski et al., 2004; Ansell & Doerr, 2000).

CONCLUSION

Our analysis of NAEP mathematics assessment data by gender reveals relatively small but consistent gaps favoring males in 2003. Although both male and female students' average scale scores continued to rise, gender gaps have not diminished. In 2003, males scored significantly higher on average than females at both the 4th- and 8th-grade levels. Because the effect sizes for the observed gender differences were generally very small, we may reasonably question the meaningfulness of those significant differences. Further analysis of gender gaps in NAEP average scale scores suggests that they are not evenly distributed across percentiles. At each grade level assessed, gaps favoring males were largest at the upper end of the percentile range. As grade level increased (from Grade 4 to Grade 8), gaps became even larger and more concentrated at the upper end of the percentile range. Those findings are consistent with our analysis of 2000 NAEP data (Lubienski et al., 2004).

To go beyond simply reporting the size of gender disparities in general mathematics achievement, we analyzed whether gender gaps varied by mathematical content strand, item type and difficulty, race/ethnicity, and SES. We also analyzed students' responses to released items, as well as responses to NAEP questionnaire items related to self-image and beliefs about mathematics. Our analysis suggests that the gender gap is not distributed evenly across mathematical content strands. At each grade level, the gaps were largest for NAEP Measurement items, with girls' average scale scores trailing boys' scores by a significant 5 to 7 points. We also found a consistent gap of 3 to 4 points in scores favoring boys across grade levels for Number and Operations items and a significant difference favoring boys for Algebra and Functions items at Grade 4. Our item analyses revealed that girls tended not to perform as well as boys on

Measurement items that required reading instruments or using indirect calculation methods nor on items that asked students to choose the best or most reasonable unit of measure. Items in the Number and Operations strand that favored boys tended to involve fractions, rational numbers, and some computational tasks; items favoring girls included computational tasks and tasks that required students to analyze and create rules for number or letter patterns. Our analysis of the released items in the Geometry and Spatial Sense strand produces mixed evidence with respect to the relationship between spatial visualization and performance by gender found in previous research (Battista, 1990; Tartre, 1990). With respect to Data Analysis, Statistics, and Probability, gender differences were found mainly in items that involved creating or interpreting information represented in a graph or picture (e.g., pie chart). Boys performed better than girls on seven of the eight such items. Item-level analysis across content strands revealed several instances in which differences in performance by gender favored boys and involved analysis of information presented on intervals; however, because of the small set of NAEP items available for analysis, further research is needed to draw conclusions about possible relationships between gender and mathematical content involving interval analysis.

Our examination of NAEP item type and difficulty suggests that items in which gender differences in performance favor males tend to be multiple choice, whereas items favoring females are more likely to require constructed responses. That finding is consistent with Ansell and Doerr's (2000) analysis of 1996 NAEP data; those researchers found that boys were more likely to outperform girls on items that did not require an explanation, whereas girls were equally likely to outperform boys on items that required an explanation. With respect to item difficulty, the distribution of items favoring boys tended to be skewed toward the most difficult category, and the distribution of items favoring girls tended to be skewed toward the moderately difficult level. In other words, proportionally more of the items accounting for the overall gender difference favoring boys were in the most difficult item category. That finding is also consistent with findings of previous NAEP analyses (Ansell & Doerr, 2000; Lubienski et al., 2004).

An analysis of interactions among gender, race/ethnicity, and socioeconomic status suggests that differences in performance by gender are small compared with differences across racial/ethnic categories. Gender gaps were found for white and Hispanic students, but not for black students, and favored boys. With respect to SES, patterns found in previous NAEP analyses (Lubienski et al., 2004) that indicated that the largest gender gaps occurred among upper SES white students were not found in our analysis of 2003 data.

With respect to student affect, our analysis of 2003 NAEP data suggests that female students are less likely than their male counterparts to like or believe they are good at mathematics; however, they are similar to males in their beliefs about their level of understanding of what goes on in mathematics class. Males and females seem to hold similar views, however, about the nature of mathematics as measured by NAEP student survey items. They tend not to believe that there is only one correct way to solve a mathematics problem, and they tend to believe that all students can do well in mathematics if they try, although that belief seemed to diminish somewhat as students got older. Our findings on student affect are consistent with those of previous NAEP analyses (Ansell & Doerr, 2000; Lubienski et al., 2004).

Gender gaps in NAEP scores and student affect described in this chapter are generally relatively small, particularly when compared with gaps related to race/ ethnicity and SES. However, the persistence of those gaps since 1990 indicates that work done over the last decade and a half to promote both gender equity and NCTM *Standards*-based instruction cannot be said to have diminished U.S. gender gaps in mathematics achievement, at least not as measured by the NAEP assessment. Scholars have raised the question of whether calling attention to small gender gaps in mathematics performance does more harm than good by confirming and perpetuating stereotypes (Fennema, Carpenter, Jacobs, Franke, & Levi, 1998b). Others have asked why scholars show more concern about girls' performance in mathematics than about boys' lack of interest in vocations that involve caring for others (Noddings, 1998). Despite our focus on gender gaps in the NAEP mathematics data in this chapter, we believe that those crucial questions are important to be mindful of as a mathematics education community. As we wrote this chapter, those questions prompted us to examine and emphasize ways in which the data showed more similarities than differences between boys and girls, such as the immense overlap in their score distributions.

We offer these descriptive data on gender differences in student affect and achievement so that disparities in educational opportunities and outcomes can continue to be monitored. However, we are fully aware that if we are to understand relationships between student affect and performance on NAEP, including interactions among gender, race/ethnicity, and SES, then further studies within schools and classrooms are necessary.

REFERENCES

Ai, X. (2002). Gender differences in growth in mathematics achievement: Three-level longitudinal and multilevel analyses of individual, home, and school influences. *Mathematical Thinking and Learning, 4,* 1–22.

Ansell, E., & Doerr, H. M. (2000). NAEP findings regarding gender: Achievement, affect, and instructional experience. In E. A. Silver & P. A. Kenney (Eds.), *Results from the seventh mathematics assessment of the National Assessment of Educational Progress* (pp. 73–106). Reston, VA: National Council of Teachers of Mathematics.

Battista, M. (1990). Spatial visualization and gender differences in high school geometry. *Journal for Research in Mathematics Education, 21,* 47–60.

Campbell, P. B. (1991). So what do we do with the poor, non-white female? Issues of gender, race, and social class in mathematics and equity. *Peabody Journal of Education, 66,* 95–112.

Elliott, J. C. (1990). Affect and mathematics achievement of nontraditional college students. *Journal for Research in Mathematics Education, 21,* 160–165.

Fennema, E., Carpenter, T. P., Jacobs, V. R., Franke, M. L., & Levi, L. (1998a). A longitudinal study of gender differences in young children's mathematical thinking. *Educational Researcher, 27*(5), 6–11.

Fennema, E., Carpenter, T. P., Jacobs, V. R., Franke, M. L., & Levi, L. (1998b). New perspectives on gender differences in mathematics: A reprise. *Educational Researcher, 27*(5), 19–21.

Friedman, L. (1995). The space factor in mathematics: Gender differences. Review of *Educational Research, 65,* 22–50.

Frost, L. A., Hyde, J. S., & Fennema, E. (1994). Gender, mathematics performance, and mathematics-related attitudes and affect: A meta-analytic synthesis. *International Journal of Educational Research, 21,* 373–385.

Gaffney, J. M., & Gill, J. (1996). Gender and mathematics in the context of Australian education. In G. Hanna (Ed.), *Towards gender equity in mathematics education: An ICMI study* (pp. 237–255). Dordrecht, Netherlands: Kluwer.

Hacket, G., & Betz, N. E. (1989). An exploration of the mathematics self-efficacy/mathematics performance correspondence. *Journal for Research in Mathematics Education, 20,* 261–273.

Hembree, R. (1990). The nature, effects, and relief of mathematics anxiety. *Journal for Research in Mathematics Education, 21,* 33–46.

Leder, G. C. (1992). Mathematics and gender: Changing perspectives. In D. A. Grouws (Ed.), *Handbook of research on mathematics teaching and learning* (pp. 597–622). New York: Macmillan.

Lubienski, S. T., McGraw, R., & Strutchens, M. E. (2004). NAEP findings regarding gender: Mathematics achievement, student affect, and learning practices. In P. Kloosterman & F. K. Lester Jr. (Eds.), *The 1990–2000 mathematics assessments of the National Assessment of Educational Progress: Results and interpretations* (pp. 305–336). Reston, VA: National Council of Teachers of Mathematics.

Ma, X. (1999). A meta-analysis of the relationship between anxiety toward mathematics and achievement in mathematics. *Journal for Research in Mathematics Education, 30,* 520–540.

Ma, X., & Kishor, N. (1997). Assessing the relationships between attitude toward mathematics and achievement in mathematics: A meta-analysis. *Journal for Research in Mathematics Education, 28,* 26–47.

McGraw, R., Lubienski, S. T., & Strutchens, M. E. (2006). A closer look at gender in NAEP mathematics achievement and affect data: Intersections with achievement, race/ethnicity, and socioeconomic status. *Journal for Research in Mathematics Education 37,* 129–150.

Meyer, M. R., & Koehler, M. S. (1990). Internal influences on gender differences in mathematics. In E. Fennema & G. C. Leder (Eds.), *Mathematics and gender* (pp. 60–95). New York: Teachers College Press.

National Council of Teachers of Mathematics. (2000). *Principles and standards for school mathematics.* Reston, VA: Author.

National Science Foundation. (2000). *Women, minorities, and persons with disabilities in science and engineering* (NSF 00-327). Arlington, VA: Author.

Noddings, N. (1998). Perspectives from feminist psychology. *Educational Researcher, 27*(5), 17–18.

Seegers, G., & Boekaerts, M. (1996). Gender-related differences in self-referenced cognitions in relation to mathematics. *Journal for Research in Mathematics Education, 27,* 215–240.

Smart, T. (1996). Gender and mathematics in England and Wales. In G. Hanna (Ed.), *Towards gender equity in mathematics education: An ICMI study* (pp. 215–236). Dordrecht, Netherlands: Kluwer.

Tartre, L. (1990). Spatial skills, gender, and mathematics. In E. Fennema, & G. C. Leder (Eds.), *Mathematics and gender* (pp. 27–59). New York: Teachers College Press.

11

Designed to Differentiate: What Is NAEP Measuring?

Beatriz S. D'Ambrosio, Signe E. Kastberg, and Diana V. Lambdin

INCREASED concern in recent years about United States students' academic performance has prompted heightened interest in the NAEP. Teachers and parents, principals and superintendents, curriculum coordinators and textbook authors, as well as business leaders, citizens, and politicians, are all interested in what can be learned from NAEP results. But what does NAEP measure?

The government has communicated the intent of the NAEP testing program through the framework that guided the construction of the 2003 NAEP mathematics assessment (National Assessment Governing Board (NAGB), 2002). According to the framework, "The results of these periodic assessments are published in the *Nation's Report Card* to inform citizens about the nature of students' comprehension of the subject, curriculum specialists about the level and nature of student understanding, and policymakers about factors related to schooling and its relationship to student proficiency in mathematics" (p. 1). Furthermore, the framework is specific in claiming increased attention focused on the assessment of students' mathematical power by "continuing deliberate attention to reasoning and communication and by providing students with opportunities to connect their learning across mathematical content strands" (p. 12). Throughout the framework, the goal of determining students' understanding and mathematical power by analyzing their performance on the NAEP assessments is quite clear and much more explicit than it has been in previous frameworks.

To what extent do multiple-choice NAEP items actually give students the opportunity to show how they can reason and communicate and how they can connect their learning across mathematical content strands in meaningful ways, as is the goal of the NAGB? To answer these questions, we must understand how the wording and structure of assessment items can affect student performance.

More specifically, examining items gives a sense of the opportunities that students have to demonstrate their mathematical power and understanding.

Before we turn our attention to actually examining NAEP items, we briefly discuss the criteria that are typically used in developing good test items. In 1967, R. L. Thorndike suggested that designing good test questions was one of the most demanding types of writing possible, and that writing good multiple-choice test items is particularly challenging. Thomas Haladyna and Steven Downing appear to have made a career of writing about the development and validation of multiple-choice items. In 1989, they assembled a taxonomy of rules for writing multiple-choice items on the basis of "a consensus of 46 authoritative references representing the field of educational measurement" (1989a, p. 38), and they investigated the extent to which the item-writing rules were supported by credible research (1989b). More than a decade later, they reprised their earlier study, examining 27 new textbooks and more than 27 new studies of guidelines for writing multiple-choice items. Using their review, they reduced the original set of 43 guidelines to 31, which they organized into four categories: content guidelines, style and format concerns, writing the stem, and writing options (Haladyna, 2004). In the third edition of his classic book *Developing and Validating Multiple-Choice Test Items,* Haladyna (2004) devoted four chapters to the theme of "developing multiple-choice test items" and another three chapters to "validity evidence arising from item development and item response validation" (statistical techniques for analyzing the validity of items by studying item-response patterns).

Critiques of standardized testing (Delandshere, 2002; Shepard, 1991; Van den Heuvel-Panhuizen & Becker, 2003) assert that psychometric design principles appear to be based on a behaviorist model of student learning. They have called for the creation of test-design mechanisms or procedures that are more attuned to current theories of learning and ways in which learners interact with the items themselves. Bass, Magone, and Glaser (2002) claim that "there are numerous psychometric techniques for analyzing assessments once they are implemented, [although] there are considerably fewer procedures available to guide task development" (p. 25). Pellegrino (2002) reiterates the same view, asserting the need for new models of assessment that are based on models of how students learn and thus more clearly assess what students know. In his view, "much of what we've been doing in assessment has been based on impoverished models of cognition, which has led us to highly limited modes of observation that can yield only extremely limited interpretations of what students know" (p. 49).

In this chapter we analyze NAEP 2003 released items with the goal of identifying those characteristics of the items that may influence student performance. We assert that student performance is influenced by much more than knowledge of mathematical content. In previous work, we addressed the role of item context in student performance (Kastberg, D'Ambrosio, McDermott, & Saada, 2005). In this chapter we extend our analysis to additional characteristics of test items that influence student performance as identified in the mathematics education literature. Beyond item context, the characteristics include language and format, the use of mathematics symbols, and the choice of distractors. We discuss and illustrate each of those characteristics by using NAEP items.

If providing the nation with accurate information about United States students' mathematics performance is a goal of the National Assessment Governing Board, then awareness of the impact on student performance of the item characteristics listed above is essential. The National Center for Education Statistics (NCES) can legitimately claim that NAEP performance reports function as the "Nation's Report Card" only if attention has been paid to those factors that may restrict some students' opportunity to share what they actually know and can do.

The goal of this chapter is to provide teachers, administrators, policy makers, and others with a framework with which to understand student performance on NAEP beyond simply considering students' responses to specific items as correct or incorrect. We also hope to heighten an awareness of the need to be critical of, and reflective about, several dimensions of items when using them for assessment purposes. Although we have focused our critique on NAEP test items, the same sort of analysis could be used with test items from any test item bank. Indeed, teachers should routinely engage in this sort of reflection when choosing items for classroom assessments or when creating their own assessment items.

Finally, we hope to help teachers understand why some of their students may not be performing as well on test items as might be expected. Even when children know the content well, some characteristics of test items may mask their true understanding. When teachers gain such an awareness, they may be able to help their students become more "test savvy" and hence more successful in showing what they know. Empowering teachers to better understand the limitations of test items used in large-scale assessments is the first step in curtailing the dangers of the lack of fidelity between learning that occurs in the classroom and what is measured on large-scale assessments (Wilson & Draney, 2004). We build our intents on research findings that suggest that teachers can use summative assessments for formative purposes and thereby influence their students' performance on large-scale assessments (Black & Wiliam, 2004).

IMPACT OF THE CONTEXT USED IN ITEMS

Research in mathematics education includes at least two perspectives on children's reactions to contexts in assessment items. Several authors have found that when children confront problems—in school or on tests—that are set in a realistic context, they may tend to ignore the realistic nature of the questions (Greer, 1993, 1997; Verschaffel, De Corte, & Lasure, 1994). They argue that children see testing as an extension of the didactical contract. Children understand that real-world contexts may appear on tests, but they believe the contexts are not to be taken seriously. We contend that children who ignore the real-world context of a problem, and instead create an oversimplified mathematical model of the situation, are often quite in tune with the didactical contract of problems situated in mathematics classes and on tests. Children who appear to ignore context are often more successful overall because their interpretations of problems are, in fact, closely aligned with the item developers' intent. The children, in essence, understand the "ground rules" of testing and instruction.

Other authors have suggested that when students confront problems that are situated in real-world contexts, they tend to perform differently than they would in solving purely numerical problems. When children do so, they seem to view the context as a tool that can allow them insight into the problem. Van den Heuvel-Panhuizen (1996) found that contexts can help students by providing powerful images and operations not implied by the numbers themselves. Kazemi (2002) found that some children do in fact pay attention to problem contexts and that their solutions often take the real world into consideration. However, the findings of Cooper (1998) and Cooper and Dunne (1998) illustrate that some children's understanding of the real world and their application of that knowledge to realistic contexts in test items can hinder performance, masking their true understanding of mathematical ideas and procedures. When Cooper asked children about their solutions to contextually rich problems from a testing situation, the children revealed their overemphasis on the reality of the problem. Yet when prompted to ignore the reality, they could usually solve the problem correctly (as intended by the test developers).

In analyzing the context of NAEP items to determine how student performance on those situated in a real-world context might be affected, we found certain items in which the context actually did serve simply as "window-dressing" (Van den Heuvel-Panhuizen, 1996) because the context was irrelevant in selecting a solution path. For example, students were asked to read a stem-and-leaf plot (see Figure 11.1). The fact that the plot represents Gloria's scores from a competition is irrelevant to the solution of this problem. Of course, the context used in this multiple-choice item can easily be ignored, but then one must wonder why it was included in the first place.

According to Kazemi (2002), constructed-response items are even more likely than multiple-choice items to prompt children to seriously consider the real-world context in which the problem is set. Indeed, from the NAEP 2003 released items we have identified several constructed-response items that require children to make decisions about just how much realism should be considered in the solution process. For example, in the item in Figure 11.2, children are told the number of bicycles and wagons in a school yard. They are then asked how many wheels are in the yard. For a child who thinks hard about the context, plenty of other "wheels" might be present in the school yard besides those from just bicycles and wagons (e.g., merry-go-round, wheelchair). The realistic count of the number of wheels that could potentially be in the yard becomes impossible to know. A child's success on an item such as this one can be greatly affected by how realistic the child tries to be, because the context of the mathematics test matters

Gloria's diving scores from a recent competition are represented in the stem-and-leaf plot shown below. In this plot, 3 | 4 would be read as 3.4.

$$
\begin{array}{c|cc}
5 & 2 & 5 \\
6 & 1 & \\
7 & 7 & \\
8 & 0 & 2 \\
\end{array}
$$

What was her lowest score for this competition?

A)   0.02
B)   1.0
C)   2.5
D)   5.2
E)   8.0

Figure 11.1. Grade 8 item involving a stem-and-leaf plot. (2003-8M10 #8)

Questions 5–6 refer to the situation described below.

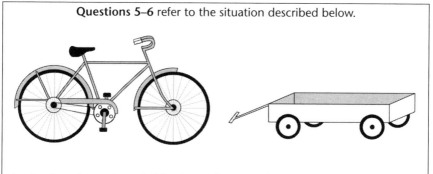

A school yard contains only bicycles and wagons like those in the figure above. On Monday there were 3 bicycles and 2 wagons in the school yard. How many wheels were in the school yard?

Figure 11.2. Grade 4 "wheels in the school yard" item. (2003-4M7 #5)

more here than the context of the school yard in obtaining the anticipated answer. Elsewhere we have described in more detail how students may attend more to the context of problems than to the mathematics when solving NAEP items that involve mathematics but that are posed in other disciplines, such as science or social studies (Kastberg & D'Ambrosio, 2004; Kastberg et al., 2005).

Mathematics educators working in the field of situated cognition would argue that children are more likely to respond correctly to contextualized problems when such problems are presented in out-of-school settings than when they are presented in a formal test situation (Lave, 1988; Nunes, Carraher, & Schliemann,

1993; Saxe, 1995). From the 2003 NAEP released data set, we observed that several of the realistic contextual mathematics problems involved money. Purchasing multiple items, saving money, and making change were some of the situations posed to the students. Students' low performance on NAEP items involving financial transactions (e.g., buying movie tickets, see Figure 11.3) may be more indicative of the difficulties children have in translating their real-world knowledge into paper-and-pencil assessments than of their ability to deal with situations involving buying and selling.

Movie tickets cost $5.25 each. If 100 tickets were sold, how much money was collected?

Answer: _____

	Correct	Incorrect
Overall performance	69%	28%
Achievement level		
Advanced	96%	3%
Proficient	89%	10%
Basic	75%	23%
Below Basic	40%	52%

Figure 11.3. Performance of 8th graders on the movie-ticket item. (2003-8M10 #2)

Only 69% of 8th graders responded correctly to the problem of determining the cost of purchasing 100 movie tickets, given the price of 1 ticket. Note that if we restrict our attention to the subset of students who scored Below Basic on the test overall, a majority (52%) were *not* successful in solving the movie-ticket problem (Figure 11.3). Yet such a high proportion of Below Basic scorers would be unlikely to struggle with this simple purchase in the real world, as indicated by the research findings of situated cognition (Lave, 1988; Nunes et al., 1993; Saxe, 1995). Those findings have shown that children and adults, even when unschooled, can easily solve problems that are more complex than this one when the problems are situated in a daily shopping or selling context.

IMPACT OF THE LANGUAGE AND REPRESENTATIONS USED IN ITEMS

Several studies have described the impact of the language used in test items on student performance (Abedi & Lord, 2001; Bass et al., 2002; Wilson, 2004).

Authors of the studies claimed that even minor changes in wording can result in significantly different performance by students. Wilson provided examples of tasks given to students with limited English proficiency (LEP) and described how simple word changes can result in very different performance by those students. Her work corroborated the findings of Abedi, Hofstetter, Baker, and Lord (2001) and Abedi, Lord, and Hofstetter (1998). Moreover, the findings applied even to students for whom English was a first language. In an extensive analysis of NAEP items, Abedi and his colleagues found that simplifying the language used in the test items resulted in improved performance by all students. Abedi et al. (2001) modified NAEP items in many ways: using shorter words, sentences, and questions; using more common and familiar vocabulary; using shorter prompts; using active rather than passive verbs; and generally clarifying the language used in the items. Figure 11.4 presents an example of a modified item.

Original problem statement:

If $\square$ represents the number of newspapers that Lee delivers each day, which of the following represents the total number of newspapers that Lee delivers in 5 days?

A) $5 + \square$
B) $5 \times \square$
C) $\square + 5$
D) $(\square + \square) \times 5$

Modified:

Lee delivers $\square$ newspapers each day. How many newspapers does he deliver in 5 days?

Figure 11.4. Delivering newspapers. Modified problem from Abedi et al. (1998, p. 21).

In using items with modified English, Abedi et al. (1998) found that "clarifying the language of the test helped all students improve their performance.... Item-level analyses indicated that the language modification of items helped students improve their performance in about 49% of the items (17 out of 35)" (p. 61). The results of subsequent studies were less conclusive in attributing improved performance to modified English; instead, they revealed the more positive impact of a combination of accommodations, of which modified language was one (Abedi et al., 2001).

Bass et al. (2002) determined, in a population of students including fluent English speakers, that "ambiguity in the question wording may have compromised the effectiveness of the item to elicit what students know" (p. 14). "The wording of some questions seemed to confuse or mislead both high-scoring and low-scoring students, although problems were more pronounced for low-scoring students" (p. 15). Bass et al. analyzed 1996 NAEP Science items that required students to perform science experiments (by following directions) and to interpret the results of the experiments.

> First, students were instructed to measure the length of a pencil weighted with a thumbtack (which serves as a hydrometer) floating above the surface of the water, in both fresh water and salt water. The pencil is marked with equally spaced letters from A (top of pencil) through J (bottom of pencil), and students are asked to observe where the water line comes to on the pencil and then place a mark on a picture of the pencil. Students are then directed to measure the length of the pencil that was above the water using a to-scale picture of a ruler. They repeat the Floating Pencil test to identify a "mystery water": They measure the length of pencil floating above the water in the mystery water and compare this finding with results from the previous tests. Throughout the task, students also were asked (a) whether the amount of water in the cylinder changes when the pencil is added; (b) how the way the pencil floats in salt water compares with how it floats in fresh water; (c) how dissolving more salt in the salt water would change the way the pencil floats; (d) how they can tell what the mystery water is; and (e) whether, when people are swimming, it is easier for them to stay afloat in the ocean or in a freshwater lake. (p. 5)

By observing students working on this problem and interviewing them, the researchers determined that the reading load of the test item affected student performance. In several instances, students were not sure what the question was asking or what they were expected to do to respond to such test items as these, in which all responses were related to the science experiment described.

Bass et al. (2002) also found children's explanations about whether it was "easier" to float in the ocean or on a lake to be very interesting. Many children drew heavily on their real-world knowledge of oceans and lakes to interpret the word *easier*. Some responded that it would be easier on the lake, since there would be no sharks or waves. A similar difficulty can be found on the 2003 NAEP mathematics item shown in Figure 11.5. How students interpret the word *quick* may relate to their success or difficulties on this item. *Quick* is probably intended to indicate speed in the use of an operation as opposed to speed in the solution of the problem. Yet in the real world, children might suggest putting all 12 boxes on a scale for a quick way to find the weight, but of course, that option was not offered on the test. Furthermore, for many 4th graders, multiplying a number (especially a double-digit number) by 12 may not seem like a "quick" way to get a solution.

Wilson (2004) found that the format in which a question is presented can have an impact on student performance. A difference in the instruction of "show your work and explain your answer" versus "use pictures, words, or numbers to explain your answer" (p. 136) can result in differences in performance by students. In the first situation, a student might feel limited to an algorithmic solution, whereas the second instruction gives the student permission to solve the

Carla has 12 boxes that each weigh the same amount. What would be a quick way for her to find the total weight of the 12 boxes?

A) Add 12 to the weight of one of the boxes
B) Subtract 12 from the weight of one of the boxes
C) Divide the weight of one of the boxes by 12
D) Multiply the weight of one of the boxes by 12

Figure 11.5. Grades 4 and 8 item on weighing boxes. (2003-4M6 #9, 2003-8M6 #9)

problem in more intuitive ways, enhancing the opportunity to assess the student's mathematical reasoning.

The work discussed above raises the question of whether the intent of NAEP test items to assess students' reasoning in mathematics is actually being realized. The complexity of the sentence structures used in some NAEP items may be testing students' ability to read and interpret complex sentences or reading passages instead of revealing their understanding of the intended mathematical concepts. We contend that because NAEP assessments are intended to be used to evaluate the mathematical reasoning of all students, an extremely important consideration for NAEP test developers is to reduce the level of demand introduced by the language used in the items.

In examining NAEP released items from the 2003 mathematics assessment, we found several examples of items in which language difficulties could explain the low performance of students. Consider, for example, the NAEP item in Figure 11.6. Only 34% of all 4th graders picked the correct option (D) for this item. A large percentage of students (53%) found incorrect answer B to be most appealing. As shown in Figure 11.6, distractor B was chosen by students at nearly all achievement levels (all except those with an advanced scale score), suggesting that most students apparently did not understand what the question was asking. A plausible explanation is that students who selected 20 as their answer were determining the number of boys in the class, whereas the question asked them to determine the number of boys and girls altogether.

This item might be a good candidate for exploring the impact on student performance that a modification of the language used in the question statement could produce. For example, the research of Abedi et al. (2001), Bass et al. (2002), and Wilson (2004) would suggest that modifying the question statement could result in improved student performance by removing confusion due to language and thus more accurately reveal the extent to which the students tested actually understood the mathematics involved. A possible modification might be the following:

> In Jean's class there are twice as many boys as girls. There are 10 girls in the class. How many children (boys and girls) are in the class?

In Jean's class there are twice as many boys as girls. If there are 10 girls in the class, how many boys and girls are there in the class?

A)   15

B)   20

C)   25

D)   30

	A	B	C	D (correct)
Overall performance	7%	53%	5%	34%
Achievement level				
Advanced	1%	37%	——	62%
Proficient	2%	52%	0%	44%
Basic	6%	57%	4%	31%
Below Basic	17%	49%	12%	19%

Figure 11.6. Performance on Grade 4 item on number of boys and girls in a class. (2003-4M7 #16)

Rewording of the question statement aside, we nonetheless wonder why such an item might have been included at the 4th-grade level, considering that a well-known line of research points to language difficulties (for adults as well as children) that arise with this sort of word problem. Because the structure of the English language suggests direct translation of words into symbols in such a problem situation, learners may naively translate the phrase "twice as many boys as girls" into "2 times the (number of boys) results in the (number of girls)." Mestre (1988) studied the difficulties of this type of question for non–English speakers and found that—

> language proficiency can influence problem solving … in the way that mathematical and natural language are structured to form text: the problem solver must be able to distinguish when a word is being used mathematically and when it is not. In addition, the solver must understand how the parts of the problem are related to each other in a mathematical sense. For example, when attempting to solve the "students and professors" problem cited earlier,[1] many students use a strict left-to-right parsing strategy. This strategy does not work in translating the problem from text to symbolic language because the mathematical meaning of the problem cannot be related to the problem's syntax in this fashion. Clearly, relying on the surface features of a text can lead to misinterpretations. (p. 216)

---

[1] The "students and professors" problem referred to here is "Write an equation using the variables S and P to represent the following statement: 'There are 6 times as many students as professors at this university.' Use S for the number of students and P for the number of professors." This problem has been examined in multiple studies (e.g., Clement, Lockhead, & Monk, 1981), and even adult students have been found to struggle in the ways described by Mestre.

Although the NAEP results in Figure 11.6 show that this item was rather difficult for all students, we wondered in particular how students with limited English proficiency (LEP) fared. Unfortunately, the NAEP Questions Tool does not allow us to separate out the performance of students with LEP. The only available information that might give us a hint about the performance of nonnative English speakers is data on the performance of Hispanic students, because they are more likely than other groups to include large numbers of non-native English speakers. For the problem in Figure 11.6, only 28% of Hispanic students picked the correct answer, compared with 38% of white students. Still, we fully realize that the Hispanic student data includes the performance of Hispanic students who are fluent English speakers; thus, any relevant conclusions about the performance of students with LEP are difficult to draw.

We found several released NAEP items in which the clarity of language was questionable. The example in Figure 11.7 illustrates the potential for difficulty in interpreting awkwardly worded questions. Although 47% of all 8th graders chose the correct answer, we note a large gap between the performance of students eligible for the reduced-price school lunch program and those not eligible. That gap suggests differences in performance by socioeconomic status. Fifty-two percent of the students not eligible for reduced-price school lunches picked the correct answer, compared with only 38% of those who were eligible. Although one should expect that students with the lowest scores overall would also have lower scores on individual items, an alarmingly low percentage, 25%, of students scoring Below Basic picked the correct answer. Thirty-five percent of the students scoring Below Basic found the answer of 80 radios most appealing, suggesting that the students found their answer by calculating the product of two numbers in the problem. The selection of that distractor could stem from struggling with the wording of the problem while trying to decide what was being asked.

We believe that understanding the factors that may affect the performance of all students is important. In particular, we are interested in tracking how certain characteristics of items may shape performance and potentially mask opportunities for all students—particularly those performing Below Basic—to show their understanding of mathematics and their ability to solve problems. We find particularly troublesome analysts' dismissal of the responses of the Below Basic students on particular items because they are not expected to perform well anyway. Their performance can be very revealing of the characteristics of test items that result in poorer performance than might otherwise be attained.

When we look more closely at the language used in the "packing radios" problem, we see many characteristics of linguistic complexity. The question is certainly not worded in a straightforward way. This question is a strong candidate for rewording, and we speculate that the rewording itself would alter student performance results. A possible rewording might be the following:

We have 15 boxes with 8 radios in each box. We want to repack the radios into 10 larger boxes. How many radios will we put in each box?

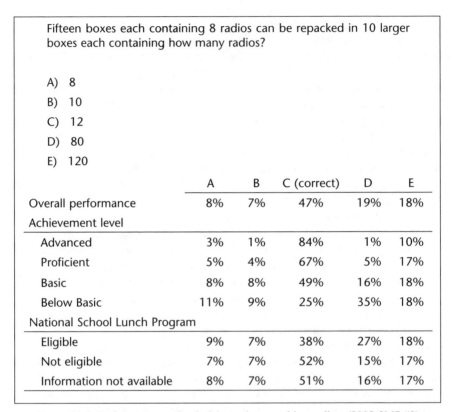

Fifteen boxes each containing 8 radios can be repacked in 10 larger boxes each containing how many radios?

A) 8

B) 10

C) 12

D) 80

E) 120

	A	B	C (correct)	D	E
Overall performance	8%	7%	47%	19%	18%
Achievement level					
Advanced	3%	1%	84%	1%	10%
Proficient	5%	4%	67%	5%	17%
Basic	8%	8%	49%	16%	18%
Below Basic	11%	9%	25%	35%	18%
National School Lunch Program					
Eligible	9%	7%	38%	27%	18%
Not eligible	7%	7%	52%	15%	17%
Information not available	8%	7%	51%	16%	17%

Figure 11.7. Performance on Grade 8 item about packing radios. (2003-8M7 #9)

Another source of difficulty for many students is symbolic mathematical language. If one goal of NAEP is to test students' understanding of symbolic language, which seems a reasonable aim, then the items used must not conflate testing understanding of symbols with testing underlying mathematical concepts. However, findings relating to students' interpretation of symbols and mathematics concepts seem difficult to separate, given the nature of many NAEP questions. For example, we believe that the question in Figure 11.8 conflates understanding of symbols with understanding of inequalities.

The question in Figure 11.8 is interesting because the overall performance of the 4th graders closely reflects the performance of all subgroups of 4th graders. Only 24% responded correctly. Although we hypothesize that English verbal language was at the heart of the difficulties in previous examples, we contend that 4th graders' lack of familiarity with mathematical (symbolic) language used in this item (viz. the greater-than symbol) may be at the heart of students' difficulty with it. The inequality symbol and number sentence probably do not yet carry the meaning for 4th graders that was expected by test developers. Moreover, the logic of sets and subsets needed to make sense of the mathematical use of such

What are all the whole numbers that make 8 – ☐ > 3 true?

A) 0, 1, 2, 3, 4, 5
B) 0, 1, 2, 3, 4
C) 0, 1, 2
D) 5

Grade 4 Performance

	A	B (correct)	C	D
Overall performance	13%	24%	15%	46%
Achievement level				
Advanced	3%	65%	16%	16%
Proficient	9%	30%	19%	41%
Basic	13%	19%	14%	52%
Below Basic	20%	17%	12%	48%

Figure 11.8. Performance on Grades 4 and 8 item involving the greater-than symbol. (2003-4M6 #20, 2003-8M6 #20)

words as *all, some,* or *none* is likely to have contributed to the complexity of this item, as well. Although the intent of this question was apparently to assess students' conceptual understanding of inequalities, performance on the item may also reflect students' understanding or lack of understanding of the symbols and words used to communicate about inequalities. We argue that modifying the language used in this item could result in significantly different results. For example, if we assume that the item is intended to test students' understanding of inequalities, then the item might be rewritten as "What are all the whole numbers that make 8 – ☐ less than 3?"

To bolster our assertion, we identified two 8th-grade NAEP items that apparently were intended to test students' understanding of inequalities. We examined the way those tasks were posed, as well as student performance on the items. The first item was the previously discussed item involving the greater-than symbol (Figure 11.8), which had been administered to 4th and 8th graders. The second item was the task shown in Figure 11.9, which does not involve the inequality symbol. Additionally, the complexity of this latter task is not compounded by the logic of sets and subsets. In Table 11.1, we see that 63% of 8th graders responded correctly to the item involving the greater-than symbol, whereas 77% of 8th graders had success with the question that did not employ the symbol (with an additional 17% of the students picking the incorrect option 10 as the correct answer, apparently responding with the solution to the equality $x + 2 = 12$ rather than the inequality $x + 2 < 12$). Clearly, the solution to the equation rather than the inequality is the most popular incorrect answer in both of the problems above.

(It was especially popular among the 4th graders when they were asked to solve $8 - \square > 3$ in the former problem.)

If the value of the expression $x + 2$ is less than 12, which of the following could be a value of x?

A)   16
B)   14
C)   12
D)   10
E)   8

Figure 11.9. Grade 8 item involving an inequality expressed in words. (2003-8M10 #3)

Table 11.1

Eighth-Grade Performance on Inequality Employing Greater-Than Symbol and Inequality Expressed in Words (2003-8M6 #20, 2003-8M10 #3)

Item Employing the Greater-Than Symbol (Figure 11.8)

	A	B (correct)	C	D
Overall performance	5%	63%	10%	20%
Achievement level				
Advanced	0%	99%	1%	1%
Proficient	1%	92%	3%	4%
Basic	5%	65%	10%	19%
Below Basic	10%	33%	16%	39%

Item employing an algebraic expression (Figure 11.9)

	A	B	C	D	E (correct)
Overall performance	1%	2%	2%	17%	77%
Achievement level					
Advanced	—	0%	0%	1%	99%
Proficient	0%	0%	0%	4%	95%
Basic	0%	1%	1%	13%	84%
Below Basic	2%	7%	5%	33%	52%

One of the striking differences in the performance of 8th graders on the two similar inequality items is in the higher level of performance of students scoring at the Basic and Below Basic levels on the inequality expressed in words (Figure 11.9). Both groups of students scored better on that item than on the inequality involving the greater-than symbol (Figure 11.8). At least two explanations for the higher success rate seem plausible. First, the question in the item in Figure 11.9

is written in simple language rather than in symbols. Second, the item in Figure 11.9 requires a single numerical answer rather than selection from sets involving multiple answers.

As we have shown in this section, the language used in the statement of NAEP items can hinder the performance of students and may mask their real understanding of mathematical concepts. In the next section we address the role of distractors in multiple-choice test items and how they may hinder students' ability to show what they know.

IMPACT OF DISTRACTORS USED IN ITEMS

Kazemi (2002) explored the impact of the format of test items on students' thinking and approach to solving mathematics tasks. In comparing students' responses to multiple-choice and open-ended items, she found that "when students approach a multiple-choice problem, their attention is drawn to the choices themselves. Focusing on the choices can lead students to use different knowledge than if the problems were open-ended, leading to higher rates of incorrect responses [on multiple choice items]" (p. 207). In Kazemi's study, the students drew on their mathematical knowledge and used mathematical reasoning much more readily when they approached open-ended items. In contrast, in solving multiple-choice items they tended to look at the choices before attempting to solve the problem. Hence the choices offered sometimes led the children to trivialize the problem or to use ineffective heuristics for problem solving. Those ineffective heuristics are described by Sowder (1989) as some sort of "short-cut" that has been useful in school mathematics, such as picking the numbers and looking for a key word associated with an operation. Kazemi (2002) also found that, at times, the graphics included along with the problem statement and intended to facilitate interpretation of the problem hindered students' approach to the problem solution, creating more confusion than support.

According to Van den Heuvel-Panhuizen (1996), growing concern has been expressed about the need to design tasks that pay adequate attention to student reasoning and student development. Changes in the presentation of a task and the choice of distractors can greatly affect the performance of students.

In our analysis of NAEP released items from the 2003 mathematics assessment, we found some consistency in item developers' choice of distractors. In items in which the solution was a numerical value resulting from the use of an operation, we noted a tendency to offer a sequence of integral values with a constant increment for the multiple-choice options (e.g., choices of 3, 4, 5, 6; or 9, 10, 11, 12; or 15, 20, 25, 30; or 46, 48, 50, 52). The four items in Figure 11.10 are representative of a much larger number of items exhibiting that pattern of distractors that we found in looking across all the 2003 released multiple-choice items.

In all four items shown in Figure 11.10, what students might actually do (correctly or incorrectly) to solve the problem seems to have been irrelevant to the

1. Estela wants to buy 2 notebooks that cost $2.79 each, including tax. If she has one-dollar bills and no coins, how many one-dollar bills does she need?

A) 3
B) 4
C) 5
D) 6

2. Kirstin wants to buy a flute that costs $240. She has saved $20 each week for 3 weeks. How many more weeks does Kirstin need to save money if she continues to save $20 each week?

A) 9 weeks
B) 10 weeks
C) 11 weeks
D) 12 weeks

3. In Jean's class there are twice as many boys as girls. If there are 10 girls in the class, how many boys and girls are there in the class?

A) 15
B) 20
C) 25
D) 30

4. Six students bought exactly enough pens to share equally among themselves. Which of the following could be the number of pens they bought?

A) 46
B) 48
C) 50
D) 52

Figure 11.10. Four multiple-choice items from NAEP 2003, all with answer options that are arithmetic sequences. (2003-4M10 #15, 2003-4M7 #14, 2003-4M7 #16, 2003-8M6 #11)

design of the item. The distractors do not appear to have been chosen according to how students might actually think about the problem. Rather, the correct answer is hidden in an arithmetic sequence of integers. The construction of distractors in this way follows the principle of numerical ordering but violates the principle of "making all distractors plausible" (Haladyna, Downing, & Rodriguez, 2002, p. 312). We question what we might learn about children's thinking, reasoning, or even computational skill from such items. In devising responses to such questions, item developers might turn back to students themselves. Students' responses to parallel open-ended items could productively be used to identify plausible distractors. Such items are more likely to produce data that are revealing of students' thinking. Researchers who have explored the proposed approach have found that it provides far more information about learning than can be drawn from irrelevant distractors (Sadler, 1998).

In other instances, the distractors on NAEP items appear to be built from combinations of numbers and operations taken from the problem. Although that method of constructing item distractors does adhere to a commonly used guideline (Haladyna et al., 2002), we contend that developing distractors using the actual mental operations or strategies that students might use to solve the problem, rather than arbitrary mathematical operations, could reveal much more about students' thinking and understanding. Using distractors that correspond to common student errors means that data about student performance can be much more useful to teachers because they can create learning opportunities for their students that fit with how the students are thinking. The item in Figure 11.11 is an example in which children's mental operations seem not to have been taken into consideration.

Sam placed cookies on a cookie sheet to form 2 rows with 6 cookies in each row. Which of the following number sentences best describes this situation?

A) $2 \times 6 =$ ▨
B) $2 + 6 =$ ▨
C) $6 \div 2 =$ ▨
D) $6 - 2 =$ ▨

	A (correct)	B	C	D	Omitted
Overall performance	83%	7%	6%	1%	3%
Achievement level					
Advanced	98%	——	1%	——	1%
Proficient	95%	1%	3%	0%	1%
Basic	86%	6%	6%	0%	2%
Below Basic	62%	19%	10%	3%	7%

Figure 11.11. Grade 4 performance on item involving choice of operation. (2003-4M7 #4)

The item in Figure 11.11 is particularly interesting if we look at the choices picked by students scoring Below Basic. Had this item been an open-ended problem, both responses 2×6 and $6 + 6$ could have been considered correct. Developmentally, some 4th graders might legitimately have offered the solution $6 + 6$. The omit rate for this problem by students scoring Below Basic was higher than for any other 4th-grade multiple-choice item released in 2003. The average omit rate for the 42 4th-grade multiple-choice items released in 2003 was 1.6%.

Whereas students scoring Below Basic had an average omit rate of 2.5%, the omit rate on this problem was unusually high at 7%. We suspect that not finding their anticipated choice of 6 + 6 among the options led a large number of students, typically those scoring Below Basic, to omit this item. A similar explanation might explain the choice of distractor B by 19% of the students scoring Below Basic. Distractor B was perhaps appealing to students for whom addition was the mental operation they had chosen to solve the problem.

In another item that required students to select an expression (Figure 11.12), 53% of the students scoring Below Basic picked distractor D (3 + 4 + 5). As Kazemi (2002) suggested, students tend to use nonefficient heuristics more often when the problem is posed in multiple-choice format. In this item, students may have decided on option D simply because three numbers were involved in the problem statement and D was the only choice that involved all three of those numbers. For whatever reason, option D was chosen by a disproportionate number of students scoring Below Basic. Using Kazemi's (2002) analysis of the format of the task, we contend that student performance might have revealed greater understanding had the same problem been presented in open-ended format.

Pat has 3 fish bowls. There are 4 plants and 5 fish in each bowl. Which gives the total number of fish?

A) 3 + 5
B) 3 × 4
C) 3 × 5
D) 3 + 4 + 5

Figure 11.12. Grade 4 item involving selection of an expression. (2003-4M7 #11)

Looking back to item 2 in Figure 11.10, we see another situation in which many students favored a particular distractor, yet that choice may represent reasonable mathematical thinking. In this problem, the incorrect choice may be due to a misinterpretation of the language rather than a lack of understanding of the mathematics. Whereas 39% of the 4th graders picked the correct answer (9 weeks), another 35% picked 12 weeks. In fact, Kirstin will take 12 weeks total to save $240. An important consideration to note is that the students responding 12 weeks apparently were able to think about the underlying mathematics of the problem, but they seem to have answered a different question than what was asked. Simply considering percentage right and wrong can lead to a misrepresentation of what 4th graders can do with mathematics when solving a rather complex problem for that particular grade level.

Another source of impact on student performance might occur when two items are placed sequentially. In blocks 2003-4M6 and 2003-8M6, which were 4th- and 8th-grade blocks containing many of the same items, Items 16 and 17 were related. In Item 16, students are asked to place the point 3/4 on a line segment already subdivided into eighths. Item 17 asks students to determine the number of eighths in three-fourths. No representation is provided in Item 17, although a representation is in view from the previous item. To an item developer or to a researcher reporting on student performance on individual items, the two items might appear independent (that is, answering one item would have no impact on how the other item might be approached) unless the researchers realize that the items were administered consecutively. Yet we contend that the items can certainly be used together to construct responses. In fact, the representation used in Item 16 could trivialize the thinking needed for Item 17. Determining how many eighths in three-fourths can become a mere counting problem for the student who has just solved Item 16 and is now confronted with Item 17. If the student realizes that the two problems are the same, Item 17 has little potential to tell us about whether students can create the representation needed to solve the problem on their own.

In sum, in the instances of distractor choice discussed in the foregoing, we notice a lack of consideration given to how children think. We also assert that this same lack of attention to student reasoning and to research on the development of student reasoning can be found by analyzing the rubrics for some of the open-ended items. Such an analysis goes beyond the scope of this chapter but can be found in Norton (in press).

CONCLUSIONS AND IMPLICATIONS

We have identified three issues in the construction of NAEP items that may affect student reasoning and consequently mislead us in interpreting what students know and can do in mathematics. First, our analysis of the role of context, language, and distractors on students' approaches to test items in general, and NAEP items in particular, suggests that careful consideration be given to item construction and its role either in supporting or eliminating inequities in testing performance. We also suggest that mathematics educators can contribute significantly to large-scale assessment development in several ways. Research on the development of mathematical ideas may contribute to more purposeful distractor selection. The use of research findings could lead to the development of items that provide more meaningful information about the mathematical understanding of students who select incorrect distractors. In that sense mathematics educators must take crucial leadership roles in large-scale test-item construction. Finally, we should actively investigate the characteristics of test items that disproportionately disfavor students of lower socioeconomic status, or students of a particular cultural or racial background, or students with limited English proficiency, so that items with those specific characteristics can be avoided in future test construction. Only when we fully understand and begin to anticipate how students may think when confronting items will we begin to construct assessments that are fair to all students, giving all students an opportunity to demonstrate fully their understanding of mathematics.

REFERENCES

Abedi, J., Hofstetter, C., Baker, E., & Lord, C. (2001). *NAEP math performance and test accommodations: Interactions with student language background* (CSE Technical Report 536). Los Angeles: University of California, Center for the Study of Evaluation, National Center for Research on Evaluation, Standards, and Student Testing.

Abedi, J., & Lord, C. (2001). The language factor in mathematics tests. *Applied Measurement in Education, 14,* 219–234.

Abedi, J., Lord, C., & Hofstetter, C. (1998). *Impact of selected background variables on students' NAEP math performance* (CSE Technical Report 478). Los Angeles: University of California, Center for the Study of Evaluation, National Center for Research on Evaluation, Standards, and Student Testing.

Bass, K. M., Magone, M. E., & Glaser, R. (2002). *Informing the design of performance assessments using a content-process analysis of two NAEP science tests* (CSE Technical Report 564). Los Angeles: University of California, National Center for Research on Evaluation, Standards, and Student Testing.

Black, P. & Wiliam, D. (2004). The formative purpose: Assessment must first promote learning. In M. Wilson (Ed.), *T owards coherence between classroom assessment and accountability* (pp. 20–50). 103rd Yearbook of the National Society for the Study of Education. Chicago: University of Chicago Press.

Clement, J., Lockhead, J., & Monk, G. S. (1981). Translation dilation in learning mathematics. *American Mathematical Monthly, 88,* 286–290.

Cooper, B. (1998). Using Bernstein and Bourdieu to understand children's difficulties with "realistic" mathematics testing: An exploratory study. *Qualitative Studies in Education, 11,* 511–532.

Cooper, B., & Dunne, M. (1998). Anyone for tennis? Social class differences in children's responses to national curriculum mathematics testing. *Sociological Review,* 115–148.

Delandshere, G. (2002). Assessment as inquiry. *Teachers College Record, 104,* 1461–1484.

Greer, B. (1993). The mathematical modeling perspective on wor(l)d problems. *Journal of Mathematical Behavior, 12,* 239–250.

Greer, B. (1997). Modeling reality in mathematics classrooms: The case of word problems. *Learning and Instruction, 7,* 293–307.

Haladyna, T. M. (2004). *Developing and validating multiple-choice test items* (3rd ed.). Mahwah, NJ: Erlbaum.

Haladyna, T. M., & Downing, S. M. (1989a). A taxonomy of multiple-choice item-writing rules. *Applied Measurement in Education, 2,* 37–50.

Haladyna, T. M., & Downing, S. M. (1989b). Validity of a taxonomy of multiple-choice item-writing rules. *Applied Measurement in Education, 2,* 51–78.

Haladyna, T. M., Downing, S. M., & Rodriguez, M. (2002). A review of multiple-choice item-writing guidelines for classroom assessment. *Applied Measurement in Education, 15,* 309–334.

Kastberg, S. E., & D'Ambrosio, B. (2004, July). *The role of contextually rich items in assessing student learning.* Paper presented at the 10th International Congress on Mathematics Education, Copenhagen, Denmark.

Kastberg, S. E., D'Ambrosio, B., McDermott, G., & Saada, N. (2005). Context matters in assessing students' mathematical power. *For the Learning of Mathematics, 25* (2), 12–17.

Kazemi, E. (2002). Exploring test performance in mathematics: The questions children's answers raise. *Journal of Mathematical Behavior, 21,* 203–224.

Lave, J. (1988). *Cognition in practice: Mind, mathematics, and culture in everyday life.* New York: Cambridge University Press.

Mestre, J. P. (1988). The role of language comprehension in mathematics and problem solving. In R. R. Cocking & J. P. Mestre (Eds.), *Linguistic and cultural influences on learning mathematics* (pp. 201–220). Hillsdale, NJ: Erlbaum.

National Assessment Governing Board. (2002). *Mathematics framework for the 2003 National Assessment of Educational Progress.* Washington, DC: National Assessment Governing Board. Retrieved October 30, 2005, from http://www.nagb.org/pubs/math_fw_03.pdf

Norton, A. (in press). What's on your report card? *Teaching Children Mathematics.*

Nunes, T., Carraher, D., & Schliemann, A. D. (1993). *Street mathematics and school mathematics.* New York: Cambridge University Press.

Pellegrino, J. (2002). Knowing what students know. *Issues in Science and Technology, 19*(2), 48–52.

Sadler, P. (1998). Psychometric models of student conceptions in science: Reconciling qualitative studies and distractor-driven assessment instructions. *Journal of Research in Science Teaching, 35,* 265–296.

Saxe, G. B. (1995). From the field to the classroom: Studies in mathematical understanding. In L. P. Steffe & J. Gale (Eds.), *Constructivism in education* (pp. 287–312). Hillsdale, NJ: Erlbaum.

Shepard, L. A. (1991). Psychometricians' beliefs about learning. *Educational Researcher, 20*(7), 2–16.

Sowder, L. (1989). Choosing operations in solving routine story problems. In R. I. Charles & E. A. Silver (Eds.), *The teaching and assessing of mathematics problem solving* (pp. 148–158). Reston, VA: National Council of Teachers of Mathematics.

Thorndike, R. L. (1967). The analysis and selection of test items. In S. Messick & D. Jackson (Eds.), *Problems in human assessment.* New York: McGraw-Hill.

Van den Heuvel-Panhuizen, M. (1996). *Assessment and realistic mathematics education* (R. Rainero, Trans.). Utrecht, Netherlands: CD-ß Press.

Van den Heuvel-Panhuizen, M., & Becker, J. (2003). Towards a didactic model for assessment design in mathematics education. In A. J. Bishop, M. A. Clements, C. Keitel, J. Kilpatrick, & F. K. S. Leung (Eds.), *Second international handbook of mathematics education* (pp. 689–716). Dordrecht, Netherlands: Kluwer.

Verschaffel, L., De Corte, E., & Lasure, S. (1994). Realistic considerations in mathematical modeling of school arithmetic word problems. *Learning and Instruction, 4,* 273–292.

Wilson, L. D. (2004). On tests, small changes make a big difference. *Teaching Children Mathematics, 11,* 134–137.

Wilson, M., & Draney, K. (2004). Some links between large-scale and classroom assessments: The case of the BEAR assessment system. In M. Wilson (Ed.), *Towards coherence between classroom assessment and accountability: 103rd Yearbook of the National Society for the Study of Education* (pp. 132–154). Chicago: University of Chicago Press.

## 12

Challenges and Opportunities in the Analysis of NAEP Mathematics Results

Frank K. Lester Jr., John A. Dossey, and Mary M. Lindquist

Over a century and a half ago, Horace Mann, secretary of the Massachusetts State Board of Education, was dismayed to learn that Boston schoolchildren could answer correctly only about a third of the arithmetic questions they were asked in a survey of subject knowledge. "Such a result repels comment," he said. "No friendly attempt at palliation can make it any better. No severity of just censure can make it any worse." In 1919, when part of the survey was repeated in school districts around the country, the results for arithmetic were even worse than they had been in 1845. Apparently, there has never been a time when U.S. students excelled in mathematics, even when schools enrolled a much smaller, more select portion of the population.

> —Jeremy Kilpatrick, Jane Swafford, and Bradford Findell
> *Adding It Up*

[M]athematics testing in the United States has been embedded in a cultural, social, and political context that has shaped the tests and the uses to which they have been put. In particular, . . . during the period from the 1980s until the end of the century, politicians and other policymakers exhibited a tendency to link student performance on state, national, and international mathematics assessments with the economic well-being of the nation. This tendency persists today.

> —Peter Kloosterman and Frank K. Lester Jr.
> *Results and Interpretations of the 1990–2000 Mathematics Assessments*
> *of the National Assessment of Educational Progress*

D ESPITE the belief presented in the media and promoted by various critics of contemporary education that students' mathematics performance was better in the "good old days" before the curriculum reform efforts of the past 15 years, the fact is that never in our nation's history has students' mathematics performance been considered satisfactory.[1] Moreover, mathematics testing has been used as a policy tool in education in the United States for more than a century (Madaus, Clarke, & O'Leary, 2003). The difference today is that the rhetoric surrounding issues of mathematics achievement is more strident and the stakes are higher. A case in point is the NAEP mathematics assessment.

The mathematics assessments of the NAEP have come to be regarded by many policymakers as the primary tool by which to judge the extent to which U.S. schools are meeting national expectations. Writing about the history of the involvement of the National Council of Teachers of Mathematics (NCTM) in preparing interpretive reports of NAEP mathematics assessments, Kenney (2004a) pointed out how much different NAEP is now from the vision of its creator, Ralph Tyler, who envisioned it as a tool to assess the U.S. national educational system and not as an evaluation of individual students' success. She noted that Tyler valued local control and did not want nationwide tests or standards. In spite of his vision, steady movement has been made toward increasing the possibility of making judgments about individual students, schools, and districts on the basis of NAEP results. Indeed, the initial legislation for NAEP called for it to be more like a census than a tool of reform. Occasionally, item developers have been able to include a few items that help mathematics educators forecast growth in a content area, but generally the use of NAEP results for such purposes has not been possible.

So how can NAEP results be used to guide our practice as mathematics teachers, teacher educators, and curriculum developers, and how can those results be used to influence national and state policy? Answering questions of this sort requires serious deliberation about a host of issues related to the nature of NAEP and its purpose. In this final chapter we raise several such issues and discuss them in terms of challenges and opportunities for the mathematics education community.[2]

---

[1] Several studies conducted before and during World War II highlighted the dire state of U.S. students' mathematics achievement (Sowder, n.d.). In particular, the computation skills of students at every level were considered to be very poor.

[2] NCTM has been almost alone among professional organizations in providing interpretive reports of NAEP findings. By law, the National Center for Education Statistics (NCES), which is responsible for administering and preparing summaries of the results, is not allowed to prepare or commission such reports. Moreover, even if NCES staff were allowed to do so, they could have a difficult time finding the sort of content area expertise that NCTM has been able to marshal to interpret the NAEP findings for mathematics educators.

CHALLENGES

Perhaps the most pressing challenges facing us in using NAEP results have to do with the influence of the No Child Left Behind legislation (NCLB) on the nature and importance of NAEP. In particular, the fact that NCLB calls for a biennial sampling of 4th- and 8th-grade students on NAEP in mathematics and reading to confirm states' progress on state assessments raises new questions: What is the purpose of the NAEP tests? How are they administered? Who runs NAEP? And how have the tests been retooled to fit NCLB? Each of those questions presents challenges to the individuals designing the assessments, administering the tests, and interpreting the results.

The single biggest challenge is one of scale; NAEP has become a huge undertaking involving an enormous investment of resources and money. NCLB calls for NAEP to administer reading and mathematics assessments at Grades 4 and 8 every other year in all states and in other subject areas as funding permits. In addition, NAEP must test those subjects on a nationally representative basis at Grade 12 at least as often as it has done in the past (i.e., every four years). Another requirement calls for administering separate, long-term-trend assessments in reading and mathematics at ages 9, 13, and 17 on a regular basis. One result of that expansion of NAEP is likely to be a significant cost increase.

Improving achievement has been the unrealized goal of federal education programs for decades. Under NCLB, federal funding would be allocated according to whether states actually succeed in that endeavor, as measured by the NAEP test. President Ronald Reagan once said in reference to arms agreements with the Soviet Union, "Trust, but verify." Although every state is committed to raising its students' achievement levels, the current administration is seeking to use NAEP to verify state achievement trends. Clearly, NAEP has changed in scope and purpose from Tyler's original vision of 40 years ago.

Consistency in sampling, privacy protections, security against fraud, and comparability make NAEP a useful testing instrument. However, the test has its limitations, and concerns are being raised about its possible impact on teaching and local control. To restructure NAEP to fit its proposed new role, lawmakers must address those limitations and concerns. With those broad issues and questions as a backdrop, we turn next to several specific challenges.

Challenge 1. Interpreting and Communicating NAEP Results in Meaningful Ways

For many, if not most, of the public (including the media), NAEP is thought of as a single entity.[3] That public perception has contributed to the confusion that

---

[3] When the results of the 2004 Long-Term Trend (LTT) assessment were released in 2005, most media reports failed to distinguish LTT from other NAEP assessments, even though LTT is very different from other NAEPs.

has too often accompanied reports of NAEP results. The fact is that over time, NAEP has evolved into three separate assessment programs: Main NAEP, State NAEP, and Long-Term Trend (LTT) NAEP.

Main NAEP, also referred to as National NAEP, is the primary program. Students are sampled across the country, and the results are intended to be representative of the entire U.S. student population.[4]

Begun on a trial basis in 8th grade in 1990 and now an integral part of NAEP, State NAEP reports achievement for 4th and 8th grades on a state-by-state basis. In 2003, all 50 states and 3 jurisdictions participated in the mathematics assessment. A significant change to State NAEP occurred in 2001 with the NCLB legislation. That legislation requires states receiving Title I funding to participate in State NAEP in reading and mathematics at Grades 4 and 8 every two years.

From its inception, State NAEP has used the same items and testing format as Main NAEP[5], and thus results from individual states can be compared with results for the nation as a whole. And beginning in 2003, Main NAEP became a composite of State NAEP results. Individuals can examine NAEP results online for each state at http://nces.ed.gov/nationsreportcard/states.[6]

The third NAEP program is Long-Term Trend. In contrast with the Main and State NAEPs, LTT NAEP uses different items, a separate national sample, and a different testing schedule. Reading and mathematics are the only subjects that have been tested since 2000. LTT NAEP used the same item pool for each assessment from 1973 until it was changed for 2003, and the sampling plan has remained the same since the mid-1980s.

The original LTT NAEP sample consisted of students ages 9, 13, and 17 who were selected using the same procedures as used in the Main NAEPs of the 1970s, 1980s, and 1990s. By retaining the same items and sampling procedures and by testing students at the same age levels, LTT NAEP could be used to determine how student performance had changed over a 30-year period.

The original LTT NAEP was administered for the last time in 2004, and the results were made public during the summer of 2005 (see chapter 2). Beginning with the 2008 LTT assessments, which is the next time they will be administered, some of the items will change, but the design and methodology used will remain constant over assessment years to maximize comparability of results over time.

---

[4] The 2005 Main NAEP assessment in mathematics was administered in schools throughout the country from January to March 2005. National assessments were conducted at Grades 4, 8, and 12. The results for Grades 4 and 8 were released in the fall of 2005. The results for Grade 12 have not yet been released.

[5] The Main NAEP includes special administrations (such as the paced audiotape estimation assessment), which are not part of the State NAEP program.

[6] In contrast with Main NAEP, State NAEP results do not include private schools. Consequently, state-by-state analyses are representative of public schools only.

The major limitation of the original version of the LTT is that the computational focus of the items was more relevant for mathematics curricula of the 1970s than for the early years of the present century. Calculators were permitted for only a few questions on the original LTT assessment. An advantage of the original and new LTT assessments over the Main and State NAEPs is that they allow us to see how students of today compare with students of the past in computational and procedural mathematics. (The LTT assessment for 2008 and subsequent years will provide for inclusion of, and accommodations for, students with disabilities and students with limited English proficiency, in accordance with the relevant policies and procedures adopted for Main NAEP.) According to the National Assessment Governing Board (NAGB) 2002 policy statement, a sample of test items from each LTT assessment will be made public, necessitating the development of new items that will not have been used on previous LTT assessments. For the 2004 LTT assessment, three blocks of items were made available on the NAEP online Questions Tool.

In short, the three versions of NAEP give us slightly different but complementary pictures of what students know and can do in mathematics. Considered together, they foster insights about what students know that cannot be obtained from any of the three assessments individually. Furthermore, by looking at all three assessments, we are better able to discern how the mathematics knowledge of today's students compares with that of students 5, 10, 20, and 30 years ago. However, communicating differences in NAEP results to various stakeholders has been a challenge for NAEP officials. This difficulty is due, among other factors, to the complexity of the NAEP design and the fact that multiple NAEPs are administered. Mathematics education researchers must begin to pursue collaborations with specific dissemination partners (e.g., Council of Chief State School Officers, Education Commission of the States, American Educational Research Association, and selected content-area teacher organizations) to facilitate gaining access to stakeholders and crafting effective communication strategies.

Challenge 2. Adjusting to the Changing Importance of NAEP

NAEP has traditionally been a low-stakes assessment because no scores are reported for students and no consequences for students, teachers, schools, or school districts were associated with the assessment results. Also, NAEP has traditionally been a voluntary assessment, and it continues to be so for students. Under the NCLB legislation, as in the past, parents of students selected into a NAEP sample must be informed before the assessment is administered that their child is not required to participate in the assessment, is not required to complete the assessment, and is not required to respond to all the items on the assessment. As a result, students who have been selected for the sample may choose not to participate, thereby raising the possibility that the assessment results are biased in some way. NAEP's new role in NCLB may not change the stakes for students at all, but it does change the stakes for schools and districts. Robert Schaeffer, a critic of the NCLB legislation, has suggested, "It's likely that you're going to see efforts to boost NAEP scores, from gamesmanship to teaching to the test to outright cheating. NAEP has been a good measure precisely because there haven't been stakes attached to it" (Toppo, 2003).

To balance the need for accurate information about what students were learning with the need to keep testing time to a minimum, NAEP was designed so that each participating student is tested for an hour and takes only a small subset of the items for her or his grade level. By pooling results from students, one can get a sense of progress for the nation as a whole. Not possible with NAEP is a way to get a good sense of any individual student's achievement, and thus NAEP is quite different from state and local accountability tests that are typically designed to identify students who are not doing well (see chapter 1).

Another difference between NAEP and state and local tests is the motivation level for students to complete the test and put in their best efforts. Because no individual scores are reported and students have no major incentives to do their very best work, we can assume that many students view NAEP as a low-stakes test. This concern is especially acute at Grade 12 because 12th graders' performance on NAEP assessments will have no bearing on their grades or their futures after they leave school. Thus we may reasonably conclude, as O'Neil, Sugrue, and Baker (1996) have suggested, that NAEP scores may actually underestimate what students are able to do.

Nevertheless, the large national sample for NAEP (about 190,000 students in Grades 4 and 153,000 students in Grade 8 took the mathematics Main NAEP in 2003) and the fact that the sample includes the lowest to the highest achieving students make NAEP the most representative indicator we have of the mathematics skills that it tests. Moreover, now that NAEP will be used in some form to monitor state testing programs as called for in the NCLB legislation, schools will need to find ways to get students to take the test more seriously. In short, NAEP is quickly moving from being an assessment that generated relatively little interest among teachers and policymakers to one that could have significant impact on school curricula, practice, and policy.

Because the NAEP assessment results, especially the percentages of students in each state meeting various achievement performance levels, will play a central role in NCLB studies of state-level performances, the outcomes of those actions must not result in changes being made in the NAEP assessments themselves. If the outcomes are challenged by the states, one repercussion may be movement to change the measures, that is, to change the NAEP assessments. However, adequate measurement of students' performances over time is impossible if the measures themselves are constantly changing.

The accountability link in the NCLB legislation will be gauged by the various percentages of students performing at Below Basic, Basic, Meeting Standards, or Exceeding Standards at the state level on state assessments and by the percentages of the students from the state meeting those criteria according to the NAEP definitions of the standards on the NAEP assessment. Central to the NCLB legislation is the proviso that all states will make progress toward having all their students performing at the Meeting or Exceeding Standards level (according to their state definitions of those terms) by the 2014 assessment (see chapter 1). To ensure that this goal is reached, states are required to show yearly progress, relative to a federally approved state plan, toward it.

At the heart of the interpretation of the data at both state and national levels is the question of the validity of the achievement levels and their associated cutoff points on the NAEP scale. That question has been the center of many discussions since the initial setting of such achievement standards with the 1992 Main NAEP (National Academy of Education, 1993).

Dissatisfaction with the processes used to set the standards initially and in subsequent adjustments focuses on the fact that the NAEP achievement levels are defined in terms of the corpus of extant NAEP item content rather than in terms of an absolute curriculum. As such, they lack the richness and the breadth that would come with a set of standards set on the curriculum. Although improvements have been made in incorporating more information from the tests and students' performance outside of NAEP on similar assessments into the setting of standards for Grade 12 for 2005, the process still lacks a curricular basis for setting standards for student performance in school mathematics as a whole.

Challenge 3. Dealing with the Complexity of the NAEP

Matters related to the design and implementation of NAEP assessments have clear implications for both the analyses conducted using NAEP data and the ways in which the results can be interpreted. The NAEP design, test administration, and analysis techniques are complex. They have been developed explicitly so that the scale scores and trend measures are as precise and reliable as possible (taking account of the current state of research in teaching and learning, content areas, and psychometrics). Techniques developed for NAEP are used in a variety of other settings in educational measurement (e.g., the international assessments PISA and TIMSS),[7] and NAEP is widely considered to be the gold standard of educational achievement survey assessment (Jones & Olkin, 2004). As the importance of NAEP increases, teachers and policymakers will have to become better informed about the procedures and processes of a NAEP administration. The complexity of NAEP is best illustrated by considering the various aspects of designing and administering the tests and analyzing and reporting

---

[7] PISA is the Programme for International Assessment, and TIMSS is the Trends in International Mathematics and Science Study. Information about each of those assessment programs can be found in chapter 2 and at www.pisa.oecd.org (PISA) and timss.bc.edu (TIMSS).

the results, in particular, the test-development process, scoring procedures, and data-analysis techniques.

The NAEP Test-Development Process

All NAEP assessments are developed to represent content area frameworks. Those frameworks are developed by the NAGB with broad input from stakeholders, including teachers, subject matter specialists, testing experts, and interested members of the general public (NAGB, 2004). The resulting frameworks specify content, outcomes, and item formats. To ensure that NAEP assessments continue to remain relevant to current educational practice, subject area frameworks are reviewed and revised approximately every 10 to 12 years.[8] If appropriate, a new framework is developed for a subject area. When a new framework is adopted, the old NAEP trend lines are discontinued and new ones are started.[9]

Each subject area assessed in NAEP has a test-development committee that selects NAEP items from a pool of items written by teachers and content specialists. During the test development, the committee meets quarterly. NAEP items undergo extensive scrutiny, review, and pretesting before operational use. Items must survive reviews by test specialists, editorial reviews, bias reviews, small-scale pilot tests, and full-scale national field tests. Additional reviews by state curriculum and testing personnel are employed for state NAEP subject areas. Statistical analyses determine whether an item is functioning as intended, and differential item functioning (DIF) analyses are completed to ascertain whether any of the items are unfair.[10] However, in recent years mathematicians and mathematics educators have had very little input in the development of items, leading to concern that the items do not necessarily measure mathematical understandings and proficiencies that are most important.

The Scoring of Tests

Scoring a NAEP assessment is an intricate business. Student response booklets are scanned so that the multiple-choice item responses can be machine-scored. Images of the student responses to the constructed-response items are presented via computer to human raters for scoring. The professional raters are carefully trained before being allowed to score student responses, and rating reliability is monitored within the assessment year through "second scoring" a percentage of the student responses. Cross-year reliability is also monitored through periodic rescoring of a set of student responses from previous assessments. If the monitoring indicates that the scoring has fallen below reliability

---

[8] The mathematics framework was revised for the 2005 assessment.

[9] Short-term trend lines are discussed in chapter 2 of this monograph.

[10] An item may go forward even though the DIF analysis flags it at a low level of DIF. A panel determines whether the DIF has any basis. In most instances the item is removed, but in some instances, it goes forward.

standards or is consistently shifting in one direction, item scores are discarded, scorers are retrained, and scoring of the item is done over. Those quality control measures over the constructed-response scoring process, although challenging to complete, increase the trustworthiness of the scoring that forms the basis of reported NAEP scale scores and trends. However, the high complexity of the scoring process increases the potential for delays in reporting results.

Analysis of NAEP Data

NAEP assessments are usually administered to groups of 25–30 students in a classroom, although exceptions are made for students who require accommodations to participate meaningfully in the assessment. Multiple subjects are assessed in the same session, as the books are designed with common sets of directions and timing. Item blocks and sections of background questions are separately timed, and the session administrator indicates when the time to complete a section is over. Although testing is done at the students' school, the mathematics test is not administered to entire classes. Because no student can realistically complete the entire assessment, the total pool of items is divided into "blocks" of items. Those item blocks are selected to meet time and content constraints. In particular, blocks differ with respect to content coverage within subject area, item type, difficulty, and number of items. The blocks are assembled into test books according to a balanced incomplete block (BIB) design. The design is balanced in that each block of items appears equally often in the total set of books, each block appears in every position in the set of test books, and each block of items appears paired with every other block of items.[11] The design is incomplete in that the conditions for position and occurrence of each block with every other block are not crossed (see Allen, Carlson, & Zelenak, 1999 for details and examples). In general, more than 20 test books are used per grade per subject.

After almost every assessment,[12] NAEP releases and replaces approximately 30% of the items in the pool. As a result, across years in NAEP assessments, item pools are not identical. Blocks of items are released, and the replacement blocks do not have precisely the same characteristics as those released. Some items are unique to the current year, although the majority of them are used for multiple years. NAEP analysis methods combine results across different test books within an assessment year and produce results that are comparable across assessment years despite changes in the item pool. The results provide information about student proficiency in the subject area and content sub-

---

[11] NAEP uses a complex variant of multiple matrix sampling called *BIB spiraling* to assign items to students. Because of BIB spiraling, NAEP can sample enough students to obtain precise results for each question while generally taking about an hour and a half of each student's time. See nces.ed.gov/nationsreportcard/pubs/guide/ques20.asp for details about BIB sampling.

[12] No items were released after the 2000 Main NAEP mathematics assessment, but items from 2003 Main NAEP assessment and from the 2004 LTT assessment were released (see chapter 1).

domains in terms of average scores and percentages of students at or above the achievement levels for the subject, as well as information about trends over time (see chapter 1).

NAEP uses analysis techniques based on Item Response Theory (IRT) (Baker, 2001; Lord, 1980) and employs analysis methods developed by Mislevy (1991), Rubin (1987), and others. The IRT item parameter estimation is completed in a context in which no student responds to more than 20% of the item pool, but the analysis results must provide an estimate of group scores on the entire assessment. This format requires tracking of the multiple book compositions, block positions within books, and the varied connections between blocks. Background variables for each student, including relevant teacher and school variables, must be matched to the correct students. Students do not respond to enough cognitive subject area items to yield reliable individual scores; however, NAEP data collection and analysis procedures have been specifically designed to provide reasonably unbiased and reliable estimates of student population and subgroup scores.

Measuring trends across time requires that assessment results be reported on a common scale. NAEP scale metrics are set at the beginning of a subject trend line. Since the analysis results are in an arbitrary metric, typical of IRT, a scale score metric is selected that is thought to be easily interpreted by the general public. As noted in chapter 2, the scale used for NAEP mathematics ranges from 0 to 500 with a 2003 average score of 235 in Grade 4 and 278 in Grade 8. Trend measures are maintained by analyzing both the current assessment data and the previous assessment data together. The common item blocks in the two assessment years are estimated with a single set of item parameters unless strong evidence of differential functioning across assessment years is found. When differential functioning occurs for an item, the item is estimated with two separate sets of item parameters, one for each year. At the end of the data analysis, the proficiency distribution for the previous assessment's data is reestimated. Once that process is completed, the reestimated proficiency distribution for the previous NAEP administration's data is transformed to the reporting metric. The same transformation is applied to the current year's assessment results, placing both years' results in the common scale score metric. Further details of NAEP data analysis procedures are available in NAEP's 1998 technical report (Allen, Donoghue, & Schoeps, 2001).

Sampling Procedures

All NAEP assessments are subject to two basic constraints: (a) NAEP must cover broad content areas and report on subdomain proficiency within those content areas, and (b) the item pool used in any assessment must meet framework specifications about item types and subdomain representation. As a result, NAEP item pools for a given grade often contain between 100 and 200 items, making unrealistic any expectation that a student could complete every item at a grade level.[13] Therefore, for all NAEP assessments, results are based on samples of students and items. Simple random sampling is neither practical nor efficient, so NAEP uses multistage complex sampling procedures. The student samples are drawn to be representative of the nation (in the national samples) or the state (in the state samples). Single-grade samples range in size from approximately 8,000 for a national-only content area to more than 150,000 for a combined state and national assessment content area. State samples are approximately 2,500 students. Certain subgroups of interest, such as minority students or students attending private schools, are oversampled so that sufficient precision in the results for those subgroups can be obtained. As a result of the disproportionate number of students from the oversampled subpopulations and the nature of the balanced incomplete block design used to collect student performance data, the resulting sample is not a simple random sample. Hence, the data must be adjusted with sampling weights in the analyses to restore proportionality.

The use of student and item samples has implications for analysis. Much of standard statistical theory and many existing software programs that implement statistical tests assume independent and identically distributed observations. NAEP data are neither independent nor identically distributed; instead, data are clustered within schools and by geographical area. Furthermore, by oversampling subgroups of interest, NAEP data violate simple random sampling assumptions. Thus, if analysis procedures that assume independence and identically distributed observations are used with NAEP data, estimates of simple descriptive statistics will be biased. Weights must be used in the analysis of NAEP data to correct for the effects of the oversampling. Estimating standard errors for NAEP target statistics is complex because using statistical tests based on simple random sampling will underestimate the actual sampling variability in the complex sample. NAEP uses a jackknife procedure to achieve a more accurate estimate of the sampling variability and thus provides accurate statistical tests of the results. (For additional information about the analysis procedures and other technical topics, see Allen et al., 1999.)

Reporting Processes

NAEP results are reported to the general public and so must be presented in as understandable a format as possible. The score reports must support a broad range of uses by researchers, educators, policymakers, politicians, and interested members of the general public. Scores are reported in print format, and a large amount of NAEP data is accessible on the NCES Web site. As has been described in chapter 1 and elsewhere (e.g., Kloosterman, Kehle, & Koc, 2004), special data tools have been developed to allow examination of NAEP results in detail, and released NAEP items (with response data information and sample student

---

[13] For the 2003 NAEP mathematics assessment, 182 items were used in the Grade 4 pool and 205 items were used in the Grade 8 pool.

responses) are also available. Although those data tools are reasonable efforts to make NAEP results more accessible, they also open up the possibility for mis-analyses by well-meaning individuals and groups who may not be well informed about the complexity of the NAEP design and sampling procedures. We say more about this concern in our discussion of the next challenge.

Challenge 4. Dealing with Changes in NAEP Procedures

In spite of the efforts to make NAEP data and results more readily accessible, the public needs to become better informed about the procedures used by NAEP in preparing and administering the assessment.

Before the 2003 mathematics assessment, procedures for preparing and administering NAEP tests in different subjects were designed independently. For some subjects, the short background questionnaire was given before the test, whereas for others, it was given afterward. For some subjects, the test was given in three 15-minute blocks; for others, it was given in two 20-, 25-, or 30-minute blocks. As a result, tests for different subjects could not be administered in the same room without instructions for one test interrupting administration of a block from another subject area and thus the processes of data collection and analysis becoming unnecessarily complicated.

To solve that administrative problem, NAEP adopted a standard test structure for all subjects—two 25-minute blocks of test questions, followed by two short blocks of background questions. Common block timings permit assessing different subjects in the same classroom, reduce the number of classrooms required, require fewer numbers of students per subject in each school (increasing precision of the findings), permit the simultaneous pretesting of questions that are not yet operational, and simplify the development of sampling weights. In U.S. history, geography, and reading, the only required change is shifting the order of the background and test question blocks; but in mathematics and science, the blocks of test questions had to be reconfigured.

NCES has always standardized the administration conditions for all NAEP assessments, but the implementation of contractor administration of all sessions is new. Before 2002, school personnel administered state assessments, although contractor personnel randomly monitored a portion of them. No meaningful differences were observed between the monitored and unmonitored sessions in the past. Beginning in 2002, the state assessment sessions were administered by contractor personnel. The effect of that change is not clear, but the change should be studied closely. The uniform administration is important as NAEP takes on a "high stakes" position, but at the same time it may detract from student motivation and comfort.

Under NCLB, NAEP has begun to play a prominent role in the evaluation of adequate yearly progress in the states, jurisdictions, and territories receiving federal Title I assistance. NCLB calls for NAEP to be used as a serious discussion tool to provide a context for state assessment scores. However, its exact role and uses are still being defined. Similarly, adequate yearly progress and how it is determined are both subjects of ongoing discussion. NAGB has devoted serious study to that policy issue (NAGB, 2002). Stakeholders must have a clear understanding of NAEP procedures, including test development, scoring, sampling, data collection and analysis, and reporting.

Challenge 5. Resolving Various Concerns Specific to the Mathematics Assessment

As we pointed out earlier in this chapter, the mathematics education research community and the NCTM have had a long history of collaboration in the preparation of interpretive reports of NAEP mathematics assessments. This collaboration is unique; no other professional education organization or research community has been as interested in studying what NAEP tells us about students' academic performance. Not surprisingly, then, mathematics educators who have been associated with NAEP and analyses of NAEP data are concerned about several aspects of the NAEP mathematics assessments. Their concerns have to do with the nature of the items developed for the assessments, issues associated with the sampling plan and data-analysis techniques, changes in the background questionnaire and the items used on the LTT assessment, and the definition of proficiency levels.

Item-Level Issues

Several item-level issues are in need of attention. Those issues have to do with how items are developed, how items are tested, and how performance on the items is analyzed. In particular, what effects will the *item development* (items are developed by a single contractor with little input from mathematicians and mathematics educators), *item testing* (large-scale pilot testing is often conducted in advance only locally, i.e., in Princeton, New Jersey), and *item analysis* (item block design complicates analysis of individual item responses) have on the potential for interpretive analyses? Item development is centered in one source rather than juried from a broader set of individually submitted items. Also, locking items in blocks in a BIB design prevents easy analysis and keeps items in the overall active item pool for too long a time. For example, if an item underperforms in providing information, but is included in a block of items that works quite well overall, it is locked into the NAEP assessment until the time comes for the entire block to be released. The BIB design also limits the use of the families of items that allow for variations of concepts and procedures; too much interpretation (and thus valuable information for teachers) must rely on single items rather than a set of items clustered around a given topic.

Item tryouts by means of local pilot testing need to be more extensive before national pilot testing is done. Although items are reviewed extensively, more time should be devoted to item development in conjunction with cognitive labs or through several iterations of obtaining information from students, particularly for extended constructed-response items. Also, careful attention needs to be given to the wording of items for students whose primary language is not English and for various other groups of students, and, of course, items need to be tried with those various groups.

Items that have p values below .1 or above .9 are generally considered inappropriate for inclusion in Main NAEP on the basis of the lack of cost-effectiveness of their return of information. However, such items can help address the performance of students who are Below Basic or Exceed Standards. To date the policy has been to administer items that measure only what is rather than what might be; that is, little or no consideration is given to including topics that are new to the mathematics curriculum and looking at change in students' growth over time on those topics. Given current policy, if items measuring knowledge of new topics were included, they likely would be excluded after their first usage because of lack of student opportunity to learn the concepts and skills related to the new topics.

Sample Size and Statistical Interpretation

Sample sizes have increased dramatically with the inclusion of State NAEP data into Main NAEP. As a result, nearly all differences between subgroups are statistically significant, thereby complicating the analyses related to performance gaps for the NCLB legislation. The increase in sample size raises such questions as "What constitutes a performance gap if most differences are significant?" and "How should performance targets for states be determined given the different levels of minority and limited English proficient populations in states?"

Data Availability Issues

NAEP interpretive reports published by NCTM have traditionally discussed items that were released to the public along with a presentation of student performance data on those items. Half the items on the first mathematics NAEP were made public, and a fourth to a third of the items on all other NAEP assessments through 1996 were released and thus are no longer used. To comply with NCLB and to ensure that a sufficient number of items would be available for the 2003 NAEP administration, none of the 2000 items were released to the public. In November 2003, blocks of items from 2003 Main NAEP assessments were released, and blocks from the 2004 LTT NAEP were released in July 2005. Not clear, however, is the policy concerning release of items with each administration. The potential inaccessibility of items will restrict the mathematics education research community's ability to perform meaningful, useful analyses.

Nature of the Background Questionnaire

The reduction of curriculum-based information to accommodate more demographic information on the background questionnaire may mean that an analysis of NAEP results in terms of curriculum and teaching methods will no longer be possible. The NAEP High School Transcript Study (HSTS) may be able to provide some details about student course taking, but only for the grades covered by individual transcripts. The HSTS is a periodic survey of the curricula being offered in U.S. high schools and the course-taking patterns of high school students through a collection of transcripts. The HSTS also offers information on the relationship of student course-taking patterns to achievement at Grade 12 as measured by NAEP. Most recently conducted in 2000, HSTS may prove to be a valuable source of information to supplement the NAEP background questionnaire because in 2000, for example, transcripts were collected for 12th-grade students who graduated from high school by the end of the collection period. Most of those students also participated in the NAEP assessment earlier that same year. To date, transcripts have been collected from students who graduated in 1987, 1994, 1998, and 2000 and will be collected again in 2005. However, before we will be able to make use of the HSTS data, we must determine the extent to which those data can be compared with NAEP assessment data.

Related data that have been omitted from the NAEP Report Cards are trends in student performance by mathematics content areas and the related information on teacher focus on material covered in the grade levels tested.

Changes in the LTT NAEP Process

The change in the items used on the LTT NAEP means that a loss of anchor on basic computational skills will result; that is, items that have been used on several LTT administrations will be lost. That loss will render very difficult over time the task of tracking students' knowledge of basic facts and their ability to perform paper-and-pencil calculations. The changes that are being planned may result in a test that will not provide any meaningful data about trends in student achievement over time.

Challenge 6. Maintaining NAEP as a Valuable Research Tool

As NAEP begins the cycle of biennial testing in the service of NCLB, the availability of data for the interpretive reports will likely suffer. Beginning with the 2000 administration, researchers engaged in interpretive analyses for the NCTM monographs were not given access to secure items (see Kloosterman & Lester, 2004); that restriction hampered their ability to draw meaningful conclusions. A procedure is now in place for viewing the secure items, but it is very restrictive. Researchers have to apply for and get permission to view the items, and, once approved, must then go to NCES to view them. Any notes taken about the items are heavily censored before being returned. Moreover, researchers will have to be much more careful than in the past about how they report information about secure items. The authors of NAEP interpretive reports will no longer be allowed to write parallel items or give a good sense of what an item was about. We expect this situation to persist as long as the high-stakes nature of NAEP remains: very few items will be released, researchers will encounter increasing difficulty gaining access to secure items, and student work may not be made available (Wilson, in press). Nevertheless, NAEP will continue to hold great promise as a valuable source of research. But before we provide support for that claim, we must discuss what NAEP cannot do for us as researchers.

WHAT NAEP IS NOT DESIGNED TO DO

The NAEP redesign policy purports to focus NAEP on what it does best: measuring student achievement. Focusing NAEP on what it does best comes with a related idea: recognizing what NAEP is not designed to do.

Although NAEP is well designed to measure student achievement and trends over time, it is not a good source of data for drawing conclusions about, or providing explanations for, the level of performance that is reported. It also does not prescribe a national curriculum, an appropriate means for improving instruction in individual classrooms, or a basis for evaluating specific pedagogical approaches.

NAEP is an example of a *cross-sectional survey*, an effective and cost-efficient means for gathering data on student achievement. A cross-sectional survey gathers data at one point in time. In the instance of NAEP, data are gathered on national and state representative samples of students at a particular time during the school year. The sample is large enough to permit reasonably accurate estimates of subgroup performance (e.g., by gender, race, and ethnicity). Change over time can be measured by administering the same survey again in subsequent years, under the same testing conditions, with samples of students that are similar to those tested earlier. Comparisons can be made within and across the subgroups and for the whole sample.

However, a cross-sectional survey cannot provide answers about what causes the level of performance that is reported. Measuring the causes of achievement would necessitate (1) a very different sort of research design, (2) specific research questions to answer, (3) pretesting and posttesting of students, and (4) comparisons of results between groups of students receiving a particular educational approach with those who are not. Although some policymakers may view such research as a worthwhile part of NAEP, the need for pretesting and posttesting alone would double the costs of NAEP testing and would require additional administrative burden on schools and more time away from instruction for students. Those added features would likely decrease school and student participation rates in NAEP. Having too few schools and students in the sample, in turn, would jeopardize NAEP's ability to provide results representative of national and state student achievement.

The best that can be done at present regarding explanation or interpretation of results is to report on background variables that may be associated with achievement. However, in many instances, the data from background questions collected by NAEP are inconclusive, and the recent cutback in the number of items on the background questionnaires exacerbates the problem. If we had better and more extensive background data about the curriculum used in the schools tested, we would still have to be careful about drawing conclusions, but at least we would know considerably more than we do now (and acquiring more comprehensive background data would add only a few minutes to the time adults need to complete the school or teacher questionnaires). Even with stronger linkages between data from the students' background questionnaires and their performances, the total NAEP design is still not adequate to support conclusions that explain why achievement is at the level reported. Clearly, the use of NAEP background data to explain or interpret achievement results should be done with caution.

OPPORTUNITIES FOR NAEP AS A RESEARCH TOOL

The main purpose of all NAEP assessments has been to monitor student achievement over time for diverse, representative groups of students. In addition, it has served the mathematics education research community as a valuable research tool. In comparison with various other federally administered achievement tests since the mid-1960s involving nationally representative samples of students, NAEP is remarkable in several respects.

First, NAEP is the only database that has collected achievement data continuously for more than 30 years. Thus, although confident claims about trends over time are difficult to make because of regular changes to the test frameworks and items, with the exception of the LTT NAEP through 2004, the simple fact is that the mathematics education community has learned quite a lot about students' performance over the past 30 years.

A second advantage NAEP has over other data sets is that for most of the nine mathematics assessments, data have been collected from three separate age groups (since 1990 from Grades 4, 8, and 12), thereby making possible the study of students' growth in mathematics performance as they progress through school.

Third, NAEP has much larger sample sizes than any of the other surveys of student achievement. During the 1990s, other surveys have included samples that are only 10% to 20% as large as NAEP for any single administration and only 1% to 5% as large as NAEP for repeated testing (Grissmer, 2003).

A fourth advantage of NAEP for mathematics education researchers is that the design, administration, and scoring of NAEP are of higher quality than in any other surveys. We can safely say that even with the limitations of NAEP outlined in this chapter, the care with which all NAEP assessments are conceptualized, administered, and scored is without peer. With those advantages in mind, we discuss several features of the current way in which NAEP is being conceptualized, administered, and reported.

With the expansion of NAEP under NCLB, NAEP began conducting biennial state-level assessments, administered by contractor staff (not local teachers). The newly redesigned NAEP has four important features. First, NAEP now administers tests for different subjects (such as mathematics, science, and reading) in the same classroom, thereby simplifying and speeding up sampling, administration, and weighting. Second, NAEP conducts pilot tests of candidate items for the next assessment two years in advance and field tests of items for precalibration one year in advance of data collection, thereby speeding up the scaling process. Third, NAEP conducts bridge studies, administering tests under both the new and the old conditions, thereby allowing the possibility of linking old and new findings. Finally, NAEP is adding more test questions at the upper and lower ends of the difficulty spectrum, thereby increasing the power of NAEP to measure performance gaps.

Shortened Time for Producing Reports

Previously, NAEP has conducted weighting, scoring, and scaling after the completion of data collection. No further reductions in reporting time could be squeezed out of the previous design. Weighting has been speeded by reducing the number of different sets of sample weights. Scoring is now conducted in parallel in distributed scoring centers. To speed scaling, NAEP will pretest questions twice, two years and one year in advance of an actual assessment. The latter pretest, with larger representative samples, will permit calibration of items before operational testing and thereby accelerate scaling. NCES will look for ways to streamline its checking and approval of draft reports. Pretesting questions two years in advance will require longer lead time for development of tests in each subject.

Equally important to researchers and those interested in more technical aspects of NAEP is the timely production and release of the technical reports detailing the actual developmental, administrative, and reporting aspects of each assessment. Those manuals are vital to accurate and informative interpretive reports of each assessment.

Bridge Studies to Ensure Comparability

Reconfiguring NAEP's test questions into blocks of different lengths in mathematics and science and changing the order of the background and assessment questions in reading could change scale parameters, reducing the comparability of current NAEP scores with those of previous assessments. The solution to that problem is to conduct supplemental NAEP bridge surveys in which the same test questions are administered under both the old and the new designs. The resulting data may permit measurements of the impact of design changes and allow appropriate comparisons of previous NAEP results with those of the new design.

Potential to Measure Achievement Gaps

The accuracy of NAEP scores for a subgroup depends principally on the size of the subgroup sample and the accuracy of the test in the range of the subgroup scores. NAEP ensures adequate sample sizes of groups for which NAEP measures gaps by targeting needed students for oversampling and, if necessary, by increasing state sample sizes.

NAGB has recognized that too much was being expected of NAEP; indeed, some of the expectations were beyond its capacity to do well (e.g., measure and report on the status of student achievement and change over time) (NAGB, 1996). NAGB also has drawn distinctions among the various audiences for NAEP products. Specifically, the primary audience for NAEP reports is the U.S. public, whereas the primary users of its data have been national and state policymakers, educators, and researchers.

A consequence of the advantages discussed above is that NAEP enables researchers to address some important research questions and issues that are very difficult to study otherwise. In addition to questions related to ongoing research on student mathematics achievement, the large sample sizes (both overall and for pivotal subgroups), data from three student grade levels, and the general high quality of the NAEP design make possible research on a wide range of important topics, among them the following:

- The effects on student mathematics achievement of national changes in student demographics (e.g., families, schools, and communities), educational resources, and education and social policies since 1970.

- The effects on student mathematics achievement of different state educational and social policies, particularly the effects of state resource–based efforts and systemic reform efforts including NCLB.

- The effects of state frameworks and assessment programs on student achievement and mathematics instruction.

- Research on minority and disadvantaged students and other groups that require large sample sizes so as to study more detailed subgroups within each population. Recent works of Kenney (2004b) and Lubienski (2002a, 2002b) are examples of recent research in those areas.

SUMMARY

The foregoing discussions outline several topics that have an impact on the design, administration, interpretation, and reporting of the NAEP mathematics assessments. Those issues change over time as the result of changes in formal or operating policies of NAGB or the various contractors employed by NAGB to ensure that the assessments are developed and carried out. The assessment itself has made significant strides in keeping step with changes in the mathematics curriculum over time (inclusion of a greater proportion of constructed-response items, shifting emphases in the assessments conducted in the 1990s to meet the changes brought on by the release of the NCTM Curriculum Standards, and the inclusion of technology in a responsible way). The overall sampling and structural features of the interpretation involve state-of-the-art approaches from statistical and psychometric standpoints.

However, for those who are involved in interpreting and reporting NAEP findings to audiences of mathematicians and mathematics educators, classroom and prospective teachers, and members of the lay public specifically interested in mathematics, certain features of the program, if changed or improved, would lend support to increasing both the validity of the program and the interpretability of the resulting data. Our preceding comments have been focused on a set of steps that would move interpretations and research based on NAEP forward and that would improve researchers' ability to draw more import from the NAEP data.

REFERENCES

Allen, N. L., Carlson, J. E., & Zelenak, C. A. (1999, July). *The NAEP 1996 technical report.* NCES report 1999-452. Washington, DC: National Center for Education Statistics.

Allen, N. L., Donoghue, J. R., & Schoeps, T. L. (2001, June). *The NAEP 1998 technical report.* NCES report 2001-509. Washington, DC: National Center for Education Statistics.

Baker, F. (2001). *The basics of item response theory.* ERIC Clearinghouse on Assessment and Evaluation, University of Maryland, College Park.

Grissmer, D. (2003, July). *Utilizing NAEP for educational research.* Paper prepared for the National Assessment Governing Board.

Jones, L. V., & Olkin, I. (Eds.). (2004). *The Nation's Report Card: Evolution and perspectives.* Bloomington, IN: Phi Delta Kappa Educational Foundation.

Kenney, P. A. (2004a). A brief history of the NCTM NAEP interpretive reports projects. In P. Kloosterman & F. K. Lester Jr. (Eds.), *Results and interpretations of the 1990–2000 mathematics assessments of the National Assessment of Educational Progress* (pp. 33–55). Reston, VA: National Council of Teachers of Mathematics.

Kenney, P. A. (2004b, April). *Performance by race/ethnicity on the NAEP Long-Term Trend mathematics items: Is the glass half empty or half full? Or another way to examine performance on the NAEP Long-Term Trend assessment: A modest proposal.* Paper presented at the annual meeting of the American Educational Research Association, San Diego.

Kilpatrick, J., Swafford, J., & Findell, B. (Eds.). (2001). *Adding it up: Helping children learn mathematics* (p. xiii). Washington, DC: National Academy Press.

Kloosterman, P., Kehle, P., & Koc, Y. (2004). Using the NAEP online tools. In P. Kloosterman & F. K. Lester Jr. (Eds.), *Results and interpretations of the 1990–2000 mathematics assessments of the National Assessment of Educational Progress* (pp. 57–68). Reston, VA: National Council of Teachers of Mathematics.

Kloosterman, P., & Lester, F. K., Jr. (Eds.). (2004). *Results and interpretations of the 1990–2000 mathematics assessments of the National Assessment of Educational Progress.* Reston, VA: National Council of Teachers of Mathematics.

Lord, F. M. (1980). *Applications of item response theory to practical testing problems.* Hillsdale, NJ: Erlbaum.

Lubienski, S. T. (2002a). A closer look at black-white mathematics gaps: Intersections of race and SES in NAEP achievement and instructional practices data. *Journal of Negro Education, 71,* 269–287.

Lubienski, S. T. (2002b, April). *Are we achieving mathematical power for all? A decade of national data on instruction and achievement.* Paper presented at the annual meeting of the American Educational Research Association. New Orleans.

Madaus, G., Clarke, M., & O'Leary, M. (2003). A century of standardized mathematics testing. In G. M. A. Stanic & J. Kilpatrick (Eds.), *A history of school mathematics* (pp. 1311–1433). Reston, VA: National Council of Teachers of Mathematics.

Mislevy, R. J. (1991). Randomization-based inference about latent variables from complex samples. *Psychometrika, 56,* 177–196.

National Academy of Education. (1993). *Setting performance standards for student achievement: Background studies.* Stanford, CA: Author.

National Assessment Governing Board. (1996). *Redesigning the National Assessment of Educational Progress.* Policy statement. Washington, DC: Author.

National Assessment Governing Board. (2002, May). *The National Assessment of Educational Progress: Design 2000–2010.* Policy statement. Retrieved September 18, 2005, from http://www.nagb.org/naep/design2000/status.html

National Assessment Governing Board. (2004, September). *Mathematics framework for the 2005 National Assessment of Educational Progress.* Retrieved September 18, 2005, from http://www.nagb.org

O'Neil, H. F., Jr., Sugrue, B., & Baker, E. L. (1996). Effects of motivational interventions on NAEP mathematics performance. *Educational Assessment, 3,* 135–157.

Rubin, D. (1987). *Multiple imputations for non-response in surveys.* New York: Wiley.

Sowder, L. (n.d.). *Why I support reform: The good old days never were.* Retrieved June 14, 2005, from http://mathematicallysane.com/analysis/goodolddays.asp

Toppo, G. (2003, November 11). NAEP may be used as a truth serum. *USA Today.* Retrieved July 15, 2005, from http://www.usatoday.com/news/education/2003-11-10-neap-usat_x.htm

Wilson, L. D. (in press). High stakes testing in mathematics. In F. K. Lester (Ed.), *Second handbook of research on mathematics thinking and learning.* Charlotte, NC: Information Age.

AUTHORS' NOTE

We wish to thank Arnold Goldstein of the National Center for Education Statistics for his assistance with various technical details discussed in this chapter.

ABOUT THIS INTERPRETIVE REPORT

This interpretive report is the result of a collaborative effort of the National Council of Teachers of Mathematics (NCTM) and mathematics educators at Indiana University (IU) with financial support from the National Science Foundation. The project prepared professional development materials and interpretive reports based on data from various NAEP mathematics assessments. The interpretive reports include two monographs, of which this volume is the second. The first is *Results and Interpretations of the 1990 Through 2000 Mathematics Assessments of the National Assessment of Educational Progress,* edited by Peter Kloosterman and Frank K. Lester Jr. (Reston, VA: NCTM, 2004) (see below).

Also Available From NCTM . . .

Joint NCTM and IU Interpretative Monograph:

- *Results and Interpretations of the 1990 Through 2000 Mathematics Assessments of the National Assessment of Educational Progress,* edited by Peter Kloosterman and Frank K. Lester Jr. (Reston, VA: National Council of Teachers of Mathematics, 2004).

Joint NCTM and IU Professional Development Materials:

- *Learning From NAEP,* edited by Catherine A. Brown and Lynn V. Clark (Reston, VA: National Council of Teachers of Mathematics, 2006). This workshop facilitator's manual and its accompanying CD are designed to help facilitators create meaningful professional development experiences for classroom and preservice teachers of mathematics at all grade levels. The activities in the *Learning From NAEP* materials are intended to help educators better understand the intricacies of assessment data and how they can use such data to support students' learning in the mathematics classroom. The workshops address students' understanding, content knowledge, assessment, and equity, and the facilitator can modify each workshop by NAEP content strand, state, or grade level.

Please consult www.nctm.org/catalog for the availability of these titles and for a plethora of resources for teachers of mathematics at all grade levels.

❋

For the most up-to-date listing of NCTM resources on topics of interest to mathematics educators, as well as on membership benefits, conferences, and workshops, visit the NCTM Web site at www.nctm.org.